THE NEOLIBERAL PATTERN OF DOMINATION

Studies in Critical Social Sciences Book Series

Haymarket Books is proud to be working with Brill Academic Publishers (www.brill.nl) to republish the *Studies in Critical Social Sciences* book series in paperback editions. This peer-reviewed book series offers insights into our current reality by exploring the content and consequences of power relationships under capitalism, and by considering the spaces of opposition and resistance to these changes that have been defining our new age. Our full catalog of *SCSS* volumes can be viewed at www.haymarketbooks.org/category/scss-series.

The Neoliberal Pattern of Domination

Capital's Reign in Decline

José Manuel Sánchez Bermúdez

Haymarket
Books
Chicago, IL

First published in 2012 by Brill Academic Publishers, The Netherlands.
© 2012 Koninklijke Brill NV, Leiden, The Netherlands

Published in paperback in 2013 by
Haymarket Books
P.O. Box 180165
Chicago, IL 60618
773-583-7884
www.haymarketbooks.org

ISBN: 978-1-60846-282-7

Trade distribution:
In the U.S. through Consortium Book Sales, www.cbsd.com
In the UK, Turnaround Publisher Services, www.turnaround-psl.com
In Australia, Palgrave Macmillan, www.palgravemacmillan.com.au
In all other countries by Publishers Group Worldwide, www.pgw.com

Cover design by Ragina Johnson.

This book was published with the generous support of Lannan Foundation
and the Wallace Global Fund.

Printed in the United States.

10 9 8 7 6 5 4 3 2 1

Library of Congress Cataloging-in-Publication Data is available.

To Iván, Derek, Ulises, Gala, Fanny and Quique, because they are the future, the nearest and dearest I have, and because, within fifty years, in spite of the wildly complicated world we are leaving them, they and their children and their children's children will be fully and wonderfully alive, even if the empiricists and immediatists like to say that "within fifty years we will all be dead." This we recognize as an excuse for washing their hands of what their present acts will reap in the future.

CONTENTS

ACKNOWLEDGEMENTS

I would like to thank the Autonomous University of Nayarit and its Council for their support in the completion of my doctoral studies and the research that enabled me to prepare this work, and to express my profound gratitude to Víctor Figueroa Sepúlveda, my friend and teacher, for his generosity in sharing his knowledge; to R.A. Dello Buono for his invaluable support and encouragement; and to both for their effort and intellectual consistency in a world full of so much inconsistency placed at the service of capital.

And finally, to Mari, because if my life has been a life, it has been because she has shared her life with me; to Omar and Magaly, the most cherished lives in my life, the lives which, although we gave them life through ours, we did not make them, because each life makes its own life; to Mireya, because she has been an anchor in my life and a source of profound feelings, always so remote and so present; and to Isadora, Mirna and Priscila, because we have been learning how to share life, which is no small thing in these times of alienation in a neoliberal labyrinth designed to kill the emotional capacity of human beings.

It is not my purpose to abuse the patience of my readers or bore them with the details of my personal emotional bonds which are a private matter. In reality, I only wish to say that I just like every one of the more than six billion human beings who inhabit this planet loves life – that brief parenthesis between two eternities which can and must be glorious. It simply doesn't seem reasonable that a handful of profit-obsessed lunatics bent on serving the logic of capital should be able to deem life insignificant and destroy it, as they have done to many millions of lives in Iraq, Afghanistan, Eastern Europe, Africa, and the Middle East. Likewise here in Latin America, some countries with devastated economic and political structures are increasingly incapable of attending the most basic needs of a growing proportion of their inhabitants and have been turning into territories controlled by bands of armed murderers.

Tepic, Nayarit, Mexico

PROLOGUE

With publication of this book by the distinguished Mexican economist José Manuel Sánchez Bermúdez, the "Studies in Critical Social Sciences" Series has made another major contribution to the field of critical political economy. In a brilliant treatise, Sánchez lays out an ambitiously systemic, structural approach to the entire capitalist system with the aim of articulating the shifting general pattern of domination. He places specific emphasis on the conditions of underdevelopment and readers will be immediately struck by the breathtaking scope of analysis put forward in this volume.

While Sánchez offers a highly structural analysis in *The Neoliberal Pattern of Domination*, it is at the same time a hopeful one. This is because its insightful analysis does not simply point to an all too familiar scenario of an overly determined fate of inescapable domination. Nor does it paint a shiny future of the new order emerging out of the throes of a collapsing "late capitalism." Rather, its contribution rests upon revealing the real and dynamic structures of a neoliberal phase of capitalism in decline while demonstrating an inescapable tendency towards rebellion. It is this fact that establishes the possibility of anti-capitalist revolutions at multiple points throughout the larger system.

The analysis presented by Sánchez probes the conditions of domination that accompany capitalist social formations. By comparing these formations as they developed historically, his analysis spans across various regimes of domination that have unfolded out of the structured shift back and forth between their "natural" and "contained" forms. By detailing this process in the context of a sequential progression across three paradigmatic periods, namely, the liberal/oligarchic, Keynesian/developmentalist, and neoliberal eras, he reveals the structural interconnections of each within the capitalist mode of production and captures their corresponding cyclical phases.

Throughout this work, Sánchez maintains his "eye on the ball," i.e., that the control of surplus is shown to be the ultimate and constant objective of the exercise of capitalist domination. In so doing, his framework incorporates the work of an impressive number of classical and contemporary analysts, the latter of which includes many distinguished Mexican and other Latin American authors. Readers will appreciate this intellectual service and the way he smoothly weaves their contributions into his discussion of their northern counterparts such as Samir Amin, Zygmund Bauman, Alain Tourane, Jean Francois Lyotard, Alain Lipietz, just to mention a few.

As Sánchez presents his expansive analysis, he develops a complex treatment of neoliberalism by employing a historical, social class analysis that penetrates the shroud of neoliberal ideology. His formulation of an explanatory framework seeks to build comprehension of the full reach as well as the structured limits of this pernicious form of capitalist domination. Among the many unique aspects of his work is the way that it goes beyond merely establishing the common link between military activity and overall capitalist state reproduction and expansion. Sánchez extends out much further in this regard to uniquely draw in the state's broader "administration of criminal activity" which in many cases closely overlaps with other militarized activities. This includes such diverse aspects as the surge of paramilitary violence, the criminalization of protest, corruption and organized criminal syndicates, collaboration with foreign military forces, and so on. His keen observations by reference to the case of Mexico will be of particular interest to the English-speaking world as he generalizes from it and develops numerous implications for the rest of the region and well beyond.

Scarcely a day goes by without news of another horrific murder scene coming out of Mexico, a vast and developing country where criminal violence has recently climbed to epic proportions. This book's analysis of the state's administration of criminal activity in recent times makes it all the more relevant beyond Mexico's borders. Indeed, the seminal theoretical work offered here constitutes an urgent call for the necessity of transition away from the savagery that neoliberalism has brought to the author's own country just as it has done in so many others.

The implications arising from the analysis contained in *The Neoliberal Pattern of Domination* are without doubt far reaching. Diverse social phenomena such as crime and state misconduct, state repression, environmental management, social movements, regulatory debates and immigration policy are shown to be fundamentally structured by a globalized capitalist logic. The imposing manner in which neoliberal globalization has shaped the development process calls out the need for a theoretical framework grounded in the larger political economy. With ecological crimes, state organized crimes, crimes against humanity and so many other human rights crimes in ascendance, the underlying nature of the capitalist state persists in manifesting a general albeit elusive character. In the final analysis, the neoliberal state is a particularly complex apparatus that must nevertheless ensure continuation of the overall process of capital accumulation regardless of growing social conflicts and raging political disputes.

In a post-oligarchic context, the modern state institutionally assumes the position of "mediator" in which it organizes, regulates and protects the "legitimate" institutions of conflict resolution that have evolved in a given national setting. This cultivation of legitimacy is part and parcel of the state's attainment of an image of a "neutral" governing body. The state as such seeks to legitimately establish the "fair" rules of the game by which all social classes must play. To facilitate this process, neoliberalism created its own particular mythology concerning the distribution of wealth, the supposedly self-correcting nature of the system, and the long term tendency towards greater equality. As the myth goes, existing inequalities are inherent but can remain at "acceptable" levels while the "magic of the market" is left to harness powerful new technologies and produce the best possible world for the greatest number of citizens. In this sense, neoliberal ideology reconstructed a worldview atop the complete denial of Keynesian "common sense."

Meanwhile, neoliberal restructuring was devastatingly effective at dismantling the regulatory and interventionist mechanisms of developing nation states, arguing that the "free market" could not tolerate any form of "state interference" in economic affairs. In ideological terms, neoliberalism sought to reconstruct market mediated consumption rights as "natural," with the market itself being the essence of democracy. As Sánchez reaffirms, the limits of the neoliberal state in its role of class mediation inevitably becomes challenged when its policies come into contradiction with the underlying reproduction requirements of the existing political economy.

Through his critical systemic approach, Sánchez thus makes it possible to see globalizing capital in the light of the very social antagonisms that it spawns at multiple levels, something which in due course generates multiple centers of resistance. For this reason, his book is essential reading at it leads us into deeper levels of analysis regarding the big questions of our time. Readers however should be forewarned. There is no neutral ground in Sánchez' provocative exposition and once inside his framework, there is no easy escape from his impassioned reasoning. In the final analysis, this book removes the Teflon from a system in decline and insists on the necessity of a radical alternative to a fundamentally inhumane system.

R.A. Dello Buono
Manhattan College
New York City, USA

INTRODUCTION

In contemporary society, it is a favorite argument of the ruling ideology that class analysis constitutes a "worn out paradigm." This paradigm, "an invention of the communists," is supposed to have died with the USSR and "real socialism" since it represented not an internal contradiction of contemporary societies but an external challenge by communism of liberalism, which was resolved with the triumph of the latter.[1]

The dominant ideology goes on to claim that the death of so-called "real socialism" and, by extension, of class analysis as a means of explaining social processes brought an end to attempts to define society in terms of larger articulations of economic, political and ideological interests of competing social classes. "Metanarratives" are a thing of the past and what prevails in the post-modern world is a multiplicity of "narratives" (Lyotard, 1984) expressed in society in numerous complex and diverse social spaces no longer defined by class-based features (Morin, 1999; Maffesoli, 1996).

According to this argument, class-based social alignments, if they ever existed, are now obsolete. Instead, the new major alignments are marked out with different delimitations: between civilizations (Huntington, 1996), between economic blocs and their "models" for the administration of capitalism (Thurow, 1992) or since 9/11 between "the civilized world and terrorism."

Thus, if we are to believe the dominant ideology, we must convince ourselves that, given the non-existence of social classes, the contemporary world is not the product of one social class in conflict with another, but of the triumph of the market economy (the "economic model") and of liberalism (the "political model"), which have emerged victorious as forces of nature, as products with no producer, as the very expression of the eternal nature of human societies.

In reality, the organic intellectuals (using an expression coined by Gramsci) of the ruling class, or, more specifically, of the hegemonic faction of the ruling class, have never been interested in explaining the mechanisms on which their class domination over the dominated and exploited class or classes is based. To clarify these mechanisms has always been the

---

[1] See, for example, Fukuyama, 1992.

task of critical thought and this task has been important from the perspective of the interests of the exploited and oppressed. But in the current phase of the development of capitalism, it seems more important than ever. This is so for at least two reasons:

First, due to its exclusive concern for increasing profit levels, capital has devastated the institutional channels that once contained its own voracity, destroying whole societies, condemning millions of human beings to economic, moral and intellectual misery and annihilating nature, placing the very existence of humanity at risk.

Second and in spite of the suffering that its domination inflicts on contemporary society, capital in the form of a handful of gigantic multinational corporations that control production and the world market, is supposed to have risen victorious. This is expressed by the rather euphoric tone of the discourse of its organic intellectuals. The working class and the socialist project appear to have been defeated; the apologists of capital claim this defeat is final, but those of us who examine the process and not merely the moment, and who like Bloch (1986)[2] have hope that humanity still has a future, believe the defeat is merely transitory.

The contribution of this study is to give visibility to both the phenomenon of class domination (which, together with exploitation, is the object of analysis most ignored and obscured by the dominant ideology) and the subject that produces it; to help dispel its apparently natural character, i.e., the presumed absence of a producer, all of which the dominant ideology uses to "explain" the very disasters provoked by capital in contemporary society.

To examine the domination of capital, this book is divided into two parts. The first part, consisting of four chapters, sets forth a conceptual framework for the analysis of the general conditions of the domination of capital over the working class, its basis and its forms, both logical and historical.

In the first chapter, I analyze the content of the domination of capital – operating as the support to capitalist exploitation by reducing the working class to obedience, subordinating it economically, politically and ideologically – as a power built around a single basic social relation that

---

[2] It should also be added, however, as Mokhiber and Weissman note, that "the future of the scattered movement against the power of the corporations is uncertain. It is clear that it has a long way to go before it overturns the iron rule of the corporations over society. But our greatest hope lies in the task of saving our lives and our planet from the grip of the corporations" (Mokhiber and Weissman, 2005b).

establishes and constitutes the essential factor in the capitalist world: the capital relation, the relation that separates producers from the means of production. The analysis of this essential relation – the relation between capital and wage-labor, the concentration of the means of production and subsistence into the hands of the capitalist class and, as a result, the dispossession and separation between producer and means of production and subsistence – constitutes the organizing principle behind this entire work, from the first to the last chapter.

In the second chapter, I identify the general forms, or logical principles, of the domination of capital: its natural and its contained form. While the content of domination is articulated through exploitation, the forms of domination express a link between the two, defined in the conditions organized by the capital relation itself.

This analysis is founded on one basic principle: that the exploitation of the working class by the capitalist class is expressed as production and appropriation of surplus-value. Capital is value that appreciates but, unlike pre-capitalist forms of exploitation, which recognized a limit in the use value and consumption of the exploiting class, the capitalist form of exploitation has an insatiable need to appropriate the labor of others, as "its constant tendency... [is its] appetite for the labor of others" (Marx, 1867: Ch. 15), which makes capital extremely reluctant to grant concessions to the working class.

As this logic is the natural tendency of capital and organizes its immediate, direct and spontaneous movement, the natural form in capitalist domination is the effort to ensure the submission of the working class to the need for the spontaneous movement of the exploitation and accumulation of capital, stripping it of the conditions that make resistance and bargaining possible; the aim is not merely to prevent workers from stopping exploitation, but even from attempting to moderate it, to bargain or negotiate the conditions of their exploitation, and to win some form of concession from capital.

In contrast, in the contained form, capital is faced with a working class, and a society in general, that has managed to establish a certain level of containment of its spontaneous movement, and so adapts its domination to these conditions. In this context, in its most immediate sense, the contained form of domination derives from the struggle of the workers to wrestle concessions from capital, to achieve some degree of recognition of its material interests.

As we are dealing with general forms, not restricted to a particular historical period but constructed through theoretical abstraction, it is possible to work with them not as periods but as criteria for periodizing the history of domination. These general forms may assume different modes of historical expression, thereby allowing us to consider the history of capitalist domination not only as a succession of periods, but also as an alternation of its general forms.

In the third chapter, I examine the concept of the pattern of domination as a historical expression of a general form of capitalist domination which, while realizing in a specific context the basic processes defined by that general form, enables the delimitation of a historical period and, therefore, the construction of a world history of capitalist domination, correlated with a world history of capitalist economics.

The concept of the pattern of domination establishes an intermediate field of theoretical and historical analysis in a description moving from the general to the specific, between a general theory of capitalist domination and actual specific national cases of domination. It defines a periodization which, on the one hand, exhibits enough features to identify and differentiate periods in the world history of capitalist domination, but which, on the other hand, given the general nature of the features, allows for a multiplicity and diversity of specific forms of domination in different nation-states in the historical period concerned.

The intention behind the pattern of domination concept is thus to identify a historical trend that may define basic outlines in the prevailing form of capitalist domination, to find basic structures, broad cycles in the history of domination that allow us to posit a periodization that can be applied to a synthetic analysis of the historical evolution of capitalist domination. This periodization would also allow the identification, beyond the infinite diversity that can be found among all the specific cases, of general tendencies in capitalist domination.

In the fourth chapter, examining the history of capitalist domination from the perspective offered by the concept of the pattern of domination, three major periods are identified, defined in their basic historical expression by developed capitalism; in the first, the natural form predominates, in the second, the contained form and in the third, once again the natural form.

In developed Western capitalism, these three periods are defined by three patterns of domination: liberal, Keynesian and neoliberal. The first and the third are historical manifestations of the natural form, while the second is a historical manifestation of the contained form of capitalist domination. The liberal pattern constitutes the first historical expression of the natural form and the neoliberal pattern is its second expression, while the Keynesian pattern is an expression of the contained form.

These three patterns of domination correspond to subordinate patterns in Latin America, which are the oligarchic pattern, the developmentalist pattern and the neoliberal pattern, respectively. The oligarchic and neoliberal patterns are the Latin American expression of the natural form in its first and second historical emergence, while the developmentalist pattern is the expression of the contained form of capitalist domination.

The fourth chapter constitutes an introduction – merely by way of an overview, as it is not the central purpose of this work – to the study of the liberal/oligarchic and Keynesian/developmentalist patterns of domination: their birth, development and decline.

The second part of the book is dedicated to the analysis of the neoliberal pattern of domination, the current form of capital domination. I have attempted to summarize its general features in four processes which, although amidst resistance and diverse internal contradictions, seem to me to constitute the essence of its dynamic: the economy, the state, the state administration of criminal activity and the intellectual and moral leadership of neoliberal capital. Each of these processes constitutes a complex object of study of a process in progress, open to future turns in the course of history, although they are all intimately interrelated, and the aim here is to capture their tendencies, their strategic purpose in the context of the evolution of the capital/wage-labor relation, without limiting them to a particular moment in their development. It is an analysis conducted more on the logical plane than an attempt to define a particular historical manifestation, although the United States and Latin America (particularly Mexico) will serve as specific historical points of reference to illustrate certain tendential lines of the process.

A chapter is dedicated to each of these processes in the second part of the book, which begins with an examination of the transition from the Keynesian to the neoliberal pattern in the fifth chapter. The sixth chapter then examines the neoliberal economy, the seventh focuses on the neoliberal state, while the eighth examines the state administration of criminal activity and chapter nine treats its intellectual and moral leadership.

Chapter Five begins with a general overview of the decline of Keynesianism/developmentalism as modes of the contained form of domination. It is noted that a political structure that articulates forms of organization and representation of the working class and forms of negotiation between classes is only viable if, at the basic level of exploitation, the capitalist class is able to assume the commitment to improve the living conditions of the working class (by means of direct wages or redistribution of surplus-value by the state in the form of indirect wages) without affecting the rate of profit. In other words, to be viable, this structure of domination requires a delicate balance between wages and profit that is only possible in the context of a certain level of development of the productive force of labor, and, therefore, a certain level of organic composition of capital. But this same circumstance says much about the limitations of the contained form of domination, which enjoyed its peak during the post-war boom and waned with the fall in the rate of profit when that boom came to an end.

In the face of the crisis, capital imposed strategic initiatives aimed at opening a new channel for the satisfaction of its insatiable appetite for the labor of others and, just as the transition from the liberal to the Keynesian form had occurred in its time, the transition from the Keynesian to the neoliberal form took place.

There is, however, a radical difference between the transitions that marked the shift from the natural (liberal/oligarchic) form to the contained (Keynesian/developmentalist) form and those of the return to the natural (neoliberal) form; while the first meant that workers around the world had managed to win some concessions from capital and improve their working and living conditions (albeit within limits), the second meant that capital resumed its normal role, rolling back the gains that the workers had made with considerable struggle.

The first transition improved living and working conditions, while the second was explicitly designed to worsen them: the reduction of direct and indirect wages, the casualization of labor, increased unemployment, and the resumption of direct control of underdeveloped nations. The global wave that constituted the different modalities of the contained form of domination disappeared, giving way to a new emergence of the natural form of capitalist domination that was imposed throughout the world: the neoliberal pattern of domination.

The sixth chapter (The Neoliberal Economy) argues that, promoted and institutionalized by organizations such as the FMI and the WTO, the so-called globalization of big multinational financial capital (i.e. its free mobility and the development of its global financial, commercial and production networks, and the simultaneous expansion of the power of the new technological revolution) constitutes a series of strategies to increase the rate of surplus-value and concentrate its production and appropriation, redefining the relation between capital and labor and between developed capitalism and the underdeveloped world.

In the seventh chapter (The Neoliberal State), I contend that, in response to the globalization of capital, nation-states assumed as their political priority the task of promoting the free mobility and global competitiveness of their capital and of making themselves competitive (i.e. attractive for the investment of global capital). The nation-states are integrated into the global network of competitiveness and subordinated to the dynamics of the globalization of big multinational capital. The workers – particularly those of underdeveloped nations – are reduced to a situation of virtual defenselessness because (contrary to the free mobility of capital) they are denied the right to move about and organize themselves internationally and are held in national confinement, with nation-states now dedicated to dismantling the concessions that the workers achieved during the period of the Keynesian/developmentalist pattern of domination and disabled as spaces for the negotiated regulation of the capital-labor relation.

The eighth chapter examines what I refer to as state administration of criminal activity and its function as a link between the economics and the politics of neoliberal capital: the state administers the vacuum of life options and the discontent provoked by neoliberal economics (casualization, unemployment, poverty, illegal immigration, etc.), while also dismantling the institutional channels for addressing the problems produced by neoliberal politics. Faced with a systemic crisis that is expressed in a multiplicity of crises (financial, fiscal, overproduction, underproduction, labor, food, health, environmental, energy and other crises) which are apparently individual and independent of one another, and with a universal crisis of legitimacy of the state permeating them all, capitalism today constructs channels not to resolve the many economic, social and political problems it generates, but to administrate them according to the logic of the state administration of criminal activity, including the diverse variants of what it calls the war on terrorism and the fight against crime.

The state administration of criminal activity is established in necessary opposition to the growing chasm opening up between neoliberal economics and politics (both radically subordinated to the logic of capital) and the needs of society. It is a strategy that attempts to legitimize to society the development of a war which, based on the needs of capital, is waged against that same society; in its specific historical expression, this means that big capital is not prepared to negotiate with labor, or to moderate its voracity, or to recognize the relevance of any of the needs of the rest of society, but, attending solely to its insatiable appetite for surplus-value, it continues on its way, imposing its interests ever more violently.

While in the seventh chapter I examine how nation-states are networked into the logic of the administration of competitiveness, in this eighth chapter another dimension of the network is examined, this time from the logic of the administration of criminal activity: the construction of what are referred to as security alliances to combat terrorism, organized crime and other emergent threats.

There is a systematic and constant effort to develop the structure that networks the nation-states – a structure that intertwines the promotion of the free mobility of capital and the administration of competitiveness and criminal activity. This effort acquires its full meaning when it is examined in relation to the dynamic of the establishment of a global financial oligarchy and the specific form of state that it seeks to organize.

The ruling faction in neoliberal capitalism is global financial capital, third-generation monopolies – the grandchildren of the national monopolies (which, associated with their respective nation-states, led after the end of the 19th century to the imperialist division of the world and the two world wars), and the children of the multinational monopolies of the post-war period; it is the culmination (still in process) of the internal tendency of capital towards concentration and centralization of the means of production worldwide.

The transformations underway in the state and in the economy of capitalism are geared toward the creation of a global financial oligarchy which personifies this global financial capital and which, amidst intense social resistance and sharp internal contradictions, aspires to control the economy and politics of the world, seeking to complement free trade with the development of a framework of networked states and a military positioning on a global scale. The economics of neoliberal capital is a device for achieving its deepest and most private goal, i.e., to concentrate all of the world's wealth, and its politics is a systematic design to position nation-states in accordance with the achievement of this purpose, establishing spaces of global political power, under the direction of a central governmental control commanding a network of subordinate nation-states,[3] which guarantee the free movement of capital and the global administration of competitiveness and criminal activity, both to strengthen its economics and its politics, and to resolve the problems of what it calls social governance; i.e. the obstacles raised by social resistance.

---

[3] It is obvious that the U.S. oligarchy is the one that most openly promotes its aspiration to hold the central position in *the power structure of globalization*. And it is also clear that there are many obstacles in its way, including, in addition to acute social resistance, opposition from other *oligarchical conglomerates* established through various economic and political channels which may potentially lead to open military conflicts. But I must stress that the purpose of this work is to study the capital-labor relation, and so the examination of the development of inter-imperialist struggles, as important as it is, is not possible here.

The ninth chapter explores the project for the future that this global financial oligarchy – already in an advanced state of gestation – offers humanity and according to which it exercises its intellectual and moral leadership over contemporary society.

The first two sections of this chapter examine the general features of this intellectual and moral leadership, constructed in a social environment founded on disorganization and reduction to isolation in order to prevent the construction of interests that would transcend individual particularities and express the recognition of a social relation, a relation between social classes, by alienating individuals in competitiveness and criminal activity, in solitude and fear. A basic outline is presented to connect economics, politics and ideology in the current historical context, in order to round out the overview of the neoliberal pattern of domination and explain why the state administration of criminal activity is ultimately established as the core of the whole system of the intellectual and moral leadership of neoliberal capital: criminalizing and dissolving class opposition against its domination, reducing society to powerlessness and legitimizing its repression and its positioning of police and military forces against society by presenting it as a response to a demand made by society itself.

This increasing priority given to the state administration of criminal activity in the ideological and practical framework of neoliberal capital is neither accidental nor provisional, but necessary, as its future trajectory requires the increasing development of necrophilia and genocide. The last two sections of the chapter offer a reflection on the project for the future, the project of civilization that neoliberal capital offers humanity, based on which it exercises its intellectual and moral leadership and its economic, political and ideological practices.

In its struggle to establish absolute monopoly – to consummate its status as a global oligarchy concentrating all of the world's means of production and subsistence – it subordinates everything to its supreme purpose and, as such, lacks the capacity for concern about anything as insignificant as the wellbeing or the lives of billions of human beings.

Any consideration or respect for life becomes irrelevant in the face of the "magnificence" of the dystopia that dazzles its contemporary personifications,[4] and subordinates them (following the concept developed by

---

[4] "Human beings and life concepts disappear from economic concepts... the theory and praxis of economics no longer take as their point of departure the real needs of men,

Marx) to an extreme fetishism; the contemporary world resembles a spaceship[5] driven by a "self-regulating system" which is "self-programmed like an intelligent machine."[6] The logic of transnationalized capital is imposed upon the nation-state in the privileged position of reason and the public interest constructed by bourgeois political science and – parallel to the lack of any institutional framework to replace it, except that which capital itself has been establishing to promote its globalization – the multitude of disasters which its domination produces and which oppress contemporary society are simply opportunities to pursue the development of that logic. The "alternatives" proposed by the voices of capital always revolve around an argument for the unavoidable necessity of further development of their policies, explaining that the problems are the result of the invariably insufficient application of those policies.

In keeping with this necessity, wholeheartedly assumed by its ideologues and personifications, to unburden capital of any consideration that opposes its self-regulation, they promote radical and total submission to the logic of capital, dismissing the old discourses, which once constituted valued political principles (human rights, humanism, justice, equality, the social contract, the public interest), as obsolete and irrelevant, or sterilizing them, stripping them of any critical potential and unleashing an active hostility toward any criticism made of the logic of the fetish.

Thus, through the reconfiguration of its pattern of domination, framed within a new, powerful and multifaceted technological revolution and developed in the context of an aggressive economic, political and ideological offensive, neoliberal capital has rendered large sectors of contemporary society defenseless and won resounding victories in the context of the class struggle, and its domination appears to be permanently established. However, belying this appearance, the current historical period of the development of capitalism displays internal contradictions that are acquiring an increasingly irresolvable nature, made evident in multiple crises which are, in turn, necessarily expressed at the level of the class

---

society loses its primacy over economics and any reflection on society vanishes... Free competition between individual economic interests is finally replacing all forms of social coexistence" (Kurnitzky, 2000).

[5] The metaphor is inspired by a proposition offered in Ianni, 1996.

[6] According to Lyotard's analysis of the *post-modern condition*, capital operates as a "self-regulated system" that is "self-programmed like an intelligent machine", which dismisses anything that opposes it, and which, although its logic aggravates society's ills, allows for no alternative or possibility for solutions to the problems it creates (Lyotard, 1984).

struggle, as capital tends to aggravate the social ills that it provokes, and opposition to its domination is becoming as necessary and irrevocable as the defense of life itself.

The purpose of the tenth chapter is to relate the historical succession of patterns of domination to the tendencies that organize the long term or life cycle of capitalism (the gestation, development and extinction of its social classes), the period from its birth as a social mode of organizing production to its death. For this analysis, there are just three periods to consider: infancy, maturity and decline.

The essential point in this analysis is the fact that the capital relation, the separation of producers from the means of production, develops together with the development of the productive force of labor and unleashes the profound tendencies, the general trends that shape the future of capitalist society and point to its end: increased labor productivity, increased organic composition of capital, concentration and centralization of capital, expulsion of the work force from the labor process, expansion of the industrial reserve army and worker overpopulation, and finally, as a result of the above, a drop in the rate of profit.

The theoretical space that allows us to link the pattern of domination with the long term history of capitalism derives from the capital relation and the development of its internal tendencies. The delimitation of each of its periods is drawn from the decisive moments in the development of the productive force of labor; i.e. from the decisive moments in the development of the capital relation. In this development lies the common basis for both the world history of capitalist economics and the world history of capitalist domination.

The relation between the historical succession of patterns of domination and the long term history of capitalism is established in accordance with the patterns of domination prevailing in developed capitalism, as it is these that define the basic features of the historical period. Thus, the liberal pattern corresponds to the infancy of capitalism, while the Keynesian pattern, the first and only historical expression of the contained form of domination corresponds to its period of maturity.

The neoliberal pattern of domination, the second historical expression of the natural form of domination, corresponds to its decline. For capital, decline means an increasing organic composition and a decreasing rate of profit, and as a result, a renewed need to increase the rate of surplus-value in a final effort to restore the level of the rate of profit, along with a renewed hostility toward making concessions to the working class, becoming even more intense as it draws closer to its end. For those dispossessed of the means of production and subsistence, it means increasing hardships and an urgent need to defeat capitalism.

The period of decline is the process moving toward the final crisis of the capital relation. The new technological revolution, while providing the basis for the restructuring of the pattern of domination, delimits the territory for the transition toward the end of capitalism. Capitalism today still has the ability to integrate a significant percentage of the world's population into its structures, but it is increasingly turning into a machine designed to produce a growing mass of human beings superfluous to it and to promote all manner of conflicts that lead nowhere, producing only more poverty, chaos, social degradation and death; such is the future that capital domination offers humanity.

The state administration of criminal activity has become a means of managing its period of decline and of configuring its governance. Thus, the current personifications of capital promise an endless war, which they claim to be against terrorism and organized crime, and insist that humankind must choose between the terrorists and them, the ones who (presumably) will fight the criminals.

It is of course an absurd and insane dilemma, the only purpose of which is to confine humanity in an irresolvable labyrinth and in meaningless conflicts with no future. It is like being made to choose from an array of images in a house of mirrors, all of them reflections of the same thing. The only expression of conflict that can offer hope for the future and possibilities for the construction of a new civilization is a class-based conflict aimed at bringing an end to the capital relation.

There is a need implicit in the development of the relation between capital and labor: to restore the connection between producers and the means of production through the social reappropriation of those means, and to use production to satisfy the needs of society rather than to profit a small group. In this way, by economizing labor time, technological progress, rather than producing a redundant population, may reduce working hours, providing more free time and work for all, and thus establish the conditions for the full development of all individuals. In opposition to the capitalist state, the historical need awaiting expression is the socialist state, the organization of free associated producers (which is completely unrelated to the state capitalism that gave itself the name of real socialism in the 20th century), the essential task of which will be to guarantee the connection between producers, organized as a worker collective, and the means of production and subsistence.

The conflict between capital and labor entails its necessary negation. The development of capital is neither eternal nor reducible to a scenario of political wills and struggles between social classes, as these struggles unfold in the context of objective conditions defined by the capital relation, which will ultimately lead to its end. It is a necessity contained in the development of necessary relations that are independent of the will and consciousness of men, but the form that this necessity takes will depend on the class struggle: it is will and consciousness in action.

Anyone who has read the novel *Moby Dick* will probably agree that what is outrageous about the story is not so much Captain Ahab's obsession with the great white whale, but the inability of the crew of the Pequod to unite and save their own lives by casting the insanity into the sea, just as humankind needs to do today with this increasingly insane Captain Ahab that is the capital relation. Without the additional insanity of obedience to a madman, Captain Ahab would be a harmless lunatic locked up in an anonymous asylum, rather than the pilot of this increasingly bleak spaceship of which we are all passengers.

But beyond the outrage, this situation poses a challenge: to understand domination and how it prevents unity in the defense of the lives of the vast, multifarious mass of human beings dispossessed of the means of production and subsistence and divided in conflict and competition against one another.

The concept of the pattern of domination, and particularly the neoliberal pattern of domination, is proposed as a means of identifying the difficulties to be overcome in order to organize, expand and win the battle against the capital relation. It is constructed to examine the conditions of the problem, not the conditions of the solution. But I believe that by explaining one, we can go a long way toward comprehending the other, as to a large extent the conditions of the problem contain those of the solution. It is to that comprehension that I wish to contribute this modest work.

PART ONE

THE DOMINATION OF CAPITAL:
ITS LOGICAL AND HISTORICAL FORMS

CHAPTER ONE

THE BASIS OF CAPITALIST DOMINATION

"The Communist Manifesto had, as its object, the proclamation of inevitable impending dissolution of modern bourgeois property... The theory of the Communists may be summed up in this single sentence: Abolition of private property."

K. Marx and F. Engels
The Communist Manifesto

To examine the nature of capitalist class domination I will adopt a series of approaches, moving from the general to the specific, on a gradual path towards the concrete. It is worth remembering that, if a trajectory moving from the general to the specific constitutes a means of getting closer to concrete reality, it is because we can find the most general and abstract qualities, developed and redefined, in the most specific situations.

As this entire work is articulated from the perspective of Marxist theory, I will begin with a few notes related to the Marxist definition of domination. It is not my purpose to offer either a synthesis or a general review of such an extraordinarily complex theoretical field, but rather to identify a few concepts that will facilitate the analysis that follows.

DOMINATION AND OBEDIENCE

Before entering the theoretical territory of Marxism, I believe it will be useful to begin with a general idea of the meaning of domination. The dictionary of the Royal Academy of the Spanish Language defines dominio ("dominion" or "rule") as "the power to use and dispose of one's possessions" (Real Academia Española, 1992). The term is thus expressed in relation to property; those who dominate use and dispose of something that belongs to them; the thing dominated is used as a possession.

The Spanish UNESCO *Diccionario de ciencias sociales* defines *dominación* ("domination") as "socially established, recognized and compelling power to control and dispose of any object: the right to use it, destroy it, or transfer it to others. The domination relation is closely associated with the institution of property" (UNESCO, 1987). Both of these dictionary definitions, insofar as they associate domination with the ownership of things, reserve the use of the term to define relationships between people and objects, not relationships between human beings. In other words, the domination relation, according to the definitions provided by both dictionaries, appears to be something foreign to human relations.

This delimitation of the concept, with social relations excluded from its definition, is of little use in explaining domination as a relationship between human beings. There can be no doubt that the crucial, essential role of such a relation in contemporary society should not be overlooked by any dictionary, however general it may be. But perhaps we expect too much of such dictionaries; perhaps it is a topic confined to the realm of political science. Yet a Spanish specialist dictionary in political science, compiled by Norberto Bobbio and Nicola Matteucci, omits the term. Apparently, they did not consider it sufficiently important to include it in their dictionary (Bobbio and Matteuci, 1981).

These omissions may be symptomatic of a lack of interest in clarifying a topic which is crucial, but problematic, conflictive, unpleasant and, it might be said, "irrelevant" for the dominant ideology. Domination is imposed, administered and developed but, from the perspective of the dominators, it is neither necessary nor advisable to turn it into a topic of discussion, interest or public reflection. It is essentially a topic of private interest, exclusive to those who dominate. The dominated need not strain their intellect studying and analyzing these types of questions.

The conversion of human beings into things, into objects belonging to other human beings, is a notion associated with the social relations of slavery. Nevertheless, in capitalism, the working class labor force is converted into a commodity, an object that becomes the property of its purchasers: the idea of treating the labor force as property is not alien to the capital-labor relation. Thus even the dispassionate notions offered by the dictionaries mentioned above tend to evoke certain aspects of the domination relation between the classes of capitalist society and the right to use, destroy and transfer, which the dominant class assumes it has over certain dimensions of the lives of the dominated classes, or over certain segments of those classes.[1]

---

[1] There is no shortage of examples to illustrate this tendency to exercise *property rights* over human beings. One need only consider, for example, the lack of protection and complete absence of rights of illegal immigrants on the border between Mexico and the United States, or the way the Mexican government has treated recent social uprisings in Atenco and Oaxaca; men and women attacked and abused by authorities immune to

Of course, my purpose here is not to explain domination as a relation between human beings and objects, but as a relation between human beings, between two groups in society; the dominant group that gives the orders and the dominated group that obeys them. "Domination," says Sánchez Vázquez, "requires an assurance of its recognition on the part of the dominated. This evidence that the other force is defeated or dominated is its obedience. In the power relation, one group gives the orders and the other obeys. Control is the quality of those who exercise the power; obedience is the quality of the dominated. Power can only exist if it dominates, and it only dominates if it is obeyed" (Sánchez Vázquez, 1999: 15–16).

Orders are not advice, or requests, or recommendations. Orders compel because those giving them have the capacity to make others obey.

SOCIAL CLASSES IN CAPITALISM

The aim here, however, is not to explore any relationship of rule and subordination, of control and obedience between any two groups of human beings, but relations between social classes. The essential relationship under capitalism, the underlying social relation between its classes, consists in the separation between direct producers and the means of production and subsistence: "the social form of production is determined first of all by a particular relation between direct producers and the means of production and subsistence. Under the regime of capital, ownership is merely the manifestation of the separation between direct producers and their means. When we speak of separation, we mean capitalists on one side and paid workers on the other, and *this is the essential relation under capitalism*" (Figueroa Sepúlveda, 1986: 8, emphasis added).

This is the essential social relation under capitalism, that which constitutes the capitalist social form: the workers are apparently dispossessed of the means of production and subsistence, which are set up against them as an autonomous power. "It is this separation that constitutes the concept of capital."[2] For Marx – and this is his general concept – the working class is made up of people dispossessed of the means of production

---

punishment, who seek in this way to make clear who the masters of society really are. Indeed, throughout the history of capitalism in general, and that of Latin America in particular, there is an abundance of evidence of the fragile line, in the eyes of the dominant class, between the dignity of a human life and the banality of a worthless object.

[2] From Marx's *Theories of Surplus Value* (as quoted in Figueroa Sepúlveda, 1986: 38).

(and, therefore, of the means of subsistence), while the capitalist class are the possessors of the means of production (expressed in legal terms as property); in its basic, general sense, the working class is made up of that great mass of human beings who lack means of production and subsistence, and are required to sell their labor-power to capital for a wage in order to survive and who are, therefore, constantly seeking to maximize their own utility, to serve a function within the complex social framework of capitalism.

This essential relation does not change according to the form taken by this autonomous power with which the direct producer is faced. The variations may have a range of significant meanings, but in terms of their essential characteristics, as constituent parts of class relations in capitalism, it matters little whether the means of production and subsistence are presented to workers distributed over multiple owners, as in the competitive capitalism of the first two thirds of the 19th century, concentrated in the hands of a few macro-capitalists, as in the great global monopolies of the "globalized" capital of the late 20th century, in the hands of the state as "nationalized" property, or in the hands of a state-organized collective owner, as in the so-called "real socialism" of the 20th century. Of course, the legal form that this separation takes is also of no real importance. In all cases, the separation between producer and means of production and subsistence remains the same and, with it, the class relation between capitalists and workers.[3]

If the constitution of the capitalist class allows variety and modifications in form without necessarily altering its essential content, the same may be said of those dispossessed of the means of production and subsistence.[4] Their existence in capitalism takes on a wide variety of forms[5] which, for the function they fulfill at the service of capital (at least with

---

[3] From this we can conclude that the self-acclaimed "real socialism" of the 20th century was merely a form of state capitalism managed by a collective of property owners organized into the "Communist Party", and into a "Socialist State", that the collapse of this system simply represented a change in its capitalist structure, and that capitalism will only be overcome with the effective appropriation of its means of production and subsistence by the producer class.

[4] For this reason it is important to understand *working class* as referring to the *dispossessed* as a group (a more inclusive concept which encompasses the diversity of forms assumed by the dominated class in capitalism) and not only to the *workers* (which tends to be associated with the industrial proletariat). On the other hand, the concepts of *middle classes* and *marginalized* seem to me inconsistent and tendentious, and as such are ideologically useful to the domination of capital.

[5] "The idea of a more or less homogeneous mass of workers is as obsolete as the idea of labor that thinks and plans as it acts" (Figueroa Sepúlveda, 1986: 57).

regard to the relationship between the working class and production capital), could be grouped into a few basic categories: active workers – divided into productive (general labor[6] and immediate labor[7]) and non-productive (monitoring and supervision tasks[8] and commodity circulation tasks); and non-active workers (the industrial reserve army, the section of the workforce that slips in and out of the dynamic of capital accumulation, and the absolute surplus population, the section that is simply surplus to the needs of capital with the many social forms that it adopts).

Not all are exploited, as not all produce surplus value, but all are dominated, subordinated to the needs of capital, and all share the same basic separation from their means of production and/or subsistence, compelled to sell their only possession – their personal attributes – to survive. Exploring diverse combinations of meanness and pettiness with wit and creativity, whether in white collars or blue collars, denizens of the noisy, suffocating atmosphere of the factory or the neat and quiet space of the office, cubicle or laboratory; tramps in the poor quarters of the cities, street walkers or beggars; the fate of all the inhabitants of the kingdom of capital is defined according to the same basic social relation – the capital relation.

The definition of domination given by UNESCO's *Diccionario de ciencias sociales*, associated with the notion of an "ecological system," offers a graphic image for the idea presented here: "domination is linked to control, which one species exercises over the material conditions of sustenance of the other species of the system. The dominant species organizes the activities of the others, assigns to the subordinate species their different ranks, stabilizes, maintains order and permits the growth of the system, integrates the activities of the different species and performs functions of coordination and control. This entails a center or focal point from which influence is exerted and an area or territory in which this control is imposed. The subordinate species are positioned in relation

---

[6] The section of the workforce engaged in scientific and technological research, and general planning of production processes, made up of a diverse range of scientists and professionals.

[7] The section of the workforce engaged in operative tasks, those who directly produce the merchandise, comprising the *industrial proletariat* in the strict sense of the term.

[8] "At first, the capitalist is relieved of manual labor. Then, when his capital grows and with it the collective labor that he exploits, he hands over the work of direct and constant supervision of the individual workmen and groups of workmen to a special kind of wage-laborer. An industrial army of workmen, under the command of a capitalist, requires subordinate officers (managers, overlookers, foremen) who, while the work is being done, command in the name of the capitalist" (Marx, 1867: Ch.13).

to the center of domination and in relation to each other" (UNESCO, 1987:743–744).

The "dominant species" in the "ecological system" of capitalism, the capitalist class, assigns ranks to different segments of the "dominated species," differentiating them and placing them in opposition against one another, which not only serves as a functional response to their needs for domination and exploitation, but also their ultimate purpose: division, opposition and competition between the dominated as a basic condition for perpetuating their subordinate status.[9]

There is nothing absurd or irrational in this proclivity of the dominated towards division and mutual competition. It is natural and necessary as the aim is to serve capital and negotiate some form of reward in return. The political project of unification of the dominated can only take root when the aim becomes not to serve, but to fight against capital. As everything in public life is at the service of capital, it is natural that the different segments of the dominated, spread throughout the economic, political and cultural framework of bourgeois society, would strive to demonstrate their qualities and qualifications of servitude and compete against each other for the positions and rewards that capital offers.

The rewards accessible to the dominated for services rendered to the domination and exploitation of capital, expressed in the context of the capitalist relation, may vary in size. But even when the rewards are few, they are not necessarily any less desirable or less provocative of division and conflict among the dominated, creating what might be called *the Ah Q Syndrome*.[10]

It is also clear that this predisposition towards division and competition among the dominated becomes even more acute when there are limited collective means of organizing their relationship with the domination and exploitation of capital; that is, so limited that they are compelled to

---

[9] "The essential condition for the existence and for the sway of the bourgeois class is the accumulation of wealth in the hands of individuals, the formation and augmentation of capital. The condition for the existence of capital is wage-labor. *Wage-labor rests exclusively on competition between the laborers"* (Marx and Engels, 1848, emphasis added).

[10] Lu Xun's tale, "The True Story of Ah Q", illustrates a case which, although extreme, is nonetheless common in our society. The story tells of two beggars fighting, with considerable fury but little energy due to their starving condition, for the *privilege* to beg on a "good" street corner. Gogol's story "The Overcoat" narrates the tragicomic efforts of a lower-level bureaucrat to win the recognition of his superiors. Hundreds of examples of such scenarios, all expressions of the *Ah Q Syndrome,* can be found by observing the behavior of sections of the dominated not only within "economic" institutions, such as capitalist corporations, but also within cultural or political institutions, such as universities or political parties.

negotiate their position in society individually. Under these conditions, the inclination towards unconditional servitude to capital will be accentuated, and individual positioning and the search for immediate alternatives will be favored, whether or not it is recognized that these contribute to the domination and exploitation of capital and, therefore, undermine medium- and long-term group and even individual interests.

The greater the lack of political organization that would grant them some level of identity and class consciousness, the greater the obligation upon the dispossessed masses to provide human beings for the unconditional satisfaction of any need of capital; from supervisors and foremen who represent it in direct labor relations to political employees who operate the state system, and including what might be called the degradation professions (torturers, hired killers, drug producers and dealers, prostitutes, sex offenders and a long list of others) if opening such sources of employment are in the interests of capital.

This is why the social structure preferable to capital is social atomization; the reduction to individual units and to defenselessness in against its domination. Bourgeois individualism is not based on a notion of each person fully realizing his or her individual potential.[11] For all of the members of the capitalist class, individualism means promotion of their capital, of their private property. For all of the members of the dominated class, individualism means individual management of their place in the structure of domination and exploitation of capital, defenselessness against and subordination to capital interests, in the hope of receiving some kind of reward for placing themselves at the service of capital.

However, this diverse mass of human beings, divided, set at odds and in competition against each other, shares the common traits of separation from the means of production and subsistence, the need to sell themselves or their personal attributes as the only way of gaining access to their means of subsistence, and job insecurity due to their dispensable nature from the perspective of capital. Both a foreman in a factory and a researcher in a laboratory, each in his or her specific sphere of activity, may be fierce advocates for capital interests while working at its service; but, under certain conditions, either one may be cast out to join the unemployment lines.[12]

---

[11] In contrast, Marx proposed that "in place of the old bourgeois society, with its classes and class antagonisms, there will arise an association in which the free development of each is the condition for the free development of all" (Marx and Engels, 1848).

[12] There is no doubt that, depending on the level and complexity of their qualifications, foremen are more dispensable than scientists. But scientists are not indispensable to

Of course, this diversity and multiplicity of forms derives from the historical evolution of capitalist society and from the different positions defined by the capitalist class for different segments of the dominated classes, according to its needs of exploitation and domination. However, two points need to be added in this regard:

1. The relative importance of each of the sections of the labor force referred to above is modified by the evolution and behaviors of capital accumulation; the composition of the working class changes with the unfolding of the tendential laws of capitalist development.[13]

2. Capitalism is a global economic system, with its social classes organized on a global scale and, as such, the spatial distribution of the different sections of the working class needs to be observed.[14]

With this in mind, to examine the composition of the working class, we need to consider its functional and spatial distribution at the global level, as well as the circumstances of the historical period and the degree of development of the tendential laws of capitalism.

EXPLOITATION AND DOMINATION: CAPITAL RELATION AND PRODUCTION PROCESS

This same essential relation, the capital relation,[15] the separation between producers and their means of production and subsistence, which establishes the social classes in capitalism, constructs the basic articulation between the economic, political and cultural dimensions of relations

---

capital; currently, certain types of highly qualified personnel in Europe and the U.S. are being displaced by competition from their colleagues in India, who offer services of equal quality at lower costs.

[13] Thus, in the 19th century, the industrial proletariat, the section of the labor force that performs *immediate labor*, was the predominant sector of the working class as a whole. Over the course of the 20th century, the section responsible for scientific and technological research acquired greater strategic importance, which it continues to hold today. And currently, due to the very same dynamic of capitalism, and the development of productive forces, the segment of the "excluded", the *surplus population*, is assuming, at least quantitatively, increasing importance.

[14] This perspective enables us to identify certain basic processes; for example, that the section that performs *general labor* tends to be concentrated in developed countries, while the industrial reserve army and surplus population tend to be concentrated in developing countries.

[15] Hereinafter, to avoid repetition, I will refer to this condition of separation between producers and their means of production and subsistence, constituting the capital/wage labor relation, as the *capital relation*.

between the classes.[16] More specifically, it constitutes the core from which it is possible to explain domination and to link it to capitalist exploitation.

Exploitation, explained briefly, refers to the appropriation of the labor of others: one part of society, constituting the exploiting social class, appropriates the labor performed by another part of society, defined as the exploited social class. Domination, as has been argued above, refers to the fact that one part of society, constituting the dominant social class, subordinates another part of society, defined as the dominated social class, reducing it to obedience.

The basis of capitalist exploitation is the capital relation: workers sell their labor-power because they lack the means of production and subsistence. Capital pays the value of the labor-power and appropriates the excess value produced by the laborer; the working class is exploited by the capitalist class through appropriation of surplus value. Capital is value that appreciates.

But the capital relation is also the basis of capitalist domination. Workers sell their labor-power for a wage in order to acquire a means of subsistence.[17] Capitalists pay for the use of this labor-power; they purchase control over it. From that moment, a relation not only of exploitation, but of control and subordination, is established within the labor process. It should also be noted that the domination relation is established as a condition that is repeated with the simultaneous occurrence of various circumstances.

The first of these circumstances is that the needs of workers are renewed and, with them, the need to renew the sale of their labor-power; "The laborer... will feel it to be a cruel nature-imposed necessity that his capacity has cost for its production a definite amount of the means of subsistence and that it will continue to do so for its reproduction" (Marx 1867:Ch.6).

The second circumstance consists in the fact that the worker's condition is one of constant uncertainty in the labor market, even more so when, as a result of technological developments, that market operates in

---

[16] "Debate in our societies is nothing more than the debate over specific *social* relations, which in turn constitute the common core of economic, political, cultural relations, etc. The economic and political spheres are never separated, for the simple reason that they are each no more than different dimensions of a single process, the process of the *social form* that constitutes the movement of societies" (Figueroa Sepúlveda, 1986: 8).

[17] "The proletariat, the class of modern laborers, who live only so long as they find work, and who find work only so long as their labor increases capital" (Marx and Engels, 1848).

the context of a large reserve army, promoting intense competition for employment among workers.[18]

The third circumstance is founded in the progressive domination acquired by capital over the labor process, which is evident in the concepts and conditions relating to the shift from formal to real subordination of labor to capital and from the production of absolute surplus value to the production of relative surplus value.

Capital separates general labor (production of scientific and technological knowledge) from immediate labor, which becomes a sphere for the application of science (Figueroa Sepúlveda, 1986: 41). Capitalist domination over the worker also now appears as subordination of the laborer to the machine (Figueroa Sepúlveda, 1986: 31). Workers are deprived of many of their productive faculties, just as before they were deprived of their means of production; "these faculties reappear now as a quality of the collective laborer and this, in turn, as a quality of capital," as a form of existence of capital and, therefore, an alien power that dominates the worker (Figueroa Sepúlveda, 1986: 34). Laborers remain separate and alienated from one another: "[they] are isolated persons, who enter into relations with the capitalist, but not with one another. This cooperation begins only with the labor process, but they have then ceased to belong to themselves... they are but special modes of existence of capital" (Marx, 1867:Ch.13).

Technological progress, systematically promoted by capital and turned into its private property, not only ensures the control of capital over the labor process but also, by promoting a constant increase in labor productivity, enables the scale of production to be increased without proportionate increases in the number of laborers. Technological progress becomes a mechanism for progressive expulsion of the labor-power involved in the labor process and, therefore, a mechanism for the creation, development and consolidation of an industrial reserve army. In other words, it becomes not only a mechanism for increasing the level of worker exploitation, but also a mechanism central to class domination as it promotes competition and division among the workers.

Thus, domination and exploitation in capitalism find a point of connection in the capital relation and the production process itself; advances in the conditions to develop the exploitation process are also advances in the

---

[18] "The 'despotism of the factory' is imposed upon proletarians who are subjected to market coercion, as they are dispossessed of everything except their own arms. And market coercion entails employment uncertainty" (Brunhoff, 1980: 226).

domination process. In the hands of capital, the usefulness of any given technology is defined in terms of its capacity to produce surplus value and, at the same time, its capacity to increase the domination of capital over labor: to ensure that capital maintains control of the production process within the factory and to contribute to the creation of a reserve labor army which will foster competition and division among workers and which therefore establishes a general condition for the domination of capital over labor.

Domination and exploitation are mutually interdependent and both are constructed on a common foundation: the capital relation. Technological progress promoted by capital develops the capital relation, as will be examined in some detail in the final chapter of this work. Once this relation is established as the dominant force in society, accepted as the social "norm," the process acquires a certain "automatism", and capital builds its domination in the realm of production itself, in the economy in general. Unlike relations between slaves and slaveholders or between servants and masters, whereby the immediate workers maintain a basic connection with their means of production, relations between capitalists and workers do not appear to require direct, constant political coercion.

And this "norm" is consolidated because, as Figueroa Sepúlveda explains, the exploitation relation conceals its nature, being distorted so as to present itself as something other than it really is: "the wage form thus extinguishes every trace of the division of the working day into necessary labor and surplus labor, into paid labor and unpaid labor. All labor appears to be paid labor."[19]

In this way, according to Figueroa Sepúlveda, the exploitation relation vanishes behind the monetary relation. "We can therefore understand the decisive importance of the transformation of the value and price of labor-power into the form of wages, or into the value and price of labor itself. All of the notions of justice to which both workers and capitalists adhere, all of the mystifications of capitalism regarding freedom, all of the senseless justifications of vulgar economics, have their basis in the form of expression referred to above, which makes the actual relation invisible and presents the exact opposite of that relation."[20] This makes it possible "to dispense with the use of coercion at the level of production and to disassociate the political from the economic" (Figueroa Sepúlveda, 1989: 47).

---

[19] Taken from Marx's *Capital* (quoted in Figueroa Sepúlveda, 1989: 47).
[20] Also taken from *Capital* (quoted by Figueroa Sepúlveda, 1989: 47).

However, a long series of historical processes are necessary before this appearance of "naturalness" can be established: "It takes centuries ere the 'free' laborer, thanks to the development of capitalist production, agrees, i.e. is compelled by social conditions, to sell the whole of his active life, his very capacity for work, for the price of the daily necessities of life" (Marx, 1867: Ch.10). And, as will be shown in the following sections, many processes are needed to preserve this capitalist "norm."

The Capitalist State and Social Power

Every state is a power organization of a class, a class that is organized as the dominant class. Political power in the capitalist state is the power of the whole capitalist class: "the executive of the modern state is but a committee for managing the common affairs of the whole bourgeoisie" (Marx and Engels, 1848). "The common affairs of the whole bourgeoisie" cover a wide range of matters, the analysis of which is beyond the purpose of this investigation. In the following chapter, I will attempt to explore this further, but in this chapter the aim is to focus on the basic point.

The basic point is that, in spite of its strength, this "automatism of the market," this quasi-automatic reproduction of the separation between producers and their means of production and subsistence, is not a sufficient assurance to maintain the capital relation. The main "common affair of the whole bourgeoisie" is to preserve and develop the capital relation, wherein politics and economics are interwoven.

It is intrinsic to the very nature of the capital relation that workers recognize in this separation the source of all their difficulties as a class, and seek to reestablish their connection with their means of production and subsistence by destroying the capitalist relation, or, in a more moderate, less ambitious scenario, seek to bargain, to negotiate the conditions of their domination and exploitation with the constant threat of hindering the "smooth running" of the affairs of domination and exploitation. And the essential task of the capitalist state is, firstly, to prevent the destruction of the capital relation and, secondly, to contribute to its development.[21]

---

[21] Its opposite, the historical necessity that has still yet to be realized, is the socialist State, the organization of the working class, whose essential task would be to ensure unity between producers, organized as a workers' collective, and their means of production and subsistence.

From the mid-19th century to the first decades of the 20th, the workers' movement, not creating a project but rather contributing to the identification of a historical necessity, developed through Marxism an acute awareness of the need to destroy the capital relation, and converted this awareness into revolutionary attempts to transform capitalist society. In that period, as in no other period since, this historical necessity entailing the destruction of the capital relation through the social reappropriation of the means of production and subsistence acquired force and intensity.

Over the course of the rest of the 20th century, the vicissitudes of the class struggle numbed this awareness, but this is not to say that the domination of the state became irrelevant; subsequently, the workers' movement, not to destroy but rather to negotiate the conditions for capitalist exploitation and domination, established complex bargaining and protest processes that necessitated constant management by the state to regulate and direct the conflicts. The state established itself as the force for order, for the reconciliation of contradictions which, if not resolved, would have led to societal paralysis.

Now in the early 21st century, as if waking from a long slumber, in an awkward process of trial and error, spurred on by the renewed voracity of capital, a new march is beginning, a long and complex march towards the future. The struggles of this huge, complex, diverse, scattered, multifaceted, passionate and conflictive segment of humanity, separated from its means of production and subsistence, articulated in the capital relation as the exploited and/or dominated class, are not a topic belonging to the past or specific to any particular period in the history of capitalism. The vicissitudes of their struggle stretch across the whole history of capitalism; the "automatism" of the market has never been sufficient assurance of the preservation of the capital relation, and in every period the state has been guarantor of its continued existence and a constant manager of its development.

As the essential task of the state is to prevent the destruction of the capital relation, political domination is coordinated to support class exploitation. In reality, the raison d'etre of political domination is to ensure exploitation. "The young Marx," argues Sánchez Vázquez, "focused his attention on the state, but the discovery of what Hegel had mythologized (the relations between state and civil society) led Marx to uncover *the real basis of the state*. In doing so, he revealed the limitations of Hegelian theory on the state, and the need to begin a critique of the real basis of social division and political power: the economy" (Sánchez Vázquez, 1999: 33, emphasis added). "*Capital* (Marx's book)," he adds, "is not purely a work of economics, unrelated to politics; it explains the real basis of politics."[22]

Exploitation is not possible unless it is sustained through domination, and domination has no purpose except as a support to exploitation. The separation of domination from exploitation, according to Sánchez Vázquez, *fetishizes* power:[23] "if the political is founded on the social, the anatomy of which is the economic, there can be no exclusively political criticism (such criticism is unfounded and insufficient on its own), but only political criticism founded on economic criticism" (Sánchez Vázquez, 1999: 34).

Economics, politics, and ideology are not self-contained fields separated one from the other. They all form part of a social power, the domination of one class over the other, based, in all its dimensions, on the same social relation – the capital relation: "Against the tradition of bourgeois thought, which views political power as absolute, Marx is a theorist of economic power, considering it in relation to political and ideological powers" (Sánchez Vázquez, 1999: 48).

The raison d'etre of the state, the power organization of the dominant class, is to provide support for the exploitation perpetrated by that class. Capitalist domination takes on diverse forms,[24] but it is essentially based on force, on the capacity of the dominant class to inflict violence upon the dominated classes, while stripping them of their capacity for violent response.

According to Lenin, "the standing army and the police are the chief instruments of state power," and, in this sense, the basic task assumed by the state is to "deprive the oppressed classes of definite means and methods of struggle for the overthrow of the oppressors" (Lenin, 1918).

---

[22] "Marx takes a new perspective on social thought, which, from Machiavelli to Hobbes and Hegel, had examined power, while exploitation remained in the shadows" (Sánchez Vázquez, 1999: 11).

[23] This is the basis of his criticism of Marcuse and Foucault: for the first, he says, "the rationale of power is technological. The technological *logos* develops in an inherent fashion, whatever may be the relations of production," and for Foucault, "the power relation [is] a network of powers (factory, school, church, family, etc.); reticulate or capillary power, which is everywhere; it is not localized in the state system or in its repressive function. He objects to viewing this network of powers as a simple projection of political power, but doesn't recognize the nexus that unites this power to the relations of production, its nature as a class and the role it plays in the class struggle" (Sánchez Vázquez, 1999: 13).

[24] The State has the "possibility of adopting diverse forms of power or of government (authoritarian or democratic) to better serve, in specific historical conditions, the interests of the dominant class" (Sánchez Vázquez, 1999: 38).

Domination is based, as a last resort, on violence, on the coercive capacity of the state and of the dominant class.

Domination is always dictatorial: "it is not a question of the practice of violence as the sole function or as one of several functions, but rather, of what is at the very heart of power... whether it is a power legitimized by the law (the so-called democracies) or a despotic or dictatorial power (not subject to any law), there is no qualitative distinction in its nature; power is based on force and on the institutions established to exercise it. Armed forces, police forces and security forces exist to dominate those who might resist or counteract them. Domination always finds latent or effective opposition, actual or potential resistance. In the relation between the dominant and the dominated, force is decisive, in its potential state as a threat or in the act itself. Power is domination and domination is insepa-rable from force" (Sánchez Vázquez, 1999: 14).

Of course, this recognition of force as the basis of state power overrides (but does not reduce the significance of) the form of enforcing obedience and, therefore, the distinction between democratic and despotic power. Whether power is democratic or despotic affects the degrees of domina-tion and the modes of obedience. An authoritarian and arbitrary regime demands total obedience, with no restrictions or legal regulations. On the other hand, democracies legalize and regulate the conditions for obedi-ence, even granting freedoms and a certain legal margin for disobedience. The difference, of course, is highly significant, as significant as the differ-ence between a Hitler and a Roosevelt; nevertheless, bourgeois democracy is still a means for bourgeois domination and in this we find its limits; in the world in general, and in Latin America in particular (consider Allende in Chile), it is well-known that the commitment of the bourgeoisie to democracy has strict limitations.[25]

Nor does this reduce the importance of ideological domination, i.e. power based not only on force, but on the control of the consciousness of the dominated. Marx, Engels and Lenin return constantly to the question of the capacity of the capitalist class to establish ideological domination

---

[25] "Bourgeois rule as the outcome and result of universal suffrage, as the express act of the sovereign will of the people; this is the meaning of the bourgeois constitution. It is the duty of the bourgeoisie to regulate the right to suffrage so that it wills the reasonable, that is, its rule. *Our dictatorship has hitherto existed by the will of the people; it must now be con-solidated against the will of the people*" (Marx, 1895); "The assertion that class rule is *essen-tially dictatorial* does not mean that dictatorial methods are invariably used, but that these methods are necessary for class rule in a sense in which constitutional methods are not" (Moore, 1957: 30).

over the dominated class;[26] domination seeks to be accepted and assumed by those it dominates. There is no domination more firmly established than that which is actively (or at least passively) accepted by the dominated.

This would mean that the capitalist class, in certain circumstances, has the capacity not only to dominate coercively, but also to obtain the consent of the dominated through its ideological domination. Gramsci took up this point and vested it with new dimensions by articulating a theoretical construction around the concept of "civil society."

According to Gramsci's analysis, the dominant class produces its ideology, its general conception of the world, and disseminates it by means of an ideological framework to society as a whole, adapting it to the conditions of the different social groups to ensure their association with, and allegiance to, its "intellectual and moral leadership" (Portelli, 1998: 17); the dominant class thus constitutes an ideological bloc under its hegemonic direction (Portelli, 1998: 22).

For Gramsci, the ideological framework constitutes the "internal articulation of civil society: an organization through which the governing class disseminates its ideology. It is the material organization created to maintain, defend and develop the theoretical and ideological front, which includes organizations whose function is to disseminate the ideology: communications media, all the instruments that enable the influencing of public opinion, libraries, circles, clubs, etc., cultural organizations (church, schools, the press)" (Portelli, 1998: 24).

Capital domination cannot be disassociated from ideological domination. Capital presents its reasons for society as a whole to obey it. Obedience "is presented as a rational matter... but it is power that determines the reasons and the criteria of the rationale, and the border between what should and should not be obeyed is historically variable... Power presents its particular interests, which it expresses as rational and universal... rational obedience is obedience for the reasons established by power" (Sánchez Vázquez, 1999: 20–21).

---

[26] Ideological power "is exercised in the realm of ideologies. It contributes to the maintenance of political power and the economic and social bases that sustain that power... Because of its capacity to mobilize consciousnesses, it contributes to the creation of a consensus of approval of the political power, to its legitimization, and to the acceptance of the general conditions of exploitation" (Sánchez Vázquez, 1999: 48–49).

Obedience and Disobedience:
Dominant Class and Dominated Class

In capitalist society, economic, political and ideological domination and exploitation are coordinated into a single social power, the rule of one class over another, based, in all its dimensions, on the same social relation, the capital relation. The maintenance of the capital relation guarantees that the obedience of the dominated class is presented as something natural, normal, automatically assumed and reiterated. As long as the capital relation is not socially questioned, the submission of the dominated operates as a form of "automatism", and political power, particularly its violent and repressive dimension, has no need to intervene. It is simply maintained, in an apparently exterior condition, as a possibility, as a reminder that capitalist private ownership of the means of production and subsistence is sacred and inviolable, as is affirmed by all the political constitutions of every bourgeois state in the world.

Paradoxically, the most recurring argument in bourgeois ideology to consolidate its control in the consciousness and the activity of the dominated, particularly in its versions for mass-consumption, is freedom: workers are free to work or not to work for whomever they want, just as women are free to buy or not to buy a particular brand of jeans; young people are free to study whatever they want to find a "good job" at the service of capital, just as the developing nations in the globalized world compete freely to attract the investment of big capital. This is the freedom offered by the capitalist market, and its underlying social relations, transmuted into the absolute concept of freedom.

The bourgeois ideology of freedom, presenting the dominated as free, is founded on the systematic promotion in the consciousness of its victims of a disconnection in their understanding of the link between the conditions of their domination and their "freedom." Its ideological effectiveness is contingent upon its ability to dull the perception in the consciousness of the dominated of their social condition, and to develop their intellectual disconnection from the reality of their situation. In this sense, particularly if the dominated do not question the capital relation and even more so if their perception of that relation is dulled so as to remain beyond their awareness, bourgeois domination not only admits but promotes a wide variety of currents of thought, a wide range of "freedom of thought."[27]

---

[27] For example, in *post-modern* contemporary society there is a wide and increasing range of all types of sects, some *scientific and philosophical*, cultural or artistic, others

The dominated must operate their margin of freedom within the field of domination structured by capital, perhaps without realizing, or perhaps without caring very much. Nevertheless, the history of capitalism abounds with evidence that, while in certain conditions capital is capable of dominating with the active or passive acceptance of the dominated, in other conditions the domination of capital does not appear to constitute a field of freedom, but a degree of oppression that is insufferable in the eyes of a certain number of its victims.[28]

In such conditions, the victims do not obey because they are convinced, but because "they have no alternative: they obey in spite of their beliefs, reasoning or better judgment... They do not wish to obey; in other cases, obedience is internalized before it is externalized. Now there is the alternative of disobedience; but certain conditions are needed for this possibility to be realized, such as the willingness of the victim to assume the risk in light of a power that could exercise its last resort – the use of force. The revolutionary struggle is a kind of act of disobedience" (Sánchez Vázquez, 1999: 21–22).

For those dispossessed of the means of production and subsistence, obedience is a necessity, and to question it, to assume disobedience as a historical possibility – not as a simple passive rejection of the power of capital, but as an active struggle to destroy it – they must question the capital relation and consider the historical conditions needed to overcome it. The reality of their situation, their subordinate position in the capital relation, cannot be resolved by a magic, illusory freedom, but by an effective, real transformation of the conditions that deprive them of the means of production and subsistence and subject them to obedience, subordinating them to the control of capital.

Only changes occurring to the capital relation can alter the reality of the condition of the exploited and/or dominated in capitalist society. Everything aimed at diverting their attention from the central axis of

---

magical, metaphysical, mystical or religious, from which people may choose, *freely*, the one that best meets their needs for intellectual, emotional and spiritual development.

[28] However, the importance and complexity of ideological domination must not be underestimated. Consider, for example, the extreme but increasingly common case in our societies, of the *surplus population*; while little has been achieved to establish some sense of *class consciousness*, not even the most influential of the mass media, the most impassioned political discourse, the most brilliant formula of distinguished intellectuals will convince them, as they watch their children starving, of the benefits of a society that has provided them with everything so that they can *"be free."*

articulation of social relations, whether presenting sublime expressions of freedom or employing the most sophisticated intellectual theorems, can only serve to consolidate the power of capital. "Freedom of the will," affirms Engels, "means nothing but the capacity to make decisions with knowledge of the subject. Therefore the freer a man's judgment is in relation to a definite question, the greater is the necessity with which the content of this judgment will be determined; while the uncertainty, founded on ignorance, which seems to make an arbitrary choice among many different and conflicting possible decisions, shows precisely by this that it is not free, that it is controlled by the very object it should itself control" (Engels, 1878).[29]

Ideological,[30] economic and political domination are not independent variables. As components of the social power of a class, their fate is linked to the evolution of the basic relation, the capital relation. It is therefore necessary to examine – and this is the purpose of the chapters that follow – how this basic relation evolves and how, with its evolution, it transforms the conditions of the domination of the capitalist class, the conditions of its social power. But first we need to consider, in a synthetic approach, the concepts of dominant class and dominated class.

For Gramsci, the state, the site for the establishment of a dominant class, is "political society plus civil society." This concept links the conditions of ideological domination with those of coercive domination, and associates, at least as a general, initial proposition, the conditions for domination with those for exploitation. The state not only organizes the domination of the dominant class over the dominated, but also ensures the cohesion of the dominant class: it provides the dominant class with "homogeneity and awareness of its function not only at the economic level but also at the social and political levels" (Portelli 1998: 49). It ensures the "organic link that connects structure and superstructure, civil society and political society" (Portelli 1998: 93).

---

29 And Engels adds: "Hegel was the first to state correctly the relation between freedom and necessity. To him, freedom is the insight into necessity: 'Necessity is *blind* only *in so far as it is not understood.*' Freedom does not consist in any dreamt-of independence from natural laws, but in the knowledge of these laws and in the possibility this gives of systematically making them work towards definite ends" (Engels, 1878).

30 "What occurs in the consciousness of the individual also varies historically; what passes through the consciousness is not a purely individual affair, but is conditioned – as every individual is a social being – by the forms of individuality determined by the different systems of social relations" (Sánchez Vázquez, 1999: 20).

In contrast, what characterizes the dominated classes is their lack of unity and homogeneity: "the subordinate classes, by definition, have not been unified and cannot be unified until they are able to become the 'state'... their history is no more than a constantly renewed attempt to unify and form a new hegemonic system and, therefore, a civil society" (Portelli 1998: 90).

CHAPTER TWO

THE GENERAL FORMS OF CAPITALIST DOMINATION

What could possibly show better the character of the capitalist mode of production, than the necessity that exists for forcing upon it, by Acts of Parliament, the simplest appliances for maintaining cleanliness and health?

K. Marx
Capital

In the previous chapter, I examined the basic features of domination as components of the domination relation that links the dominators and the dominated class in capitalist society. These features were examined as static elements, without capturing their movement, as if they were parts of a building. But in capitalist society, nothing is ever static. As a metaphorical image, the idea of a building is inappropriate. It might better be described as a boat, sailing constantly over stormy seas; like the Pequod, commanded by the obsessive Captain Ahab, tirelessly and incessantly chasing the great white whale of profit.I If the entire relation of domination and capitalist exploitation, that is, the class relation as a whole, is expressed in the capital/wage-labor relation, in the separation between producers from the means of production and subsistence, the key to all movement in the class relation lies in the development of the capital relation.

In this tireless chase after its Moby Dick, the capitalist class develops the capital relation; it is therefore necessary to investigate how the relation develops and how, based on this, it is possible to understand the movement of capital domination, to distinguish the basic forms that it takes in that movement and to periodize its history. In the previous chapter, I presented the content of capitalist domination. The aim here, based on that content and on an initial analysis of the development of the capital/wage-labor relation, is to identify its general forms, and to use these in the next chapter to propose how to examine and periodize the history of capital domination. While the content of domination is articulated through exploitation, the forms of domination express a link between the two, defined in the conditions organized by the capital relation itself.

The Development of the Capital Relation:
Tendencies and Time Periods

To examine the movement and development of the capital relation, there are two propositions in Marx that I consider fundamental. The first of these is found in the preface to *A Contribution to the Critique of Political Economy*, in which Marx asserts that, in the social production of their existence, men necessarily enter into social relations that are independent of their will and consciousness.[1] The second is found in the *Communist Manifesto*, in which Marx states that "all history is the history of class struggle."[2] Taken in isolation, the first proposition appears to be determinist, while the second seems voluntarist. In reality, both fall within a single theoretical framework that links exploitation and domination, economics and politics; the necessary regularities, which are determined by objective social relations, are developed through social practice. The necessary tendencies of the development of capital unfold through the struggle between social classes: basically, the struggle of the capitalist class to subordinate the working class to the needs of capital, and the resistance of the working class against that subordination. Thus, to understand the development of capitalism, an analysis of the forms of exploitation and accumulation and their developmental tendencies is as important as an analysis of the forms of domination and resistance through which they unfold.

For the case of capitalism, Marx undertakes an analysis of these social relations, "inevitable and independent of the will and consciousness of men," in *Capital*, in which he demonstrates that these relations can be broken down into various developmental tendencies, general trends that organize the progress of capitalist society and that mark out its limits: increased labor productivity, increased organic composition of capital, the concentration and centralization of capital, the expulsion of labor-power from the labor process, the expansion of the industrial reserve army, and the consolidation of a worker surplus population; finally, he shows how these tendencies are expressed in downward pressure on the rate of profit.

---

[1] "In the social production of their existence, men inevitably enter into definite relations, which are independent of their will, namely, relations of production appropriate to a given stage in the development of their material forces of production" (Marx, 1859: Preface).

[2] "Ever since the dissolution of the primaeval communal ownership of land, all history has been a history of class struggles, of struggles between exploited and exploiting, between dominating and dominated classes..." (Marx and Engels, 1883).

He also suggests that the same tendencies that push down the rate of profit generate counter-tendencies, such as constant reduction of capital and an increase in its technical composition more intense than the increase in its value-composition. The search for counter-tendencies by capital to avoid the drop in the rate of profit covers a wide range of possibilities, but the basic counter-tendency, which ultimately supports all others, is to increase the rate of surplus-value. In this way, capitalist development is, inevitably, development of the productive force of labor. This development is expressed in the tendency of the rate of profit to fall, a trend which must be slowed down or temporarily reversed through the implementation of counter-tendencies. These tendencies, which organize the historical time of capitalism, running from its birth as a social mode of organizing production through to its death, articulate its long term; the historical duration of the capitalist mode of production.

With this basic theoretical proposition, an field of analysis has been established[3] for the study of the historical development of capitalism as a series of phases of economic expansion, the fundamental condition for which is the existence of a historical set of economic, political and ideological circumstances that ensure a rate of profit that is satisfactory for capital, and phases of depression resulting from the exhaustion of the conditions that ensured an increased rate of profit during the period of expansion that preceded it. The efforts of the capitalist class during the period of depression will therefore be focused on searching for new historical modes to increase the rate of profit once again.

Between one stage and another there is a basic continuity in terms of the tendential laws of capitalist development; each stage begins with the levels of labor productivity, organic composition and concentration of capital with which the previous stage ended. From that point, the capitalist class must undertake the task of historical restructuring in order to reactivate the rate of profit.

This is how the new economic, political and ideological modes that will ensure the profitability of capital are defined, and also how the members of the capitalist class who will be able to operate successfully in the new conditions are determined; each historical era defines the dominant faction of the capitalist class, the faction that will be able to operate in the new circumstances. Ultimately, this is the faction which, by saving itself, saves capitalism as a whole.

---

[3] See, for example, Hirsch, 1979.

These phases or stages make up the middle term of capitalism; based on the analysis of the long cycle or Kondratieff cycle,[4] various authors have proposed periodizations which generally outline four periods of expansion (1770 to 1830; 1850 to 1873; 1896 to 1914 and 1945 to 1967) followed by their corresponding periods of depression (1830 to 1850; 1873 to 1896; 1914 to 1945 and 1967 up to the present). Dabat associates the long Kondratieff cycle with the concept of historical stages, or the "structural historical form of capitalist development in the industrial era" (Dabat 1993: 163). According to his proposition, the phase of expansion of the Kondratieff cycle corresponds to a historical stage of capitalist development, while the phase of depression corresponds to a period of transition between one stage and another.

Thus, the development of the capital/wage-labor relation can be examined on different analytical levels; the historical phase articulates the specific conditions for the expansion of capital but, viewed in succession, each phase constitutes a moment in the course of the overall historical time of the life of the capital relation. The analysis of the middle term offers explanatory dimensions and precise historical meanings when considered in relation to the long term.

There is no doubt that the features produced by the conditions of the long term and middle term in the development of capitalism are of great significance for the analysis of the development of the domination of capital and its forms. Chapter 10 of this study is dedicated to the analysis of these relations but, to identify the general forms of capitalist domination, we need first to examine the most direct and immediate features of the capital relation in the consciousness and practice of capitalists.

THE SPONTANEOUS MOVEMENT OF CAPITAL AND THE GENERAL FORMS OF ITS DOMINATION

The exploitation of the working class by the capitalist class consists in the appropriation of surplus-value; capital is value that appreciates. Unlike pre-capitalist forms of exploitation, which recognized a limit on the use value and the consumption of the exploiting class, the capitalist form of exploitation has an insatiable need to appropriate the labor of others: "If machinery be the most powerful means for increasing the productiveness of labor, i.e., shortening the working time required for the production of a

---

4 See, for example, Amin, 1975.

commodity," states Marx, "it becomes *in the hands of capital* the most powerful means... for *lengthening* the working-day beyond all bounds set by human nature. It creates, on the one hand, *new conditions by which capital is enabled* to give free scope to *this its constant tendency*, and on the other, *new motives* with which to whet *capital's appetite for the labor of others*" (Marx, 1867: Ch.15, emphasis added).

Value, as pure condensation of work-time, is separated from use value; capitalists don't exploit to consume, but to accumulate, and they accumulate to exploit further, thereby generating a necessary dynamic of development, structured within a context of specific social contradictions. The capitalist and the capitalist class, the personification of the exploiting party in this social relation, is the personification of capital. The contradictions and needs of incessant appreciation and accumulation of capital are assumed as interests of the capitalist class: "Strictly speaking, it is capital, and not 'the capitalists', that governs the process, imprinting its global logic on the decisions which, stoked by individual capitalists, are taken by the state" (Thwaites Rey and Castillo, 1999).

The existence of the working class, the personification of the exploited party in this social relation, is an absolute condition for the existence of capitalist society. Without an exploited class there can be no exploitation or exploiters; there can be no capital, no capitalists, and no accumulation. The two social classes are constituent parts of the capitalist social relation, structured within a context of necessary relations, "independent of their will and their consciousness." However, the capitalist, as the attentive and diligent personification of capital, is necessarily active in this relation. Capital accumulation is a contradictory process, fraught with hurdles and obstacles that must constantly be removed for accumulation to continue, until new obstacles appear. Capitalists must therefore necessarily establish themselves as an organized class. It is not enough that each individual capitalist attend to the needs of reproduction and accumulation of his own capital; the class as a whole must set up forms of organization that will permit it to attend to the general needs of capital accumulation.

The main obstacle to exploitation and the accumulation which that exploitation must produce is, of course, the resistance posed by the exploited against their exploitation. The capitalist class organizes itself into a state to pursue its own interests, i.e. to overcome the resistance of the workers and attend to the needs of exploitation and capital accumulation, whatever name it may give those interests and needs: progress, civilization, or simply the laws of the market. By organizing itself into a state, the exploiting class also becomes the dominant class, endowed with the conditions required for the creation of the social order it needs to pursue its interests, imposing that order on the dominated class. From this perspective, the history of capitalism can be analyzed as the history of the struggle of the capitalist class to create the social order that capital requires for its development.

The capitalist social relation involves one pole, the dominant, capitalist class, necessarily organized and active in pursuing its class interests, while for the opposite pole, the dominated working class, the situation is more complex. Depending on the modes of domination and resistance, the working class, viewed from the perspective of its organization as a class, will assume one of three general modes:

· Disorganized – the situation that Marx calls the "class in itself," simply existing as a reality in the system of production relations, as a basis for capitalist relations of exploitation;
· Organized, with an independent class organization to fight for its class interests – the situation that Marx calls the "class for itself";
· Organized, under terms compatible with bourgeois domination, restricted within the framework of what Lenin calls "trade unionism."[5]

Thus, on the side of capital, we have the "appetite for the labor of others," a constant tendency, an insatiable need, a logic that organizes its spontaneous movement, present throughout its historical cycle, and each and every one of the historical stages of its development, regardless of the period analyzed, is a short or middle term; this logic, this tendency, organizes the immediate, direct, spontaneous movement of capital. On the other side, we have the working class, which may assume different modes and levels of organization and of capacity for resistance, depending on the circumstances of the class struggle in its economic, political and ideological context.

Based on this dual set of circumstances, we can identify two logical forms, two general forms of capitalist domination: its natural form and its contained form. In its natural form, capital organizes a type of domination

---

[5] The following quote of Kautsky's, cited by Lenin, defines "trade unionism": "The object of the mass strike... cannot be to destroy state power; its only object can be to make the government compliant on some specific question, or to replace a government hostile to the proletariat with one willing to meet it half-way. But never, under any circumstances, can it (the proletarian victory over a hostile government) lead to the *destruction* of state power; it can only lead to a certain *shifting* of the balance of forces *within the state power*" (Lenin, 1918: Ch. 6).

appropriate to the needs of its spontaneous movement, as it is structured based on the movement imposed by individual capitalists, while in its contained form, capital is faced with a working class, and a society in general, that has managed to establish a certain level of containment of its spontaneous movement, and so adapts its domination to these conditions. The general features of each of these forms of domination are examined in the following section.

THE NATURAL FORM OF THE DOMINATION OF CAPITAL

The natural tendency of capitalist class domination is the effort to ensure the subjection of the working class to the needs of the spontaneous movement of exploitation and capital accumulation, to ensure the obedience of the exploited class, its subordination to the needs and interests of capital, divesting it of the conditions that would make any resistance or bargaining capacity possible. This means not only preventing them from stopping the exploitation, but even from attempting to moderate it, to negotiate the conditions for their exploitation, or to win some concession from capital.

In defense of its right to quench its insatiable need for the labor of others, capital, like an old, meticulous spiritual guide, is hostile to any sin of resistance, whether of thought, word or deed.[6] However, given that the basic condition for resistance is organization, the capitalist class is, at least in principle, particularly hostile to any form of organization on the part of the working class.[7] Capital needs a flexible working class; malleable, manageable, easily manipulated, constantly adapted and adaptable to the diverse and changing needs of capital accumulation.[8] Any resistance from the working class is viewed by the capitalists as an intolerable obstacle "to progress, civilization, and the laws of the market." This form of domination requires certain conditions, assumes a certain dynamic and has certain limits.

---

[6] "In the domain of Political Economy, free scientific inquiry meets not merely the same enemies as in all other domains. The peculiar nature of the materials it deals with, summons as foes into the field of battle the most violent, mean and malignant passions of the human breast, the Furies of private interest" (Marx, 1867: Preface to the 1st German Edition).

[7] Organization, according to Poulantzas, is the condition for the exercise of a specific class practice (Poulantzas, 1973: 128).

[8] It is no coincidence that the favorite slogan of capital in these times of globalization is "to make labor relations more flexible."

The general conditions for this form of domination are the weakness and lack of organization of the workers, on the one hand, and a state permissive of "private initiative" (i.e. spontaneous, individual movements of capital by each individual capitalist) on the other. The workers have suffered some political and ideological defeat, and capital has transformed and developed the capital relation with some technological revolution which, on the one hand, increases its control on manufacturing and, on the other, increases the surplus worker population, superfluous to the needs of capital appreciation. In light of the weakness of the working class, the state assumes the role, as Marx and Engels describe it, of "a committee for managing the common affairs of the whole bourgeoisie" (Marx and Engels, 1848), as the mere expression of the logic of capital.

Under these conditions, each individual capitalist will search for the strategies that best suit him to increase his rate of profitability, with no concern as to whether the outcome degrades the workers, society in general and the environment, because attending to his long-term preservation, although a condition for reproduction for capital itself, is not necessarily worthwhile from the perspective of immediate profitability. And, in so far as his actions yield competitive advantages over other capitalists, these others will imitate his practices and even outdo them;[9] the logic of competition between capitalists contributes to the activation of a spiral of growing social degradation, even to the detriment of their own long- and medium-term interests.

However, according to Marx, "capital, which has such 'good reasons' for denying the sufferings of the legions of workers that surround it, is in practice moved as much or as little by the sight of the coming degradation and final depopulation of the human race, as by the probable fall of the earth into the sun" (Marx, 1867: Ch. 10). By way of explanation, he adds, "looking at things as a whole, all this does not, indeed, depend on the good or ill will of the individual capitalist. Free competition brings out the inherent laws of capitalist production, in the shape of external coercive laws having power over every individual capitalist" (Marx, 1867: Ch. 10). The more the process is abandoned to the initiative of individual capitalists, i.e. the more absent the capitalist state is in the regulation of their behavior, the

---

[9] "The division of labor within the society brings into contact independent commodity producers, who acknowledge no other authority but that of competition.... [and] denounces with equal vigor every conscious attempt to socially control and regulate the process of production" (Marx, 1867: Ch. 14).

less control capitalists actually have and the more capital governs the process.

Because "the first birthright of capital is equal exploitation of labor-power" (Marx, 1867: Ch. 10), the individual capitalist who best embodies the logic of capital – for example, the one who establishes the longest working day (if, given the technical combinations between duration and intensity, this proves a profitable option) or the one who best organizes the army of workers at his disposition, "making labor relations more flex-ible and globalized" – will be the one who sets the pattern for all other capitalists to follow, regardless of the processes of degradation that these initiatives may unleash upon society. The limits on this form of domina-tion depend on the extremes to which capital itself will go before it places the general conditions for its reproduction at risk and provokes the grow-ing resistance of workers, of society in general and, ultimately, the inter-vention of the state to moderate and regulate its actions.

The resistance of the workers must be organized in such a way so as to compel the capitalist class as a whole; restraining one individual capitalist would probably only result in his bankruptcy, without resolving anything in terms of the general mode of class relations. The trade union battle, bringing one group of workers into confrontation with one individual cap-italist, is not enough. To break this form of domination, workers must achieve a certain level of general organization in the form of class organi-zation. When it reaches its limit, this form of domination offers a number of possible conclusions:

· The struggle of the workers provokes the capitalist state, representative of the whole capitalist class, to regulate and moderate the excesses of capitalists.
· The struggle of the workers ultimately destroys the capital relation.
· The workers fail in their attempt and capital continues its work of destruction and degradation.

In the first case, the natural form of domination of capital shifts to a con-tained form. In the second case, capitalist society moves towards social-ism. In the third case, at least while the failure of the workers persists or until the capitalist state itself reacts, society and nature will continue to suffer the effects of a growing process of degradation.

In summary, with the natural form of domination, the spontaneous movement of capital, the movement arising from its internal logic, from its insatiable need for surplus-value, from its exclusive attention to its own interests, in the absence of a "general public interest" being imposed upon them, degrades society and the environment and generates a feedback loop that can only be contained through the establishment of social limits imposed not merely on one individual capitalist, but on the capitalist class in general; limits which, in a capitalist society, only the state can establish, but which it will only impose as a result of the struggle of the workers.

THE CONTAINED FORM OF THE DOMINATION OF CAPITAL

The state, as the "capitalist collective," as the representative of the general interests of capital, may, on its own initiative, contain the excesses of private capital, especially when these excesses have reached the extreme of placing the reproduction of capital itself at risk. However, the theory and history of capitalism show that large-scale intervention by the state to systematically regulate the excesses of capital only occurs as the result of a prolonged struggle on the part of the workers.

A brief review of the chapters "The Working-Day," "Cooperation" and "Machinery and Modern Industry" in Marx's *Capital*, eliminating all references to specific historical issues and processes, serves to identify the general moments marking the introduction of the contained form of the domination of capital:

> "The creation of a normal working-day," says Marx, "is the product of a protracted civil war... between the capitalist class and the working class... In the capitalist, the greed for surplus-labor appears in the straining after an unlimited extension of the working-day... *'Après moi le déluge!'* ["After me, the flood"] is the watchword of every capitalist and of every capitalist nation. Hence capital is reckless of the health or length of life of the laborer, *unless under compulsion from society*" (Marx, 1867: Ch. 10, emphasis in original).

Neither capital nor its state will transform, on its own initiative, the natural form of its domination into its contained form: "the capitalist 'rationality' implied in the state as the 'ideal capitalist collective', which assumes the reproduction of both poles of the capitalist social relation, cannot be explained solely as a direct product of the needs of capital, but must be understood as the result of the struggle and the relative strength or weakness of the labor pole to impose the limits of its own reproduction as a class... it is labor-power itself that compels capital to guarantee its reproduction, that awards 'rationality' to the capitalist state as a project of general social reproduction, while at the same time providing the elements for the continued existence of the system through their legitimation" (Thwaites Rey and Castillo, 1999).

The first condition for the appearance of the contained form of the domination of capital is thus a process of complex and intense worker organization and struggle, a class struggle, which places the workers in confrontation not (or not only) with individual capitalists, but with the state, the general representative of capital. Secondly, as a result of this struggle, the containment must be imposed on capital by the state, and must assume a form that is binding, coercive and legal: "The English Factory Acts... curb the passion of capital for a limitless draining of labor-power, by forcibly limiting the working-day by state regulations, made by a state that is ruled by capitalist and landlord" (Marx, 1867: Ch. 10).

Thirdly, the restrictions will meet with violent opposition from capitalists: "The working-class was everywhere proclaimed, placed under a ban, under a virtual law of suspects. The manufacturers had no need any longer to restrain themselves. They broke out in open revolt... against the whole of the legislation that since 1833 had aimed at restricting in some measure the 'free' exploitation of labor-power" (Marx, 1867: Ch. 10).

Fourth, if restrictions cannot be prevented, the capitalists affected will demand that they be imposed upon all, to prevent disparities in their "right to equal conditions" in the exploitation of the workers and competitive disadvantages. The Factory Acts in England, the first labor legislation enacted by a capitalist state, began as a set of special laws for mechanical spinning and weaving mills, but the industries subject to the regulations wanted an even playing field, since "the first birthright of capital is equal exploitation of labor-power by all capitalists," (Marx, 1867: Ch. 10), and so demanded the universal application of the legislation.

Fifth, the restrictions should include the workers themselves, to prevent the possibility that competition between them, job uncertainty and unemployment may compel them to submit defenselessly to the conditions imposed by capital: "For protection... the laborers must put their heads together and, as a class, compel the passing of a law, an *all-powerful barrier that shall prevent* the very workers from selling, by 'voluntary contract', themselves and their families into slavery and death" (Marx, 1867: Ch. 10, emphasis added).

These conditions are the first signs of the transition toward the contained form of capitalist domination. But there is one other condition essential to defining the possibility of consolidating this transition: "When the barons of industry submitted to what they had not been able to prevent, and even reconciled themselves to the outcome, the force of resistance of capital began little by little to weaken" (Marx, 1867: Ch. 13). In other words, capital finds some kind of compensation: if the working day is restricted, the intensity of the work is increased; if wages are increased, worker productivity increases. Capital does not easily accept a reduction in its rate of profit and surplus-value but, when compelled by the circumstances, it agrees to share the fruit of new advances in labor productivity and intensity.

This means that a crucial condition for the consolidation of the contained form of domination is that it be supported by advances in labor productivity, i.e. that the mediation concerned be supported by increased rates of exploitation and profit. If capital cannot find a form of compensation, it will maintain constant and incessant opposition to any limitation upon "freedom" and "free enterprise" and will defend its unrestricted right to exploit labor. These are the circumstances for the transition from the natural form to the contained form of domination: "that first conscious and methodical reaction of society against the spontaneously developed form of the process of production," and the workers win concessions, wrestled with considerable struggle from capital (Marx, 1867: Ch. 15).

The dynamic of the contained form of domination then begins to appear: "what strikes us, then, in the English legislation of 1867 is, on the one hand, the necessity imposed upon the parliament of the ruling classes, of adopting in principle measures so extraordinary, and on so great a scale, against the excesses of capitalist exploitation; and, on the other hand, the *hesitation, repugnance and bad faith* with which it lent itself to carrying those measures into practice" (Marx, 1867: Ch. 15, emphasis added). As the hesitation, repugnance and bad faith in the administration of the concessions won by the workers shows, the contained form of domination does not put an end to the class struggle, but establishes a structured framework for constant bargaining between capital and labor, mediated by the state, in which each concession made by capital to labor is disputed time and again, inch by inch, denied whenever capital can deny it, and conceded only when there is no alternative.

The state no longer appears here as the organized arm of capital, giving full rein to the "free initiative" of the capitalists and nothing to the profoundly subjugated initiative of the workers, but intervening, "mediating," regulating the dispute between workers and capitalists, defending the "reasonable" and the "possible," orchestrating a complex social framework that channels, orders, structures and limits the bargaining between the classes.

This form of domination reaches its limit when the accumulation of capital is faced with a crisis situation, i.e. a reduction in the rate of profit: "invariably, states Marx, the crises follow a period of a general rise in wages when the working class receives a genuinely larger portion of the commodities produced for consumption each year. It seems, therefore, that capitalist production entails conditions that do not depend on good or ill will, conditions that only fleetingly tolerate this relative prosperity of the working class, and always in the nature of a storm-bird, a harbinger of the crisis."[10]

A capitalist economic crisis is always, essentially, the result of a reduction in the rate of profit; whatever the specific historical circumstances may be that have brought about the crisis, capital and its state will turn on the workers to raise the rate of surplus-value and restore the level of the rate of profit and, in circumstances of a crisis in capital accumulation and a drop in the rate of profit, they will consider it totally inadmissible and absolutely impossible to grant concessions to the workers: "the recovery from the state of crisis will always be accompanied by an intense attack on the living conditions of the masses" (Figueroa Sepúlveda, 1989: 133).

From that moment, capital and its state will make every effort to dismantle the system of concessions established during the period of the contained form of domination. Workers will try to hold onto the concessions, which represent veritable historic victories won with great effort and intense struggle, with blood shed and lives sacrificed by whole generations; however, having reached its limit, the logical way out offered by this form of domination is a return to the natural form. The workers, after a reasonably long period that placed them in a political and ideological context in which they could negotiate with capital and its state rather than struggle against them, are unlikely to find the ideological and political conditions necessary to turn this crisis in capital accumulation into a revolutionary crisis that could bring about the destruction of the relation of capital to wage-labor.

With the return to the natural form of domination, and in a context of new historical circumstances, in a new stage of the life cycle of capitalism, of its middle and long term, the workers once again find very narrow avenues for negotiation; capital unleashes its natural logic, its spontaneous movement, and the workers will once again have the opportunity (and the need) to struggle against capital, to disobey it, to oppose its economic, political and ideological domination.

---

[10] Quoting from *Capital* (Figueroa Sepúlveda, 1989: 133).

The General Forms and the Basis for Distinguishing Them

The class struggle, under the conditions of the contained form of domination, acquires a distinct framework, a means of processing the conflict between the classes that is different from the means applied under the conditions of the natural form of domination; this framework is constructed based on the conditions for negotiating the concessions that capital is willing and able to grant the workers and/or that labor is able to wrestle from the capitalists.

In the establishment of this framework, the relationship between dominant and dominated is not necessarily democratic. What distinguishes one general form of domination from the other is not their degree of democratic or authoritarian development (although we may acknowledge its importance), but the recognition (or lack thereof) of the material interests of the workers; i.e, the distinction does not lie exclusively in the political sphere, as it is deeply rooted in the economic sphere, in the conditions for exploitation of the workers and in the development of the capital relation.[11]

Nor does the distinction between the forms of domination lie in the sphere of ideology; the hegemony of the bourgeoisie, although expressed as "intellectual and moral leadership," according to Gramsci's analysis, is not a purely ideological matter. This hegemony requires material support: "for the dominant class to 'convince' the other classes that it is the ideal group to ensure the development of society, that is, that its own interests are mixed up with the interests of the general public, it is necessary to foster, within the economic structure, the development of the forces of production, and *the* (relative) *improvement of the standard of living of the masses*" (Thwaites Rey, 1994, emphasis added).

Marx, Engels and Lenin analyze the capitalist state as essentially founded on its coercive capacity, what Gramsci calls "political society." Gramsci uses the term "East" to define societies under a backward form of capitalism, with a gelatinous civil society. On the other hand, in the societies of advanced capitalism, in which the bourgeoisie has established a

---

[11] A brief reference to the case of Mexico may clarify this idea: it is clear that Mexico's post-revolutionary, developmentalist "social authoritarian State" maintained a much greater commitment to the interests and material needs of workers than the current "neoliberal State", officially labeled "democratic" or, at least, "in transition toward democracy" (see, for example De la Garza, 1988). We thus find that *"democracy"*, restricted appropriately, can prove *more exclusionary* than a form of "social authoritarianism" that regulates social demands, negotiating, granting or rejecting them.

solid "civil society," the phenomenon of domination appears much more complex. The bourgeoisie has set itself up as the hegemonic power, capable of exercising intellectual and moral leadership over society as a whole. This is Gramsci's "West."

East and West (although they have Eastern and Western Europe as specific historical referents) do not refer to geographical territories; rather, they constitute theoretical constructions that explain two different forms of domination in capitalism. In the East, the workers are ideologically, and even politically and organically, distanced from the capitalist state. In the West, they are closely associated with the state, organized under its hegemony through their integration into civil society; the dominant class exercises its power not only through coercion, but also by constructing a series of mechanisms for ideological transmission and successfully imposing its world view, its philosophy, its morality, its customs and its "common sense," which fosters the consent of the dominated to their domination.

However, to understand Gramsci's notion of "civil society" and the "hegemony" of the dominant class as a simple framework for ideological production and dissemination would be to disassociate politics from economics, the "superstructure" from the "structure"; it would mean subscribing to an idealist approach to analyzing the relation between the social classes.[12] If the bourgeoisie in the West appears to be hegemonic, this is not due simply to its capacity for ideological production and dissemination, but to the fact that it has established a social framework in which ideological production and dissemination and the organization of "civil society" are closely associated with bargaining for and granting better material conditions in the lives of the workers.[13]

Thus, in the East, "coercion and force appear as a consequence of the failure of the bourgeoisie to present itself to society as 'society itself', and consequently to be able to fulfill commitments to other classes. Because for the dominant class to be able to present the state as a body of the people as a whole, this representation cannot be entirely false; the state must

---

[12] Nevertheless, in many of Gramsci's interpreters, the explicit analysis of the material basis of consent is absent, as is the structural role that this should have in the analysis.

[13] "Overcoming vulgar economics – which requires emphasizing the importance and complexity of the 'intellectual and moral' dimensions of bourgeois supremacy – should not mean falling into an idealist notion that assumes the possibility of the construction of general consent, hegemonic production and non-coercive rule without any reference to the material conditions in which social power relations are expressed" (Thwaites Rey, 1994).

take on some of the interests of the dominated groups" (Thwaites Rey, 1994).

In the natural form of domination, as analyzed above, capital is reluctant to assume any commitment to the interests of the dominated, resulting in a distancing and growing conflict between dominated and dominant. In the contained form of domination, the state, compelled by the struggle of the workers, assumes the task of regulating the relation between classes and negotiating concessions for the workers.

What I refer to here as the natural form of domination can be understood in part as Gramsci's East and in the basic theoretical propositions of Marx, Engels and Lenin,[14] while to understand the contained form of domination, Gramsci's West offers the best point of reference. However, making an effort at abstraction as I have attempted to do in this chapter in order to identify general forms of domination, without merely focusing on the description of periods, helps to resolve a number of additional problems.

First, the natural form, unlike Gramsci's East, does not necessarily refer to a backward or outdated form of capitalism, belonging to a remote and forgotten past;[15] as a general form of capitalist domination it is not limited to a specific historical period, but may reappear at any time, and this possible reappearance will be pregnant with different meanings if the time of its reappearance is analyzed in relation to the life cycle of capitalism, with the long term of the capitalist mode of production, which is addressed in Chapter 10 of this work.

Second, the contained form of domination is, as even its name suggests, provisional. Of course, viewed in historical time, all forms of domination are necessarily provisional, but this is very much contrary to what capital, by its nature, demands. We could not conclude that this is the form that "came to stay," the stable form of capital domination, as a misreading of

---

[14] I refer here to Lenin insofar as the analysis of the form of domination is concerned. With regard to the form of struggle and victory over capitalist domination, I feel that there are crucial differences between Marx and Lenin, and that Gramsci is much more consistent with Marx: there is a considerable distance between the Leninist "vanguard party" (which represents, leads and, finally "liberates" the proletariat) and the Marxist proposition ("the emancipation of the proletariat can only be the work of the proletariat itself"), just as there is between state capitalism, now long gone (which referred to itself as "real socialism") and the effective socialization of the means of production and means of subsistence, i.e. the real destruction of the *capital relation*.

[15] For example, Portelli associates the "East" with pre-capitalism (Portelli, 1998: 143), which would mean there would be nothing to learn from the "East" to explain the forms of domination of the present day.

Gramsci and his analysis of the West might lead us to assume. It is clearly the strong form of capitalist domination – strong in the sense that it is the form that is presented as legitimate to the dominated and is therefore the most susceptible to ideological manipulation to the benefit of capital domination. For this same reason it is more important, in theoretical, ideological and political terms, to determine at what time and under what conditions it appears in the life cycle of capital and whether it may possibly reappear.

Third, my purpose is not simply to reproduce Gramsci's East and West with another name, but to seek out more general features, to attempt an abstraction and to identify general forms of capitalist domination. If general forms can be found (and not merely forms associated with specific, unrepeatable historical conditions), it will then be possible to examine them, not as periods in the history of domination, but as criteria for the periodization of the history of domination, or general forms subject to different modes of historical expression. We may thus consider the history of capitalist domination not only as a series of periods, but also as an alternation of forms of domination which, in their succession, acquire different historical meanings, associated with their position in relation to the long term, the life cycle of capital.

Fourth, if with these general forms we can periodize the history of domination, we can identify variants within the same period in which a particular general form pervades, diverse and specific historical examples which nevertheless correspond to the same period in the history of capitalist domination and share certain essential features; in other words, differentiated examples sharing the same historical territory, the same general form of domination. This will be explored further in the following chapter.

CHAPTER THREE

THE PATTERN OF DOMINATION:
HISTORICAL FORMS OF CAPITALIST DOMINATION

Present-day bourgeois society, no less than its predecessors, [has been exposed]
as a grandiose institution for the exploitation of the huge majority of the people
by a small, ever-diminishing minority.

F. Engels
Karl Marx

In the work of Marx, as well as in that of Engels and other Marxists (Lenin and Gramsci in particular), we can find the basis for a general theory of capitalist domination. On the other hand, there is a vast number of individual studies of capitalist domination in specific countries and in particular periods. The natural space for the organization of capitalist domination is the nation-state. It should therefore not be surprising that the study of specific examples of capitalist domination naturally entails the study of specific nation-states.

World History of Capitalist Domination

It is my belief that between these two extremes (a general theory of capitalist domination and specific national cases of such domination) an intermediate theoretical and historical framework can be established, which would allow us to delimit general historical periods of capitalist domination. This would involve a kind of periodization which, on the one hand, exhibits enough features to clearly identify and differentiate historical periods, but which, on the other hand, given the general nature of those features, allows for a multiplicity and diversity of forms of domination by nation-states in the historical period concerned. In other words, if the theory and history of capitalism shows that this periodization is viable, the periods identified would allow us to explain, in a description moving from the general to the particular, the specific features that the phenomenon of domination assumes in different situations, but all in the context of a period of world history.

A proposition of this type may seem wildly ambitious in a world where the domination of capital appears spread across so many different nation-states, each one claiming to be a sovereign, autonomous, independent product of its very particular past and absolute master of its future, suggesting that each state should prove radically different, with its own, unique and exclusive history. However, in spite of this claim to individuality, capitalist states all belong to the same historical time. There is no doubt that each state organization has its specific characteristics, but all have a shared history, a world history of capitalist domination, which is grounded in world capitalist economic history.[1]

The intention behind the construction of this field of analysis is to identify a historical rhythm, to find basic structures, broad cycles in the history of domination that allow us to posit a periodization that can be applied to a synthetic analysis of the historical evolution of capitalist domination. This periodization would also allow the identification, beyond the infinite diversity that can be found among all the specific cases, of general tendencies in capitalist domination.

PATTERN OF DOMINATION

If we assume this proposition as a starting point, the second challenge we face lies in the construction of criteria for periodization of this still presumed world history of capitalist domination. This problem was partly resolved in the previous chapter with the identification of general forms of capitalist domination with the capacity to operate as criteria for the periodization of its history, while acknowledging that such criteria are prone to adopt different modalities of historical specificity. General forms, while enabling us to periodize the history of domination, also make it possible to identify variants within the same period in which a particular general form prevails; diverse and specific historical examples which nevertheless correspond to the same period in the history of capitalist domination and share certain essential features. In other words, they allow us to identify

---

[1] "Marxism views the global economy not as a simple sum of its national parts but as a powerful, independent reality created by the international division of labor and by the global market, which, in our times, dominates every national market. The forces of production of capitalist society swept away national boundaries some time ago. (...) The specific features of a national economy, as important as they may be, constitute to an increasing degree the elements of a higher unit known as the global economy, on which, ultimately, internationalism is founded," Leon Trotsky (as quoted in Ayala and Figueroa, 2001).

differentiated examples sharing the same historical territory, the same general form of domination.

The general forms proposed permit us to periodize the history of domination because they assume a particular manifestation in a specific period, organized into a pattern of domination. This means that a pattern carries out the basic processes defined by a general form of domination in a specific manner. Pattern of domination is therefore the name that I propose to designate the historical manifestation of the general form of capitalist domination that prevails in (and so delimits) a particular historical period. A pattern of domination shapes a specific historical period in the world history of capitalist domination.

In short, the proposition is based on the following premises:

1. It is possible to construct an object of study called world history of capitalist domination, grounded in world capitalist economic history; i.e., a world history of the development of the relation between capital and wage-labor.
2. This history can be periodized according to general forms of capitalist domination.
3. The historical manifestation of a general form constitutes a pattern of domination, and the period of its prevalence constitutes a period in the world history of capitalist domination.

The general forms of capitalist domination, according to the analysis of the previous chapter, are its natural form and its contained form. The proposition thus assumes that, beyond the particular features of the numerous nation-states, we can delimit periods in the world history of capitalist domination in which either the natural form or the contained form predominate, expressed in one or several patterns of domination.

These periods are like historical waves sweeping across a beach. One wave washes up here, crashes against a rocky outcrop over there, penetrates deeply into one area while barely touching another, drifts off to one extreme while scarcely approaching the other. But in the end, this wave washes over the whole beach, and is distinguishable from the one that preceded it and from the one that follows.

Obviously, the viability of this proposition needs to be tested against the political history of capitalism, which is what I will attempt to do in the following chapters. However, to prevent the proposition from being reduced to an essentially empirical, historicist discovery, it must be positioned in relation to the theory of capitalism, giving it theoretical grounding. This will be the purpose of Chapter 10, to relate the periods of the world history of capitalist domination, the historical succession of patterns of domination, with the tendencies that organize the long term, or life cycle, of capitalism from its birth through to its death: infancy, maturity and decline.

IMPERIALISM: DEVELOPMENT AND UNDERDEVELOPMENT

Up to this point I have examined the possibility of constructing a theoretical and historical framework that would link the level of the pattern of domination directly with the nation-state. However, the historical reality of capitalism makes it necessary to introduce an intermediate level between the two. Since the emergence of imperialism, the world has been characterized by two poles: the developed pole and the underdeveloped pole. My examination so far has been of relevance to the developed pole, and so, to complete the panorama, it is necessary to consider the situation in the underdeveloped pole.

According to Víctor Figueroa Sepúlveda, the developed/underdeveloped dichotomy characterizes "the essential relation of the imperialist system" (Figueroa Sepúlveda, 1989: 13), and the difference between one and the other constitutes the basic problem in the capital/wage-labor relation, and the conditions for the development of that relation. In developed capitalism, capital separates general labor (scientific and technological research, creation of new media and processes, i.e. expansion of the forces of production and growth of the productive power of labor) from immediate labor (the implementation or operation of the products designed by general labor).

In contrast, in underdeveloped capitalism, capital does not organize general labor, which means that its relation with wage-labor is dependent on the general labor produced in developed capitalism; it is a form of capitalism that can only function by importing the products of the technological development of developed capitalism – capital equipment, intermediate goods, even consumer goods (Figueroa Sepúlveda, 1989: 53–55) – although, obviously, in order to be able to import, it needs to export. This situation unleashes a range of processes; those of interest to this study are outlined below.

Developed capitalism sells the products of both general labor and immediate labor to underdeveloped capitalism, which only sells products of immediate labor. This asymmetrical relationship translates into a systematic transfer of value from the underdeveloped to the developed world. Underdeveloped capitalism contributes to the stimulation of accumulation in developed capitalism, while its own accumulation is limited. The result of this is that its capacity for absorption of labor-power is lower, and a surplus population, superfluous to the needs of capital, will be a constant in its societies; the imperialist relation thus organizes an "uneven distribution of unemployment" (Figueroa Sepúlveda, 1989: 149) around the world.

Wages will tend to be permanently low, on the one hand because the surplus population pushes them downward, and on the other because keeping them low becomes one of the conditions that underdeveloped capitalism needs to export and, therefore, to be able to import. "The *absolute surplus population* in Latin America," explains Figueroa, "not only contributes to the establishment of a low level of the value of labor-power as it imposes limitations on the demands of active workers, but also contributes to shaping the *life aspirations* of the workers" (emphasis in original). "Their demands tend to be limited to very elemental questions... the workers of the active army use up much of their energy and their struggle *in defense of their jobs*... while... at the heart of the absolute surplus population... *survival becomes the life aspiration*" (Figueroa Sepúlveda, 1989: 114–115, emphasis added).

The nature of underdeveloped capitalism thus produces at least four consequences at the political level that need to be emphasized:

1. As the bourgeoisie of the underdeveloped countries acquires the means for both the exploitation of immediate labor and for their own expansion from the developed countries (i.e. from the developed pole of imperialism), this relationship with the developed pole contributes to the position of the local capitalists as the dominant class. As such, the underdeveloped bourgeoisie will tend to be pro-imperialist; imperialism also creates a social and political base for its reproduction in the underdeveloped countries;[2]

2. The bourgeoisie representing underdeveloped capital is always dependent on the bourgeoisie representing developed capital. However, as technological progress pushes the sectors in which the underdeveloped pole has its exports toward the developed pole, the tendency is toward a constantly decreasing need on the part of developed capital

---

[2] "Capital as personified by the Latin American bourgeoisie is not capital in general, but *underdeveloped* capital, which at the same time makes it the carrier of the relations represented by underdevelopment and its main social and political base of support" (Figueroa Sepúlveda, 1989: 91).

for underdeveloped capital, which thus faces increasing difficulties in making itself useful; in other words, increasing difficulties in building an export sector under the condition of underdevelopment;[3]

3. The economic and political weakness of underdeveloped capital compared to developed capital will therefore tend to deepen, while developed capital will tend to take what it needs from the region of the world "entrusted" to underdeveloped capital directly without the mediation of the latter;

4. It is a given that in the underdeveloped pole of the imperialist system, where unemployment and poverty reign and where life aspirations are reduced to defending your job (if you are employed) or to surviving (if you are unemployed), the political structures are fragile and unstable. The underdeveloped world appears to be a permanent inhabitant of Gramsci's East: "underdevelopment constitutes the weaker pole in the system, which makes it possible for capital under imperialism to concentrate the most palpable manifestations of its contradictions in the underdeveloped world" (Figueroa Sepúlveda, 1989: 149).

THE FORMS OF DOMINATION IN THE UNDERDEVELOPED WORLD

The question is thus whether in the tragic world of underdevelopment it is possible to differentiate patterns of domination; whether, in the state that represents the political organization of underdeveloped capital, the natural form of domination is the only possible form, or whether there is something that can reasonably be identified with the contained form of capitalist domination.

To answer this question, we need to review the theoretical production that identifies the specificities of capitalism in underdevelopment. Figueroa Sepúlveda, examining the historical process of Latin America, distinguishes two forms of economic growth in the conditions of underdevelopment.[4] The first he calls absolute or "outward" growth: absolute because in the underdeveloped pole no growth is possible without exporting in order to be able to import; export production is favored, the

---

[3] Food and raw material production is still "evolving and is an object of progress... this suggests that the region (Latin America) may be stagnating in the exportation of basic products... Technical progress allows developed countries to reduce their dependence on our countries" (Figueroa Sepúlveda, 1989: 164–165).

[4] Two forms of economic growth reflecting particular *patterns of industrial colonialism,* historical forms that express the basic tendencies of underdeveloped production in a particular way" (Figueroa Sepúlveda, 2001: 12).

fate of the economy is linked to the development of exports and the under-developed economy does not control its own development. The second is relative or "inward" growth: although it depends on the growth of exports, accumulation is aimed at the internal market (Figueroa Sepúlveda, 1986: 153–155).

Of the features which, according to Figueroa Sepúlveda, characterize each of these forms of growth, a few of relevance to our topic are outlined below:

In conditions of absolute growth, as it involves the use of competitive capacity at an international level, the predisposition toward openness to and dependence on foreign capital is accentuated. The efforts of the state are not focused on the unification of the nation or on the development of the internal market, but on clearing obstacles to international trade; the design is strengthened to keep wage levels down, as this becomes a "comparative advantage." Because it needs to operate with a high organic composition, the capacity for absorption of labor-power is greatly reduced, unemployment rises and competition between workers intensifies. This type of growth fosters a concentration of wealth and a gap between the poles of rich and poor, and is characterized by authoritarianism in the political sphere and free trade in the economic sphere (Figueroa Sepúlveda, 1989: 154–159).

In relative growth, industrialization, aimed at the internal market, diversifies the branches of immediate labor and expands internal demand; the state establishes mechanisms for the protection of this industry, creates an infrastructure aimed at facilitating internal transactions and, in general, unifies and fosters the development of the internal market. The number of workers expands, their organization is strengthened within set limits and, if the process displays a certain continuity, wages should grow, albeit slowly. This form of growth is characterized by an interventionist state that is developed in the manner of a direct capitalist (Figueroa Sepúlveda, 1989: 160–164).

Thus, as described above, if the political sphere (i.e. the sphere of domination, of regulation of relations between social classes) is inseparable from the forms of economic organization, and if the basic distinction between the general forms of capitalist domination lies in the recognition or denial of the material interests of the workers, it is clear that the only possibility in underdevelopment[5] for some mode of the contained

---

[5] At least in the Latin American case, which is the case examined here, although it is highly probable that the whole underdeveloped world shares the same essential characteristics.

form of domination to arise is associated with the relative or "inward" growth of its economy and the role taken by the nation-state in this form of growth. In this case, the underdeveloped economy disconnects to a certain extent from the global market and the local state acquires a certain capacity to regulate the dynamics of the national economy, and, therefore, to regulate relations between social classes.

On the other hand, under conditions of absolute or "outward" growth, workers will face enormous difficulties in establishing a political space to moderate capital, as at least three phenomena occur which render impossible the creation of anything vaguely resembling the contained form of capitalist domination:

1. The local state cannot establish institutions for the containment of capital or negotiation between classes, as wage levels need to be kept low as a "comparative advantage" to promote exports and as part of the "offer" to attract investment by foreign capital;
2. Local underdeveloped capital will itself face difficulties due to competition with the developed pole, and it tends to be expendable for developed capital, which generally appropriates the economic sectors and natural resources that interest it;
3. Underdeveloped capital tends to use all the mechanisms at its disposal to extract greater surplus-value from the workers, in an effort to survive the competition posed by developed capital.

It is thus clear that the conditions of absolute or "outward" growth, structured in a context of "free trade" and openness to direct investment by imperialist capital, require the establishment of the natural form of domination.

COMMAND OF THE DEVELOPED POLE OF THE IMPERIALIST SYSTEM

As the underdeveloped pole needs to import as a prerequisite for any process of economic growth, its fate is tied to the behavior of its export sector, while the fate of this sector in turn depends on the process unfolding at the developed pole of the imperialist system. The transitions from one form of economic growth to another are not the result of internally generated or internally controlled processes. They do not arise, as in the case of developed capitalism, from the process of internal class struggle, nor from a fall in the local rate of profit, but from a crisis occurring at the center: "it is a fall in the rate of profit at the center that unleashes all the contradictions inherent to accumulation in the underdeveloped pole in their most extreme form. Recessions do very little or nothing, while the crisis lasts, to restore conditions for growth, as this will depend on economic developments at the center" (Figueroa Sepúlveda, 1989: 194).

This means that since the form of domination in underdevelopment is linked to its form of economic growth, which is in turn associated with processes defined in developed capitalism, the patterns of domination at the underdeveloped pole will tend to be connected, to correspond as a subordinate form, to the patterns of domination at the developed pole, as both are tied to the same global economy, under the command of the developed pole of the imperialist system.

While the organization of the patterns of domination in developed capitalism is defined by its own internal dynamics of class struggle and economic behavior, in underdeveloped capitalism the pattern of domination is associated with economic dynamics that are neither generated nor controlled internally, but by the development of the capital/wage-labor relation at the center; it is the developed pole of the imperialist system that imposes the basic tendencies of capitalist domination at the global level.

The Centrality of the Relation between Capital and Labor

According to the above, the concept of pattern of domination to explain our object of study (i.e. the way in which capital dominates labor) needs to include at least three interconnected dimensions: the organization of the relationship between the state and capitalists; the organization of competition between capitalists; and the way in which the developed pole of the imperialist system organizes its relation with the underdeveloped pole. To clear up any possible confusion, it is worth concluding this chapter with some reflections on the nature of the relationship between these dimensions and the object of study.

With regard to the first dimension – the relationship between the state and capitalists – it is my belief that it is not the relation that defines the form of domination, but rather, that the reverse is true: the form of domination defines the relation. It is the weakness or resistance of the workers that determines whether the state will leave the management of class relations to the free initiative of capitalists, to the supposed consensus between capitalists and individual workers, as occurs in the natural form of domination, or whether the state will intervene in these relations and manage them, organizing a forum for negotiation between the classes, as occurs in the contained form of domination.

The second dimension – competition between capitalists – is, at least in relation to the object of study here, a derivative of the first. The degree to which the state will allow free competition between capitalists or intervene to regulate that competition is determined by the form of domination. Under the conditions of the natural form of domination, competition is free; however, under the conditions of the contained form of domination, competition must necessarily be regulated or channeled by the state. It is therefore clear that it is not the form of competition between capitalists that defines the form of domination, but rather the other way round.

With regard to the third dimension – the relation between the developed and underdeveloped poles of the imperialist system – I indicated above that it is the developed pole that establishes the pattern of domination at the underdeveloped pole, while the organization of the patterns of domination at the developed pole are determined by its own internal dynamics of class struggle and economic behavior. Therefore, it is ultimately the form of domination at each pole that defines the relationship between the two poles of the imperialist system, and not the other way round. This means that the form of growth (relative or absolute), with its full range of consequences, which the developed nations impose on the underdeveloped world, is more closely linked to the struggle of the workers at the global level than to capitalist and state management of underdevelopment.

THE DOMINANT FACTION OF CAPITAL

The analysis of the historical succession of the patterns of domination also entails an analysis of the successive dominant factions of the capitalist class. Each pattern of domination is associated with the domination of a dominant faction of the capitalist class. The concept not only requires an understanding of the general form of domination of the period, but the identification of the specific subject behind that domination.

While the general question for the analysis of the relations of domination is "How does the dominant class dominate?," the basic question in the analysis of the pattern of domination is "How does the hegemonic faction of the dominant class dominate?." If, in general, we view capitalist domination as a producer of the social order that the capitalist class needs to pursue its interests, the concept of a pattern of domination raises the question of how a specific faction of the capitalist class, established as the hegemonic force in a specific period, organizes a particular social order.

The Production Workshop of Domination Strategies

A pattern of domination results from a combination of ideological, political and economic circumstances and class practices that express wills and intentions in conflict, operating in a context of structural relations with a tendential development, independent of will and consciousness. However, in this section my intention is to highlight the intentional, voluntary, conscious component of the pattern of domination; it is necessary to examine the creation of political initiatives by the dominant class in conflict with the resistance of the dominated, its strategic intentionality and its political will, not as a spontaneous result of the activities of government and private capital, but as a systematic effort to establish a methodology of domination.

The problem exists in all periods of domination but, as will be shown in the following chapters, the need for a concept that examines this becomes more obvious as capital makes an increasingly systematic effort to put science at the service of its domination; class domination becomes a matter of design and scientific application, a result of something that might be called the "production workshop of domination strategies."

This concept is analogous to the workshop of technological progress proposed by Víctor Figueroa Sepúlveda as a place "where the productive applications of science are processed" (Figueroa Sepúlveda, 1989: 41). For the development of the productive force of labor (i.e. for the development of the relation between capital and wage-labor), there comes a time when purely empirical knowledge is not enough and it is necessary to organize science to carry out general labor as a specific form of productive labor, in a task of growing complexity and magnitude. Similarly, the history of the domination of capital demonstrates the inadequacy of purely empirical knowledge, and the task of domination becomes a matter of scientific production and application with the establishment of a "production workshop of domination strategies" as a place where the political applications of science are processed.

Capital turns to science for answers to its problems of both exploitation and domination.[6] Like the workshop of technological progress, the

---

6 Although the basis of the relation between capital and wage-labor lies in the separation of workers from the means of production and subsistence, capitalism makes a range of other expropriations and constructs diverse needs of exploitation and domination that require science for their development: "the separation of workers from the means of production in the economy, from the means of war in the army, from material means of administration in government, from the means of research in the academic institution and

production workshop of domination strategies constitutes "a complete, integrated network" (Figueroa Sepúlveda, 1989: 42) connecting political parties, trade unions, universities, business and professional associations, think tanks and government departments. Its task is to provide capital with mechanisms for domination and to promote incentives for competition and division among workers, thereby hindering the construction of viable alternatives. It conducts scientific and technological research with military and law enforcement applications and produces everything from geoeconomic and geopolitical designs to strategies for mind manipulation. And at its helm is the state, increasingly connected to the major monopolies, coordinating its strategic coherence.[7]

This concept is useful for analysis, but also for political purposes. It is analytically useful because, if domination and its forms are not a spontaneous product but, at least in part, the result of strategic class designs, we need a concept that enables us to identify where and how such designs are structured. It is politically useful because examining the subject of the process (the class, faction or power group) helps to expose the most basic resource of bourgeois ideology: to present the order of capitalist society as an expression of human nature, the needs of capital as natural needs and the process of capital as a natural process without a subject, in order to discourage inquiry by the dominated who seek the cause of and the solution to their woes. If, as their ideologues take for granted, the laws of the operation of capital are as natural and eternal as the law of gravity, the woes of the workers are natural, eternal and irremediable and the only rational response is resignation.[8] But if capital is a social and historical product, resignation is not only irrational but impossible.

---

the laboratory, is a common decisive factor both to the modern military-state political enterprise and to private capitalist economics" Max Weber (as quoted by Portantiero, 1981: 17).

[7] "In the United States we find... from the direct enlistment of intellectuals, scientists and academics in State and Defense department programs (see the *Report of the Panel on Defense Social and Behavioral Sciences, Trans-action,* May 1968), to the incorporation of social scientists into operations designed and piloted by the Pentagon and the CIA against revolutionary movements (Irving Louis Horowitz: "The Life and Death of Project Camelot", in *Professing Sociology,* Aldine, Chicago, 1968), and even the use of private foundations (the Ford Foundation and many others) and ad hoc associations (Congress for Cultural Freedom, etc.) effectively coordinated by the U.S. Administration to organize both intellectual and media initiatives in order to promote the objectives of the United States" (Vidal-Beneyto, 2002).

[8] The *laws of the market* are, in bourgeois discourse, analogous to the *laws of nature* and, particularly in neoliberalism (which in reality is a *theology*), they have the same logical structure as the *laws of God.*

For decades, capitalist states, particularly the imperialist ones, have been developing the "production workshop of domination strategies," perfecting the applications of science in designs of both domestic and foreign policy.[9] Every nation-state and every local government has its offices of experts, but organizations like the CIA, the FBI and the Pentagon, accustomed to designing strategies with global reach, are veritable repositories of political wisdom, shining stars in the universe of the "production workshop of domination strategies." As are the most sophisticated offices of the IMF and the World Bank which, particularly in the current period of neoliberal globalization, design global economic policy while their experts prevent the social and political effects of those economic policies and define what they refer to as governance and governability strategies (usually preceded by the elegant qualifier democratic); in other words, strategies for imposing the economic policy that the major global corporations need without inciting protest, or for defusing protest and reducing it to irrelevance. These offices issue instructions, particularly imperatives for the governments of underdeveloped countries, both to design policies that will make their countries more competitive and attract the investment of capital, and to fight extreme poverty, reform their education systems, empower "civil society" or strengthen "local governments."

Moreover, all this wisdom, this monopoly of knowledge and information, is concentrated in stable social groups removed from public scrutiny, protected against any kind of democratic control, far from the vicissitudes of political-electoral processes. In the United States, governments come and go, Democrats and Republicans alternate in power, but the CIA, the FBI, and similar organizations, remain as undisputed pillars of the "production workshop of domination strategies," and are constantly developing their knowledge.[10]

The state "penetrates more deeply into society and concentrates societal intelligence and the capacity for command, in a dual process of concentration of activity and monopolization of knowledge," and the new forms of organizing the relation between governors and governed

---

[9] For example, the *Cold War* and the *fight against "the communist threat"* at the peak of the post-war period offered vast territories of experimentation and development, just as the so-called *"fight against organized crime"* does today.

[10] "The fact that the historical development of political and economic forms has seen the rise of the 'career' civil servant, technically skilled in bureaucratic work (civil and military), is of primordial importance in political science and in the history of forms of government" Gramsci (as quoted by Portantiero, 1981: 49).

"strengthen the relative position of the power of bureaucracy (civil and military), of high finance and of all authorities in general, relatively independently of the fluctuations in public opinion" (Portantiero, 1981: 34–54). Centralization of class power runs parallel to the concentration of capital produced by financial capital,[11] monopolization and imperialism; as capitalism develops, the organized forces of the major monopolies and the state grip firmly on the reins of economic and political power.

---

[11] See Lenin's definition of the merging of banking and industrial capital (Lenin, 1916: 226).

CHAPTER FOUR

THE HISTORY OF CAPITALIST DOMINATION

In any given society, the striving of some of its members conflicts with the striving of others, [and] social life is full of contradictions. Marxism has provided the guidance – i.e. the theory of the class struggle – for the discovery of the laws governing this seeming maze and chaos.

V.I. Lenin
Karl Marx

In the previous chapter I argued that, beyond the specific features of each of the many different nation-states, it is possible to identify periods in the world history of capitalist domination in which either the natural form or the contained form has predominated, and that the historical manifestation of a general form constitutes a pattern of domination in such a way that its period of prevalence is effectively a period in the world history of capitalist domination. The purpose of this chapter is to examine the viability of this proposition by analyzing the political history of capitalism (if only in a general historical outline) in terms of the concept of the pattern of domination.

Pattern of Domination and Periodization

If we look back over the history of capitalism, we find a long historical period of formation and consolidation of the capitalist relation as the dominant relation, running from the 16th century (exploration of the world, new discoveries, construction of the first colonial empires, development of manufacturing and formation of a global market) up to the end of the 18th century. This was the period of transition from feudalism to capitalism; the capitalist class, first under the direction of commercial capital and later under that of productive capital, embarked on a process of transformation from feudal society to establish the social order necessary for the assertion and development of the capitalist production relation. As interesting as it might be to analyze the modalities assumed in the establishment of the bourgeois class as the dominant class during the long process of transition from feudalism to capitalism, this is not my purpose here.

If we consider the history of domination in capitalism once it had been established as the dominant relation in the economic and political spheres, i.e. from the end of the 18th century, beginning in England with the Industrial Revolution, which lay the foundations of modern industry, and with the bourgeois revolutions – particularly the French – which set up the capitalist class as the dominant class (in other words, as the state), up to the present, we find three major periods in the history of capitalist domination, defined in their basic historical expression by developed capitalism: in the first, the natural form of domination predominates; in the second, the contained form, and in the third, once again the natural form.

In developed Western capitalism, these three periods are defined by three patterns of domination: the first by the liberal pattern, the second by the Keynesian pattern and the third by the neoliberal pattern of domination. The first and the third are historical manifestations of the natural form, while the second is a historical manifestation of the contained form of capitalist domination. The liberal pattern constitutes the first historical expression of the natural form while the neoliberal pattern is its second expression. These three patterns of domination correspond in Latin America to the oligarchic pattern, the developmentalist pattern and the neoliberal pattern of domination, respectively. The oligarchic and neoliberal patterns are the Latin American expression of the natural form in its first and second historical emergence, while the developmentalist pattern is the contained form of capitalist domination.

In the previous chapter, I used the image of a wave washing over a beach to explain how I understand the historical development of each pattern of domination; my intention is not necessarily to suggest a homogeneous or globally simultaneous situation, but to identify a historical trend that could define the basic features of the prevailing form of capitalist domination, to find basic structures or general "cycles" in domination. The aim here is to establish a kind of periodization which, beyond the infinite diversity that can be found in the wide range of specific features, will allow the identification of the general tendencies in capitalist domination. As will be shown in Chapter Ten, these tendencies are associated with the long term, the historical cycle of capitalism.

To provide further context for this study, what follows is a brief outline of the characteristics of the first two of these periods in capitalist domination and of the patterns of domination that define them (liberal and oligarchic; Keynesian and developmentalist). The analysis of the neoliberal pattern will be taken up in Part Two.

THE FIRST EMERGENCE OF THE NATURAL FORM

As mentioned above, capitalism was established as the dominant relation in the economic and political spheres in Western Europe towards the end of the 18th century, beginning in England with the Industrial Revolution, which laid the foundations of modern industry, and with the bourgeois revolutions (particularly the French Revolution), which established the capitalist class as the dominant class. From that point on, capitalism began to transform the rest of the world, exporting commodities, exporting capital, importing commodities, transforming production structures and, in short, transforming social relations around the world.

Capitalism was born in Western Europe, but once born, it would foster, engender and condition its successive births in the rest of the world, transforming but also combining with the local, "traditional" forms of domination and exploitation, in accordance with the historical pre-capitalist forms in each region of the world where capital would be introduced. Most of the products of these successive births, particularly those in which capital developed into imperialism, would be deformed, incomplete forms of capitalism: underdeveloped capitalism.

The general form assumed by this process is described by Marx in *Capital: .".*.[I]n any given economic formation of society, where not the exchange-value but the use-value of the product dominates, surplus-labor will be limited by a given set of wants which may be greater or less, and here no boundless thirst for surplus-labor arises from the nature of the production itself. But as soon as people, whose production still moves within the lower forms of slave-labor, corvee-labor, etc., are drawn into the whirlpool of an international market dominated by the capitalistic mode of production, the sale of their products for export becoming the principal interest, the civilized horrors of over-work are grafted onto the barbaric horrors of slavery, serfdom, etc." (Marx, 1867: Ch. 10).

I believe that it is possible to demonstrate that the form of domination that capital establishes around the world at its birth, and which develops during the course of its infancy, corresponds to the characterization I have offered of the natural form, and that, as capitalism develops into imperialism, in the gestation of underdeveloped capitalism the domination and exploitation of capital comes into being by combining with the forms of domination and exploitation of the local pre-capitalist classes, at least unless capital introduces its own specific forms.

In Western Europe, this combination was the result of a compromise between the nascent bourgeoisie and the feudal state which was settled relatively quickly in favor of capitalist domination. Conversely, in the rest of the world the combination was between an already globally dominant bourgeoisie and local powers which, in this way, for better or for worse, initiated their transition toward capitalism – underdeveloped, in almost every case, apart from a few exceptions such as Japan – but which were already associated with the accumulation of capital; as such, these are forms of capitalist domination.

The result is that from its birth the form of domination in the underdeveloped world was linked to its form of economic growth, and the patterns of domination at the underdeveloped pole would tend to be connected, to correspond as a subordinate form, to the patterns of domination at the developed pole, as both are tied to the same global economy, under the command of the developed pole of the imperialist system.

An example of this is the connection between European despotism and Asian despotism, as analyzed by Marx in his examination of European domination in India. This connection, which resulted from an insatiable need of capital to appropriate the labor of others, which is uncontained in the historical circumstances of its birth, gave rise to a particular historical manifestation of the natural form of capitalist domination through its combination with a specific pre-capitalist form of domination: "to characterize the working of the British East India Company," explains Marx, "it is sufficient to literally repeat what Sir Stamford Raffles... said of the old Dutch East India Company: '...actuated solely by the spirit of gain, and viewing their subjects with less regard or consideration than a West India planter formerly viewed a gang upon his estate, because the latter had paid the purchase money of human property, which the other had not, employed all the existing machinery of despotism to squeeze from the people their utmost mite of contribution, the last dregs of their labor...'" (Marx, 1853).

The emergence of the natural form of domination as a general historical form (although it has assumed diverse modalities or patterns of domination, particularly differentiated between developed and underdeveloped capitalism) marked the beginning of the historical cycle of capital, spreading around the world as unevenly as the spread of capitalism itself. This form was introduced wherever capitalism was born, over the course of a period of time beginning in the late 18th century and running throughout the 19th.

An examination of the spread of the natural form of capitalist domination, tracing its historical path from its birth and introduction around the world, is beyond the scope of this study. I will therefore limit my study of this historical panorama to the presentation of the general features that this form assumed as the liberal pattern of domination in developed capitalism, particularly in England (which was the hegemonic state at the global level during the period), and as the oligarchic pattern of domination in Latin America.

Liberal Pattern of Domination

The first real period of bourgeois domination was organized under the liberal pattern, the prevailing pattern in developed capitalism, and the natural form, as a general historical form assuming diverse modalities or patterns of domination, defines an entire period of world history: the beginning of the historical cycle of industrial capital and its spread around the world over a period of time beginning in the late 18th century and running throughout the 19th century.

This period begins with the Industrial Revolution; at the heart of the production process, in the capitalist factory, labor had been effectively subsumed by capital,[1] representing a major defeat for the worker. As I indicated in the first chapter, capitalist domination over the worker by this time also appeared as subordination of the laborer to the machine. Workers were deprived of many of their productive faculties, just as before they had been deprived of the means of production; by developing the productivity of labor, capital created its own reserve army and intensified competition among workers.

In short, the Industrial Revolution stripped workers of the possibilities of bargaining or negotiation with capital which they had achieved for factory conditions. These transformations, occurring at the level of the capital/wage-labor relation, in the relations of exploitation and domination as these were expressed within the sphere of production itself, were complemented by transformations occurring in the sphere of politics and ideology.

---

[1] See Marx's discussion of relative surplus-value (Marx, 1867) and his explanation of the concepts of *formal and real subsumption* (Marx, 1863).

The bourgeoisie had already established a specifically capitalist technical base – the machine – and was preparing to transform the productive
structure of Europe and of the whole world, as the Industrial Revolution
began to demonstrate its enormous transformative potential. In the political sphere, the era of bourgeois revolutions began; throughout this period,
the bourgeoisie gradually consolidated itself as the dominant class in
Europe, essentially leaving behind the political forms of compromise with
the feudal classes – the absolutist state in particular – which had characterized the last phases of the transition from feudalism to capitalism.

In these revolutionary processes, at least at their most radical moments
(particularly in France in the late 18th century), the bourgeoisie led the
people (i.e. of the oppressed and exploited classes) against feudal oppression and exploitation. It set itself up as the representative of a project of
civilization that offered liberty, equality and fraternity in a context of constant progress under the aegis of reason to manage relations with nature
and relations among human beings themselves. Affairs among human
beings were no longer under the control of divine will: there is nothing
more than humanity. Humans have inalienable rights, and people agree
on the modes of their relations through a pact or contract to ensure a level
of order that guarantees well-being and happiness for all.

At the beginning of the liberal period, workers found themselves
defeated in the sphere of production and subsumed in the political, ideological and organic spheres, as part of the "people," under the political and
ideological direction of the bourgeoisie. And on this foundation of worker
defenselessness, the liberal structure of domination was built. Since abso-
lutism, the bourgeoisie had already been fighting to establish "property
rights," and its first act upon establishing the bourgeois state was to guarantee capitalist property, i.e. to give legal status to the relation that separates direct producers from the means of production and subsistence.[2] In
this way, the capital/wage-labor relation was affirmed as the basis of the
new society, thereby bringing into effect the whole range of the "necessary
relations, independent of the will and consciousness of men" that characterize capitalism.

Having legally affirmed the capital relation, the separation between
producer and means of production, as the inviolability of property, and

---

[2] "Private property, which constitutes the basis of bourgeois society, occupied the central position in liberal theory and the constitutional systems of the period: to ensure the
inviolable character of property and the power to dispose of it freely, guaranteeing the
unimpeded development of industry and commerce" (Kuhnl, 1978: 50).

reduced the workers to a state of defenselessness, the liberal pattern of domination led to private agreements, to negotiation between free and equal individuals, in the determination of the conditions of sale and use of labor-power. According to Kuhnl, "the law had to be limited to the regulation of formal relations between individuals; it could not hope to determine the content of the private sphere, including the area of production and distribution of goods. The state and the law could only fulfill the function of guaranteeing the basis of bourgeois society – private property – and of setting the general framework in which the free competition of economic entities and opinions could occur. Individuals, legally free and equal, had to regulate their mutual relations through freely determined private agreements" (Kuhnl, 1978: 48).

"The state," adds Kuhnl, "has the sole function of setting general rules regarding the movement of private individuals and of protecting their liberty and their property, but must remain neutral with regard to the content of the agreements established between them (state as 'night watchman'). Bourgeois society was elevated to the sphere of private autonomy, *while public authority was subordinated to the needs of private life*" (Kuhnl, 1978: 53, emphasis added). In this way, according to the dominant ideology of the era, an order is assured in which the people regulate their affairs freely themselves, without resorting to violence, in a rational manner in which material justice would arise of its own accord (Kuhnl, 1978: 55); liberalism proclaims "liberty and progress" on behalf of all human beings.

It is clear that relegating the regulation of relations between social classes to "the private sphere" when the working class has no means of defense effectively hands control of the process over to private capital and to the logic that organizes its spontaneous movement. There is no need to explore here the terrible excesses produced by the private agreements, the negotiations between free and equal individuals, in the forms of labor exploitation imposed by capital: excessively long working days, reduction of wages, health problems, abuse of female and child labor, etc. Marx documents these in detail, particularly in the chapters "The Working Day" and "Machinery and Modern Industry" in Volume I of *Capital*.

The picture that characterizes the liberal pattern of domination is completed with liberal democracy and bourgeois individualism. With regard to liberal democracy, there are three dimensions worth highlighting: the delimitation made between the "public" and "private" spheres, the form of expression of inter-bourgeois relations and the form of organization of the political relation between capital and labor.

The first aspect has already been partly addressed above. The public sphere, which organizes the activities of the state, is clearly delimited; it has the sole function of setting general rules regarding the movement of private individuals and protecting their liberty and property. Everything else falls within the private sphere and is beyond the authority of the state; the state must remain neutral with regard to the content of the agreements established between free and equal individuals.

It should be added here that democracy is a form of administration of the public sphere – a form of administration of state activity. The limits of the public sphere are therefore also the limits of the territory of democracy; everything excluded from the public sphere is also excluded from the administration of democracy. In other words, in the liberal state, the content of the agreements established between free and equal individuals are not a public affair, nor are they subject to any regulation arising from the state's administration of democracy. They are simply matters excluded from the public agenda.

In relation to the second aspect – the form of organization and expression of inter-bourgeois relations – it should be noted first of all that, in this first stage of the life cycle of capitalism, ownership of the means of production and subsistence (i.e. the capital/wage-labor relation) was spread out over a large number of capitalists. In its first stage, the liberal state was the political expression of competitive capital, in the phase of free capitalist competition: it was this multiplicity of capital owners that gave rise to the liberal state in its first stage, prior to the rise of imperialism in the last third of the 19th century. The periodical elections of governments and their control by legislative bodies reflected the conditions of inter-capitalist competition and the need to prevent the state from being used by individual capitalists to promote their accumulation over that of their competitors.

Of course, the bourgeoisie has never been a homogeneous class at any time in its history. It has always been divided into groups and factions, and inter-bourgeois conflicts are reflected in the struggles for control of the state. However, in this period (as never again in periods that followed), the state was the state of the whole bourgeoisie, and its status as a democratic institution, specifically the principle of the division of powers, operated efficiently. In the subsequent periods, as we will see later, the state favored the interests of one faction of the capitalist class and, consequently, executive power acquired a clear preeminence over the other powers that constitute the formal institutions of bourgeois democracy.

In relation to the third aspect – the form of organization of the political relation between capital and labor – liberal democracy radically excluded non-owners (i.e. the workers); it was democracy exclusively for the owners (i.e. capitalists and landlords). Owners ensured their control of "private" affairs through private agreements between free and equal individuals, as well as control of "public" affairs. Civil rights were based on property and income or revenue for three reasons: first, because property owners were the ones who paid the taxes that the state had to decide how to spend, thereby giving them the right to participate in the decisions that affected the public interest; second, because only an educated person could be expected to have the capacity for discernment to decide on matters of public interest, and access to education depended on having sufficient resources; third, because only property could provide men with the free time necessary to be able to exercise their political rights (Kuhnl, 1978: 56).

In light of the above, it is no surprise that voting rights in liberal institutions were limited to property owners "to avoid the perils of demagoguery" and that universal suffrage was viewed as "a favor done to ignorance, vulgarization and brutalization of public life... an opportunity to unleash the forces of stupidity, superstition, malignancy and lies, and selfish and vulgar interests," which must be opposed by the "the upper classes, the properly instructed classes" (Kuhnl, 1978: 58). And, finally, it should be noted that bourgeois individualism[3] on the one hand reflected the conditions under which relations among capitalists themselves were established, the nature of the relations of competition under which each property owner necessarily operated; it was a society in which each individual attended to his property, to his interests, and to the expansion of his capital.

However, analyzed from the perspective of the relation between capitalists and wage-laborers (and this is the fundamental aspect for the topic examined here), bourgeois individualism constitutes a proposition to erect a structure of domination. Faced with the organized economic, political and ideological force of the capitalist class, laborers, relying only on "their individual effort," as the liberal ideology proposes, are defenseless: "The history of the regulation of the working day... prove[s] conclusively that the isolated laborer... when capitalist production has once

---

[3] The criticism of bourgeois individualism does not imply a denial of the importance of the individual; in Marx, in clear contrast with the so-called "real socialism" of the 20th century, a socialist project of liberation only has meaning if it guarantees the full realization of the individual (See for example Fromm, 1978; Mészáros, 1978).

attained a certain stage, succumbs without any power of resistance" (Marx, 1867: Ch. 10).

During the liberal era, there was clear and open hostility to any form of working class organization. Individualism was nothing more than an ideology, a conception of the world of which the bourgeoisie hoped to convince the workers. It was not merely a recommendation or suggestion; workers who were not convinced of the wondrous virtues of individualism and, in spite of it, sought to promote unions or any other type of organization, would have to face the aggressive, organized violence of the state. Clearly, according to the logic of the liberal pattern of domination, worker organization is an intolerable attack against liberty and against the ordering principle of social life: the private agreement between free and equal individuals.[4] With this situation, the best of all possible worlds had arrived in the eyes of the bourgeoisie and, for the first time in capitalism, the end of history was proclaimed. There were no more social classes, no more oppression, no more exploitation; all these social curses belonged to the feudal past. Now, each individual could carve out his own destiny by his own effort.

This was the discourse of modernity, the discourse of a class that was quite clear about the exact limits of its identification with the interests of "all men"; but it was also an optimistic discourse of a class that believed itself capable of managing progress and happiness for all, although, of course, more for some than for others.[5] However (and this is the point at which an examination of the Keynesian pattern of domination begins), the development of capitalism itself created the space in which the first forms of working class organization and resistance would take shape. But first, an examination is needed of the Latin American correlate of the liberal pattern: the oligarchic pattern of domination.

---

[4] "With the victory of liberalism, social assistance measures were suppressed due to their incompatibility with the principles of free economic expansion, legal equality of persons and non-intervention of the State in the economy; as a result the working-day grew longer and female and child labor increased. As *any form of labor association was prohibited under very severe laws,* the affected parties accepted the work conditions imposed upon them. The submission of the workers to discipline and obedience would not have been possible without the help of the bourgeois State" (Kuhnl, 1978: 81, emphasis added).

[5] "A class in an upward phase like the bourgeoisie tends to develop an optimistic interpretation of its social function and of the world in general. The basis of the liberal conception of the world rests on the conviction that history constitutes a rational evolution toward superior forms of life; man learns to dominate nature with increasing ability and will ultimately subject the development of society to the demands of reason. Man is conceived as naturally good and capable of attaining perfection; he only needs the opportunity to develop freely. Together with the doctrine of natural rights and the natural

Oligarchic Pattern of Domination

During Latin America's time as a Spanish colony, the predominant production relation was slavery,[6] although even then it was a slave-based economy within a dynamic emerging from the global market, commanded by commercial capital.[7] The crisis of colonial domination was linked to the crisis of commercial capital domination in the global market and the emergence of productive capital; England and France's defeat of Spain was an expression of the defeat of commercial capital by productive capital.

For the Latin American, essentially agro-mining oligarchies, independence meant breaking the "colonial pact"; i.e. breaking the commercial monopoly exercised by the Spanish crown over its colonies and, as such, the possibility of opening up "freely" to global trade and diversifying its external market. The project of the Latin American oligarchies consisted in entering the global market; they viewed themselves, as they always had, as export producers.[8] And, since export production is organized to meet needs that develop outside it, the oligarchy lacked a project of internal transformation, other than the project of adapting to export needs.

This same lack of a project for internal transformation explains why, during the first decades of the 19th century, with the global capitalist

---

equality of all men, optimism and humanism form part of this basic conception. This optimistic, humanist faith in progress also characterized the philosophy of history in this period" (Kuhnl, 1978 39). Needless to say, the bourgeois discourse in relation to history – the discourse of "modernity" – contrasts violently with contemporary "post-modern" discourse.

6 "The production relation that tended to be predominant and stable was slavery. This constituted the basis of operations for large-scale production aimed at exportation; it offered the use of a massive work force that was compelled to work under the harshest conditions... The Spanish colonial 'mita' or 'cuatequil' [systems of forced labor] differed from classical slavery, but nevertheless constituted slavery. The same is true of the peonage or retainer... The 'peón' (general laborer) *was not* a free laborer with the ability to sell his labor-power as a commodity, but a slave tied to the plantation and to the will of the land-owner" (Figueroa Sepúlveda, 1986: 211).

7 "In our case, the result of the Conquest and colonization could not have been a simple slave-based economy. From the beginning, the aim was to organize the exploitation of labor and production directly in order to increase exchange-value. What arose here was therefore not a slave-based economy in the sense of the social relation represented by slavery constituting the nucleus around which society is organized and its movement is determined; rather, slavery was set within another dynamic, which emerged from the developing global market" (Figueroa Sepúlveda, 1986: 212).

8 "The productive intentionality of the dominant classes continued to be export production, both because there was no internal market and because they showed no interest in developing local industry... production continued to depend on external demand" (Figueroa Sepúlveda, 1986: 219).

economy in crisis and the development of the oligarchic export economy blocked, the Latin American oligarchies, incapable of organizing themselves into nation-states,[9] developing their internal markets and fostering transformations to their productive structures and production relations, took refuge on their rural estates and in their local regions, dedicating themselves to destroying one another in internal conflicts,[10] awaiting, like a giant Macondo,[11] the longed-for rise of the exporter age;[12] this age would not come until the second half of the 19th century, and would only be consolidated with the arrival of capitalist imperialism.

The Latin American oligarchies, the dominant class of this Macondo, without an external market to give their production a purpose and a target, could only suffocate in their solitude, carrying on for three quarters of the 19th century with the same strategies and productive capacities that operated in colonial times, trying to change as little as possible and to profit as much as they could. According to Carmagnani, instead of renewing the pre-existing economic, social, political and cultural structures, the oligarchies tried to promote them and give them a new direction, seeking to reconcile the old elements with the new, establishing a new order that did not change a single fundamental mechanism already in place (Carmagnani, 1984: 10, 12).

Only with the arrival of imperialist capital would significant changes occur in the Latin American economy, although even then the oligarchies attempted to preserve their basic forms of domination into the 20th century. And in this way of constructing their historical project, although slavery was legally abolished with independence, there was no room or

---

[9] Indeed, several institutions of the colonial past defended by the *conservative* current within the oligarchy, such as the military and ecclesiastical authorities, aided by the absence of an internal market, operated as forces to block the process to establish a nation-state. See, for example, Ricaurte Soler (as quoted in Cueva, 1993: 46).

[10] The inter-oligarchic struggles did not end because an internal solution was found, but as the result of the economic growth produced by demand in the countries of developed capitalism; the oligarchy on its own was never capable of finding a way of establishing itself as a nation-state or organizing a national economy. "After 1880, the new integration of the Latin American economies into the global economy favored and strengthened all of the oligarchies. Thanks to economic growth, inter-oligarchic struggles came to an end" (Carmagnani, 1984: 98).

[11] Macondo, the fictional town in Gabriel García Márquez's epic novel *One Hundred Years of Solitude*, has often been interpreted as a metaphor for Latin America in the 19th and early 20th centuries.

[12] "The weak and scattered efforts to promote capitalist production found no echo among those who controlled economic power, who showed practically no interest whatsoever in the 'nation' in terms of its development. Rather, they sat waiting for the benefits that independence might bring in terms of diversification of the external market" (Figueroa Sepúlveda, 1986: 217).

need to transform either the production relations, or the forms of domination that the oligarchy exercised over the workers. In other words, there was no transformation of their immediate structure, because in a general sense there were indeed enormous transformations; in the colonial era, the global market was controlled by pre-capitalist commercial capital, while from the Industrial Revolution on it was controlled by productive capital and, more specifically, industrial capital, i.e. capital equipped with machinery as the basic means of labor. And, by the end of the 19th century, it was imperialist capital that commanded the global market.

Thus, analyzing the situation as a whole, oligarchic domination after independence was not a pre-capitalist form of domination, but a capitalist form, constituting the oligarchic pattern of capitalist domination, at the service, initially, of industrial capital, and subsequently, toward the end of the 19th century, of imperialist capital. It was the modality assumed by the first emergence in Latin America of the natural form of capitalist domination: "The fact that we now not only call the plantation owners in America capitalists but that they are capitalists is based on their existence as anomalies within a world market based on free labor."[13]

The oligarchic pattern created a structure of domination in which political power appeared personified and under which the dominated had no rights or means of defense. According to Ianni, boss, chief, colonel, cacique, leader, etc. were the various names given to this personified power (Ianni, 1977a: 161). The natural home of the power figure was the rural estate, where it was embodied in the landowner and exercised over the laborers. But in the mines and the few factories that existed at the time, the boss also exercised this same type of power over his workers.[14]

The personification of power means autonomy and free will in the exercise of domination and the correlates of this personification are: first, the absence of a free market for labor-power, second, coercive recruitment of labor-power by various means (advances, indebtedness, sharecropping, agrarian contracts, etc.);[15] third, work conditions characterized by an

---

[13] From Marx's *Outlines of the Critique of Political Economy, Vol. 1* (as quoted in Figueroa Sepúlveda, 1986: 220). "This does not impede, but rather entails," adds Figueroa Sepúlveda, "their non-capitalist behavior *in relation to the labor they exploit.*"

[14] Even the so-called "middle classes" had the quality of a bureaucratic or professional "clientèle", at the service of the oligarchic *boss* not only in terms of their employment but also in social and political terms (Quijano, 1977: 148).

[15] "Wherever free labor is the rule, the laws regulate the mode of terminating the contract. In some States, particularly in Mexico, slavery is hidden under the form of 'peonage'. By means of advances, payable in labor, which are handed down from generation to generation, not only the individual laborer, but his family, become, *de facto*, the property of other persons and their families" (Marx as quoted by Figueroa Sepúlveda, 1986: 211).

extremely long working day, obstacles to the organization of unions and a total absence of social rights; fourth, worker consumption established in accordance with their minimum physiological needs; and fifth, the use of force by the state to support the personal power of the oligarchs.

This form of domination is expressed in the form assumed by the oligarchic economy. Unlike the bourgeois economy of the countries of developed capitalism, in Latin America neither the oligarchy nor the imperialist bourgeoisie were interested in the development of an internal market; as such, they had no interest in the complete liberation of the work-force or the creation of a free labor-power market. Of course, they also had no interest in producing any kind of political transformation even vaguely resembling anything that could be defined as "bourgeois democracy," and they certainly had no interest in granting any kind of rights to the workers. The crisis for this pattern of domination would originate in the struggles of the workers and the breakdown of its economic substratum.

The oligarchic pattern of domination constitutes the political correlate of the "primary export economy," the first historical manifestation of absolute growth or "outward growth," with which Latin America would ultimately be incorporated into the underdeveloped and dominated pole of the imperialist system. I conclude this brief exploration of the characteristics of the oligarchic pattern of domination with three final observations.

Firstly, with this form of growth, the Latin American economy assumed an external focus, while internally its lack of organization was accentuated: "The branches of primary-export production under imperialist and incipient local capitalism were individually connected to and governed by the needs of metropolitan capitalism" (Quijano, 1977: 117).

Secondly, foreign capital, particularly from the point at which U.S. capitalists replaced the British, ultimately appropriated all of the most profitable activities, thereby displacing the local oligarchies. Carmagnani points out that, unlike the British, who concentrated their investments in the business and financial structure, U.S. capital invested directly in the productive structure (agriculture, livestock, oil and industry), displacing the local oligarchy and reorganizing the productive structure to adapt it to its own needs, to such an extent that the most profitable sectors of the Latin American productive structure were in the hands of U.S. capital at the onset of the crisis of 1929 (Carmagnani, 1984: 181, 186, 193). And the reality is that, in the final analysis, the developed bourgeoisie is always necessary for the underdeveloped bourgeoisie, while for the former the latter is always, in principle, dispensable.

Thirdly, the forms of domination and exploitation and the brutal attitude toward the working and living conditions of the laborers hardened to the extreme, and workers were subjected to a process of absolute impoverishment.

The Contained Form in History

The liberal pattern of capitalist domination (and its correlates in the underdeveloped world) ultimately provoked a mobilization of workers without precedent in history, and the early 20th century saw a worldwide emergence of the masses and the birth of the mass society; the period defined by the natural form had come to an end.

The second period of bourgeois domination was organized under the Keynesian pattern, the prevailing pattern in developed capitalism, and the contained form, as a general historical form assuming diverse modalities or patterns of domination, defined a new era in world history. The transition from the natural form to the contained form covers a long period beginning in the final decades of the 19th century and basically culminating in the 1930s. The contained form reached its mature expression with the onset of World War II, and maintained its prevalence until the global economic crisis that began at the end of the 1960s. This form assumed three basic modalities: the Keynesian pattern in the U.S. and Western Europe; the developmentalist pattern in Latin America and, with different variants and limitations, throughout what came to be called the Third World – the portion of the underdeveloped world that underwent some process of industrialization; and the third modality, constituted by what we could call the Soviet pattern of domination, the variant of state capitalism constituted by "real socialism."

Only the general features of the Keynesian pattern and the developmentalist pattern in Latin America are examined here; but first, what follows is a brief outline of the process of transition from the liberal to the Keynesian pattern both in Europe and the United States. This was the fundamental process that established the period of the contained form of capitalist domination, the process that made room for the possibility of both the developmentalist pattern and the Soviet pattern.

Transitions to the Contained Form: Western Europe

For over one hundred years, from the revolutions of 1848 to the popular revolutions after World War II, and even into the 1950s, Europe would be the stage for decisive confrontations between capital and labor, the confrontations that have defined the history of humanity up to this time.

In Europe, for the first time in human history, the working class became self-aware, creating its own "conception of the world" and its own "civil society," and organizing itself into a multitude of labor and political organizations that sought not only to improve their situation within the capital/wage-labor relation, but to destroy the relation itself. For the first time in human history, the working class became a subject of history. But the decisive events in this long struggle took place after World War I, over the course of the 1920s – the "tragic decade" for the worker movement. Below I attempt to outline the process leading to the key moments of that decade, in order to situate my discussion in the context of the crisis and transformation of the liberal pattern of domination.

The liberal pattern of domination faced a crisis with the working class struggle and, as the working class had become organized and established as a subject of history, the crisis for this first emergence of the natural form of capitalist domination had two possible conclusions: the revolutionary transformation and destruction of capitalism, or the restructuring of the forms of capitalist domination.

As discussed above, during the liberal era there was clear and open hostility toward any form of working class organization. According to the logic of the liberal pattern of domination, worker organization was an intolerable attack against liberty and the ordering principle of social life: the private agreement between free and equal individuals. However (and this is a point stressed by Marx in the *Communist Manifesto*), the development of capitalism itself created a space in which, inevitably, the first forms of working class organization took shape: the factory. With the expansion of capital, factories and the number of workers multiplied; the expansion and the accumulation of capital also multiplied the number of workers in a single factory, under the command of a single capitalist.

The proletariat was in the process of establishing itself as a revolutionary class, and this process, as Claudín points out, had two facets: on the one hand, the constant deterioration – both absolute and relative – of the living conditions of the proletariat, which compelled them to rebel; and on the other, the factory as a breeding ground for unity, organization and class consciousness (Claudín, 1976: 20–21). It should be noted that, according to Marx's analysis, the first aspect explains the condition of the need for rebellion, a particularly intense need under the conditions of capitalist liberal domination. The second aspect offers the condition for the possibility of rebellion.

At the beginning of the liberal period, the central goal of capitalist domination was expressed in the effort to eliminate the possibility of worker rebellion, specifically focusing on preventing the creation of forms of class organization. Only when this effort to prevent worker, union or party organization proved futile did the form of domination begin to undergo changes, and the liberal pattern of domination in Western Europe began to move toward new forms of domination, pushed by the struggle of the workers and provoked by a series of economic transformations that were underway.

At the end of the 19th century, capitalism in Western Europe entered its imperialist phase. The structure of capital changed, the capitalist class experienced a profound process of internal differentiation and a new hegemonic faction emerged within it: the financial class, a product of the merger of industrial capital and banking capital. Imperialism is, according to Lenin's classic definition, monopoly capitalism, or financial capitalism established as a monopoly (Lenin, 1916). As Figueroa Sepúlveda points out, this is the period of a new division of labor: in the capitalist factory, immediate labor, associated with operation, is separated from general, scientific labor, associated with processing the development of productive forces (Figueroa Sepúlveda, 1986). This division of labor constituted the basis for the rise of the imperialist phase of capitalism, as it redefined three fundamental relations (Figueroa Sepúlveda, 1986):

1. In the relation between the capitalist class and the working class, the real subsumption of labor changed its mode of operation with the appearance of general labor in the final decades of the 19th century, and the production of relative surplus-value was systematized thanks to this new division of labor.

2. Competition between capitalists was resolved in favor of the capitalists who appropriated the conditions to ensure the renewal of their technical mode of production, the development of productivity in their enterprise; the monopolization of general labor and of its results to promote technological development became the basis of capitalist monopoly.

3. In the global capitalist social structure, two regions were consolidated: a developed region, made up of countries where capital itself generated the conditions for the establishment and renewal of its technical mode of production; and an underdeveloped region, which lacked this capacity and had a constant need to turn to the developed region to establish and renew its technical mode of production. The monopoly of general labor held by the developed countries became the economic (and even political and military) basis of the imperialist relation between the developed and underdeveloped regions of the world.

By the final decades of the 19th century, financial capital was already structured and widespread, giving rise to the financial oligarchy, the faction of capital which, from that point on, would hold the reins of power in capitalist society. From that time, the state was placed at the service of financial capital, and the social order that the state would strive to create would be in line with the interests of financial capital.

After the major revolutionary crises of 1848 and 1870, it became evident that the liberal pattern of domination was coming to an end. To survive, capitalist domination needed to be restructured; reform of the system of domination was essential to prevent revolution, and the economic transformations already underway would support this reconstruction of domination. In 1895, in his introduction to Marx's book, *The Class Struggles in France*, Engels made the first reference to the transformations that the form of domination was undergoing. Considering that the main political element of change was the organized presence of the masses throughout Europe, he writes: "the mode of struggle of 1848 is today obsolete in every respect."

The arguments put forward by Engels to explain this obsolescence cover a wide range of issues, including changes to the military dimension of domination. However, there are two issues Engels mentions which I believe are central to my analysis.

The first of these is the issue of democracy and the right to vote, as a right seized by the workers from the capitalists with considerable struggle, and the benefits they obtained from this right. In particular, the workers and German social democracy "have used the franchise in a way which has paid them a thousandfold and has served as a model to the workers of all countries... [the franchise has been] transformed by them from a means of deception, which it was before, into an instrument of emancipation" (Engels, 1895).

The second is the new meaning of the nation-state and democratic institutions in the class struggle. Until then, electoral democracy, limited to the participation of property owners, had been a simple instrument for organizing the dominant class; but now, according to Engels, with the "successful utilization of universal suffrage... an entirely new method of proletarian struggle came into operation... It was found that the state institutions, in which the rule of the bourgeoisie is organized, offer the working class still further levers to fight these very state institutions" (Engels, 1895).

It is clear that Engels, a revolutionary socialist, is not interested in bourgeois democracy as a means of "improving" capitalism, but rather as a path toward its revolutionary transformation. The "thousandfold" benefits brought by the franchise are not recorded by Engels merely as improvements to the situation of the proletariat within the capitalist system, but as a framework for the spreading of the struggle for socialism under the new conditions of bourgeois domination. As early as his discussion of the *Principles of Communism*, he had written that "democracy would be wholly valueless to the proletariat if it were not immediately used as a means for putting through measures directed against private property and ensuring the livelihood of the proletariat" (Engels, 1847).

For Engels, democracy is the space in which to convert the socialist project into a project of the masses, assumed by and comprising the vast majority, which was the only possible response to the new conditions of bourgeois domination. In all revolutions up to 1848, says Engels, "one ruling minority was overthrown, [and] another minority seized the helm of the state in its stead and refashioned the state institutions to suit its own interests... And these features... appeared applicable, also, to the struggle of the proletariat for its emancipation; all the more applicable, since precisely in 1848 there were but a very few people who had any idea at all of the direction in which this emancipation was to be sought" (Engels, 1895).

But fifty years later, affirms Engels, "the time of surprise attacks, of revolutions carried through by small conscious minorities at the head of masses lacking consciousness is past. Where it is a question of a complete transformation of the social organization, the masses themselves must also be in on it, must themselves already have grasped what is at stake... But in order that the masses understand what is to be done, long, persistent work is required, and it is just this work that we are now pursuing... everywhere the unprepared launching of an attack has been relegated to the background... no lasting victory is possible for them [socialists] unless they first win over the great mass of the people... Slow propaganda work and parliamentary activity are recognized here, too, as the immediate tasks of the party" (Engels, 1895).

It goes without saying that history has not taken the direction that Engels expected. The social democratic parties in Western Europe ended up directing reforms and abandoning the revolutionary project, and the international workers' movement suffered an irremediable collapse in the face of the revolutionary crisis that led to the first imperialist world war. What should have been the construction of a space in which to promote the independent organization of the working class was ultimately turned into a space compatible with bourgeois domination, which complicated that domination, but did not destroy it.

To resolve the problem that the mobilization of the masses and the crisis in the liberal pattern of domination posed for the bourgeoisie, it was necessary to "abandon the concept of the linear relation of the individual to the sovereign, and locate that relation within the analysis of the organizations that ensure the reproduction of domination" (Portantiero, 1981: 16). The reality of capitalism at the beginning of the 20th century was "a reality of groups and institutions and could not be tackled using the notion of the individualist contract" (Portantiero, 1981: 12); the reconstruction of capitalist domination could only be based on the recognition of the centrality of the worker organizations.

In this context, in 1917, in the midst of a revolutionary crisis on the rise, Max Weber outlined the basis for the reconstruction of the bourgeois political system as a "state of the masses," asserting that the political left (social democracy and the unions) would have to play a central role. The masses, mobilized and determined to participate politically, could not be treated as passive objects of the administration; however, as they think in immediate terms, they are exposed to emotional influences and tend to practice "street democracy." This meant that "rationally organized parties" and a "mature trade unionism" were needed: "the best guarantee against the fickle political moods of the 'Spartacists' was the integration of the trade unions and of social democracy into the political system" (Portantiero, 1981: 14).

And indeed, the social democratic parties had been moving toward "rationality and responsibility"; in the context of the imperialist war, they had aligned themselves with their respective national bourgeoisies and had concentrated their political efforts on modifying the forms of domination rather than destroying domination itself. For Bernstein, it was a process of transition toward the "neutrality" of the state, while Cunow asserted that "we are the state"; both viewed the capitalist state as a neutral space, with "instrumental potential to protect different social interests according to the historically variable capacity manifested by whichever social sector predominates in that originally empty space" (Portantiero, 1981: 28). For Kautsky, the pressure of the organized masses modified the essence of the state itself: "if it becomes the instrument of an exploiting minority, this is not due to the nature of the state but to that of the working classes, their disunity, their ignorance, their lack of autonomy or their inability to struggle" (Portantiero, 1981: 28).

Such was the path of gradual transformation of the pattern of domination taken by the processes of capitalist restructuring in the 1920s and

1930s in Western Europe. The crisis of 1929 produced two major political responses: on the one hand, an advance in the process of transformation of the liberal pattern toward a contained form of domination and, on the other, the brutal response of fascism and the destruction of the best sectors of the worker movement, while the parties of the Second International attempted to consolidate new forms under capitalist domination and the parties of the Third International led the workers from one defeat to another, unable to make sense of the process of capitalist domination that was taking place or of its political effects on the masses.

Following World War II, with the fall of fascism, having overcome the crisis produced by the emergence of "people's democracies" in Eastern Europe and with relations with "Sovietism" relatively stabilized, Western Europe began to consolidate and develop the Keynesian pattern of domination. Meanwhile, in Eastern Europe, where the forms of domination had been left untouched by the restructuring that had occurred in Western Europe from the end of the 19th century onwards, the conditions of the old liberal pattern of domination remained in effect, and in Tsarist Russia, the Bolsheviks, "a small conscious minority at the head of masses lacking consciousness," seized power and built societies based on state capitalism, first in the former Russia and then in a wide region of Eastern Europe. The Bolsheviks, after the elimination of a large portion of the old revolutionary guard, turned into the pigs in Orwell's Animal Farm[16], a new form of bourgeoisie.

Thus, in Western Europe, the restructuring of the forms of domination allowed the bourgeoisie to defeat the proletariat in the revolutionary crises that occurred in the first decades of the 20th century, while in Eastern Europe, specifically in Russia, the victories of the people's revolutions merely brought new forms of administration of capitalist development. The working class was thus defeated on two fronts.

Nevertheless, a major change had occurred in the structures of domination; for the first time in the history of capitalism, the bourgeoisie recognized the need to accept a compromise with the proletariat, and the

---

[16] This analysis does not attempt to examine the peculiarities of the so-called "real socialism" of the 20th century, but I believe its essence lies in the difference between *nationalization*, which reproduces the separation between workers and means of production, and *socialization*, the genuine appropriation of the means of production directly by the worker: "the fact that capital is entirely centralized under the command of *a single corporation* does not negate its *capitalist nature*" (Figueroa Sepúlveda, 1989: 56). In all other respects, Orwell's novella appears to me to be extraordinarily astute.

"bipolarity" that emerged in the post-war world between "real socialism" and "the Western democracies," as they called themselves, would open up the possibility for processes of "national liberation" in the former colonies of the empires of the late 19th century and for the promotion of "developmentalism" in part of the underdeveloped world. The post-war world thus became the stage for the different modalities assumed by the contained form of domination around the globe, with every advance made the result of major popular struggles.

The conditions of the first cycle of bourgeois domination were maintained for much of the 20th century in the backward nations of Europe and the rest of the world, but the intense, generally popular and specifically working class struggles undertaken in this context resulted in particular modalities that introduced the conditions of the second cycle, although in no case did they lead to socialism.

The proposition outlined by Engels to pursue the struggle for socialism under the new conditions of bourgeois domination thus sank into oblivion, and his theoretical framework would be developed only by the solitary Gramsci, while locked away in a prison by the Italian fascists. In spite of all that called itself "socialism" during the 20th century, from the celebrated leader who claimed that in its struggles for national liberation Africa was moving "from tribalism to socialism" (Jaffe, 1976), to those who celebrated any case of nationalization as "socialism," the 20th century was a century of capitalist development and restructuring of the forms of capital domination over the working class.

Capital not only expropriated the means of material production from the working class, but also the means of intellectual production and the administration of their collective affairs. The basic problems of capitalist domination and, therefore, of its defeat, relate to the separation of producers from the means of production as an essential characteristic, as discussed in the first chapter, but also to the separation between intellectual and manual labor, between general and immediate labor, and the separation between governors and governed, as problems arising from the first problem, while also constituting developments of it. Capitalism cannot be overthrown with the replacement of one "elite" for another that reproduces the same basic conditions of domination; it is necessary for the masses, the working class in itself, to appropriate the means of production, of manual and intellectual labor and of government of society.

The "socialist" left of the 20th century fell far short of pursuing this true, profound and radically revolutionary task. In the Soviet Union, the idea of the establishment of the working class as the dominant class and therefore of the conditions for the genuine defeat of capitalism and its transformation into socialism disappeared from the moment that the SUCP destroyed the Soviets as institutions of real power. From that moment, the "representatives of the proletariat," the self-declared "revolutionary vanguard," took charge of the administration of state capitalism. With the Cultural Revolution in Maoist China in the 1960s, the notion made a brief reappearance, which was radically concluded with the coup d'état of the seventies after Mao's death; today, the Chinese Communist Party is an efficient administrator of the development of neoliberal capitalism.

Both the social democratic left (heirs to the Second International) and the communist left (heirs to the Third International) were made up of bourgeois elites; the social democrats orchestrated their inclusion in the "political class" of Western capitalism while the communists became the administrators of the state capitalism that they referred to as "real socialism." However, both contributed to configure a new form of capitalist domination which, in spite of all the differences existing between its individual modalities, has one feature that is common to all of them: the acceptance by capital of a compromise with the working class. As a result of working class and popular movements around the world, a profound transformation in the pattern of domination occurred and, during the height of the post-war period, capitalism showed the most civilized face it has ever worn. In the history of capitalism, working class and popular organization and struggle has been the basic condition, not for the transformation of capitalism into socialism (a mission yet to be fulfilled), but simply for the civilization of capitalism; without worker organization and struggle there can be no revolution, but there can also be no reform that improves the plight of the workers under the conditions of capitalist domination and exploitation.

The Transition in the United States

In the United States, the conflict between capitalists and workers did not come close to the level of intensity that it had in Europe. According to Coriat, the process in the United States was focused on the struggle between capitalists and specialist workers organized under the AFL (American Federation of Labor)[17] and was resolved with the plundering of

---

[17] The racist and xenophobic AFL, incapable of organizing a class struggle against capital was, on the other hand, an efficient defender of the trades: "As a practice very much of

worker knowledge and the systematic imposition of the forms of operation designed by the capitalists in the tradition of Taylorism and Fordism
(Coriat, 1992).

What is important to note here is that Taylorism and Fordism, the
"rationalized" workshop, the production line and continuous flow manufacturing would all play a significant role in the consolidation of the
Keynesian pattern of domination; with the rise in productivity and labor
intensity that they promoted and the consequent rises in the rates of surplus-value and profit, the conditions were established for capital to grant
concessions to workers, while at the same time consolidating the domination of the former over the latter.

According to Taylor, "it will be possible to pay higher wages and reduce
the number of work hours," evidently without reducing the rate and level
of profit (Coriat, 1992: 35), and indeed, even increasing them because, furthermore, "cost prices would be reduced in such proportions that our
internal and external markets would expand considerably" (Coriat, 1992:
34). As Coriat notes, World War I created extraordinarily favorable conditions for the establishment of Taylorism and Fordism, and set the United
States on the road toward becoming the biggest industrial power on the
planet.

The crash of 1929, the result of a "lack of adaptation between the new
production and consumption structures",[18] gave new impetus to the organization and the struggle of the workers in Europe and in the United States
itself: "the working class, whose strength had been broken, found in the
crisis a source of unity and recuperation... This new effectiveness of
worker resistance must be considered in the interpretation of the huge
range of 'social reforms' that marked the initiation by the state of an
entirely new administration of labor-power and of the accumulation process and, more precisely, of the relation between labor-power and capital
accumulation" (Coriat, 1992: 95).

KEYNESIAN PATTERN OF DOMINATION

According to Coriat, it was Keynes who would complete the picture. Taylor
and Ford created the theory and the practice of mass production in the

---

the working class aristocracy, the defense of the trades was pursued with the most impla-
cable sectarian spirit and selfishness... Racism and xenophobia were constituent parts of
the ideology of the AFL" (Coriat, 1992: 14).

[18] "Mass production (the product of Taylorism and Fordism) requires the distribution of
sufficient purchasing power in the form of wages and income" (Coriat, 1992: 93).

workshop, while Keynes created the theory and practice for the type of state and regulation that mass production required (Coriat, 1992: 88); his general theory "formalized the conditions for the existence and reproduction of the mechanisms of mass production" (Coriat, 1992: 97). For Keynes, the demands of the workers were legitimate; the challenge lay in responding to those demands or perishing. A new method of administrating labor-power was a political necessity (Coriat, 1992: 98).

The new content of "labor policy" assumed by the state was defined during the "New Deal," and during World War II this new content would spread definitively throughout the developed capitalist world: the minimum wage, the reduction of the length of the working-day, compensation for workplace accidents, and unemployment insurance (Coriat, 1992: 98). The state was established as the general operator of the reproduction of wage-labor, the general administrator of the concessions that capital would grant labor; for the first time in its history, capitalism appeared to acquire a certain 'exteriority' as a "system situated above social classes," establishing a legal framework which, firstly, regulated the direct relation of exploitation (the conditions for the purchase and use of labor-power, such as the length of the working day, overtime, child labor, wages, etc.), secondly, defined indirect wages (family allowances, health and education services, medical insurance and retirement pensions) which ensured the cheap reproduction of labor for capital, and thirdly, restructured unemployment and disability assistance.

For the first time in the history of capitalism, wages (as the sum of direct wages paid by the employer to the worker, and indirect wages, as value redistributed by the state) paid for the full value of labor-power, at least for one section of the working class. As Suzanne de Brunhoff notes, "direct wages permit the 'reconstitution' of the worker during the period of employment, but not for the 'maintenance' of the unemployed or the ill, or for the costs of family maintenance"; direct wages are thus lower than the value of labor-power (Brunhoff, 1980: 226).

Under the conditions of the liberal pattern of domination, whereby the labor relation is abandoned to the "agreement between two free and equal owners," the laborer, owner of his labor-power, is responsible for his own maintenance, and this deficit produced by unemployment, illness, age and/or additional family responsibilities is compensated for by community or family support for the worker, or by "the charity and benevolence of the employer," as it is not considered a right of the worker, but a donation made by the employer. Thus, also for the first time in the history of capitalism, the labor relation ceased to be the result of the supposed "free agreement between willing individuals" that the liberal pattern of

domination had always postulated, and instead became a contract negotiated collectively by workers' unions; with the regulation of the state, class
relations and exploitation were given a contractual quality based on the
wage/productivity relation.

Collective contracts and negotiated agreements would place capitalist
practices in a new context in the management of labor-power. For the first
time in the history of capitalism, at the height of the crisis of 1929, the right
of workers to organize and collectively bargain their work conditions and
remuneration was recognized. Promoted by Roosevelt (with the opposition of the National Manufacturers Association) the National Industrial
Recovery Act established that "wage-laborers would have the right to organize and collectively bargain with the assistance of representatives of
their choice, free of obstacles or coercion on the part of employers or their
agents in the appointment of those representatives or in the organization
of unions or of any other concerted activity aimed at collective bargaining,
assistance or mutual protection" (Coriat, 1992: 100). Shooting at union
leaders and workers[19] was no longer the preferred "bargaining strategy" or,
at least, was no longer the only strategy of the capitalists.

Of course, the conditions of the contained form of domination did not
eliminate employment uncertainty, the basic uncertainty inherent to the
condition of the worker in capitalism, but the establishment of worker
rights had the effect of moderating the uncertainty of the workers and the
arbitrary acts of capital.

DEVELOPMENTALIST PATTERN OF DOMINATION

In developed capitalism, Keynesianism offered an economic response to
the crisis – a response that developed and acquired its definitive outlines
after the crisis of 1929, reorganizing its conditions for exploitation and
accumulation – and a political response, addressing the situation of the
emergence of the masses by restructuring the pattern of domination. The
economic restructuring – a rise in labor productivity, in the rate of surplus-value and in the rate of profit – provided the material circumstances
that allowed capital to make concessions to the workers and, on this basis,
to restructure their domination.

---

[19] Coriat notes that in the United States, "the dominant phenomenon of the 1920s con-
tinued to be anti-worker violence... and during the crisis, union members were shot at in
Ford factories" (Coriat, 1992: 101). It is worth remembering that a decade later in Europe, the
Nazis massacred militant workers of both the Second and Third International.

In underdeveloped capitalism around the world, over the course of several decades and in a general context of economic crisis, a process of emergence of the masses also occurred, in some cases as a veritable insurrection against poverty, exploitation and oppression. The different modalities assumed by domination during the first stage of capitalism were no longer capable of containing the rebellion of the masses; this marked the erosion of the first emergence of the natural form of domination in the underdeveloped world, and its movement toward the different modalities assumed by the contained form of domination in the underdeveloped world. This emergence of the masses provoked a diverse range of responses, but in all of them there is one essential player, the state, and two structural axes: the initiation of industrialization processes and the restructuring of the conditions for domination.

To industrialize the underdeveloped world of this period – that backward, colonized world anchored in primary export production aimed at the imperialist metropolises – it was necessary to reformulate their relations with the countries at the developed pole of the imperialist relation, and to initiate a series of projects that only direct and decisive state intervention in the economy could bring about. The result was a new type of state, the product of the transformation or destruction of the state of the first period of the natural form of domination; the uprising of the masses provided the political impetus necessary to adapt or transform the old state apparatuses and build new ones, with the capacity (although in varying degrees and modalities) to promote the implementation of new economic and political projects. However, in all cases, in spite of this emergence of the masses and of workers, and given the conditions of the underdeveloped, largely agrarian economies, leadership of the process remained in the hands of the bourgeoisie.

"Real socialism," an extreme case of nationalization of capital (means of production and subsistence) and of conversion of the capitalist state into the main player, constituted one of the responses. It began with the Bolshevik revolution of 1917, and expanded with the "socialist" revolutions after World War II in Eastern Europe. Various countries in Africa and Asia, subject to the colonial regime imposed by imperialist powers, saw the rise after World War II of what were generically referred to as "national liberation movements." As a result of these struggles, some Asian countries (China, part of Korea and Vietnam) took the path of "real socialism," with variants of and even in conflict with the "Soviet model." In the rest of Asia and the regions of Africa that were able – some for the first time in their history – to establish something resembling a "nation-state," various nationalist and developmentalist projects were initiated.[20] At least some parts of the underdeveloped world in Asia and Africa achieved a notable transformation and a certain degree of progress in the industrialization process,[21] although in most cases without overcoming their status as underdeveloped nations.

In Latin America, the "populist" regimes (the governments of Getulio Vargas in Brazil, Juan Domingo Perón in Argentina and Lázaro Cárdenas in Mexico being among the most significant), in the context of a growing situation of emergence of the masses[22] and of the effects of the crisis of 1929 and the consequent collapse of the Latin American export sector,[23] moved from the "primary export economy" (the first historical manifestation of the form of absolute or "outward" growth), to "import substitution industrialization" (a form of relative or "inward" growth), and from the oligarchic pattern to the developmentalist pattern of domination. They thus established new forms of economic growth and of domination that began to stabilize in Latin America's largest countries from the 1940s on. With the export market closed, the local bourgeoisie had to develop the internal market to continue their production and, at the same time, to face the challenge of restructuring their domination over the workers.

It is worth recalling briefly here our earlier discussion that relative or inward growth is characteristic of an interventionist state that assumes the role of direct capitalist, and that industrialization aimed at the internal market diversifies the branches of immediate labor and expands internal needs; the state creates an infrastructure geared toward facilitating

---

[20] "At the end of the war, African and Asian societies at the periphery of the global capitalist system were still subject to the colonial regime. The center/periphery polarization had taken the form of a contrast between industrialized and non-industrialized regions. The revolt of the peoples of Africa and Asia, the product of half a century of ideological and political restructuring around the new notion of nationalism, began in 1945" (Amín, 2003b).

[21] "After their political independence, the peripheries entered an era of industrialization, although their development was uneven... this gave rise to a growing differentiation between a semi-industrialized 'Third World' and a Fourth World that had not yet begun to industrialize" (Amín, 2003b).

[22] In Mexico, the great rural worker uprising of 1910 had been defeated but not crushed, and throughout Latin America the proletariat was growing in numbers and achieving certain levels of organization and combativeness: "The most solid cores of the working class were consolidated first in export production. Driven by their poverty... they began their campaigns for better working conditions very early" (Figueroa Sepúlveda, 1986: 168).

[23] "With the great crisis that began in 1929 and lasted until the Second World War... export production collapsed and absolute growth fell into serious discredit" (Figueroa Sepúlveda, 1986: 169).

internal transactions in general, unifying and facilitating the development of the internal market while simultaneously promoting export production as a crucial aim of "inward growth." The number of workers expands, their organization is strengthened within set limits and, if the process exhibits a certain continuity, wages should grow, albeit slowly.

The dominant ideology is no longer "free trade," but the promotion of interventionism[24] and a type of "nationalism" limited in two respects. Firstly, this nationalism never meant overcoming either underdevelopment or the subordination of the Latin American economies to the developed pole in the industrialist relation. Industrialization in the Latin American countries that were able to initiate it took the form of "import substitution," operating on the basis of pre-existing needs and always relying on production processes designed by the developed pole, mainly the United States. Secondly, what it did mean was a redefinition of the industrialist relation marked by one basic fact: the crucial condition for relative or inward growth is relative isolation from developed countries.

Based on these two conditions for the Latin American nationalism of the era, the whole process of restructuring the pattern of domination can be explained. The state, in redefining the relation with the imperialist metropolises, achieved a margin of autonomy and of directorial capacity over the national economy, and ensured its relative isolation from the developed nations; the development of the internal market and of import substitution industrialization permitted the diversification of immediate labor with the procedures of relative surplus-value production imported from the developed countries. The process of redefining the relation with the developed world was presented ideologically as anti-imperialist nationalism or revolutionary nationalism. In this context, the pattern of domination was restructured; the introduction of procedures of relative surplus-value production and job growth enabled the negotiation of concessions for the workers who at the same time were organized and controlled by the state, in accordance with the requirements of national unity as a supposed condition for addressing the needs of the so-called anti-imperialist struggle. The conditions for restructuring domination also defined its limitations and its fragility. This process is explored further below.

---

[24] "The state, instead of limiting itself to regulating and enforcing the standards of economic activity, acts directly as an economic agent" (Ianni, 1984: 148).

First of all, the Latin American developmentalist state not only established mechanisms for the protection of national industry; it also nationalized foreign companies, specifically to take back control of key natural
resources in the structure of the export sector of the national economy,
and to ensure control of strategic sectors of the economy with state or
mixed companies, while reformulating the conditions for the entry and
exit of foreign capital and the conditions for its association with local
capital.

Only in this way can we understand descriptions like that offered by
Ianni of the Mexican state in the era of President Cárdenas (1934–1940) as
the main decision-making center, with the capacity to expropriate and
redistribute assets for political and economic reasons determined by the
state, and to impose the modes of ownership and use on private, national
or foreign property in accordance with the national interest (Ianni, 1977b:
20).[25] Ianni adds that during the Cárdenas presidency, government participation in the national economy was expanded and systematized with
a global agricultural, industrial and educational plan, becoming the "organizing, dynamic and coordinated vanguard of production relations" and
of public and private accumulation (Ianni, 1977b: 14–15).

This margin of autonomy and of directorial capacity over the national
economy for the developmentalist state in Latin America could only occur
under conditions of relative or inward growth. It does not exist in conditions of absolute or outward growth, as shown in the examination of the
oligarchic pattern, and as will be seen with the neoliberal pattern. In these
cases, the capacity of the state to direct the economy is practically nonexistent and the intervention of capitalists and imperialist states is direct;
imperialist capital directly appropriates the most profitable activities,
and the subordination of the underdeveloped economy to the needs of
the developed world is direct and immediate. Relative growth, while it
does not mean either overcoming underdevelopment or breaking with
imperialism (i.e. it does not constitute a national project[26] in the strictest

---

[25]   This was the case not only for the Mexican state, but for all Latin American states that
were able to move toward developmentalism: "Between 1930 and 1950, government powers
related to the economy and the economic role of the Latin American nation-state grew
enormously" (Ianni, 1984: 135).

[26]   'National project' here refers to "a program that brings together a range of anti-imperialist measures with the aim of breaking the subordination of the nation and the economy... Substitution industrialization was merely a strategy adopted by the local bourgeoisie
driven by conditions which they did not create... it was not applied outside the context of
developed countries, and certainly not against their interests... Whether or not the capitalists of developed countries interfere *directly* in our affairs is unrelated to the *essence* of

sense), it does mean that neither capitalists nor imperialist states intervene directly in the direction of the national economy.

Secondly, the development of the internal market diversified the branches of immediate labor, expanded internal needs and allowed the introduction of methods of production of relative surplus-value and job growth. Under the conditions of the oligarchic pattern and of the predominance of the primary export economy, the real subsumption of immediate labor spread in export production, but in goods consumed internally (wage goods) there was no real subsumption or productivity-based growth. "The production of relative surplus-value would come with relative growth when the internal market took the central focus in the economy... It is in this type of growth that the general tendency of capital toward the production of relative surplus-value occurs... It constituted an element of the first transition, which took place when the worker movement had risen up in protest against the length of the working day and existed as an organized, expanding force" (Figueroa Sepúlveda, 1986: 184).

Increased productivity, real subsumption of labor to capital, production of relative surplus-value, a rise in the rate of surplus-value and the rate of profit, in the context of the emergence of the masses, created the conditions whereby capital (not without first complaining, resisting, and assuring that the end of the world was nigh) could view the prospect of granting concessions to workers as tolerable, as part of the process of restructuring its mode of domination.

For the first time in the history of Latin America, "the government recognized the right of urban and rural workers to defend their interests and to fight to have them respected" (Ianni, 1977b: 23). They recognized the workers' social, economic and political rights; rights as workers and rights as citizens. Among these was the right to freedom of movement, which liberated the workers from the forms of coercive labor relations that predominated in the oligarchic pattern of domination. The labor market was formalized, legislation was passed to regulate labor relations, and education, safety and public health programs were introduced, along with unionization, paid holidays, health care, protection for pregnant workers and maternity leave, free elementary education and the right to vote in elections (Ianni, 1984: 136, 139). The labor relation became a contractual relation supervised by the state, offering contract conditions on the length

---

underdevelopment and imperialism, and should be treated as a question relative to the historical form" (Figueroa Sepúlveda, 1986: 171–172).

of the working day, a minimum wage and the rights to join a union and to strike. Rights and duties were established for both wage-laborers and employers. But in this process of granting concessions, the state also organized and controlled the workers.

The ideological framework upheld under the new form of domination was developmentalist nationalism, which advocated harmony between social classes in the name of the national struggle for economic emancipation and diversification, against socioeconomic backwardness, oligarchy and imperialism. Societal peace was presented as a prerequisite for achieving the economic emancipation of the country and bringing social welfare to all of the people; to give the country back to the people, it was necessary to strengthen cooperation between capital and labor and the arbitration of the state (Ianni, 1984: 149). But an ideological framework in itself is never a sufficient condition for structuring domination. Populism, as a starting point, as a moment of transition to the developmentalist pattern of domination, constitutes a mode of direct and organic relation between the state, the "populist" party and official unionism.[27] Unionism is bureaucratized and formalized: "The union structure is established as a bureaucracy tied to or dependent on the state apparatus; its possibilities of organization, initiative and interpretation of the interests of the class it represents are delimited... state unionism politicizes the proletariat according to the guidelines and limitations established by the regime... the state-party-union system is developed as a central column of populist power" (Ianni, 1984: 146–147).

In Mexico, this system of political domination was stabilized and perfected more than in any other Latin American country. The (urban and rural) worker masses were classified in organizations directly linked to the state, set up in opposition and mutual isolation so as to turn their different interests into instruments of control. All compromises were negotiated with the union leaders, with no participation whatsoever by the worker base. The leader, the benefactor responsible for everything achieved "within the possibilities," authoritatively directed "his" union. And the leaders, as elite clientele, were offered part of the booty (for this is really what it amounted to) of the state: deputations, senate positions, etc.

---

[27] "Priority is given to the union organization associated with the state apparatus... non-populist union organizations are marginalized and even suppressed. At the same time, the government reformulates the functional and organizational requirements of unionism to keep it dependent on the state apparatus and limited to the purposes of populist policy" (Ianni, 1984: 145).

The leaders were leaders because they had government support: "in the definition of the power held by the leaders themselves, their connection with the state is decisive and therein lies *the essence* of corporatist domination" (Córdova, 1979: 36, emphasis added). The state supports the official leaders and represses any union movement organized against corporatist domination in the hope of creating an independent union. "What followed the conversion of the official party into a corporate machine," adds Córdova, "was no more than a prolonged process of perfecting the system of domination by and through organization. Once the mobilizations ended, organization, now turned into an instrument of political power, rapidly developed into a veritable prison for the organized workers, as a power that they could not question, invincible and insuperable" (Córdova, 1979: 34).

And for rural workers, whom the neoliberal governments had invited to become agricultural entrepreneurs to compete with the multinational agricultural corporations, the outcome was even worse. While it is true that agrarian reform responded partially to a very old rural demand, "rural workers became the most politically degraded sector of the masses. In the very process of agrarian reform developed by the Cárdenas government, a colossal institutional network was woven which organized their production and their whole lives" (Córdova, 1979: 36).

"Such is, in general terms," concludes Córdova, "the gigantic structure of domination that weighs upon the worker masses" (Córdova, 1979: 38). Nevertheless, organized workers, with certain recognized rights and more or less secure and stable access to their means of subsistence, were, in fact, the fortunate ones; alongside them co-existed millions of "marginal" workers, the immense majority of the working class, who were not unionized.

This solid structure of domination ensured the Mexican State of decades of political stability. But other Latin American states did not attain the level of perfection achieved by the Mexico, and workers were able to establish their own political organizations and make their demands heard. Domination became unstable, and the states violently reasserted it; even during the height of World War II, the period of maturity of the developmentalist pattern of domination, the history of Latin America was plagued with coups d'etat and violent authoritarian regressions.

The core problem lay in a nationalism that never sought to overcome underdevelopment, and in the fragility of underdevelopment itself, which rendered the state incapable of establishing a stable form of domination that would mean, at least to some degree, an improvement in the working and living conditions of the workers: "what accumulation in underdevelopment lacks most is continuity... Accumulation in underdevelopment is constantly disrupted by the imbalances that are inherent to it" (Figueroa Sepúlveda, 1986: 164, 173).

And yet, the developmentalist pattern constitutes the most civilized form that capitalism in Latin America has adopted to date and which, most probably, it will ever adopt. In spite of its considerable limitations, the developmentalist state created a political space that workers had never enjoyed under the conditions of the oligarchic pattern, and which they do not enjoy now under the neoliberal pattern of domination. For this very reason, the military violence and coups d'etat were aimed at "putting an end to processes of growth in which the decisive role of the state apparatus in guiding development *stimulated the growing activism of the popular sectors*" (Arceo, 2002, emphasis added).

State Administration of Concessions

The transformations that took place with the move from the direct, exclusionary and brutal methods of the natural form of domination in the first stage of industrial capitalism to those of the contained form (particularly in the modality of the Keynesian pattern of domination), were so profound that it is worth attempting to offer a general outline of them.

The emergence of the masses provoked by the crisis in the natural form in the first period of capitalist domination and, in particular, in the liberal pattern of domination in the countries of developed capitalism, revealed the inadequacy of purely empirical knowledge. Therefore, the task of domination became a matter of scientific study and application, with the establishment of what I earlier proposed to call the "production workshop of domination strategies," the place where the political applications of science are processed. What follows is a brief outline of how this workshop operated under the conditions of the Keynesian pattern of domination.

THE CAPITALISTS AND THE WORKERS AND THEIR REPRESENTATIVES

The underlying premise here is the recognition that "the main political element of change is the organized presence of the masses" (Portantiero, 1981: 25); in the developed capitalist nations (and throughout the world), what marked the shift from the natural form of domination to the contained form was a situation of emergence of the masses. From that time on, the capitalist state operated in association with an "organized worker movement," and expressed in that association is the basic design of domination as state administration of concessions.

Insofar as the capitalist state responded to some worker demands, assuming the administration of some of the conditions for worker reproduction and organizing the institutional framework of negotiation between the classes, it lost its exteriority to the organized workers: "this modified state could no longer be viewed narrowly as an 'administrative committee' of the bourgeoisie" (Portantiero, 1981: 25). Worker organizations, parties and unions underwent a process of profound transformation; their purpose was no longer to struggle against, but to negotiate with capital. Their nature, their scope and their structure were radically altered; they lost their external, antagonistic position in relation to the capital power structures and were institutionalized as elements of the state.

The construction of a space for negotiation between the classes requires, according to Weber's formulation, "rationally organized parties" and a "mature unionism" (Portantiero, 1981: 14–15), and the agreement of these parties and unions consists in "participating in the responsibility of government" and abandoning "the negative sterility toward the state to which they had been driven by the intransigence of the system." In other words, the basic agreement consists in accepting the unquestionable nature of the capitalist order.

Whether as a moment in the evolution of the struggle of capital against independent, revolutionary worker organization, or as the result of the defeat and destruction of revolutionary organizations, the workers were channeled into "respectable" worker organizations[28] which were recognized by the state as agencies for political and labor representation of the workers; the interests of the social classes and groups were organized and represented at the national level in order to structure the dynamics of negotiation and reconciliation of interests.

Antagonism between workers and capitalists, the revolution and the socialist project were presented as things of the past. Now the "conflicts" were subject to rules of bargaining between "negotiators." The workers (or rather, their organizations, parties and unions) became "rational negotiators" with capital and were contained within the logic of capital itself; the scope of "rationality" in the negotiation was limited by the level of

---

[28] These organizations may have been pre-existing, like the European social democratic organizations, or created *ad hoc* by the State itself, as in the case of the *state corporatism* of underdeveloped capitalism.

capital's rate of profit. A reduction in the rate of profit would inhibit investment, reduce employment and work against the interests of the workers;
the notion of "rationality" established a space for negotiation and of "common interest" between the classes.

The whole scope of negotiation was thus delimited by one basic principle: a rise in wages (both direct and indirect) depends on an increase in
productivity and on the various imperatives arising from the needs of
restructuring, competitiveness or modernization of capital. In a certain
sense, the workers became co-responsible for the efficient operation of
"their capital," whether private or national; their interests appeared to be
tied to the effective running of the company where they worked and the
economy of their country, in competition with other companies and other
countries.

Thus the agenda for negotiation and for what was negotiable also
acquired exact, predefined parameters. The public institutions that
administrate part of the value of labor-power, according to Suzanne de
Brunhoff, "are constantly the site of class confrontations with regard not
only to their establishment, but to their form and size, and are only developed through compromises between the classes... These institutions...
constantly orientate administration relative to the demands of the work"
(Brunhoff, 1980: 236, emphasis added).

This delimited territory provides the structure for the endless bargaining that keeps worker organizations permanently occupied; not only do
they negotiate the rights of the workers and the definition of the *"rights
holders"* (Brunhoff 1980: 248), but also, "the application of certain institutional guarantees are the object of struggles... some of the capitalists act
outside the agreements of their class as a whole... and the uncertainty of
the outcome of the claims forms part of the insecurity of the proletariat.
*There is no strictly progressive evolution in the integration of workers into the
system, not even in the case of the 'stabilized' sector of the proletariat*"
(Brunhoff, 1980: 252).

Along with these transformations – not of form but of content – of
worker organizations, a separation occurred between the worker base and
the organizations representing it. There developed the widespread application of what Coriat calls the policy of substitution, which "consisted in
depriving the unions of the general assistance functions that made them
popular with the workers" (Coriat, 1992: 55). Until this time, unions had
organized first aid and mutual assistance funds for accidents, illnesses or
unemployment, in an expression of class organization, cohesion, solidarity and consciousness.

Now, state institutions offered a better guarantee than what could be offered by the unions and their resistance practices, in terms of length of the working-day, regularity in employment, collective life and disability (illness or accident) insurance, old-age pensions, guarantees against unemployment, illness and unjust practices; such guarantees no longer came from working class organizations, even if it was the union that participated in the negotiation process representing the interests of the workers.

This is where a second point of separation occurred between the worker base and its organizations; negotiation involved a bargaining process that takes place between worker representatives and employers, with the regulation of government representatives. In this process, the worker base is a passive observer, with no role as an active player;[29] to a large extent, union practices and the outcomes obtained from them are alienated from the participation, decisions and wishes of the worker masses. There is a policy of alienation of workers from their organizations which is complemented by the policy of substitution and the two converge into one strategic purpose: to confine the worker masses to political passivity.

At the same time, the new modalities of capital accumulation, mass production and consumption gave workers new reasons to appreciate, regulate and protect their jobs. Under the new conditions, which included not only labor and wage conditions but lifestyle conditions as well, capital not only put an end to "the chronic state of insubordination," but also reduced the mobility and absenteeism of workers, as well as delays or carelessness on the job, and "ensured the provision of a select and docile work force" (Coriat, 1992: 57, 59). Credit systems were developed for the purchase of durable consumer goods and workers acquired the conviction that their jobs not only ensured their maintenance and well-being today, but also in the future: "retirement is earned slowly, everyday, through submission and work" (Hatzfeld, as quoted in Coriat, 1992: 84).

While the industrial reserve army was incorporated, organized and controlled, not abolished but kept on reserve, at the disposal of the fluctuating needs of capital accumulation, the active industrial army was assured of job stability, guarantees for the future and levels of consumption and

---

[29] The conversion from *active player* into *passive observer* is constantly promoted by bourgeois ideology. This is the meaning behind the ideology of the *hero* incessantly promoted in U.S. cinema and, in general, the meaning behind all *spectacles*: soccer in England was the sport of the workers until it was turned into a *spectacle* and the workers into *spectators*.

well-being that workers in the 19th century and early 20th had never even dreamed of. Such is the reward for political apathy and submission in the workplace. But political apathy and workplace submission have a more solid basis that is not limited to real or supposed worker conformism. The traditional forms of protection against unemployment and illness (the union, the family, the community) also constituted the social territory where, in the 19th century and first decades of the 20th, attitudes and political positions were processed; in working class neighborhoods, in their bars, in the heart of their family and community relations, the political positions of the workers were defined in relation to the various socialist projects.

The transformations produced by the new mode of capitalist development destroyed these social spaces and fragmented the social organization of the workers; they were individualized, isolated, atomized, disintegrated, and confined, in the best of cases, to the nuclear family.[30] This left them with no social space in which to construct a political position as a class. It was the transformation of the living conditions of the workers that constituted the basis of the transformation of their values, beliefs and attitudes, of their entire culture: "a new mass culture as a reconstruction of a collective personality that required the introduction of profound changes to everyday life" (Portantiero, 1981: 57).[31]

The risk that the emergence of the masses implied for the capitalist system was resolved in a way that the liberals of the 19th century never would have imagined. Its political design was centered on disorganizing, excluding and repressing the workers, while for Weber (according to Portantiero) the problem of domination is a problem of the sociology of organizations: "contemporary reality is a reality of groups and institutions...

---

[30] Hirsch identifies several processes that led to the disintegration of neighborhood, professional and family relations and the replacement of the community with a conglomerate of isolated workers and consumers. The material and physical reproduction of workers became more dependent on capitalist production of goods and services and geographical and professional mobility, and the constant process of disqualification and re-qualification, the intensification of labor and constant unemployment all contributed to the process of destruction of the traditional channels of production and lifestyles. In this process lies "the genesis of the modern education system under strong political control; social disintegration and the establishment of wage-labor required a special agency of control that would not only provide certain qualifications, but also control the social conditioning of youth. As the family, the community and the neighborhood lost their influence, they were replaced by institutions such as the police, the classroom and social work" (Hirsch, 1996: 24–25).

[31] Portantiero adds (quoting Gramsci) that "the new work methods are indissolubly linked to a specific way of living, thinking and feeling about life."

This recognition of the central nature of groups and institutions as an analytical unit is the basis of his [Weber's] conception that only with a sociological perspective is it possible to penetrate the essence of the political context" (Portantiero, 1981: 12).

As the masses "think in immediate terms," Weber argues, "they are exposed to emotional influences" and, when they are disorganized, they tend to practice "street democracy"; however, "an uncoordinated mass can never govern itself, but is governed, with the only change being to the method of choosing the heads of government... 'democratization' *does not necessarily mean an increase in active participation by the dominated"* (Portantiero, 1981: 14, 18, emphasis added). The counterpart to this reduction of the masses to passivity and expectancy is the activity of "the leaders." As in the soccer spectacle, the players are the experts, the specialists, the representatives of the workers, the capitalists and the government: "the new corporatism did not seek consensus so much through the occasional approval of the masses, but through continual negotiation between organized interests... the stability of the system required a much more bureaucratic and centralized kind of negotiation" (Portantiero, 1981: 21).

As Gramsci explains, "in modern civilization all practical activities have become so complex and the sciences have become so intertwined with daily life that every practical activity tends to require a school to produce its own leaders and specialists... Any problem that needs to be resolved is first examined by experts and analyzed scientifically" (as quoted in Portantiero, 1981: 55).

The Science of Capital

The exploration above highlights the multifunctional nature that science acquired in the design of capital domination and in the direction of the strategic processes under the conditions of the Keynesian pattern: breaking up the workers, alienating them from their social environment, their neighborhood, community and even family relations, destroying the space in which their processes of class organization, cohesion, solidarity and consciousness took place, reducing the worker masses to passivity and separating leadership from the masses, defining those workers who could act as representatives qualified to bargain with capital and even defining the scope of the negotiable between the classes and, in general, resolving problems related to the "sociology of organizations."

For example, "the state of chronic insubordination" of the workers, of mobility, absenteeism, delays and carelessness in the workplace, was a problem which, at the end of the 19th century and beginning of the 20th, greatly preoccupied the capitalists and their hired intellectuals.[32] For Ford, the problem was resolved by influencing the living conditions of the worker population. How to achieve this constituted a specific object of scientific research. If experts on the topic did not exist, it would be necessary to create them. Capital identified its problems and looked for answers: "This era marked the beginning of cooperation between academically trained experts (sociologists, psychologists, psychotechnicians, etc.) and business leaders. Ford set up a 'sociology department' and a body of monitors and inspectors... Their basic mission was to go out to the homes of workers and the places they frequented in order to monitor their general behavior and, in particular, how they spent their wages" (Coriat, 1992: 57).

With the results of this research, Ford turned the wage rises into a means of control over all of the living conditions of the workers; he determined which workers could benefit from higher wages (adults with at least six months in the job, not women or underage workers); and he established internal regulations to define the conditions for hiring (including impeccable morals, cleanliness, no alcohol, smoking, games or bars) and firing. The selection was strict and the benefits could be withdrawn at any time (Coriat, 1992: 57, 59).[33]

Another example may further illustrate this idea. While the National Association of Manufacturers, anchored in the past, proclaimed that "we, the employers, are responsible for the work carried out by our workers" and resorted to physical violence to "discipline" the workers, Taylor assured that there was no need to assert employer authority; the personal army of that authority was reduced or eliminated, as thenceforth enforcing its authority was a "scientific" exercise (Coriat, 1992: 32). Science, placed at the service of capital domination not only investigated problems and proposed solutions, but also, once the worker representatives had renounced the possibility of a non-capitalist option and, together with the representatives of capital and government, agreed to operate within the scope of possibilities offered by the logic of capital, science became

---

[32] In both the U.S. and France, "the sessions and communications of the engineers were focused first and foremost remuneration systems. At the beginning of the 20th century, the use of wages seemed to be the least risky method of keeping laborers in their place" (Coriat, 1992: 52).

[33] Gramsci also reflects on the meaning of the processes occurring at this time: "The puritan initiatives (in sex life, in prohibition of alcohol, etc.) have this meaning in the U.S.: to modify habits and customs in order to develop 'the new type of person demanded by the rationalization of production and labor'" (Portantiero, 1981: 57).

the spokesperson for the needs and possibilities of capital, entrusted with the task of presenting the rationale of capital in irrefutable terms, not as a capitalist whim but as a natural law, and thus became an indispensable aid in discussions between the representatives of capital and of labor.

The capitalist use of science, overdetermined by the needs of exploitation and domination, inevitably result in a concentration of knowledge; Ford, while explaining the achievements attained through rationalization in his factory, boasted that 95% of "his" workers specialized in "a single operation that *the stupidest individual* would be capable of learning within two days" (Coriat, 1992: 45, emphasis added). Indeed, from the perspective of the logic of the needs of capital, to reduce the largest possible number of workers to stupidity (i.e. to make them more easily manipulated) is no small achievement if it contributes to a rise in labor productivity and in the rate of surplus-value.[34] There is a possibility of stupidity and productive capacity coming into conflict with one another; the problem would then lie in finding the optimal combination in accordance with the prevailing technological designs and the composition of the collective of laborers. But this is just what science is for – to solve these types of problems.

THE WORKING CLASS AND ITS INTERNAL RELATIONS

The transformation of relations between the working class and the capitalist was necessarily combined with a transformation in the relations inside the class itself. The working class became more heterogeneous and differentiated[35] and, as a result, in the context of the processes underway at this time, more incapable of initiating large-scale group actions. The worker parties and unions were transformed from organizations promoting the political interests of the class into bureaucratic apparatuses integrating the masses that received legal privileges and public funding. They filtered and channeled demands, making them compatible with the conditions of the system. They manipulated public opinion and tended to

---

[34] The combination of Fordism and Taylorism means "a strict separation between the conception of the production process (which is the task of the area of methods and organization) and the performance of standardized and formally prescribed tasks" (Lipietz, 1997); Taylorism takes capital appropriation of the conditions for the performance of *immediate labor* to its most radical extreme.

[35] Suzanne de Brunhoff distinguishes between an integrated proletariat that receives a direct and indirect wage, one that receives only partial benefits, a lumpenproletariat that receives assistance, migrant workers, etc. (Brunhoff, 1980: 244–245).

concentrate their public monopoly, controlling the coordination of groups and monopolizing their methods of organization (Hirsch, 1996: 29–30).

Within the unions and worker parties, a layer of technical and political experts is created, conservative in nature and with its own interests. Decisions are delegated, meaning that they pass from the base to the "leader or representative," and the union or party base, increasingly amorphous, has no means of control over its "representative." The struggle for leadership positions became sordid and brutal, the vertical structure promoted corruption and irresponsibility among the leaders,[36] who administrated concessions more and more for themselves and less and less for the workers as a whole and who, together with the employer representatives (in reality the representatives of the great monopolies) and the government officials, ultimately constituted what Hirsch calls the corporatist bureaucratic regulation cartel (Hirsch, 1996: 31).

THE STRATEGIC PROPOSITION IN THE KEYNESIAN PATTERN OF DOMINATION

The shift from the liberal pattern to the Keynesian pattern of domination constituted what Gramsci calls a passive revolution: "a process of transformations from on high, recovering a portion of the demands of those below while taking from the latter all autonomous political initiative" (as quoted in Portantiero, 1981: 44). The concessions made to workers administrated by the state did not address all of the problems, nor were they offered to all of the workers, but they allowed the state to restructure domination on a global scale: "Only government initiative was capable of giving assistance a *strategic global character*: maintenance of ghettos, of underemployment, of poverty, not as breeding grounds for disorder, but as elements of capitalist reproduction"[37] (Brunhoff, 1980: 245, emphasis added).

The worldwide emergence of the masses, which sparked the crisis for the liberal pattern and all the modalities of the first emergence of the natural form of domination and placed at risk the domination of capital itself for the first and until now the only time in history, was resolved with

---

[36] For a detailed description of this type of relation see Almeyra, 2004.

[37] The fact that the system of worker assistance and security developed by the "welfare state" achieved essentially political goals is demonstrated by its "cyclic rhythm", which "depends on its main functions: maintenance of social order and reinforcement of workplace discipline... The system of assistance and security is not static, but expands and contracts depending on the state of social relations." When there is a mass strike combined with social upheaval, public assistance expands (Brunhoff, 1980: 245–246).

a strategic initiative by the capitalist state to restructure its domination; the administration of concessions for the workers acquired a strategic global character to restructure and, for an entire historical period, preserve the domination of capital without further challenges. The workers did not find their own strategy to oppose this strategy of capital and, since then, the initiative, the control of the process, has been in the hands of capital.

A brief summary of the discussion of this chapter will show how the pincer was closed on the workers on two fronts:

1. The transformations produced by the new mode of capitalist development fragmented the social organization of the workers; they were now individualized, isolated, atomized, disintegrated, and confined to the nuclear family;

2. Worker organizations, parties and unions underwent a process of profound transformation. Their nature, their scope and their structure were radically altered; they lost their external, antagonistic position in relation to the capital power structures and were institutionalized as elements of the state. It was as if worker organizations had been expropriated and turned into a part of the power that dominated them.

To these two it would be necessary to add a third front: the "production workshop of domination strategies," which organized the ideological and cultural messages to be circulated in society, in conjunction with the education system and the mass media. They monopolized the space for public communication and developed scientific applications to understand and influence the culture, ideology and behavior of society: surveys, interviews, publicity, propaganda, marketing, etc. Capital and its ideological universe thus invaded the everyday world of the working class.

Following the great scare provoked by the uprising of the masses around the world with the crisis of the first emergence of the natural form of domination came decades of learning for the capitalist state and of unlearning for the workers who, by the end of the prevalence of the different modalities assumed by the contained form of domination, had forgotten much of what they had learned during those extraordinary decades when they tried to take heaven by storm. Of course, as has been and will be the case throughout the history of capitalism, the struggle of the workers against capital was still present, but it no longer reached the level of a hegemonic dispute.

PART TWO

THE NEOLIBERAL PATTERN:
SECOND EMERGENCE OF THE NATURAL FORM OF DOMINATION

CHAPTER FIVE

THE TRANSITION TO THE NEOLIBERAL PATTERN OF DOMINATION

"Capitalist production comprises conditions independent of good or bad will, conditions which permit the working class to enjoy that relative prosperity only momentarily, and at that only as a harbinger of a coming crisis."

Karl Marx
Capital, Vol. II

THE END OF THE CONTAINED FORM OF DOMINATION

The Keynesian pattern of domination in particular (and the contained form of domination in general) was the result of a particular set of economic and political circumstances. First of all, it involved a transformation of the political institutions, whatever form they may have assumed – "Western democracy," "pluralism," "real socialism," "Third World populism and developmentalism," or "societal or state corporatism" (Schmitter, 1992) – which articulated some form of organization and representation of the working class and which, therefore, coordinated some form of negotiation between classes.

The capitalist state modified its position within the structures of domination according to the needs of exploitation and the circumstances of the class struggle. In the liberal pattern of domination, the state was the focal point for the organization of the capitalist class, the regulation of relations between capitalists and the repression of attempts at reform or revolution on the part of the workers. Under this arrangement, domination gradually grew more complicated. When worker and popular struggles infiltrated the space occupied by the nation-state, it became a space where the different modalities of the contained form of domination were processed.

This is a point worth highlighting. Throughout the 19th century, the socialist worker movement assumed a bourgeois-democratic[1] mission: to ensure the broadest and freest conditions of organization for the struggle

---

[1] "They need political liberty in order to unite all the Russian workers extensively and openly... but millions of people cannot unite unless there is political liberty" (Lenin, 1903).

in order to improve the living conditions of workers under capitalism and in the name of socialism, and to promote the rights of the people, freedom of assembly, of speech and of the press, of residence and of occupation. Political freedom, Lenin claimed, would not liberate the workers from poverty, but it would provide them with the weapons to fight against it.

These weapons are the basic democratic rights which the capitalists only recognized after massive worker struggles, in the context of the contained form of domination, and which the natural form of domination did not recognize, either in its expression as the liberal pattern or (although on a different scale) the neoliberal pattern.[2]

Secondly, it is important to note that a political structure of such a nature is only viable if, at the basic level of exploitation, the capitalist class is able to assume the commitment to improve the living conditions of the working class, by means of direct wages or redistribution of surplus-value by the state in the form of indirect wages, without affecting the rate of profit. In other words, to be viable, this structure of domination requires a delicate balance between wages and profit that is only possible in the context of a certain level of development of the productive force of labor, and, therefore, a certain level of organic composition of capital. How this complex balance was achieved is explained by Keynesianism and Fordism and the basic principle of negotiation that they established: to make all wage increases depend on an increase in productivity.

But this same circumstance says much about the limitations of the contained form of domination, which enjoyed its peak during the post-war boom and waned with the waning of the boom itself, when capital's rate of profit began to decrease. It must be added that, to afford the nation-state sufficient capacity to regulate class conflict through institutionalized mechanisms within the state apparatus, it was necessary for it also to have the capacity to regulate the economy, i.e. for the national economy to operate, to a certain degree, under the regulation of the nation-state. The basic condition that would make this possible was the "relative disconnection of the national economies from the global market by means of political controls; economic sovereignty of nation-states and restricted international mobility of capital" (Hirsch, 1996: 97). It is no coincidence

---

[2] Lenin suggested that "nations are an inevitable product, an inevitable form, in the bourgeois epoch of social development. The working class could not grow strong, become mature and take shape without 'constituting itself within the nation', without being 'national' (though not in the bourgeois sense of the word)" (Lenin, 1914). Neoliberal "globalization" has invested the matter of belonging to a nation-state with new complexities, such as the location of working class organization and struggle.

that, at the onset of the crisis that brought the end of the post-war boom, capital called for "free international mobility."

THE TRANSITION TO THE NEOLIBERAL PATTERN OF DOMINATION

Because the basic principle of negotiation between capitalists and workers established among the conditions for all variants of the contained form of domination was the tying of wage increases (direct and indirect) to increases in productivity,[3] the material support necessary for their political structure was a gradual and sustained rise in labor productivity; and as the technological structure that sustained Keynesianism in the developed countries was Fordism, consistent increases in labor productivity were made possible through the nature of Fordism as a technological system that would accept new incremental innovations.[4] The crisis of Fordism therefore meant that as a technological system it had exhausted its possibilities for the development of incremental innovations and, unless it could be replaced with a new technological system through a new technological revolution (Pérez, 1986), labor productivity would remain stagnant.

With productivity stagnating by the end of the 1960s, and an institutionalized political structure that allowed workers to negotiate and demand better wage, work and living conditions, the rates of surplus-value and of profit began dropping notably in the mid-1970s and the capitalist crisis, an expression of the fall in the rate of profit, became widespread. With this crisis, the economic basis for the political model was broken and the crisis of Fordism was expressed, at the level of the structures of domination, as a crisis in the Keynesian pattern of domination.

From that moment onward, the whole strategic design of the capitalist class was constructed around one basic purpose: to reverse the drop in the rate of profit and increase the rate of surplus-value. To do this, capital needed to resolve two problems: first, to break out of the limitations of Fordism as a technological system in order to raise labor productivity and increase the rate of surplus-value (i.e. capital needed to introduce a new technological revolution, to give a new boost to the development of the capital/wage-labor relation); and second – what we might call its ulterior

---

[3] In other words, any wage increase was contingent on an increase in the rate of surplus-value and the rate of profit.

[4] For an explanation of the concepts of *technological system* and *incremental innovation*, see Pérez, 1986.

motive, based on the tendential orientation of class interest – to reduce the working class to defenselessness, destroying even the fragile shelter represented by Keynesian institutionalism.

This was based on what for capital were three irrefutable facts: one, that under the circumstances of the drop in the rate of profit, it was necessary to cancel the gravy train and remove all the concessions granted to workers during the Keynesian period; two, that workers must not hinder the process of reorganization of the conditions for exploitation and accumulation which the capitalists were compelled to carry out; and three, that capital no longer had any interest, need or capacity to offer concessions to workers; on the contrary, it had to ensure that all new increases in productivity, intensity and/or working hours translated directly into rises in the rates of surplus-value and profit.[5]

In other words, the drop in the rate of profit renewed the always insatiable need of capital to appropriate the labor of others, and pushed it to restore the natural form of its domination under the new historical conditions. Moreover – and this is no minor detail – the political threat that compelled capital to accept the Keynesian compromise no longer appeared to exist. The unions and revolutionary worker parties that had threatened capital in the late 19th and early 20th century were no more; they had been eliminated by fascism or subsumed into the political structures of the Keynesian pattern of domination. Now they were unions and parties whose purpose, in the context of capitalism (whatever modality it might adopt), was to negotiate and administrate reforms, not to promote revolutions.

It must be remembered that reformism is internal to capital and reform is therefore subordinate to the needs of capital reproduction. Reformist parties and unions respond to the needs of capitalism, and what capitalism needed, under the new historical circumstances, was to increase the rate of surplus-value. There was no reason to expect them to pose any effective resistance against capital's new strategic initiative. After some ineffectual whining over the new misfortune of the working class (while helping to defuse any serious attempt at resistance[6]), they dedicated

---

[5] "The compatibility of capital profits and the well-being of the masses had come to an end… and the bases for the compromises between social classes likewise disappeared" (Hirsch, 1996: 88).

[6] "The leaders of the socialist parties have become one of the main bastions of the new order. The heads of the major unions have transformed into the biggest dampers on worker and popular protest. The old communist parties are beating a retreat in the political wake

themselves to administrating their own transition from Keynesian corporatist bureaucratic regulation cartel to monolithic neoliberal party.[7]

With the collapse of the Keynesian pattern, the contained form of domination in developed capitalism, it wasn't long before its subsidiary forms likewise collapsed. The real socialism of the Soviet Union, with its economy stagnating from the late sixties onward, exhausted from the effort of maintaining the arms race imposed upon it by the United States during the Cold War and unable to participate in the renewed technological race, attempted to modernize its capitalism, and in so doing aggravated the chaos and the crisis in its economy, causing serious deterioration to the living conditions of the vast majority. This provoked more resentment against the nomenclature and further discrediting of "real socialism."

The nomenclature, the managing elite in real socialism, however, did not lose either the political initiative or control of the process, and not only was the discontent and mobilization of the workers (which lacked political coordination) successfully defused, but the move from state capitalism to neoliberal capitalism was presented ideologically as a response to a popular demand, a move toward "democracy and universal prosperity." The Soviet Bloc in Eastern Europe didn't take long to collapse, and the rest of the "real socialist" world also underwent a shift toward neoliberal capitalism (China did so with great success), abandoning in every case the old forms of relations between social classes and the commitments to the welfare of the workers.

As a historical form of capitalist development and as a modality of the contained form of capitalist domination, "real socialism" was no better or worse than others of the same period, and the positioning of the USSR as a "superpower" helped to contain the voracity of the United States. The tug of war between the two "superpowers" opened up a certain range of possibilities for the underdeveloped nations in the area of international policy, until then the exclusive territory of the imperialist countries. They thus established the Non-Aligned Movement, demanding a New International Economic Order that would allow them to industrialize and seeking to negotiate the prices of their raw materials as a bloc. But the collapse of the Soviet Union left the United States as the only "superpower" in the military sphere and the underdeveloped nations' room to maneuver was drastically reduced with the new imperialist offensive.

---

of the socialist parties, in parallel with the restorationist about-turn of the CPs in Russia and the countries of the East" (Ayala and Figueroa, 2001).

[7] Both expressions are taken from Hirsch, 1996.

But as supposed "socialism," its worst features and its collapse – enthusiastically cited as the "collapse of socialism" by the ideologues of the bourgeoisie around the world – created serious confusion and disillusionment among the workers who still show no sign of rising up in a new formulation of the socialist project. The "fall of socialism," converted by the spokespeople of the bourgeoisie into the end of history, in supposed confirmation of capitalism as the natural social organization of humankind, as its only possibility, helped to discourage and defuse any worker response to the shift in the form of domination.

Meanwhile, Latin American developmentalism, which had never sought to overcome underdevelopment, had also reached its limit. On the one hand, the policy of import substitution, with the national market relatively isolated from competition on the global market, had enabled industrialization through the importing of obsolete production methods, devalued in the developed world but still useful in the productive structure and market conditions of underdeveloped nations. In this way, industrialization through import substitution reproduced, deepened and perpetuated underdevelopment, creating an interminable spiral of import needs.[8]

On the other hand, Latin American developmentalism opened up new possibilities of appreciation for imperialist capital through the exportation of obsolete constant capital[9] and the establishment of subsidiaries, in alliance with local capital, within the Latin American economies. From the mid-1950s on, the presence of subsidiaries of U.S. monopolies within the Latin American economies – particularly the more industrialized ones – was a growing trend. By the seventies, U.S. capital constituted the hegemonic faction of capital within the most industrialized Latin American countries, and, from within, it would pressure these countries to adopt new modalities of growth.

By the end of the 1960s, Latin American developmentalism had reached its limit with a process of industrialization that substituted imports, which in fact required increasing quantities of imports, creating an industry incapable of competing on the global market and therefore incapable of exporting – that is, incapable of financing its import requirements.

---

[8] "The internal production of goods substitutes their importation, but creates new import needs for intermediate and capital goods" (Figueroa Sepúlveda, 1986: 162).

[9] "This is why the U.S. bourgeoisie wasted no time in attempting to *promote* industrialization (in Latin America), based precisely on obsolete material in the countries themselves" (Figueroa Sepúlveda, 1986: 173).

From the end of the sixties on, the foreign debts of Latin American countries began to rise, and by the late seventies and early eighties, an external debt crisis arose which, due to the increase in interest rates imposed by the Reagan administration, reached astronomical proportions until Latin America was forced to undertake "structural adjustment" programs.[10] "Inward growth" became a new modality of "outward growth," no longer as "primary export economics," but through the creation of a new pattern of industrial colonialism (Figueroa Sepúlveda, 2001), and the developmentalist pattern of domination disappeared to give way to the neoliberal pattern.

In Latin America, as with the collapse of "real socialism," the crisis in developmentalism magnified the negative image of this socioeconomic system, thereby facilitating the presentation of the transition from developmentalism to neoliberalism as a "transition to democracy and modernity." With the military dictatorships in South America, capital achieved two goals. First, it crushed the popular struggles that had taken advantage of the political space opened up by developmentalism, at least to the extent of recognizing certain worker rights, encouraging some form of nationalism and questioning the fragility and weakness of the underdeveloped world, the chronically subordinate pole in the imperialist relation, to guarantee better working and living conditions for workers. And second, it paved the road for the emergence of the new pattern of domination and exploitation.

With these goals achieved, these dictatorships (along with finely-tuned authoritarian corporatist regimes like that of Mexico) initiated what was officially referred to as the transition to democracy; the era of the dictatorships, the spokespeople for capital announced festively, had come to an end, and a new era of civic maturity and development of "civil society," progress, respect for human rights and diversity, etc., had begun. Throughout Latin America, a new era of economic progress was proclaimed, while in Mexico the discourse went even further and, with the signing of the North American Free Trade Agreement with the U.S. and Canada, the government asserted, with unequivocal certainty, that the

---

[10] "The process of change had one fundamental point of support: the debt crisis, which had been stimulated by the United States and which was precipitated by the abrupt change in its monetary policy. The actions of the IMF and the World Bank would thus prove decisive, as they made the aid offered to cope with the rise in interest rates on the debt and the total paralysis of the voluntary flow of funds conditional upon trade liberalization, economic deregulation and privatization of the public sector" (Arceo, 2002).

country was leaving the ranks of the underdeveloped once and for all and entering the "First World."

The capitalists successfully presented their strategic initiatives, aimed at opening a new avenue to satisfy their appetite for the labor of others, as the solution to the social ills of the previous period (ills which they themselves had created), and thus won the support of society for their new projects, at least until the new ills provoked by the new initiatives become evident and the hope inspired by the "new solutions" begin to fade, at which point the cycle is initiated once again, with the proposal of some new "solution."

There is, however, a radical difference between the transitions that marked the shift from the natural form to the contained form and those of the return to the natural form. While the first meant that workers around the world had managed to win some concessions from capital and improve their working and living conditions (albeit within limits), the second meant that capital resumed its normal role, rolling back the achievements that the workers had fought so hard to win.

The first transition improved living and working conditions, while the second was explicitly designed to worsen them: the reduction of direct and indirect wages, the casualization of labor, increased unemployment, and the resumption of direct control of underdeveloped nations. The global wave that constituted the different modalities of the contained form of domination disappeared, giving way to a new emergence of the natural form of capitalist domination that was imposed throughout the world: the neoliberal pattern of domination.

In order to examine the neoliberal pattern of domination, I have attempted to synthesize its general features into four processes that I believe constitute the core of its dynamic. Although they are intimately related, each of these processes requires separate analysis, and each one constitutes an object of study of a process in progress, open to future turns in the course of history. The aim here is thus to capture their tendencies, their strategic purpose in the context of the capital/wage-labor relation, without tying them to a particular moment in their development. It is thus more an analysis on the logical plane than an attempt to define a historical manifestation, although the United States and Latin America (particularly Mexico) will serve as specific historical points of reference to illustrate certain tendential lines of the process. Another chapter is dedicated to the analysis of each of these processes later in this work.

In Chapter 6, I provide a review of neoliberal economics: the so-called globalization of big multinational financial capital, based on free international mobility of capital and the deployment of the power of the new technological revolution, with special focus on the internationalization of productive capital, as well as its translation into a new pattern of industrial colonialism. This involves a complex series of processes whose strategic purpose is to increase the rate of surplus-value and concentrate its production and appropriation on a global scale, redefining the relation between capital and labor and between developed and underdeveloped capitalism.

Chapter 7 will then analyze neoliberal politics, the transformations produced by capital at the government level: nation-states are disabled as spaces for the regulation of the capital-labor relation, dedicated to dismantling the concessions won by the workers during the period of the Keynesian-developmentalist pattern of domination and subordinated to the dynamic of globalization of big multinational capital. The workers, particularly those in underdeveloped countries, are reduced to a situation of virtual defenselessness, as their right to move freely and organize themselves internationally is denied, and they are held in a kind of national confinement.

In Chapter 8, I examine the intersection of the two previous points and the response to neoliberalism. While neoliberal economics provokes social discontent, neoliberal politics dismantles the institutional avenues for its expression; the capitalism of today has established no avenues for the resolution of many of the economic, social and political problems it generates, but merely administrates them while continuing on its course. State administration of crime replaces state administration of concessions as the central pillar of the pattern of domination.

Chapter 9 then attempts to contribute to an understanding of the future project, or project of civilization, which neoliberal capital offers humankind, on the basis of which it exercises its intellectual and moral leadership and applies its economic and political practices. This chapter also completes the overview of the neoliberal pattern of domination by providing some basic outlines to link economics, politics and ideology in the historical context of neoliberal capitalism.

CHAPTER SIX

THE NEOLIBERAL ECONOMY

News coverage and political discussion on social, economic and political problems focused on just about everything but the corporation. That seemed upside down to us... Not many of the world's problems just happen. There's usually a party responsible. And in many, many cases, that party is a multinational corporation – or a group of multinationals.

Russell Mokhiber and Robert Weissman
"Self Interview: On the Rampage"

As always, the party directing the process was developed capital. Its first responses were announced at the onset of the crisis in the late 1960s and, from the 1980s onward with the initiation of a new technological revolution, big capital unleashed a strategic counteroffensive that would structure the new conditions for exploitation and accumulation and the new conditions for domination. The neoliberal pattern of domination was established as the political framework, the structure for domination, corresponding to the neoliberal economic model. Based on the proposition of the concept of a pattern of domination as a general characterization of capitalist domination in a specific historical period, my purpose here is to trace the broad outlines of the process, viewing them as trends in progress, particularly with regard to class relations and the imperialist relation in Latin America, without attempting to study their historical manifestations.

It is worth clarifying at this point that, as the main purpose of this work is to analyze the capital-labor relation, no more than a brief examination is offered of the effect that the inter-imperialist struggle (with the developed pole of imperialism redefined in three major regional blocs) has had in guiding the process, particularly through the initiatives of the United States and its competitive strategies against the other blocs. It must be stated, however, that as a result of a deficiency in state administration of development (Figueroa Sepúlveda, 1992), the United States has wasted no time in launching strategies to compensate for its disadvantages and increase competitiveness with its most efficient rivals, characterized by a drastic disregard for the effects that the behavior of its corporations have on the environment, a seriously inequitable and exploitative attitude toward its "backyard," an aggressive policy to impose unstable and flexible labor relations on workers and the use of military force as a resource in the promotion of economic competitiveness. In today's world, the United States is an energetic and resolute promoter of barbarism.[1]

Neoliberalism is a global offensive against the workers to reestablish the conditions for the production of surplus-value, and this is the central dimension of the process. But it is also necessarily an expression of an intensely revived inter-capitalist and inter-imperialist battle to appropriate surplus-value; without doubt, the specific course being taken by the dynamic of neoliberalism is partially explained on this level. However, the systematic examination of this element is beyond the scope and the purpose of this work.

FREE MOBILITY:
NEOLIBERAL INTERNATIONALIZATION OF CAPITAL

In my analysis of the Keynesian pattern I stressed one basic fact: all of the institutions that regulated the capital-labor relation were constructed at the level of the nation-state. This is a feature shared by all of the different modalities assumed by the contained form of domination; the working and popular classes found a voice in the space of the nation-state and, for the first time in the history of capitalism, workers were afforded political, economic and social rights, as well as relatively broad freedoms of organization, at least for negotiating better living conditions under capitalism. Throughout the world, the working class and workers in general made gains in terms of organization and their capacity for struggle in order to wrestle concessions from capital, which were coordinated within their respective nation-states.

I also stressed that, to afford the nation-state sufficient capacity to regulate class conflict through institutionalized mechanisms within the state apparatus, it was necessary for it also to have the capacity to regulate the economy (i.e. for the national economy to operate, to a certain degree, under the regulation of the nation-state), and that a relative disconnection of the national economies from the global market was necessary, as

---

[1] For an interesting examination of the contributions of the United States to the rampant barbarism of today's world, see Saxe-Fernández, 2006.

well as the regulation of the international mobility of capital by means of political controls.[2]

It is true that during the post-war boom, financial capital, particularly that of the United States, reached a new stage in its process of internationalization, and the subsidiaries of its big monopolies spread throughout the world – to Europe, Japan, and, of course, Latin America. But this occurred within the context of the international regulation system defined by the Bretton Woods Agreement, which gave the nation-state the capacity to organize its own national regulation system.[3] In other words, the internationalization of big financial capital during the post-war boom did not destroy Keynesian regulation of the nation-state, but rather operated within the framework organized by that regulation. However, Keynesian internationalization was established on the basis of neoliberal internationalization.[4] In effect, faced with the crisis provoked by the drop in the rate of profit, and constricted by an institutionalism coordinated at the level of nation-states, capital needed a different kind of internationalism from that offered by Keynesianism, an internationalism that would allow it to restore the conditions of the natural form of its domination: an internationalization founded on its free international mobility.

The strategy of big financial capital (particularly its most internationalized form) and of the imperialist states (particularly the United States) to destroy the Keynesian pattern of domination consisted precisely in destroying the nation-state's capacity for economic regulation (specifically, its capacity to regulate relations between capital and wage-labor) by promoting the free international mobility of capital: "the more liberalized the markets are, the narrower the political room for state action will be" (Hirsch, 1996: 75). Specifically, free mobility of capital involves deregulation and the removal of all hindrances to free enterprise, but it does not mean no state intervention. The offensive of the financial oligarchy calling

----

[2] "Fordism was basically organized under the nation-state structure. It revolved around the expansion of internal markets on the basis of broad state intervention and institutionalized class compromises" (Hirsch, 1996: 88).

[3] "The institutions established under Bretton Woods – according to which macroeconomic tensions were basically resolved at the national level, as each State could employ its own monetary and fiscal instruments to pursue full employment, but had to ensure levels of growth of demand and prices compatible with the external balance" (Arceo, 2002).

[4] "The interpenetration of capital on a collective scale shattered national production systems and initiated their restructuring as segments of a globalized production system" (Amín, 2003b).

for free mobility sought to ensure the transition from Keynesian state regulation to regulation "by the markets," that is, by the direct and immediate
needs of capital appreciation. The state would continue to intervene in
class relations, but its intervention would no longer be under the auspices
of a political pact; rather, it would be overdetermined – regulated, it could
be said – by "the markets," by the interests of big internationalized capital.
The intention was thus to reestablish a state that not only permits but
vigorously supports the actions of "private initiative" (i.e. the actions of
the big international monopolies); a state adapted to the conditions of the
natural form of domination, to weaken and disorganize the workers and
destroy the different modalities of the "social pact" that were structured
during the era of the contained form of domination.

The Keynesian state was transformed into the neoliberal state and
quickly began implementing the project that drove it: "all the conquests of
civilization that gave shape to the modern state (which today capitalism
destroys or negates) were the result of huge and bloody struggles. Through
the worldwide defeat inflicted by Capital on Labor by the end of the 1980s,
financial capital was crudely reproducing, on a scale never seen before
and with advanced technology, many of the prevailing features of the last
quarter of the 19th century, from the imperialist wars of colonial conquest
to child slavery, the return of 10–12 hour work-days and the elimination of
labor regulations. It has been reconquering the space it had been forced to
give up, and reducing the political spaces of those whom it exploits,
oppresses and dominates. Only social resistance, which varies from country to country, places any limits on it" (Almeyra, 2007).

MONEY-CAPITAL AND COMMODITY-CAPITAL

This section examines the nature of this new internationalization of
capital, based on its free mobility. For this examination, it is necessary
to distinguish between the different functional forms of capital –
money-capital, commodity-capital and productive capital – not only
because they follow distinct rhythms and processes, but because they
have different meanings in the global structure of capital domination. In
this section, I will review the internationalization of money-capital and
commodity-capital, leaving productive-capital for the following section.

Money-Capital

Arceo examines the general framework which, by imposition of the
United States, the IMF and the World Bank, led to the "replacement of

the institutions agreed in Bretton Woods with a new system based on the deregulation of international financial markets and flexible rates of exchange" (Arceo, 2002), freeing up geographical and functional competition between different types of financial institutions, progressively dismantling the barriers to the international movement of capital and the internal regulations for financial markets and foreign currency transactions, and increasing the importance of the funds controlled by the multinationals. But what is important to highlight is that there is, at least, a twofold political meaning behind this process:

First, "in this system, the discipline imposed by the system of fixed exchange rates is replaced by *the discipline imposed by the private capital market* through the threat of a massive withdrawal of funds" (Arceo, 2002, emphasis added). Assured of the free mobility of capital, the market and not the state is now the one setting the rules of the game; the mode of relation between state and capital is radically redefined.

Second, the Bretton Woods system, which "aimed at making it possible in each country to control financial capital and award a central role to productive capital (by virtue of the commitment to guarantee full employment for the working class), was replaced by another system, in which... big financial capital regains a central position within the bloc of dominant classes"; in other words, financial capital is favored over productive capital.[5]

It should be noted that Arceo is clearly not speaking of financial capital in the broadest sense, as capital resulting from the merger of banking capital and industrial capital, but in a limited sense, as money-capital and its various functions (credit markets, stock markets, derivative exchanges, etc.). Financial capital in the limited sense may be a functional mode of financial capital in the broadest sense or it may be a differentiated faction of capital, but what is important here is that under the neoliberal system the financial function of capital is favored over the productive, which means that financial modes of appropriation of surplus-value are favored

---

[5] The relation between productive capital and financial capital in this phase of capitalist development has particular features which are beyond the scope of this analysis: "a crucial aspect of the constitution of global information capitalism is the contradictory interrelation that has been established between production and financial circulation. There would seem to be a lack of correspondence or counterpoint between these two spheres, as exchange rate speculation and volatility have translated into a series of regional financial crises, some of which have created momentary systemic instability that affects the growth of global production. However, the increasingly globalized financial system has come to play a key role in guaranteeing the cyclical reproduction of the new production base, whose turnover rates have been considerably accelerated with an extremely high potential for overproduction or overaccumulation" (Dabat et al, 2004).

over the modes of production of surplus-value and this results in the breakdown of the Keynesian pact.[6] Having been liberated from government regulation and assured of free international mobility, a global money-capital market was established and big financial capital discovered wonderful opportunities to appropriate value in extraordinary quantities.

In the 1970s and 1980s, in the context of the stagnation of productivity and the reduction of the rate of profit, companies responded by raising the prices of their products, speculating on foreign currencies, shifting their capital, provoking devaluations and inflation, and raising the interest rates to their debtors (Latin American governments being a notable case). While shattering the Keynesian strategies of state regulation of the economy, these actions provoked a massive transference of riches (both public and private) and the deterioration of the living conditions of the masses. And with governments closing the pincer by freezing wages while companies raised prices and profits, real wages dropped and a significant proportion of wage funds was converted into profit for capital.

The results were so satisfactory for big capital that, even while productive capital was restructured and the effects of the new technological revolution unfolded, the same recipe continued to be applied. In 1995, a major speculative attack[7] occurred and the world filled up with phantoms – dragons, tequilas, sambas, tangos, all with the generic surname effect (i.e. the Dragon Effect, the Tequila Effect, etc.) – as savage as the legendary monster known as the chupacabra, the first reports of which also emerged in the mid-1990s. No government could explain where these phantoms came from or how to control them but, in a matter of minutes, just as the chupacabra sucks the blood of its victims, they sucked up savings and wealth, leaving poverty and debt in their wake.

Capital thus found a means of appropriating wealth which was wonderful in one sense, but also plagued with internal contradictions. At the same time, it began to erect the framework of the new form of

---

[6] "Article 6 of the [Bretton Woods] agreement made it possible to control the international movement of capital; this control was considered by its creators to be a central element in order to prevent the interests of productive capital and of each society from becoming subject to the demands of financial capital, as had occurred in the period prior to the Great Depression" (Arceo, 2002).

[7] Speculative attacks that translate into major mass expropriations and conversions of public and private resources which, before and after 1995 and with diverse variants, have occurred periodically, coming to form part of what David Harvey calls "accumulation by dispossession" (Harvey, 2004).

domination. The liberalization of the international movement of capital and the processes that it provoked gave rise to the construction of a "new" form of political discourse: the omnipotence of market forces, which no human power could possibly oppose, according to the explanation offered by confounded governments to their dismayed and depressed citizens. It was exactly the same explanation that the Old Testament prophets used for the power of God, only now it was not God's design that ruled us, but market indicators.

The ideology promoted by capital, grounded in the new form assumed by social relations, hearkened back to the eras before the Enlightenment and the great cultural movements of the 18th century, in a move toward new versions of medieval obscurantism.[8] The logic of capital was placed above the state, the privileged position of reason and the public interest constructed by bourgeois political science, and the door was opened to allow the wildest irrationality to be unleashed. Human beings, individually or collectively, governing or governed, no longer directed the process that constituted the essence of their social reality; capital appeared to be beyond the control of human will. More than ever, it was capital and not capitalists that governed.

Under the conditions of neoliberalism, class relations appear to be regulated by the market – i.e. by an abstract entity; neither capital, nor its personification, the capitalist, appear directly or immediately involved. It is now necessary to search for them in order to identify them and to restore the knowledge and awareness of the social relation between the capitalist class and the working class, which is being expressed in this behavior of the markets. This is the result of the permissiveness, acceptance and resolute support of any initiative by capital to increase the level and rate of profit of a liberal state, which gives way (to capital); this is why the first task assumed by the neoliberal state is the dismantling of practically all political controls over the activities of capital. The economy was "autonomized," converted, in accordance with the natural form of domination, into an "independent" sphere, regulated only by the immediate and insatiable thirst for surplus-value.

Under the conditions of the liberal pattern, workers had before their eyes, as in the novels of Dickens, Balzac and Zola, the personification of

---

8 Thus we find *God* becoming increasingly present in neoliberal discourse, *legitimizing* government decisions, particularly (but not exclusively) in the United States: *politics*, a matter between human beings as it *has been understood* since Machiavelli, is now being converted back into *theology*, at least in the discourse for mass consumption.

the social relation that dominated and exploited them: the despotic, cruel, fat-bellied capitalist with the black suit and gold chain. Under the conditions of the Keynesian pattern, the visible party responsible for the behavior of capital was the state and its governors. But now, the producer of the workers' hardships has disappeared and there is nobody to blame or to fight against; where does this Mr. Market live, exactly?

This transmutation of the world of social relations into a divinized world of things, this extreme fetishization that has occurred under the conditions of the neoliberal pattern and the use that domination by capital makes of it, must be borne in mind during the discussion that follows. In redefining its relation with the nation-state, with the liberalization of financial capital as the starting point, capital redefined the whole structure of its economic, political and ideological domination.

Commodity-Capital

The process of freeing up the circulation of commodity-capital has been rather more uneven and turbulent. On the one hand, there has been a trend toward an increased opening up of national economies in order to permit access to manufactured commodities on the international market. This trend points to the shaping of a global capitalist market in line with the interests of big internationalized capital as a whole, an expression of its need and aspiration to have one single, unified world market at its disposal. The fulfillment of this purpose was the aim of the GATT, and of its successor, the World Trade Organization.

But on the other hand, the current conditions of inter-imperialist competition have led to the shaping of three regional blocs, each with their own "spheres of influence," and to the stagnation of the general advances negotiated in the GATT and the WTO; so far, what has occurred in this area is not so much globalization as regionalization, and its future development will continue to depend on inter-imperialist competition. Even the United States, the biggest advocate of free trade, "the form under which it promotes the establishment of international regulations aimed at ensuring the liberalization of trade and investments, is... strictly controlled by an agenda that reflects the priority and interests of 'its' capital" (Arceo, 2002). For example, it simultaneously promotes "free trade" where and how it suits its aims, and the establishment of Latin America as an area of its exclusive influence.

The free mobility of commodity capital, less spectacular in its immediate results than has been its twin, money capital, is nevertheless associated with much deeper consequences. The restructuring of the markets goes hand in hand with the restructuring of production: the technological revolution and global rationalization of production, the destruction or absorption of non-competitive capital, the redistribution of production on a global scale and, therefore, of industrial employment and unemployment and, in the losing regions and countries, mass migration, hunger, and a desperate search for ways to survive. Thus, to complete the picture, it is necessary also to engage in an examination of productive capital.

GLOBAL PRODUCTIVE CAPITAL

The above discussion makes it clear that the new modality of internationalization of money-capital and commodity-capital, while bringing profound changes to the relation between capital and the state, constitutes one of the pincers with which the pattern of domination will be radically altered. What follows is an examination of the other pincer, the transformation of productive capital. I have given this phenomenon its own section because it is here in the direct production relation where the essence of the capital/wage-labor relation lies. The behavior of money capital and commodity capital express the struggle for the appropriation of surplus-value, but it is only in production that surplus-value is produced; the strategic purpose of the offensive of capital lies in the restructuring of the conditions for exploitation of the workers.

Although it may seem unnecessary, it is worth recalling here a few basic truths, which should really be common sense but which tend to be overlooked in the habitual ideological discourse of the neoliberal world, which fosters the notion that capital appreciates without the need for workers. Money-capital, particularly if it operates in speculative global waves, is extraordinarily profitable, but it can only transfer value; and for it to be transferred value must first exist – it must first have been produced. And to take control of the commodity market, it is first necessary to produce commodities. The secret of the whole capitalist universe, as Marx explained, lies in the production of surplus-value, and the transformations to the mode of operation of money-capital and commodity-capital only find their true meaning when they are linked to transformations to productive capital, re-establishing the unity of the M-C-M cycle which defines the unity (albeit with mediating and contradictory factors) between the three forms of capital.

The first steps in the new internationalization of productive capital were actually made as early as the late 1960s and, since then, the strategic purposes pursued by capital in this process have gradually taken shape. While in those years, capital in the developed nations was being suffocated by the institutions created under the conditions of the Keynesian pattern of domination, outside, in the underdeveloped world, were huge reserves of labor-power: "These reserves were practically inexhaustible, as capital could rely on hundreds of millions of workers in Asia, Africa, Latin America and even the 'socialist' countries" (Fröbel et al, 1981: 39). The tally of "competitive and comparative advantages," of treasures simply waiting to be plundered, was truly stunning. In this wondrous collection of countries, real wages were between 70% and 80% lower than those paid in developed countries, the working day was considerably longer, labor productivity was equivalent for similar processes, the work force could be hired and fired virtually at whim, a greater labor intensity could be imposed and the size of the reserve army allowed "optimal" selection of the work force.[9] Moreover, a global labor-power market would constitute such effective competition against workers in developed countries that, with a little care, the labor and wage conditions in developed countries could be brought as close as possible to those of the underdeveloped nations.

The strategic purposes of capital are now clearly delineated: to create the political conditions, on one hand, and the technical conditions on the other, to convert these reserves of labor-power into a veritable worldwide industrial reserve army. The technical conditions to make this possible were already present, at least in embryonic form, in *Taylorism and Fordism*: "the development and refining of the technology, which enables the deconstruction of complex production processes into elemental units to the point that even an unqualified work force could be adapted, without difficulties and within a short period of time, to carry out the fragmented tasks" (Fröbel et al, 1981: 40).

In this way, a central aim for the organization of the subsequent technological development would be the growth of this capacity to organize the production process for the efficient exploitation of this potential worldwide industrial army reserve: "technology that allows the choice of location for industrial production to be less dependent on geographical distances. This technology includes modern transport systems for rapid

---

[9] For a list of the "wonders" see Fröbel et al, 1981: 39–40.

and relatively economical transportation between the points of final or intermediate production and the centers of consumption... and also included are the telecommunications systems, data processing systems and other means of organizing production" (Fröbel et al, 1981: 41). "Under the imperative of capital appreciation, it became necessary to reorganize (at the global level) the manufacture of those commodities whose production process could be broken up into elements... and to compare... from the perspective of cost, all of the possible subdivisions of the production process, in order to find the subdivision that would allow the lowest production costs with a global optimization, as well as the development of the most suitable production technology" (Fröbel et al, 1981: 45).

After centuries of evolution, capital, realizing a long-cherished dream, now had the technical capacity to organize its production process on a global scale and, with the technical solution already in place, it was on the verge of overcoming the political challenge: to break the resistance of the workers and ensure free mobility for productive capital. A certain level of technological development allowed it to initiate the political offensive, and its political success enabled it to launch the technological offensive: "the implementation of new technologies," says Hirsch, "is not the origin or cause, but the purpose of globalization" (Hirsch, 1986: 89); and, he adds, "the capitalist reaction to the crisis of Fordism consisted in a technological offensive, the political economic condition for which was the globalization of capitalist relations and the associated modification of class relations on an international scale" (Hirsch, 1986: 109).[10]

From the end of the 1960s on, the big corporations of the developed nations began to relocate segments of their production processes – the most labor-intensive and least demanding in terms of technical qualifications – to underdeveloped countries, especially to those where there was political stability (in some cases the product of a coup d'etat and a subsequent military dictatorship), and where the unions were weak, labor-power was abundant and wages were low. Thus, in a pincer motion, they exploited the reserve army of underdeveloped countries and weakened the worker movement of the developed nations: on the one hand, because they produced unemployment and, when this began to rise, employed workers tended to feel privileged, to moderate their demands and to try to

---

[10] Hirsch asserts that "the radical liberalization of commodities, services, money and capital is the necessary prior condition for the renewed systematic rationalization of the labor process in capitalist production, and this, in turn, is associated with the destruction of the Fordist class compromise and its institutional bases" (Hirsch, 1986:89).

avoid placing their jobs in jeopardy; and on the other, because the relocation had not only technical but political criteria: "a series of industrial
restructuring projects were implemented, aimed explicitly at relocating
the work force away from branches or regions that had shown *the highest
combative force* in the battles of the late sixties" (Thwaites Rey and Castillo,
1999, emphasis added).

This is an essential point which needs to be emphasized. The internationalization of money-capital and commodity-capital can operate
equally among developed countries and between developed and underdeveloped countries. But the internationalization of productive capital must
necessarily operate in such a way that it links developed capital with the
reserve army of labor in the underdeveloped countries; its raison d'être
essentially lies in the promotion of opposition between the workers of the
developed and underdeveloped worlds. As this new capital initiative met
with success (i.e. as the bureaucracies ruling the unions and worker parties showed their inability to challenge capital's offensive), it took on larger
dimensions, and the free trade zones which were negotiated in the late
1960s as restricted areas for the establishment of assembly plants[11] began
to expand. In the 1980s, especially after the collapse of the Soviet Union,
the developed nations began to organize their expanded free trade zones
in the underdeveloped world encompassing whole countries and regions,
and the formation of an international labor-power market and access to
an international industrial reserve army became competition factors in
the inter-imperialist struggle.

In their respective spheres of influence, to ensure free mobility for their
productive capital, the developed nations promoted the elimination of
trade barriers, not only for the movement of commodities and capital but
for raw materials and equipment, as well as changes to customs systems to
make corporate imports and exports exempt of taxes. These were the necessary conditions for the work force of the underdeveloped world to
become the real (and not merely the potential) industrial reserve army for
the capital of the developed countries.

With the advance and development of this process, its vast scope began
to be recognized: "as a long-term strategy, the free worldwide circulation
of capital was established as an unprecedented weapon for conditioning
the labor pole. As in capitalism no investment means no generation of

---

[11] For example, the United States and Mexico negotiated parts of their border zone,
Europe relocated assembly plants to northern Africa, and Japan did the same in Southeast
Asia.

productive activity and therefore no work, the shortage of capital for production is managed as a form of blackmail against workers: 'if you don't acquiesce to the new conditions that we believe necessary to recover profits, we won't invest, ergo, you have no work, ergo, you cannot reproduce your living conditions'... The fragmentation, flexibilization and casualization of labor are thus correlates to the loss of bargaining power of the classical industrial worker" (Thwaites Rey and Castillo, 1999). While capital was internationalized, the working class was not; it remained trapped in an institutional space, defined by the nation-state, which had been emptied of content, and was no longer capable of organizing an effective space for negotiation between the classes. And, in the absence of any form of institutionalism that could organize an international forum for negotiation, the working class was trapped in a situation of virtual defenselessness.

Capital took control back again; the conditions for purchase and use of labor-power were no longer open to negotiation. Capital sought to assume direct control of working conditions and establish its conditions unilaterally. With its globalizing offensive, unilateral regulation by capital was reestablished. The victories of the working class, which seemed firmly established under the conditions of the contained form of domination, have been virtually destroyed under the conditions of the neoliberal pattern of domination. As productive capital has ensured its free international mobility, decisions regarding the location of its segments are made based on an analysis of the global (not the national) situation[12] and corporations organize a worldwide production network: "what is original about this imperialist phase is not that capital reaches beyond national borders. Nor is it the fact that the multinationals invest massively in manufacturing, both in semi-colonial countries and within the imperialist countries themselves. What is new is that the industrial units of the big corporations, which operate in a disconnected manner, have come to form a worldwide production network, redefining the dimension of the industrial processes... This means that the conception of the product, the financing, advertising, marketing and production of the different parts of the product and its assembly are distributed throughout different countries and at the same time integrated into a single structure that uses

---

[12] "The gigantic multinational corporations organized product manufacturing in combined form in various parts of the world, taking advantage of the inequalities of each country, and particularly the differences in wages and work conditions... surplus profits are based on the use of inequalities between nations" (Ayala and Figueroa, 2001).

the conditions for production around the world to maximize profits" (Lipietz, 1991).

With the political challenge overcome, worker resistance neutralized or weakened and capital's free international mobility assured, with open access to the work force of different countries (a global labor-power market resulting from a combination of workers from both the developed and underdeveloped worlds), capital was able to proceed with the technical rationalization and definition of the optimal composition of its worker collective, taking advantage of the differences offered by a nationally segmented labor-power market. Technical needs in the sphere of the company, like market indicators in the sphere of society, became the impersonal and irrefutable voices for the logic of capital. After a rigorous technical, scientific examination of the worldwide range of options for alternative locations for each fragment of the production process, made possible by the free international mobility of capital, the optimal location is determined; the criterion, of course, is maximum global profitability.[13]

Multinational financial capital, the dominant faction of the Keynesian pattern of domination, has now become global financial capital and the "relay subsidiaries" have been transformed into "workshop-subsidiaries" (Arceo, 2002) – subsidiaries responsible for handling one part of the production process, while the final product is assembled at a central location. The product of each of the subsidiaries is not merchandise, but elements of its production capital that are circulated from one point to another as a result of the technical division of labor in the company's production process; thus, a significant part of "international trade" has come to involve the circulation of products within corporations. The companies' location criteria are fine-tuned with sophisticated mathematical procedures in order to determine the optimal combination, considering the technology employed, the location of the other subsidiaries, markets, competition, availability of natural resources and raw material supply sources, etc. But what is significant here is the position of the workers in this new scale of technical rationalization established by capital, as the strategic purpose of neoliberal globalization is to change the relation between the capitalist class and the working class and to increase the rate of surplus-value in order to restore the rate of profit.

---

[13] "The spatial deconstruction of corporate functions has led to a decisive strategy of rationalization and maximization of profits" (Hirsch, 1996: 74).

The new technology, unlike the rigid production structure of Fordism, is flexible, as its means of production are less specialized and can be reconfigured quickly to carry out different tasks or to change from the production of one model or product to another[14] – microelectronics, numerically controlled machine tools, robots, automation of transformation activities and auxiliary or peripheral activities, programmable equipment that allows flexible production of a varied and constantly changing range of goods and services. "Diversity and flexibility have replaced the uniformity and repetitiveness" typical of Fordism and mass production (Pérez, 1986). Flexibility in production has changed business management and, together with telecommunications, organizes new conditions for competition and competitiveness between companies: total quality and just-in-time management, zero stocks, and synchrony between all of the production functions and the market. And this, in turn, changes the combination of machines and workers in production. There is a constant search for greater mobility and a more fluid capacity for response to variations in the market and in competition. Technological change has become more dynamic; computerized design is integrated into the production process, reducing costs and times between innovations. Product life cycles are growing shorter, with the appearance of successive products and families of products, and productivity and innovation have become everyday, decisive aspects of competitiveness. "Research, development and design engineering centers tend to be integrated with one another and to be associated with the production process and with short- and medium-term strategic management and programming" (Pérez, 1986).

In response to all of these possibilities (which the dynamic of competition turns into demands) for flexibility, the big global monopolies have established worldwide production and distribution networks, with plants of different sizes in different locations, including flexible and interconnected contractors and subcontractors, with an interconnection that "involves the transcontinental and interregional generation of flows, the

---

[14] "A new generation of less specialized means of production, through numerical control, the incorporation of microprocessors in the control of machine tools and the resulting redesign of those tools... Thanks to the possibilities opened up by microprocessors, the machine designed to carry out one given task on the production line for a specific product is replaced by a tool that can be configured quickly to perform different tasks, making it possible to go from the production of one model or product to another and obtain high rates of productivity with lower costs per product" (Revelli, 2004).

daisy chaining of activities into networks and constant interaction between a growing number of participating agents" (Dabat et al, 2004: 39). The free international mobility of capital enabled the initiation of a technological revolution which, in turn, is consolidating and demanding ever greater mobility: "the historic transformation that global capitalism is experiencing has its main driving force in the revolutionary changes to the technology base, which are opening up huge possibilities of interconnection of human activities in different continents, countries and locations. Innovations in the fields of information technology and telecommunications have brought about a structural and spatial-temporal change that encourages a new form of organization of social, economic and political activities, characterized by its capacity to have repercussions over large distances in a form of interconnection that is increasingly intense, systematic and rapid" (Dabat et al, 2004: 39). Having thus flexibilized the operation of productive capital, free from the technological rigidity of Fordism, it is clear that capital would need flexible labor-power, free of the contractual rigidity of Keynesianism.

The new structure of productive capital is incompatible with a single market and labor contract in which all the workers enjoy stability and the same labor and social rights, as was structured under Keynesian regulation; instead, it requires a new labor market that is flexible and segmented. The international mobility of capital, its free access to a global market of nationally segmented labor-power, enables it to create this ideal labor market; the political offensive and the technological offensive come together and the worker collective is segmented, flexibilized and globalized. As capital finds different types of workers in different parts of the world, and given that the different stages in the production process require different worker qualifications, the geographical location of the different segments of productive capital are defined to a significant extent by the professional and political status of the workers.

General labor will tend to remain concentrated in the developed countries as always, while immediate labor, depending on its level of complexity, will tend to be relocated in underdeveloped countries – not for the production of independent commodities, but as segments of the technical division of labor in a company's production process. And, in keeping with this segmented and globalized labor market, capital will generally organize different contractual conditions. In the segments that require workers with greater technical ability, autonomy, responsibility and cooperation, capital will offer better labor and contractual conditions, including job stability, and these positions will usually be concentrated in the developed nations.

On the other hand, for the segments that require easily replaceable workers, those with fewer technical requirements, capital generally rejects any compromise with labor and establishes what Lipietz calls bloody Taylorism: external and hierarchical control of the labor process according to the classical Taylorist method, but "without the social compensations of the golden age of Fordism" (Lipietz, 1997), and these positions will usually be concentrated in the underdeveloped nations. In these cases, flexibility[15], a real or supposed technical necessity, often quickly turns into casualization: "to make companies more competitive at the expense of job security standards, increasing labor intensity and deregulating the conditions of worker protection" (Sotelo Valencia, 1999: 118–119). This means debased employment and wage conditions, job instability, the absence of legal protection, and the nonexistence of union activity.

Thus, in the context of a segmented and globalized worker collective, a single company can combine different strategies within the same production process, with a technological design coordinating the whole, for the extraction of surplus-value ranging from the most barbaric and primitive modes of production of absolute surplus-value to the most refined strategies for the production of relative surplus-value. For example, subcontracting schemes often serve not only for technical flexibilization, but also for worker casualization; imposing working days over the legal limit, liberalizing severance procedures and evading employer obligations such as the provision of medical insurance, holiday pay, profit sharing, overtime, etc.

In this way, a polarized labor market is established. At one end is a relatively small core of qualified workers who enjoy social security, usually guaranteed by the company itself, as a reward (given that it is no longer a right) for their loyalty and membership of "the family." At the other end is "an army of 'soldiers of fortune', a work force 'external' to the corporate community, extremely mobile, in certain aspects 'nomadic' and deprived of job guarantees; workers with no identifying references, a solitary crowd of freelancers with minimal qualifications, prepared to accept employment according to the logic of the auction" (Revelli, 2004). Revelli suggests that this tends to constitute "a 'caste-based' labor market, structured into 'separate bodies', each one with a differentiated legal status" (Revelli, 2004).

---

[15] Flexibility: "the adaptation of labor markets to technological innovations and the changing rhythms of the economic cycle... accompanied by... training and relocation of workers" (Sotelo Valencia, 1999: 118).

So far, I have analyzed the neoliberal offensive as a two-stage process. In the first stage, a technological foundation essentially inherited from Fordism and Taylorism enabled an initial political offensive in the late 1960s and early 1970s, with the relocation of segments of the work process to free trade zones in underdeveloped countries in order to weaken worker unionism in the developed nations and, in general, to shatter the institutionalism that coordinated the Keynesian pattern of domination. The success of this offensive allowed the initiation of a second stage in the 1980s, with the full deployment of the technological offensive, internationalizing productive capital, restructuring it with the results of the new technological revolution, and turning the underdeveloped nations into something like a (more or less) global free trade zone, to turn their surplus population into an industrial reserve army and organize a (more or less) global labor-power market.

A general overview of the political results obtained with the launching of its technological offensive shows that the outcome could not have been more satisfactory for capital. The composition of the active industrial army has been profoundly transformed and now bears hardly any resemblance at all to the relatively homogeneous masses of workers who all shared the same rights under Fordism. Now it is made up of castes of workers who, on the one hand, establish differentiated labor and contractual relations with capital and who, on the other hand, are of different nationalities, which means that, as belonging to a nation and a nation-state involves differentiated histories and structures, they are subject to differentiated social, cultural and political configurations.

Capital has been globalized, appropriating the monopoly of free mobility in the globalized world, excluding the workers; this monopoly and its preservation forms the basis of the neoliberal pattern of domination. This is why capital, which is such a globalphile with respect to the globalization of its affairs, is so profoundly globalphobic in relation to any attempt at globalizing worker resistance and struggle.[16] The nation-state, a space of oppression and exclusion under the conditions of the liberal pattern, was transformed by the struggle of the workers into a place of negotiation and

---

[16] Former Mexican presidents Ernesto Zedillo and Vicente Fox afforded us highly graphic and educational illustrations of how the State functions in its current *natural form* of domination. Zedillo taught the world that to be a true "globalphile" in all issues related to the "globalization" of capital means being totally "globalphobic" toward the "globalization" of worker issues. Fox taught us how to respond to any call for social justice: "And what's it got to do with me?"

institutionalized debate between the classes under the conditions of the Keynesian pattern. Under the conditions of the neoliberal pattern, particularly in the underdeveloped nations, it was turned into a prison for detaining and immobilizing workers, reducing them to virtual impotence against a capital that moved freely around the world.

In reality it is, on a different scale and under a new set of historical circumstances, a return to the 19th century, when the worker movement assumed a bourgeois-democratic mission, as discussed in the introduction to this chapter. The workers of the 21st century face the need to fight once again for the recognition of their basic freedoms of residence and occupation, of assembly, of speech and of the press, so that they are no longer deemed illegal aliens or criminals when they commit the offense of doing something that only capital is authorized to do: to move around. The unions, limited to the national arena (added to the fact that they tend to be controlled by a bureaucracy more concerned with defending its caste interests than producing a class policy[17]), do not have the capacity to organize all of the workers, or negotiate with the company, but only with a section of it, a segment which, like the lizard's tail, is dispensable for capital if the need arises.

Neoliberalism has revoked the workers' right, formally recognized since 1929, to "organize and collectively bargain their work and pay conditions." The workers of the 21st century lack the basic conditions for organization to open even the tiniest space for collective bargaining with capital, much less to fight for better living conditions under capitalism. And in light of this inability of the workers – so far – to organize a global resistance, capital systematically organizes global competition between groups of workers,[18] violently exacerbated by an unprecedented expansion not of the reserve army but of the surplus population on a global scale, as a result of technological change, the new internationalization of capital and the destruction of the production structure based on the old technology, all with particularly catastrophic effects for the underdeveloped nations.

---

[17] For example, in Mexico nobody in their right mind would even dream that the bureaucracy of the Confederación de Trabajadores Mexicanos (Confederation of Mexican Workers) might be interested in producing an *effective* policy for the defense of workers' rights.

[18] "The opportunities for 'relocation' to countries with low wage costs allows a capital with no territorial ties to set up work forces tied to different countries into competition against one another and to override national labor legislation and collective wage agreements" (Romero, 1998).

The workers of the underdeveloped countries compete with one another (wages in Mexico prove excessively high, so the 'maquiladoras' are relocated to China[19]) while also competing with the workers of the developed countries, who are forced to accept the freezing or lowering of their wages and the worsening of their working conditions (fewer benefits) to prevent the company from relocating to some underdeveloped country brimming over with starving unemployed workers. Under these conditions, the only trend to be expected is one of continued decline. Under the Keynesian pattern, labor legislation and union action prevented employers from unilaterally imposing their conditions but, if there is no containment, no social mechanism of defense, necessity will compel the workers to accept increasingly worse work and wage conditions.

The trend is exacerbated because the corporations and imperialist blocs (especially the United States with its reserves of labor-power in Latin America) use low wages as a deliberate competitive strategy: "competition from the NICs of Asia and even of Latin America appears to have the power to impose a single standard upon the whole world: constantly falling wages and increasingly flexible wage contracts... which will provoke a general erosion of social protection (social dumping)" (Lipietz, 1997). Even in Europe, where the worker struggles of the late 19th and early 20th centuries reached a higher level of intensity than in any other part of the world, and where governments appeared more cautious in the dismantling of the Keynesian pact, the trend pushing a "downward adjustment" is visible and the spokespeople for capital announce that "the welfare state has become a threat to the future... it is too expensive if compared on a global scale" (Martin and Schumann, 1997: 12–13).

The alternative that capital offers everywhere is to reduce wages, dismantle social security, eliminate severance payment costs, etc., i.e. to make the degradation of labor rights universal in order to "be competitive" and preserve existing jobs.[20] Or to share the poverty, for example, using

---

[19] "From the year 2000, a process of gradual dismantling (of maquiladoras) began due to their migration to other countries in spite of the fact that Mexican labor is among the cheapest in the world, and that the work conditions are, for 70% of the workers, exhausting, inadequate and extremely hazardous to their health... in China they are paying wages of 50 U.S. cents per hour, without benefits, unions or other obligations, in comparison with the 2.50 dollars paid on average in Mexico" (Villegas Dávalos, 2004: 29).

[20] In Mexico, according to the newspaper La Jornada on Wednesday, December 21, 2005, the president of the National Minimum Wage Committee "acknowledged that Mexican workers have to choose between a very low wage increase and unemployment and added that 'the first is preferable'."

"part-time employment"; instead of one worker with an eight-hour work-day, two with a half work-day and (of course) half pay. The fact is that what the few need is so much (Warren Buffett has only 62 billion dollars, Carlos Slim a mere 60 billion, and Bill Gates as little as 58 billion)[21] that what they can offer the many is little. Thus, the only realistic solution from the perspective of capital is that the luckiest workers should share this little with the less fortunate.

At a time when humankind enjoys the most impressive productive capacity ever dreamed of, the reality is that there is very little for many. And, as these many, in response to the distribution of this little, have so far been unable to establish a united front of labor against capital, it is natural that the distribution of the little should become a point of opposition and conflict between groups of workers: the Ah Q Syndrome, as explained in earlier, becomes universal.[22]

Workers in developed countries in particular, lacking even a minimal political vision of class, have initiated a fight to defend their privileges over the hordes of Third World immigrants. This fight is doomed to failure because it confuses the enemy and the nature of the process, so that all that is achieved is a fight against their own interests and the revival of the most perverse manifestations of racism and xenophobia, playing into the hands of right-wing parties and, in extreme cases, the neo-Nazi ultra-right. But it cannot be otherwise while the workers continue to play with the cards that capital has dealt them.

Industrial Colonialism: The Subordinate Region of Global Capitalism

In the preceding sections, I have argued that the neoliberal pattern of domination took shape as an offensive by capital against labor, which was initiated in the developed countries against the workers of the developed countries, in response to the reduction of the rate of profit that brought an end to the post-war boom – and with it, the Keynesian pact – and which had the basic objective of establishing a global labor-power market

---

[21] According to the report in the magazine *Forbes* of the richest men in the world in 2008.

[22] "The fight for the increasingly scarce resources changes the nature of confrontations: previously, for example, workers confronted their employers to obtain better wages, in a vertical relation, but now, regions or groups confront one another to redirect the lean budget offered to others toward them instead, and this horizontal conflict, instead of creating solidarity as in the case of vertical conflict, creates animosities and violence that tend to breed and grow" (Almeira, n.d.).

through the conversion of the surplus population of the underdeveloped nations into an industrial reserve army for the capital of the developed nations. To do this, capital launched a new internationalization strategy based on the free international mobility of productive capital and on a new technological revolution, thereby destroying the basis of the Keynesian pattern of domination and initiating a massive process of global historical dimensions in an attempt to increase the productivity of labor, the rate of surplus-value and the rate of profit. I have posited that the essential purpose of the internationalization of productive capital lies in the promotion of opposition between workers in the developed and underdeveloped worlds.[23]

However, while globalization began as an offensive against the workers, it also quickly became an offensive against underdeveloped capital (and the underdeveloped state) in order to concentrate and centralize the production and appropriation of surplus-value. For example, U.S. Secretary of State Colin Powell explained the noble purposes driving their government in relation to Latin America as follows: "Our objective with the FTAA is to ensure control for American corporations of a territory that runs from the North Pole to the Antarctic; free access, without any hindrance or difficulty for our products, services, technology and capital throughout the hemisphere."[24] His words neatly express the trend in the world today: supported by the developed states, developed capital seeks to appropriate the entire underdeveloped world as a space for production and appropriation of surplus-value.

A necessary step for the internationalization of productive capital, of course, is to persuade the underdeveloped countries of the benefits of opening up to the free circulation of capital and, therefore, of dismantling all forms of protection of local industry and state regulation established during the period of the developmentalist or "socialist" pattern of domination. The uneven results of this varied task of persuasion (which has ranged from coups d'état and military invasions to financial crises and restrictions followed by generations of structural adjustment plans) and

---

[23] "The expansion of the new order to the periphery has been one of the fundamental pillars of the process of capital transnationalization. It is the capacity of capital to organize a production process on a global scale, locating each of its phases where its cost is lowest, that has facilitated the gradual recovery of the rate of profit through an offensive against labor, driven by competition between workers with markedly different wage levels and the expansion of the industrial reserve army in the areas of greatest resistance to the deterioration of living and working conditions" (Arceo, 2002).

[24] As quoted in Dimas, 2002.

the different forms of resistance posed against the process are indicative of the uneven advances in the process of liberalization of the underdeveloped world to developed capital in Asia, Africa, Latin America and Eastern Europe. The FTAA project expresses the trend, with regard to the U.S. approach to Latin America, but with uneven levels of development in different parts of the Americas, NAFTA being its most finished product.

However, with at least part of the underdeveloped world brought within range of free mobility, capital's next step is to select where to establish what segment of its productive capital. Diverse factors influence this decision, including geoeconomic and geopolitical factors arising from competition between the three major imperialist blocs, administration by the local state to create a "good economic and political environment" for multinational corporations (i.e. public investment in constant and variable capital), industrial organization, transport costs and the location of markets, and the availability of natural resources in the country or region in question.

In this regard, there are two factors of particular significance. The first relates to the different national conditions of labor-power, which essentially define the location and segmentation strategies for productive capital; the aim is to coordinate the optimal combination of worker collectives in terms of wage levels, labor rights, technical qualifications and skills, lack of political organization, worker discipline, etc. The second involves the possibilities of industrialization in the underdeveloped world, which have come to depend on the location strategies of the big multinationals and, therefore, as the other side of the coin, on the countries' ability to make themselves attractive to those multinationals.

All of the underdeveloped countries that have opened up to the free international mobility of capital have left behind the industrialization strategy of import substitution. Now, it is basically the administration of the work force made available to big multinational capital that determines the possibilities of industrial development in the underdeveloped world: "it is a new kind of enclave economy, through the development of an updated version of the peripheral exporter model, in which the exploitation of natural resources is replaced, with similar results, by *cheap labor*" (Arceo, 2002, emphasis added).

For example, U.S. multinationals have an interest in NAFTA, an agreement that is typical of inter-imperialist contradictions, as part of a competitive strategy against the European and Japanese multinationals within the U.S. market, but based on cheap labor in Mexico: "the MNCs looked for competitive advantages in Mexico to win back positions in the heart of the

U.S. market... The form adopted by the new pattern of industrial colonialism in Mexico is directly in line with the interests of big U.S. corporations in relation to competition within their own national market... U.S. corporate investment takes the form of the annexation of a strip of Mexico to its own internal market *as low wages and other advantages justify dealing with other countries"* (Figueroa Sepúlveda, 2001: 26, emphasis added).

In the previous section, I analyzed the internationalization of productive capital as a global offensive against workers. My purpose in this section is to highlight a different dimension: the internationalization of productive capital and its strategies of profit maximization as central to the possibilities of industrialization in underdeveloped nations and the effects of this dynamic on their production structure. From now on, their possibilities of industrialization will depend on being chosen by the big corporations as the location for some segment of their production processes, and this situation becomes more drastic the more open the underdeveloped country is to the free mobility of capital in all its forms (not just in production, but also money-capital) and, as a result, the more drastic its renunciation is of any attempt to maintain an autonomous strategy of industrialization and protection of its internal market. China is an example of selective openness to production capital and commodity capital, while Mexico is an example of indiscriminate openness.

Opening up to the productive capital and commodity-capital of the developed nations necessarily involves a process that contributes to the destruction of the local industrial base, as underdeveloped capital is not competitive.[25] It therefore means mortgaging the future to become an attractive option for the establishment of segments of multinational productive capital and to compete with other countries in a similar situation in terms of their cheap labor-power, their basic source of international competitiveness; under these conditions, competition is inevitably based on constantly falling wages and increasing casualization of labor. Social dumping thus becomes a basic competitive strategy.

What were known in the now long forgotten days of Keynesianism and developmentalism as developing countries have disappeared, and in their

---

[25] In Mexico, it is easy to document hundreds of cases of whole companies and industrial sectors that have disappeared as a result of trade liberalization. One of these is the production of automotive harnesses: "the independent producers of harnesses established in Mexico during the phase of import substitution industrialization... disappeared or moved into the spare parts market. Mustafá Mohatarem comments that 'small, inefficient and corrupt Mexican producers have gotten out of the game.'" (Carrillo and Hinojosa, 2003).

place appear what are referred to as newly industrialized countries (NICs), industrialized in pieces, with fragments of production processes: "workshop-subsidiaries within the global strategy of the multinationals – in their worldwide production network – which maintain minimal ties with the local economy as they do not form part of a wide network of local suppliers" (Arceo, 2002). Developmentalism, whose inability to overcome underdevelopment constituted its limitations and its crisis, was replaced with a new pattern of industrial colonialism (Figueroa Sepúlveda, 2001),[26] which, as it develops, distances the underdeveloped countries even more than before from the conditions for the performance of general labor, as it involves a reduction even more drastic than before of the performance of immediate labor. Under developmentalism, commodities were produced; under neoliberalism, only a segment of the production process of a commodity is assumed.

However, as an industrialization strategy, Lipietz claims with a hint of irony, it has its advantages: "the technical composition of capital in these companies is particularly low. This industrialization strategy thus avoids one of the drawbacks of the import substitution strategy: the cost of importing capital goods" (Lipietz, 1997). And this is as it must be, because the purpose is precisely to take advantage of cheap labor by relocating the more labor-intensive segments of the production process. The one small problem with such an advantageous strategy is that the production structure of the underdeveloped countries is radically transformed, increasing economic and political subordination to the needs and interests of the developed pole of the imperialist relation while the working and living conditions of the workers are severely deteriorated. If, as I explained in the first chapter, domination defines a basic relation in which one group orders and others obey, with the conditions of the neoliberal pattern of industrial colonialism, developed capital sought to establish new and powerful reasons to be obeyed in the underdeveloped world.

The separation of producers from the means of production and subsistence, the separation that constitutes the capital/wage-labor relation, acquires a new dimension. While developmentalism was founded on a specific configuration in the distribution of the means of production which gave a special place to the state and to underdeveloped capital, neoliberalism promotes a massive process of concentration of the means

---

[26] A brief description of the "pattern of industrial colonialism" is offered in Section 3.4 of this work.

of worldwide production into the hands of the big capital of the developed countries; the big multinationals are leading a process aimed at destroying underdeveloped private capital, privatizing and transforming state capital and deindustrializing the underdeveloped nations, turning them into maquiladoras for partial production processes, subordinate links in the production chain (Gereffi, 2006) that makes up their global factory. Manufacturing activities have been concentrated into a few sectors and a few corporations – basically big multinational monopolies or oligopolies – and, after fifty years of developmentalist efforts, the old industrialization has been destroyed and any attempt to build a national industrial system has been abandoned.

Capital and the state in the underdeveloped countries have even lost control of primary production and the capacity to ensure national production of the foods their population needs, as well as control of their basic resources. Not only do the agri-food multinationals enjoy the conditions and possibilities for organizing the production and marketing of all food products worldwide, but also, as they control global scientific and technological research (biotechnology, genetic manipulation, nanotechnology, etc.), they have a plan to control and monopolize worldwide food production; in their strategic project, they seek to ensure a monopoly in food production from the beginning, from seed production, thereby disabling any other source of production. The development of this project represents, for the first time in history, a drastic break away from traditional agricultural production, the production that has fed mankind since the dawn of civilization.[27] Inward growth, which has its political correlate in the developmentalist pattern of domination, has been replaced by a new modality of outward growth, with a strict, direct subordination to the needs of the developed pole, no longer as producers of raw materials and food products, but of labor-power, and the neoliberal pattern of domination provides the political framework for the new form of exploitation and accumulation.

The imperialist relation between development and underdevelopment has been redefined, determined by the process of neoliberal internationalization of the capital of the developed nations (particularly by the internationalization of productive capital) and, although it is a process in

---

[27] The huge importance, not only *economic* but *political*, of this control of both food production and strategic natural resources worldwide should not be underestimated (see, for example, Klare, 2002 and ETC Group, 2008).

progress that is arousing growing popular opposition and resistance, it has generated trends in its development that can be summarized as follows:

First, as it de-industrializes underdeveloped countries (i.e. destroys the industrial production plant that they constituted during the developmentalist period), it produces a new industrialization, no longer anchored in underdeveloped capital, but associated with the internationalization of the productive capital of the big monopolies and their criteria of profitability, and set within a process of concentration and centralization of capital, concentration of production and appropriation of surplus-value worldwide.

Second, the workers of the underdeveloped world are converted into an industrial reserve army for the developed world, and subjected to a strategy of internal division and competition, in a downward adjustment process that also drags down the workers of the developed world.

Third, with the new levels of labor productivity worldwide (a product of the development of the effects of a multifaceted new technological revolution, together with de-industrialization and the destruction of traditional agricultural economies in underdeveloped countries), there has been a widespread increase in unemployment, in the surplus population and in social exclusion, leading to various processes of social degradation and desperate searches for ways to survive.

The historical cycle of underdeveloped capital is coming to an end and this is one of the processes that define the trajectory of neoliberalism as a specific historical period. Although with uneven results, depending on the resistance encountered along the way (popular resistance more than resistance from underdeveloped capital itself or from its state), developed capital has initiated a massive process of enormous historical significance, to take direct control of everything of interest to it in the region of the world historically subjected to the rule of underdeveloped capital. Developed capital, which for centuries has coexisted with its underdeveloped counterpart, now has sufficient power to transform the production structure of the whole world. Viewing the process within the broader historical landscape, the death of underdeveloped capital should not be a reason for anyone to mourn. However, it should be borne in mind that under developmentalism, for all its faults, the complex framework of production in the underdeveloped world which connected private and state capital, together with non-capitalist forms of production such as traditional agricultural production, provided a means of subsistence for many millions of human beings. The well-advanced process of its destruction is provoking an enormous social upheaval, not only due to the crisis between underdeveloped capital and labor, but because it will inevitably lead to a crisis situation for the capital/wage-labor relation as a whole.

There are still remnants of traditional agricultural production and underdeveloped private and state capital in the production chains of the big multinationals, but, as the process develops, these countries cease to be underdeveloped (i.e. administrators of underdeveloped capital differentiated from developed capital) and become something that we might call the subordinate region of global capitalism, which tends to unite the negative characteristics of their underdeveloped past with new ones derived from their increased vulnerability to the developed pole of imperialism.

CAPITAL AND THE GLOBAL FINANCIAL OLIGARCHY

At this point it would be useful to turn briefly to the agents of the process, the producers and beneficiaries of the neoliberal order – the dominant faction of the neoliberal pattern of domination. As has been shown, the freeing up of the international movement of all functional forms of capital (money, commodities and production) has tended to develop in degrees, in modalities and at rates which, to a large extent, result from the circumstances of inter-imperialist competition. The establishment of a truly global market is unlikely until the inter-imperialist struggle is resolved one way or another.

However, with the development of this global market, although still in its infancy, it is worth noting that, within the space of "free mobility" opened up for big capital, competition has been exacerbated[28] and, to deal with it, an intense process of corporate reorganization and global centralization and concentration of capital has begun, with mergers and acquisitions between big monopolies – manifestations of an intensified fight for production and appropriation of surplus-value.[29] The number of corporations is constantly shrinking while their size and market share

---

[28] "The wind of competition has become a storm, and the real hurricane still lies ahead of us" (Heinrich von Pierer, President of the Siemens global consortium, as quoted in Martin and Schumann, 1999: 15).

[29] "In the decade from 1990 to 2000, the rate of mergers and acquisitions increased to a level never seen before, beginning in 1990 with a total of 462 billion and closing in the year 2000 with an incredible peak of 3.5 trillion U.S. dollars, representing an increase of 7.5 times the initial level" (Ribeiro, 2007).

grows, leaving a handful of huge global oligopolies controlling the economy of the planet.

According to a report published by the Action Group on Erosion, Technology and Concentration in 2004, of the 100 biggest economies in the world, 51 were companies and the rest were countries. The combined sales of the 200 biggest corporations in the world represented 29% of worldwide economic activity, and the global value of corporate mergers and acquisitions jumped to 1 trillion, 950 billion U.S. dollars – a leap of 40% compared with 1 trillion 380 billion dollars in 2003: "it's no secret that transnational corporations wield unprecedented power to shape social, economic and trade policies" (ETC Group, 2005b); they are the tyrannosaurs of the world market, deciding on everything from who produces and where, to what reaches the consumer, with what quality and at what price.[30] Far from slowing down, the rate of capital concentration and centralization continues to accelerate: "according to the market analysis firm Thomson Financial, the total value of corporate mergers and acquisitions in 2006 reached 3.79 trillion U.S. dollars, representing a 38 percent rise in these types of transactions over 2005. According to the firm Dealogics, the total value was even greater, topping 3.98 trillion" (Ribeiro, 2007).

The intensity of competition demands a faster dynamic of technological change. The positioning of the oligopolies in the market is the result of the rapid introduction of innovations, and the strategies to protect their technological monopoly intensify: "often overlooked," notes Silvia Ribeiro, "but with enormous power, is the growth of market dominance through intellectual property oligopolies, manipulating patent expiration with minimal modifications to extend the life of patents, and, associated with this, the strengthening of global technology cartels" (Ribeiro, 2007). Competition revolves around "economies of scale" (optimization of the product range), "economies of location" (proximity and response speed) and "economies of specialization" (market niches), and for a single

---

[30] Wal-Mart, for example, according to the report, "is the world's largest corporation and the world's largest purveyor of food. A titanic power in global retailing, its corporate conduct affects business practices (labor, trade, environment and technology) all over the planet. The company has 1.7 million employees; an estimated 138 million people shop at Wal-Mart every week." It is no coincidence that, as the report adds: "thirteen years ago, due to pressure from the United States, the UN Center on Transnational Corporations in New York was shut down and the intergovernmental community lost its capacity to monitor global corporate activity. The United States is undoubtedly less enthusiastic today about corporate monitoring than it was in 1993... ETC Group notes that access to corporate intelligence is increasingly harder to come by" (ETC Group, 2005b).

corporate giant to achieve these three types of "economies," it must structure flexible global networks with plants of different sizes in different locations (Pérez, 1986).

Financial capital (in the strict sense), commercial capital and productive capital comprise the global financial capital that organizes its process
of domination and exploitation with an internationalization that is quali-
tatively different from that developed during the Keynesian pattern of
domination; it is the dominant capitalist faction in the era of the neoliberal pattern of domination, which acts "in global markets through global
transactions, with global visions and perspectives, with a global composition of capital and a global distribution of profits" (Arceo, 2002).

These are third generation monopolies: the grandchildren of the
national monopolies which, established by their respective nation-states
in the late 19th century, led to the imperialist division of the world and the
two world wars, and the children of the multinational monopolies of the
post-war period. The financial oligarchy that personifies this global financial capital constitutes what Petras calls the global ruling class, the select
club of billionaires who control the economy and the politics of the world,
who have been joined by the nouveau riche billionaires, made wealthy by
the processes of privatization of the underdeveloped and ex-socialist
countries (Petras, 2007).

Together with the "front line politicians and scientific leaders of the five
continents," these billionaires constitute "the new 'global brain-trusts'
who will point the way 'toward a new civilization'... the new lords of the
planet... the global players" (Martin and Schuman, 1999:35).[31]

---

[31] Martin and Schumann add: "358 multimillionaires put together are as rich as two billion five hundred million people – nearly half the world's population" (Martin and
Schumann, 1999: 35).

CHAPTER SEVEN

THE NEOLIBERAL STATE

A compact ruling elite seeks to plan, direct, structure and order all human activity on the planet, backed up by their huge economic and financial power. So vast is this power that these elites no longer even think in terms of the planet, as they consider the whole world to be their planet.

Salbuchi, Adrian,
El Cerebro del Mundo: La cara oculta de la Globalización

The neoliberal economy is associated, in a logical interrelation, with a mode of positioning of the state and a mode of configuration of the social sphere; a model designed with the purpose of concentrating all of the world's wealth (regardless of the poverty, unemployment and degradation of working and social conditions that this may cause) is what defines the neoliberal state and its social order. In the preceding chapters, I examined the essential dynamic of the neoliberal pattern of domination as an offensive launched by the capital of the developed nations against the workers of their own countries, with free international mobility of capital as a condition for reestablishing (on a new scale) the conditions for the natural form of domination, and the necessary inclusion of the underdeveloped world (Latin America for the purposes of this analysis) as a condition for the conversion of its surplus population into an industrial reserve army for the big capital of the developed countries. Neoliberalism is a radical offensive on the part of big financial capital against the working class of the whole world and, given that it seeks to concentrate the production and appropriation of surplus-value into the hands of the big capital of the developed world, it also constitutes an offensive against underdeveloped capital.

This offensive assigns to the states of the developed pole in the imperialist relation the task of ensuring free mobility for their big capital, at least in the underdeveloped region that constitutes the sphere of influence of each imperialist bloc. Hirsch describes the neoliberal state as a

competition-based nation-state[1]. But its competitiveness is a feature arising from its basic nature: its permissiveness, its acceptance and its resolute
support of all capital initiatives to increase the mass and rate of profit. This
is why the first task assumed by the neoliberal state (as discussed in the
previous chapter) is to dismantle practically all of the political controls
over the activities of capital.[2] The economy is "autonomized," converted,
in accordance with the natural form of domination, into an "independent"
sphere, regulated only by the immediate and insatiable thirst for surplus-
value. Only when free international mobility for capital has been assured
do states compete against one another to make themselves attractive to
capital investment; capital moves freely from one country to another,
nation-states compete to attract it, and the workers, lacking an institutional structure that would enable them to negotiate with internationalized capital, are trapped in institutions restricted to the sphere of the
nation-state.[3] Nation-states, which were once places for the economic and
political coordination of national capital, now acquire a new function: to
assure, within their respective territories, the conditions for the reproduction of global capital by imposing a specific political order on their working class, thereby preventing the globalization of the workers from
accompanying the globalization of the capitalists.

In effect, the result is a return to the absence of political, economic and
social rights for workers. In the 19th century, under the liberal pattern of
domination, the workers lacked rights at the level of the nation-state. At
the end of the 20th century and the dawn of the 21st, capital and the imperialist states are organized internationally and, once again, the workers are
confined to the ghettos that are the dwelling places of the world's pariahs,
people with no rights – only now those ghettos are nation-states.[4]

---

[1] "The State in globalized capitalism may be defined as a 'competition-based nation-
state'. This is a State whose policy and internal structures are determined decisively by the
pressures of 'international competition for the optimal position'" (Hirsch, 1996: 99).

[2] Hirsch himself points out that "States abandon political control over the markets...
and the interests of internationalized capital become direct determining factors for
national government policy" (Hirsch, 1996: 97).

[3] *"Although the relations of exploitation are global, the conditions for those relations are
established nationally"* (Thwaites Rey and Castillo, 1999).

[4] "The globalization of capital," says Hirsch, "relies on competitive nation-states and on
the inequalities arising from them," and he adds that "the basic meaning of the nation-state
type of political organization for the capitalist class [is]: it confines populations within
national borders, but not capital... it creates the structural possibility of politically and
economically dividing human beings and social classes to set them up in confrontation
against each other... The political organization of the individual state can be manipulated
by dividing the holders of labor-power and setting them up in confrontation against each

What follows is a brief outline of how this new confinement of workers to the ghetto of the people with no rights occurs. Firstly, I will examine the state in the developed world, with particular reference to the United States; I will then turn to the underdeveloped world (which has now become the subordinate region of global capitalism), with particular reference to Latin America and Mexico. There is no need to explore the absurd theory that "globalization" represents the "end of the nation-state"[5]; all the conditions for the new stage of capitalist development necessarily require the strengthening of nation-states – particularly imperialist ones – as they are the political instruments of the big multinational corporations.

On the one hand, we have the organization of inter- and supra-state institutions and mechanisms over which there is no public control, as they exist outside the public controls established within the framework of the nation-state; national governments and international institutions cooperate with multinational companies to organize the process of global accumulation, consolidating its basic condition – free international mobility for capital.[6] Of course, this is not a question of nations but of classes. The states of both developed and underdeveloped nations are emptied of democratic content: "the 'spaces' and institutions that define the basic parameters of an economy that cannot be understood except on a global scale are now the International Monetary Fund, the World Bank, the 'technical' bodies of the European Economic Community, etc.; centers, for all intents and purposes, removed from the 'democratic' decision-making mechanism... The result is the tendential 'political' emptying of the 'state-form'... its transformation into a body that executes decisions made in the headquarters of the 'multinationals'" (Revelli, 2004).

On the other hand, the regulation of class relations remains firmly tied to the nation-state and tends to become more authoritarian the more limited the state's capacity is to mediate and contain the voracity and pillaging of capital and the more international competition forces the trend of downward adjustment. Although the three imperialist blocs (the U.S., Japan and the European Union) seek to create their own international institutional frameworks, adapted to the expansion of their capital, the

---

other... this enables the reciprocal and systematic oppression of national populations" (Hirsch, 1996: 76, 98–99).

[5] For an example of the defenders of this idea, see Ohmae, 1997.

[6] "The most fundamental political decisions are disconnected from the democratic processes of determination of the will and the interests of the people... political decisions are made in direct negotiations between governments and powerful multinational consortia" (Hirsch, 1996: 100).

United States, the surviving "superpower" of the previous period, is the main promoter of international institutions and standards; its efforts have been aimed at redefining the functions of the old Bretton Woods institutions (the UN Security Council, the International Monetary Fund, the World Bank and NATO) in which it holds a hegemonic position and veto powers, in order to promote its international interests, while also promoting the creation of new institutions such as the World Trade Organization (which emerged from the now defunct GATT).

Through these international institutions, the United States has gradually appropriated the "right" to limit the activities of other states (including developed states) and to decide which government – especially in the case of underdeveloped nations – is compatible with the international order promoted by the U.S. itself. It has thus been gradually turning into an imperialist state that recognizes no law but its own.[7] Nevertheless, at least until the inter-imperialist struggle is resolved or takes a different turn, insofar as developed countries are concerned, these institutions are the forum in which their agreements and disagreements are processed. On the other hand, the relation they seek to establish with underdeveloped nations is one of direct command and obedience, under penalty of condemning the disobedient states to the dangerous world of the (as the U.S. calls them) rogue states, the axis of evil, the terrorist states[8]; the world of the potential victims of one of the preventive wars unilaterally declared by the United States, as recently occurred in the case of Iraq.

The governments of the underdeveloped nations are given instructions, required to provide guarantees of obedience, and positioned in competition against each other, and their good or bad behavior is evaluated and endorsed. And through this paternal and loving tutelage, they make the transition to democracy, in spite of the fact that the social base of the imperialist relation within the underdeveloped countries – their local

---

[7] With regard to the 'national security strategy of the United States of America', Rossana Rossanda notes that the U.S. "has buried the period following the Second World War when the United Nations and its Charter became the only forum for decision making and the only source of legitimation of relations between States. The United States denies both the content and the method; they are the ones who decide the universally valid ends, identify the dangers and proceed to impose them by any means necessary. It is better if others follow them, but not essential." Rossanda, 2003.

[8] In this world of *disobedient* States can currently be found – for different reasons, undergoing distinct processes and not forming any kind of common front – North Korea, Iran, Cuba, Venezuela, Bolivia, etc., while others (Afghanistan and Iraq, for example) have been *punished* and, with their *rebellion,* have become a problem that seems unresolvable for the U.S. government.

agents – is a constantly shrinking minority, more distanced from society, exhibiting increasingly authoritarian behavior and more and more dependent on domination strategies designed abroad.[9] This extreme subordination of the underdeveloped pole to the developed pole in the imperialist relation is the political expression of the economic transformations that the underdeveloped world has experienced[10] under the neoliberal pattern of industrial colonialism, as examined earlier.

Regalado Álvarez stresses that it is an offensive launched by the imperialist nations "against the principles of sovereignty, self-determination and independence of (underdeveloped) nation-states, which are subjected to a growing number of transnational legal frameworks and corresponding coercive mechanisms to guarantee their compliance" (Regalado Álvarez, 1999); the imperialist states – the United States in particular – transnationalize their legislative, executive and judicial functions through so-called transnational laws that are "unilateral" or "extraterritorial," and impose international treaties and supranational institutions (both global and regional). The result of all this is a drastic reduction of the sovereignty of these states and, along with verification, control and penalizing mechanisms, the organization of what is known as international "governance"[11], which applies not only to matters concerning international relations, but also the internal functioning of states. Much more than during the previous period, the "production workshop of domination strategies" is located outside the underdeveloped countries, as the imperialist states assume direct control over the underdeveloped world.

---

[9] In reality, there is no contradiction in describing increasingly authoritarian regimes as making a "transition to democracy" if it is taken into account that, in the neoliberal dictionary, "democracy" essentially means "agreeable to the United States." Thus, for example, Iraq was invaded, as President George Bush explained repeatedly, to "restore democracy." On the other hand, "terrorist" is defined as "troublesome to the United States"; in the "new U.S. police State... the government decides who the terrorist is and does not need to present evidence to support its decision... The central principle is that anyone can be or cease to be a terrorist at any moment, depending on changes to foreign policy or in business" (Saxe-Fernández, 2006: 239).

[10] "Although over the course of the history of neocolonialism in Latin America and the Caribbean, the national bourgeoisies enjoyed certain spaces undisputed by imperialism for their reproduction as a social class, and held at least a portion of the power of the nation-state, these bourgeoisies are now being absorbed and destroyed by the multinational financial oligarchy and, consequently, the level of political power they are able to exercise is being reduced" (Regalado Álvarez, 1999)

[11] "The 'governance' of international institutions reduces the essential functions (of the underdeveloped State)... dividing and distributing the functions of the State and putting padlocks on its economic role" (Almeyra, n.d.).

In the case of Latin America, in addition to the institutions, treaties and agreements that perform global functions (the International Monetary Fund and the World Bank, the World Trade Organization, the UN General Assembly, the Multilateral Agreement on Investment, etc.), others of a regional character, promoted directly by the United States, also have an influence. The "Washington Consensus," the OAS General Assembly, the Initiative for the Americas, the FTAA, NAFTA, and others[12] are in many cases simple transmission channels for decisions made in increasingly private and centralized locations, increasingly distant from the control of the societies of either developed or underdeveloped countries. Underlying the new institutionalism of bourgeois domination is a private "production workshop of domination strategies" that defines public government policies.[13]

In underdeveloped countries, the result is dramatic: "the 'formal democracies' are increasingly formal, to the point that they no longer decide anything of importance. Customs policy is determined by the WTO; economic and financial policy is determined by the IMF and the 'national development plans' have turned into the 'structural adjustment plans' of the World Bank" (Ayala and Figueroa, 2001). Once the line of command and obedience in the imperialist relation between developed and underdeveloped poles is established, the developed nations demand guarantees of obedience from the underdeveloped. The first of these guarantees is, of course, free mobility for their capital, the establishment of a trade system that is as open as possible, and the removal of any government restrictions on the degree of integration of local production with multinational productive capital.

This is followed by a cascade of as many additional demands as the submissiveness of the local government and the resistance of the public will allow,[14] including guarantees against the risk of expropriation,

---

[12] To even attempt a list of the webs that the United States has woven around Latin America – particularly Mexico – in the social, economic, political and military spheres is beyond the scope of this work; it is also important to note that to a great extent, many of the projects developed in this area are not disclosed to the public (see, for example, Saxe Fernandez, 2007). Regarding U.S. military positioning in Latin America, see Petras, 2002.

[13] The role played by so-called 'think tanks' in the development of public policy should also be considered. See, for example, the strategic guidelines for the U.S. government in relation to Latin America proposed in the Santa Fe documents (Committee of Santa Fe, 1980; 1988), and the articles by Abu-Tarbush, 2005 and Salbuchi, 1999.

[14] The projects for the FTAA and the Multilateral Agreement on Investment (MAI) reveal that the big multinationals certainly don't lack imagination in establishing their demands. The FTAA, according to Estay, ensures "the most complete facilities and

unrestricted remittance of profits, the elimination of any restrictions on the activity of transnational capital, the reduction of taxes, the provision of an adequate infrastructure, the resolution of problems related to transport, customs barriers, etc., and, of course, the flexibilization of labor legislation, which means the reduction to as close to zero as possible of all workers' rights.

Among the wide range of demands that may be imposed on underdeveloped states, there are two that require particular attention. The first is the demand to privatize public goods and services, which were the support and basis of national development during the developmentalist period. This demand has two objectives: an economic one, as the state transfers profitable businesses to financial capital, usually at bargain prices. But there is also a political motive: to ensure regulation by the market, dismantle the regulatory capacity of the state, reduce its intervention and, in this way, defuse electoral risks. The levers of the economy are privatized and delivered to multinationals, and the state is deprived of a significant source of revenue which, together with the tax privileges offered to the multinationals,[15] aggravates its financial crisis, making it more dependent on foreign financing and virtually destroying any degree of national independence.[16] The state loses the capacity not only to direct the economy but even to finance it, resulting in a fiscal and budgetary crisis, larger debts and greater dependence on international financial capital.

---

guarantees to foreign capital, and in particular to the major corporations of the hemisphere (the vast majority of which are U.S. companies), putting these companies in a position to establish the best of all possible scenarios for their full penetration into the economies of Latin America and the Caribbean" (Estay, 2004). And the MAI, according to Borón, "proposes no less than the unconditional surrender of society, represented by the State, to all the dictates of capital... it is a kind of one-sided 'International Treaty of Investor Rights' and a constitutional charter that sets forth the conditions for the full hegemony of transnational capital" (Borón, 2001).

[15] The result of these tax privileges for multinationals is, on the one hand, that taxes on wages increase while taxes on profits fall and "tax havens" abound: "the Cayman Islands, with its 14 square kilometers and its 14,000 inhabitants, has five hundred banks and thousands of registered companies and, of course, is the meeting place of a veritable *Who's Who* of barely disguised captains of finance and industry. In this way, capital evades national jurisdiction" (Almeyra, n.d.)

[16] "If the threatened denationalization of electricity and petroleum – already decapitalized and disconnected from the economy and the scientific and technological development of the nation – were carried out, it would fatally accentuate the State's budgetary crisis and increase even more the dependence of companies and the government on the policies of the International Monetary Fund, the World Bank and the U.S. Office of the Treasurer. In other words, it would plunge Mexico into a payments crisis, subjected to insistent demands from globalization and neoimperialism for the delivery of more wealth, resources and territory" (González Casanova, 2000).

This loss of capacity to direct the economy imposed on underdeveloped states is complemented by a second demand: to "autonomize," to change the mode of operation and decision-making in key institutions related to the design of government economic policy; in other words, to disconnect them from local decisions and tie them to external institutions, as part of the "governance" of international institutions.[17] A reflection offered by González Casanova illustrates the point: "the autonomy of central banking from the Mexican government and its integration into the network led by the World Bank increased the authority of the international organizations and major powers over investment and public spending programs in Mexico... The autonomy of central banking deprived Mexico of the possibility of facing the crisis with a monetary and investment policy aimed at promoting the growth of the internal market" (González Casanova, 2000).

During the period of the developmentalist pattern of domination, the bourgeoisie of the Latin American nations was assigned the role of promoting a relatively autonomous process, although always within the limits of underdevelopment, and the local states were given some capacity to direct the process. But under the neoliberal pattern, through the imposition of the "generations of reforms and structural adjustments" that constituted successive adaptations to the demands of big capital, the imperialist bourgeoisie has taken direct control of the most profitable activities in the economies of underdeveloped countries, and local states have generally turned into offices at the service of transnational monopoly capital, reduced to managing the development of the general operating conditions and the supply of labor that each country offers to transnational capital.

With these conditions established,[18] it is evident that states – particularly the underdeveloped ones – are positioned as "competition-based nation-states," according to Hirsch's definition. And this need to compete to attract transnational capital is imposed by the state on all groups and social classes (with the exception of course of transnational capital itself), while at the same time any opposition to it is repressed. States compete to

---

[17] This is, of course, part of a systematic strategy to *sterilize* democracy, as the local spokespeople for *globalization* themselves admit: "it is the necessary institutional armor of democracy against the distrust aroused by its *seasonal* and *fast-paced* politicians" (Luis F. Aguilar, as quoted in Camil, 2005).

[18] "Winning competitive capacity became the aim of States *from the moment that* big capital had successfully imposed its free market system" (Figueroa Sepúlveda, 2001: 21, emphasis added).

attract global capital, making the creation of optimal conditions for that capital their fundamental political priority and becoming caught in a spiral which – viewed from the logic of capital – has no limits, as capital will always demand more and will always seek out, among the different national scenarios, the one that offers it more.[19] Its establishment within specific national boundaries is always provisional and, the moment a better offer appears, it will move on without any regret whatsoever; the chief concern of the states thus becomes not only attracting investment from global capital, but preventing it from leaving.[20]

The circle is closed with the evaluation (and the corresponding reward or penalty) not only of the obedience of local governments, but of their initiative and active involvement in responding to the needs of capital. There is a direct and brutal manner of evaluating the behavior of states, which is simply withdrawing from the territory of a state that has failed: "the activity of the market itself, if there is full freedom of international activity at the global level, tends by its own nature to give financial capital greater disciplinary power... Its mass withdrawal from countries open to its activity in response to a policy that it rejects brings penalties which are greatly feared in terms of exchange and financial crises and contraction of the real economy" (Arceo, 2002).[21]

Capital flight from a country is the most extreme consequence of a negative evaluation, but capital has designed detailed procedures to inform the states of their desires and needs, i.e. their criteria for a positive evaluation. Ultimately, the main intention is not to punish, but to foster appropriate government behavior and, to this end, clear and exact instructions are required, as well as flexible adaptation and corrective mechanisms

---

[19] "The struggle to attract investments is at the same time a constant effort to deepen the impoverishment of the workers and move resources toward big business... In this way, the financial oligarchy reproduces its world, as if its ravenous hunger for profit could never be satiated" (Figueroa Sepúlveda, 2003: 40).

[20] For example, in spite of its geographical proximity and the existence of NAFTA, U.S. companies decided to move their maquiladoras from Mexico to China, in search of labor-power that is even cheaper than that offered by Mexican workers: "How could Mexico respond to this new situation? By reinforcing the same old mechanisms; i.e. pushing down the cost of its labor, introducing 'pending' reforms related to opening up to foreign investment and enhancing tax incentives to attract that investment" (Figueroa Sepúlveda, 2001: 40).

[21] On the same topic, Hirsch points out that the threatened response to any measure that affects capital profitability is the *flight* of that capital: "this reaction of capital has been made possible because there are now almost no political barriers to its international mobility, and because the technical conditions for the flexible relocation of production are constantly improving" (Hirsch, 1996: 98).

that will bring about specific day-to-day practices in government institutions. The general recipe for success, according to the experts on the topic, consists of the following: "companies and government institutions need to be agile, quick to change processes, intelligent in their ability to understand customer needs and demands, and mentally prepared to accept new concepts and offer original services" (Cortada and Hargraves, 1999: vii). It goes without saying that, for neoliberal states, the most important (and almost the only) customer is the multinational corporation.

Thus, following the instructions of their priority customer, they embark on an endless search for what they call excellence, quality, relevance, integration into the globalized world; in a word, a search for competitiveness, defined as "the country's ability to attract and retain investment."[22] But it is also an assessable competitiveness: "it is not enough to be competitive, it is necessary to be assessed," i.e. to be recognized by the customer as competitive. And to be assessed, it is necessary to specify the assessment criteria. Various hardworking institutions contribute to this specification process, including the World Economic Forum, the World Competitiveness Center and the International Organization for Standardization (ISO).

The World Economic Forum, created "thanks to the contribution of the world's 1,000 foremost corporations, contributes to economic growth and social progress, with an entrepreneurial spirit, in the global public interest... The Forum serves its members and society by promoting collaboration between entrepreneurs, politicians, and other leaders in society, with the aim of defining and discussing fundamental issues on the global agenda... In 1995, the World Economic Forum was recognized as a consulting body by the United Nations Economic and Social Council."[23] And, as an outstanding contribution to the fulfillment of its noble goals, every year the Forum publishes its Global Competitiveness Report.

The World Competitiveness Center[24] whose annual report, "the most renowned and comprehensive report on national competitiveness," assesses 61 national economies using 312 different criteria, grouped into four competitiveness factors. A basic obstacle to competitiveness highlighted in its reports is "institutional inefficiency"; i.e. the existence of "barriers that make it impossible for global capital to establish itself in a

---

[22] This is the definition of "competitiveness" offered by the Mexican Institute for Competitiveness (IMCO). See their website: http://www.imco.org.mx/
[23] The information included here has been taken from the World Economic Forum website: www.weforum.org
[24] http://www.imd.ch/research/centers/wcc/index.cfm

particular region," and the general formula to overcome this lack of competitiveness lies in offering "moderate working costs, more flexible work conditions, less environmentally rigorous legislation, and a certain level of political stability with institutions that offer confidence and infrastructure" (Rosselet-McCauley, 2010).

The International Organization for Standardization (ISO), in response to an agreement by the World Trade Organization, produces international industrial and business standards (ISO standards), the purpose of which is the coordination of national standards in order to facilitate trade and information exchange: "in the context of competitiveness policy, the aim is to adapt goods and services to international standards."[25] ISO 9000 and 9001 standards organize processes for "continuous improvement in the customer and market relation focus... affecting quality management of products and services... establishes a comprehensive system by supporting competitiveness through quality management," and it is expected that they will be adopted not only by companies, but by government, educational and other institutions. Competitiveness thus becomes measurable and assessable; the rules of "competitiveness," the desires of the "customer," are specified exactly. External assessment becomes a mechanism for the imposition of decisions, and the criteria and assessment scales become instructions or public policy templates, the primary source from which the policies of every state are drawn. But thanks to new information technologies, the states of underdeveloped countries are subjected to a level of supervision never seen before, placed on a network – on the international competitiveness network. But the process of international interconnection doesn't stop there, as the external assessment criteria are taken on as their own by the governments of the countries. In Latin America, several different governments have promoted the creation of local replicas of the World Competitiveness Center in order to perform their own internal evaluations applying the center's criteria. Some examples are offered below.

The Corporación Andina de Fomento[26] for the development of what it calls its strategic project, the Competitiveness Support Program, received assistance from Harvard University's Center for International Development to set out the conceptual base for its activities and, "under the leadership of Professors Michael Porter and Jeffrey Sachs, the center provided

---

[25] The quotes in this paragraph have been taken from the ISO website (http://www.iso.org/iso/en/ISOOnline.frontpage)

[26] http://www.caf.com/view/index.asp

the research and documentation necessary for the creation of a competitiveness agenda and the discussion of public policy."[27] In Mexico, in February 2004, on the occasion of the opening of the Mexican Institute for Competitiveness (IMC), then President Vicente Fox declared: "I share the vision of this group of entrepreneurs. I believe that this will be of great strategic use to our country, in order to make competitiveness *the top priority* on the economic agenda and turn this instrument into a true competitive advantage" (Fox, 2004, emphasis added).

In a report prepared by the IMC, this valuable institution "of great strategic use" which, as indicated above, defines competitiveness as "a country's ability to attract and retain investment," asserts that "in recent years Mexico's competitive position has deteriorated," and among the causes of this grave situation, highlights that the "lack of flexibility of labor regulations provokes the growth of the informal sector, as it is more costly and complicated to execute contracts in accordance with the law" (Instituto Mexicano para la Competividad, 2003). It is not surprising that the findings of Mexico's competitiveness institute regarding the country's lack of competitiveness coincide fully with the recommendations of the International Monetary Fund: "To increase potential growth and maintain competitiveness, it is essential to reform the energy and telecommunications sector and the labor market, including the reduction of obstacles to the hiring and firing of workers and the reduction of non-wage costs" (Cason and Brooks, 2004b).

Guatemala's National Competitiveness Program (PRONACOM), which is supported by various international organizations, such as the World Bank, the U.S. Agency for International Development and the Inter-American Development Bank, describes competitiveness as a global proposal for civilization, as the true reason, discovered at last, for human existence. The program explains that competitiveness has a macro level (all of the general policies: exchange, monetary, financial, taxation, tariffs, and security and justice, among others); a meso level (joint work activities involving public, production, labor and academic sectors); a micro level (training and citizen organization needs for proactive confrontation of the different challenges posed), and concludes by presenting its meta level: "the construction of an environment suitable for competitiveness at the level of ideas, culture, and social and political organization, in which the

---

[27] Information obtained from their website (http://www.caf.com/view/index.asp?).

different social groups share the same values and attitudes."[28] And, as a fitting reward for so much effort, Latin America has its own Competitiveness Report. In 2002, the first Latin American Competitiveness Report was published "in collaboration with Harvard University's Center for International Development," with the purpose of "complementing the World Competitiveness Report published by the World Economic Forum" (Revista Inter-Forum, 2001).

All of these centers promoting competitiveness assert that it is "a task involving everyone" (each and every one of us is human capital and, if we take on the task appropriately, we constitute social capital), which means that all of society is subordinated to the supreme goal of becoming attractive to transnational capital. For example, the Latin American Center for Competitiveness and Sustainable Development (CLACDS) considers it necessary "to promote changes in public policies, corporate strategies and civil society initiatives" (Fernández Lagraña, 2006). And to promote this "task involving everyone," they establish what might be labeled Competitiveness Promotion Brigades. In the suburbs, offices, schools, universities, government departments, political parties and unions, those most prone to catching the Ah Q Syndrome virus are recruited, motivated by the expectation of winning some reward, in imitation of the zeal and diligence of Jehovah's Witnesses, to preach the supreme command: be competitive. In a quasi-religious ritual, which generally follows the same pattern, they assert with fearful solemnity that "globalization is a risk" but, they add with a smile from ear to ear, "it is also an opportunity." They then go on to explain in detail what to do to take full advantage of this wonderful opportunity.

The task of the brigades (the due fulfillment of which is periodically subjected to external assessment to determine whether they are still worthy of being rewarded) is to translate the needs of global capital, the desires of the customer, into guidelines for organizing the daily activities of their community and, in order to prevent any dissidence, to represent the reality principle ('this is what we need'), while promising some kind of reward ('if we develop ourselves as human capital and as social capital'). The brigades constitute a social scaffolding which, supported by the networks of power deployed from the think tanks and global institutions in an environment characterized by the destruction or absence of a collective construction of alternatives, result in a relatively effective social

---

[28] Information taken from the PRONACOM website, http://pronacom.org/web/index.php.

leadership. In Gramsci's terms, they form part of the civil society of neoliberalism; part of the downward network that disseminates the neoliberal conception of the world and connects.

To complete the panorama of the submission to their interests that the multinational corporations demand of nation-states, we should also consider the concept of risk rating, defined as "an opinion on the solvency and security of a particular financial instrument issued by a given institution" (BBV, n.d.). Country risk is supposedly an objective measurement of the capacity of a country to assume its financial debt commitments at the international level; the rating is issued by Risk Rating Companies – Duff & Phelps, Standard & Poor's, Moody's Investors Service, Goldman Sachs, and Chase-JP Morgan being among the most important. The greater the risk, the more expensive the credit for the country that assumes the commitments. However, it is also a means of political positioning of international financial capital, and raising the risk rating can function as a warning or as a reprisal from investors for some political behavior that disturbs them.[29] And in the context of the panorama of submission and external assessment, it should also be remembered that the U.S. government (the only indispensable state in the world is the United States) implements unilateral certification processes for the "good" or "bad" conduct of sovereign nations, reports on the human rights situation in other countries, and demands alignment with its policies regarding the "war on drugs," the "war on terrorism," "preventive wars," etc.

The official name for this whole process of submission to the interests of transnational financial capital and – in the case of Latin America – submission to U.S. government supervision, is transition to democracy. Around the world, neoliberalism proposes as a political model the establishment of formal democracy; although the institutions and processes of liberal democracy continue to operate, "the essential political decisions are disconnected from the democratic processes" (Hirsch, 1996: 100).

Neoliberal democracy is, in reality, "a new historical form of authoritarian state" (Hirsch, 1996: 101), operating on the basis of one basic

---

[29] Two brief examples illustrate this idea: Standard & Poor's gave its customers a timely warning and raised a yellow alert based on the possibility that if leftist candidate Andrés Manuel López Obrador and the Party of the Democratic Revolution (PRD) won the Mexican presidency, the country's economic policies could suffer dramatic changes (Consuegra, 2006); and Goldman Sachs established a 'Lula-meter' tracing a connection between *country risk* and the increasing likelihood of Lula Da Silva assuming the Brazilian presidency, with the malicious intention of frightening part of the electorate (Dudley, 2002).

restriction: a drastic restriction of choice. The states cannot and must not do anything other than ensure free mobility for capital, compete to attract it and administrate the work force entrusted to them. A rigid conditioning is imposed, as inescapable as if it were a divine law; according to neoliberal ideology, nobody controls globalization, it cannot be modified in any way, everything must be adapted to its demands and there is no other possibility of progress. Neoliberal democracy is democracy that de-politicizes and de-citizen-izes, if by politics we mean (in the theoretical tradition dating back to Rousseau) a collective effort to define and construct a social order that guarantees all individual rights, and by citizenship we mean the right to participate in the definition of the social order. It produces democracies that are sterile, unstable, and incapable of contributing to the constitution of the social order.

In liberal democracy, citizens are legally defined as the owners of the means of production, and workers are excluded from this right. In what we could call Keynesian democracy, the workers, through the construction of a corporate forum of negotiation between the classes, acquire a certain degree of citizenship. But neoliberal democracy establishes two types of citizens; first-class or real citizens, who make the decisions that define the social order, and second-class or imaginary citizens, who merely vote to choose the political personnel that will administrate the social order defined by the first-class citizens.

The real citizens are hard to find because, being modest by nature, they shy away from unnecessary publicity. But I have already examined how all important political decisions aim at the creation of a system of organizations and political institutions beyond the scope of democratic control, and how the states have become subordinate to the interests of transnational capital and the institutionalized structures that it has created (the World Trade Organization, International Monetary Fund, World Bank, etc.), shaping a "hierarchically structured framework of states, international organizations, multinational consortia and mafia-type criminal organizations," (Hirsch, 2000), a "compact ruling elite that seeks to plan, direct, structure and order all human activity on the planet, backed up by their huge economic and financial power. So vast is this power that these elites no longer even think in terms of the planet, as they consider the whole world to be their planet" (Salbuchi, 1999).

The imaginary citizens have a fleeting and cyclical existence. They appear during each electoral period, vote and then disappear again. But thanks to them, the rulers within the so-called political class are chosen; those entrusted with the administration of the local governments, responsible for offering the most profitable conditions possible to capital at the expense of the well-being of their societies. Although all members of the political class (who are "uniform in appearance and conscience, primarily concerned with material privileges and their own private interests," free of ideology, as for them "politics is a 'job', a vehicle for pursuing a career and an opportunity for personal enrichment") belong to the "monolithic neoliberal party" (Hirsch, 2000), they are segmented into secondary parties in order to organize electoral competitions and win the votes of the imaginary citizens, thereby creating "a branch of mass media show business."[30]

In the electoral competitions, the parties make promises that cannot be kept, their social base disintegrates or is distanced from them, and "the negative image and breakdown of state institutions are accentuated, along with the separation of real politics from the electoral process" (Regalado, 1999).[31] In the developed nations, Hirsch notes, the political class seeks legitimacy by promoting a kind of racist and nationalist "welfare chauvinism"[32], calling for solidarity among "those who have and earn more" against the enemy, the outsiders, particularly immigrant workers; immigrant bashing is thus a popular campaign strategy. The goal is not for the workers in developed countries to improve their working and living conditions by reorganizing their mode of relating to and their capacity for negotiating with capital, but to defend and preserve what's left by fighting immigrant workers.

But in the underdeveloped countries, where the level of class conflict is necessarily more acute, specifically in Latin America, even neoliberal democracy represents a certain degree of risk and discomfort for the masters of the world, especially when social movements break the electoral monopoly of the political class. Such has not been the case in Mexico, firstly because the political class that rules the country – the local version of the monolithic neoliberal party, organized into three main parties (in simple terms, the right-wing PAN, the centrist PRI and the leftist PRD) – is

---

[30] "In the competition between party machines, the primary aim is to differentiate the product using commercial propaganda industry techniques, and to organize and promote show fights with high viewer ratings, whose presentation and realization poorly conceal the basic conspiracy between the opponents" (Hirsch, 2000).

[31] Almeyra suggests that "merely institutional politics, when parliamentary institutions don't count, leads to the integration of the parties into the state machine and into the logic of capital: corruption, seizing good positions, and unprincipled voting" Almeyra, 2004).

[32] "They are transformed into *apartheid* regimes, which exhaust all their energy in the militant repulsion of anyone who might threaten the privileges that still remain" (Hirsch, 2000).

increasingly disconnected from the needs of Mexican society,[33] as its political priority is to do business,[34] which is why the members of the political class belong to the parties.[35] Their political activity depends more on the mass media than their connection with the citizens,[36] is based on advice from the United States,[37] is lacking in principles[38] and fails to resolve national problems.[39] But it is also because this same political class

[33] "Political reforms have led the country to the creation of a political class that only represents itself, distanced from the life of its society and of its voters. This political class does not feel compelled to explain to society its view of the world and the future, or to account for the empty promises made by its members when the time comes for them to commit to the insipid hollowness of fighting to the death for political seats and for positions and budgets" (Blanco, 2006).

[34] "The law permits the creation and operation of political parties to turn into a business with funds from the treasury and no relation to the public function that defines them" (Bendesky, 2003).

[35] "Under 'normal' political conditions, the internal conflicts of the parties would already have given rise to new formations, as they are irresolvable. But this doesn't happen because of the persistence of the *monopoly on registration, the key to all prerogatives.* The result is that the diversity that actually exists is not expressed institutionally, but instead has the effect of paralyzing the internal organization of these parties, or is fabricated to reflect the position of their candidates. Can a grouping of individuals with no ideology, prepared to sell out to the highest bidder, be called a 'national' party?" (Sánchez Rebolledo, 2006, emphasis added).

[36] "The parties and the sphere of politics are out of touch with the problems that concern society, as their analyses and proposals have been reduced to campaign spots" (Zermeño, 2003); "they see the democratic game as an exercise in image and marketing" (Sánchez Rebolledo, 2003); "the television duopoly will receive close to 8 billion pesos from the political class in payment for air-time to broadcast their campaign spots" (Rascón, 2005).

[37] "Under the pretext of "'democratizing' Mexican public life, different U.S. government departments – and in particular the National Democratic Institute (NDI) and the International Republican Institute (IRI), international arms of the two main parties in the United States – have been advising Mexico's three main parties for at least four years, and for [the elections in] 2006, the U.S. Agency for International Development will provide them with technical, political and financial support" (Garrido, 2005).

[38] "That Mexican democratic politics has turned into a circus says much about the speed of adaptation of the local politicians to international trends, and much as well about the surprising degree of disintegration of the ruling groups that command Mexico's longest-standing political formations" (Cordera Campos, 2006); "abundant use of undeclared income, derived from the treasury, but also from organized groups with illegal interests, open buying of the vote, shameless electoral mobilization and manipulation, and forced abstention... what is worrying is the apparent apathy of the public toward extreme displays of political immorality and, at the same time, the victorious reassertion that the traditional mechanisms to prevent electoral fraud have a future." (Hernández López, 2006).

[39] The Editorial of the Mexican daily *La Jornada* on Thursday, January 19, 2006, offered a harsh examination of *Mexican democracy,* asserting that "democratic processes, when they have existed, have not translated into responses to the serious social problems in the country, which remain unresolved, if not exacerbated... the parties have made a great display of ineptitude, a lack of principles and the widespread deterioration of their internal organization."

has been very careful to keep social movements excluded from real access to electoral contests, which is to be expected of the right or the center, although somewhat surprising in the case of the left. Yet in spite of the existence of a strong social opposition to neoliberalism, the priorities of the leftist PRD do not go as far as the construction of a politically unified anti-neoliberal front;[40] rather, the party is highly susceptible to the Ah Q Syndrome.[41]

Nevertheless, all evidence points to the fact that a majority of Mexicans have voted in two presidential elections for candidates of the left, more out of disgust with the center and the right than for the merits of the left itself; the first was Cuauhtémoc Cárdenas in 1988 and the second was López Obrador in 2006. But in neither case did the left show either the capacity or the willingness to oppose the frauds perpetrated by the other members of the political class, being satisfied simply to be members of that class – second-class members – but members nevertheless.[42] Under these circumstances, elections are merely a source of discouragement and will only serve either to roll back processes to construct collective alternatives by promoting the individualist cry of "every man for himself" (in a scream or a whimper) as the only option, or to push society forward in search of new spaces for organization, resulting in an increased concentration of politics in social movements.[43] Nevertheless, according to the U.S. government, Mexican democracy is worthy of praise.[44] In other countries – Bolivia and Venezuela, for example – active social movements have

---

[40] For example, *Comandante Tacho* of the Zapatista Army of National Liberation (EZLN) explained that PRD senators voted against the *Cocopa Law,* "because if a peace agreement had been reached, the Zapatistas would have entered open politics," and "they thought that they would lose all their customers" (Bellinghausen, 2003). Meanwhile, Subcomandante Marcos offers a long list of insults inflicted by the PRD on the EZLN (Marcos, 2005).

[41] Luis Hernández Navarro explains how politics operates with the PRD in the Mexican state of Oaxaca, home of the resistance movement the Popular Assembly of the Peoples of Oaxaca (APPO): "Among the techniques that a former governor of Oaxaca claims to have put in practice to control the Party of the Democratic Revolution (PRD) in the state is to give away minivans to its leaders. 'It never fails,' he says. 'The group that ends up with nothing fights to the death with the one who takes the minivan. The ones who win owe you a favor. The others mention it to their colleagues. You kill two birds with one stone...'" (Hernández Navarro, 2007).

[42] For a reflection on the political significance and forms of operation of these kinds of parties in the current climate, see Petras, 2007.

[43] For an explanation of this phenomenon, see Almeyra, 2003a.

[44] "The president of the United States, George W. Bush, received the president elect of Mexico, Felipe Calderón Hinojosa, describing the elections of July 2 as 'open and honest'... Bush welcomed Calderón warmly and even stated that he was 'very proud' of the presidential elections in Mexico" (Herrera and Brooks, 2006).

participated in electoral processes and have won them, establishing governments which, in a context fraught with limitations and difficulties (as the pathways open to the underdeveloped world are rough and narrow), endeavor to develop a political agenda differentiated from neoliberalism. For the U.S. government, these efforts constitute an emerging threat, complementary to "narcoterrorism, corruption and organized crime" (Cason and Brooks, 2004a).

Thus, from the perspective of the U.S. government, in Latin America (and, it could be said generally, in the underdeveloped world as a whole) there are two fundamental socio-political trajectories: one that constitutes a quasi-perfect democracy (i.e. that has successfully blocked social resistance to the neoliberal design) and one that constitutes an emerging threat (where some public space has been structured to seek out alternatives to neoliberal domination).

However, not only from the U.S. perspective but from the perspective of neoliberal capital in general, democracies, both in the developed and underdeveloped world – even the quasi-perfect ones – are fragile and need additional support to keep them from turning into emerging threats. This is a point worthy of a more detailed examination. In the following chapter, I will discuss the form assumed by this additional support, aimed at ensuring the order that neoliberalism imposes on society.

CHAPTER EIGHT

THE STATE ADMINISTRATION OF CRIMINAL ACTIVITY

Police everywhere, justice nowhere.

Students of the *Sorbonne* in 2007

In the preceding chapters, I have examined neoliberalism as a process launched on a global scale by the capitalist class, specifically by its dominant faction, to ensure the transition from Keynesian state regulation to regulation "by the markets," i.e. by the direct and immediate needs of capital appreciation. Its fundamental principle is that the direct and immediate needs of capital appreciation regulate everything and are not regulated by anything: practically all the political controls on transnational capital activities are dismantled, and the economy is "autonomized," turned into an "independent" sphere as required for the natural form of domination, regulated only by the immediate, insatiable thirst for surplus-value. As its purpose is both to raise the rate of surplus-value and to concentrate the sources of its production and appropriation, neoliberalism produces a radical transformation in relations both between capital and labor worldwide and between the developed and underdeveloped worlds in the context of the imperialist relation.

Imperialist capital rationalizes its cycle on a global scale, and this results (in addition to direct intervention in the political management of the underdeveloped nations) in the establishment of a new pattern of industrial colonialism (which, as its unfolds, tends toward the destruction of the industry built during the developmentalist period and the annexation of the underdeveloped countries to the economy of the developed world, thereby turning them into assembly plant countries), and in the organization of global competition between workers by establishing a nationally segmented global work force.

The neoliberal economy and its state are mutually related and complementary, but they also constitute a basic structural contradiction: while the neoliberal economy provokes profound social problems, the neoliberal state dismantles the institutional channels that would be capable of processing alternative solutions to these social ills. In spite of the excessive growth of problems afflicting society, the state is systematically disabled as a space for the regulation of the capital-labor relation, dedicated instead to dismantling the concessions won by the workers during the period of the Keynesian-developmentalist pattern of domination and subordinated to the dynamic of globalization of big multinational capital. The result is a lack of spaces for processing solutions to the problems which, as they develop, tend to produce different degrees of political crisis. In the following two sections (the neoliberal construction of society and the neoliberal ghetto), I offer a review of the general conditions for this contradiction, while the third (state administration of criminal activity) will be dedicated to an analysis of the form that neoliberal capitalism has assumed in order to operate with it.

Neoliberal Construction of Society

I will begin with a brief review of society under the conditions of neoliberal domination. To this end, it is worth highlighting two of the outcomes of the processes examined previously: first, the workers are 'atomized', reduced to managing their relation with capital individually and to seeking out individual options for subsistence; second, many workers suffer a severe decline in living and work conditions, both in developed and in underdeveloped nations, although much worse in the case of the latter.

Neoliberal Individualism

The first outcome is associated with the basis of the neoliberal pattern of domination: while in the previous stage (the different modalities of the contained form of domination) capital organized workers corporately, in this stage, capital disorganizes, atomizes and pulverizes in order to dominate the workers, particularly in underdeveloped countries. In these countries, opening up to markets results in the collapse of the industry established during the developmentalist period, replaced with the *maquiladora* or offshore assembly plant as a predominant form in industry, and with unemployment on the one hand and casual employment without labor rights on the other. This provokes the growth of the informal sector and of exclusion and, as necessary correlates, chaos, anomie, and social disorder.

Zermeño describes the situation created by neoliberalism as the spread of "the assembly plant economy with its appalling implications for human, working and living conditions, its broken and impoverished families, and its devastated natural environment," leading to a situation of "adversity and disorganization, rife with unhappiness... unemployment, violence and crime... anomie, decadence, destructiveness, disintegration, savagery, chaos, negativity, anti-social perspectives... depression, desperation, a lack of future... poverty as dehumanization, as deterioration of the human individual, as a return to barbarism... The formal world of manufacturing, trade and services stagnated, becoming regressive and throwing huge contingents of workers, employees, merchants, businessmen and almost all youth into the informal sector, into any kind of business, contraband, piracy, begging, stealing, drugs and crime" (Zermeño, 2005: 15, 16, 20, 21); the world created by neoliberalism is "a world with destroyed players and without progress, but rife with clans, mafia bosses and submissive gangs made up of ragged youth terrified by insecurity and unemployment" (Zermeño, 2005: 23).[1]

Under the conditions of the new correlation of forces between social classes, capital is not prepared to tolerate dialogue with organized workers: "neoliberalism... seeks to command a society of atomized individuals. It doesn't want negotiators; it wants solitary sellers of their individual labor-power and citizens defined by the consumption of commodities rather than by their entitlement to rights" (Gilly, 2004). To this end, neoliberalism proposes a new version of the old, well-known bourgeois individualism, aimed at three different types of individuals: the employed, the unemployed, and the company.

Among the fortunate ones, those who have employment, individual rights are disassociated from the social order and turned into privileges granted by capital, and a new form of domination is constructed which replaces organized negotiators with atomized individuals. It is not merely that, with the weakness of unions and the proliferation of flexible and casual employment, each worker has to negotiate work and pay conditions individually with the company, but that, to become worthy of this privilege, workers must surrender all consciousness of differentiation from capital; capital requires workers to belong to the company, and to build their identity with the company.[2]

---

[1] "Growing numbers of people in our societies, particularly in countries of uncontrolled openness like Mexico, have been disconnected, their patterns of cohesion and culture violently affected, disordered, atomized and pushed to extreme situations of anomie, violence and degradation" (Zermeño, 2005: 29).

[2] While "the Taylorist factory was based on the idea of a separation and structural counterpoint between the main parties involved in production... in the 'integrated factory'... workers must, consciously and voluntarily, 'surrender' their own intelligence in the

There is no longer any place for workers to organize, oppose or differentiate themselves from capital, or even to build a forum for discussion and negotiation; in this sense, the relation between the classes is depoliticized, reduced to individual particularities, and any sense of universality is broken, as the construction of interests that would transcend individual particularities, that would express the recognition of a social relation or a relation between social classes, is rendered fragile, if not impossible. While among those with employment neoliberal individualism promotes a situation of submission, defenselessness and reduction to individual negotiation, for the unemployed and marginalized it results in an anomic, desperate search for forms of subsistence, including crime, illegal migration and the "informal" sector. This issue will be discussed in more detail later.

Capital universalizes the discourse of "individual rights" and, as a logical consequence (according to its particular logic) it only allows dialogue between individuals, between equals; the individual company negotiates with the individual worker and, more generally, the individual company claims its rights as an individual. This is the rationale behind the assertion by General James T. Hill, commander of the United States Southern Command, that "radical populism" (identified as one of the "emerging threats") "undermines the democratic process, as it reduces, rather than increases, individual rights" (Cason and Brooks, 2004a); obviously, the "individuals" he is referring to are the big corporations with more economic and political power than whole nations. Of course, the problem is not that companies, even the huge multinationals, call themselves individuals, but that they impose a legal and political structure that treats them as such; the discourse of "individual freedom" and "individual rights" thus becomes a simple construction of the domain of the most powerful as unregulated space, the simple use of economic, legal and political force[3] and the reduction of the workers to defenselessness.

The core of neoliberal domination lies in its capacity to break up the social domain and promote individualism (in its neoliberal version) and

---

production process. Between the labor-power system and company management there must be established a cultural, existential continuity, a common perspective that allows no fractures... 'to build' a totally new collective identity, rooted in the territory of the factory... to secure loyalty and availability.... to subsume the existential dimension of labor-power itself under capital... to identify the subjectivity of the work with the subjectivity of capital.... to make belonging to the company the only subjectivity possible" (Revelli, 2004).

[3] Mokhiber and Weissman consider it necessary to remind us that corporations *are not individuals*: "In spite of the fact that the law often treats corporations as if they were real human beings, and in spite of the efforts of corporations to present themselves as part of the community, corporations are essentially and fundamentally different from real people and should not be granted the same rights as people of flesh and blood... For example,

free competition (i.e. not subject to any legal regulation) between workers (between employed workers and other employed workers, between employed and unemployed workers, and between workers in developed countries and workers in underdeveloped countries). As it destroys the social regulation of the class relation, neoliberalism hinders the construction of a collective order and promotes a wide range of particularities with one basic purpose: to prevent any chance of structuring a class-based political front by pushing class conflict out of view and rendering it harmless to neoliberal domination.

The Global Depreciation and Degradation of Labor

The second outcome mentioned above is so self-evident that it hardly needs emphasizing.[4] "Considered in its most abstract expression," remarks Gilly, "neoliberal capital expansion that is not subject to any controls or laws can be summarized as a universal, global process... of depreciation of labor-power on a worldwide scale, through the incorporation of hundreds and hundreds of millions of new human beings into the capitalist labor market, and the disqualification or expulsion from that same market of millions of others whose labor has become as obsolete or superfluous as the machinery that is also replaced. Competition without laws or regulation of workers within the global wage-labor market and its consequent global depreciation in relation to the mass of commodities produced would thus be the ultimate meaning of neoliberal deregulation" (Gilly, 2004).

The workers are subjected to a dynamic aimed at breaking legal restrictions and regulations, which, together with the technological transformations and the reorganization of transnational productive capital on a global scale, generates poverty[5] and unemployment, while a large proportion of the employment that survives is casualized.[6]

[in the United States] they have managed to evade a large number of reasonable regulations related to advertising by claiming that they violate individual rights under the First Amendment" (Mokhiber and Weissman, 2005b).

   [4] For a systematic exploration of this topic, see Chossudovsky, 2002.

   [5] Even as questionable as their criteria for measurement are, the figures provided by the World Bank illustrate the enormous dimensions that poverty has reached in the world today: in the year 2000, 1.1 billion people in the world were living on less than one U.S. dollar a day, and 2.74 billion on less than 2 dollars; together this represents two thirds of humanity (World Bank, 2003). According to data published by the FAO, 224 million people in Latin America and the Caribbean live below the poverty line and more than 55 million suffer from malnutrition.

   [6] According to the International Labor Organization, "the number of unemployed remained at an all time high of 195.2 million in 2006," and "the ILO reported only modest

The Neoliberal Ghetto

The issue of the dismantling of state institutions as viable spaces for workers to coordinate some form of political defense against the voracity of capital needs to be examined on two levels: first, at the level of the nation-state, especially those of underdeveloped nations; and second, at the international level. In relation to the nation-state, again the evidence speaks for itself. In chapters 6 and 7 of this work, I analyzed the process that has led to the dismantling of the government forms of the previous period and the establishment of the forms of the neoliberal state, and I pointed out that the purpose of these transformations is, specifically, to destroy any space for capital to compromise with labor and to make the state increasingly impervious to any democratic recourse whereby workers might be able to express their interests and needs.

The result of this is what some authors have referred to as the "crisis of the political"[7]: the breakdown of the system of public representation and the rejection of the political class, made up of corrupt, servile, dishonest and irremediable politicians who invariably go unpunished. Social problems increase while the "politicos" fight for the popular vote by making promises that nobody believes and playing their trump card of filtering information to the media to create scandals that demonstrate that their opponent is worse than they are.[8] In terms of the second level, the lack of

---

gains in lifting some of the world's 1.37 billion working poor – those working but living on the equivalent of US$2 per person, per day – out of poverty... there weren't enough decent and productive jobs to raise them and their families above the US$2 poverty line" (ILO, 2007). This means that unemployment and casual employment that yields an utterly inadequate income for the worker affects a total of more than 1.5 billion workers. Added to this is child labor: 246 million children in the world work and some 171 million do so in hazardous situations, subjected to various forms of slavery, prostitution and pornography, or in armed conflicts, among other illegal activities. 1.2 million children are enlisted in forced exploitation in the sex trade, which in Latin America is mostly aimed at tourists (UNICEF, 2005).

[7] In Europe, Castells explains, "there is much talk of personal insecurity, crime, violence, loss of national identity (threatened by the invasion of immigrants and the supranational nature of the European Union), of jobs in danger and social security without a future, of a world dominated by multinationals, of lives alienated by technology, of governments dominated by arrogant bureaucracies in Brussels or in Washington, of an American superpower out of control, of a European Union that is faint-hearted globally and technocratic in Europe, of financial markets where our savings evaporate without explanation, of media dominated by sensationalism, and of corrupt, servile and dishonest politicians" (Castells, 2001).

[8] The *political class* staggers from one *scandal* to the next, but nothing is ever corrected or punished. They are simply scandals that are *useful* to the media: "the media has placed itself at the very heart of politics, where the opinions and decisions of the public are

an international institutional framework whereby workers can express their interests is such that even an institution like the International Labor Organization acknowledges what it refers to as the "deficiencies in governance" of globalization: "the global markets have grown rapidly without the parallel development of economic and social institutions necessary for their smooth and equitable functioning... market opening measures and financial and economic considerations predominate over social ones... these rules and policies are the outcome of a system of global governance largely shaped by powerful countries and powerful players. There is a serious democratic deficit at the heart of the system. Most developing countries still have very limited influence in global negotiations on rules and in determining the policies of key financial institutions. Similarly, *workers and the poor have little or no voice* in this governance process" (World Commission on the Social Dimension of Globalization, 2004, emphasis added).

Of course, it is not surprising that at the international level there is no institutional framework whereby workers can express their interests, either as citizens or as workers, as globalization is a class-based design. It is structured precisely to deprive the rights of workers, not to recognize them; the whole design is globalphilic in relation to the interests of big capital and globalphobic where the interests of workers are concerned.[9]

---

formed... politics has to be adapted to a media language that has three rules: simplification of the message, personalization of policy, and the predominance of negative messages discrediting the opposition over positive messages with little credibility. All of this leads to scandal politics as a basic weapon for gaining power by taking out the opponent... all the parties have made the denunciation of corruption a favorite weapon" (Castells, 2001). In Mexico, this *institutional disablement* has reached spectacular levels in the federal government in cases such as the Savings Protection Banking Fund (FOBAPROA) and in state governments in cases such as that of Mario Marín, the "gober precioso" ("dear governor") of Puebla, and Ulises Ruiz, governor of Oaxaca: "the large-scale disintegration of society, as can be seen in the way in which political and economic power is exercised... moral decline on public display... Impunity is what prevails, along with its counterpart, the increasingly conspicuous absence of firm measures by the State to protect its citizens. In the face of the evidence, practically all discourse rings hollow. The *gobers preciosos* are now a metaphor in Puebla for the networks of complicity, abuse and arbitrariness that are rampant.... the outbreaks of violence, the persistence of insecurity, the con artists and swindlers on every corner and in every public office" (Bendesky, 2006).

[9] The spokesperson for these concepts *par excellence* is former Mexican president Ernesto Zedillo, who, while a radical *globalphile*, proved profoundly *globalphobic*, archnationalist and even xenophobic, on issues not related to the interests of big transnational capital: *outraged* by the presence in Chiapas of an international human rights committee, Zedillo asserted that "these 'progressives' from abroad who consider Mexico a country of 'oppression, persecution, injustice and mistreatment of indigenous people' need to understand that it's up to Mexicans to establish their own laws and resolve their internal

Even in the realm of the unions, where the capacity of the workers to compel capital to negotiate once seemed an irreversible achievement, the obstacles are enormous. Gallin explains that the incorporation of the work force of the so-called "former socialist" and "former developing" nations has added billions of workers to the global labor market controlled by transnational capital, who have entered that market with their own particular political backgrounds ("it would have taken a miracle for the international union movement to rise above the weaknesses of its members; it would have needed to wipe out forty years of history"), some social democratic, others Stalinist, and the rest repressed and/or corporatist: "the countries that play an important role in the global labor market and that determine the conditions on the bottom of the scale are countries where the people were severely repressed, such as China, Vietnam or Indonesia, or where they are suffering the consequences of a tough repression in their recent historical past, as in Russia, Brazil or Central America. Or they are 'hard democracies', countries where democratic forms are observed but where social power relations are established according to undemocratic rules, such as India, Mexico or Turkey" (Gallin, 2000).[10]

On the level of civil rights, the construction of a framework of international governability that would civilize neoliberal globalization, resolve its "serious democratic deficit" and give rise to the "social considerations" that have so far been ignored, has been a constant proposal of the international social movement, for example, at the World Social Forum, which has identified "the need for a global governability to regulate the new international economic powers... and to fight for the globalization of social rights," (Díaz-Salazar, 2004), and has proposed "a different globalization that includes solidarity from the bottom up, the globalization of human rights, the socialization of democracy as a universal value...

---

problems... "we Mexicans are quite right to be outraged and upset by this situation... the solution to the problems in Chiapas will be internal... we Mexicans, without the need of intervention, without the need of foreign interference, will resolve our own problems.'" (Vargas, 1998; Urrutia, 1998). Thanks to this *selective globalphilia,* after completing his term as president he joined the board of directors of three multinational corporations which had benefited during his presidency (Union Pacific Corp, Procter & Gamble and Grupo Desc) as well as being appointed chairman of a UN committee (Villamil, 2010).

[10] To this already complicated panorama should be added the fact that "the global rate of unionization is below 13% (163 million union members out of 1.3 billion wage-laborers, and this rate would drop to half as much or less if we also take workers in the informal sector into account)" (Gallin, 2000).

the universalization of care for the Earth and its ecosystems" (Boff, 2003). But the inequity that plagues neoliberal globalization, both between social classes and between developed and underdeveloped nations, is not due to "deficiencies in its governance"; on the contrary, its governance is designed to make this inequity governable, denying workers not only rights as citizens but even as laborers, while capital organizes its domination on a global scale.

It is a political design created by capital, personified by the big multinationals and by the nations of developed capitalism, particularly the United States (the "powerful countries and powerful players" to which the ILO makes a vague reference), the result of a systematic and explicit effort on the part of what I have named the production workshop of domination strategies. For example, in response to the social mobilization of the 1960s, an analysis published in 1975 titled "The Crisis of Democracy: Report on the Governability of Democracies" (Crozier et al, 1975), ordered by the Trilateral Commission, an initiative of David Rockefeller that brought together the big business leaders of the U.S., Europe and Japan, asserted that "the social expectations of citizens and their demands on the state have risen considerably, while the capacity and resources of the latter to satisfy them have fallen, generating frustration and rejection. Therefore, to propose greater participation by citizens in public life and demand greater responsibility and involvement by the state, far from making our democracies more governable, aggravates their deficiencies... Thus the solution consists in reducing civic participation, modernizing the management of society and entrusting it to social players (companies, associations, interest groups) and a few institutions which, by coordinating their interactions, will be able more easily to reconcile their antagonisms and resolve their conflicts" (Vidal-Beneyto, 2002).

Inequality and anti-democracy in neoliberal globalization cannot be understood as a problem of "deficiencies of governance," as there is no intention to correct this supposed deficiency by strengthening democracy and incorporating "social considerations" or the interests of "the workers and the poor" as the ILO suggests. The question that preoccupies neoliberal capital is not how to incorporate the interests of the workers, but how to pursue its efforts to satisfy its interminable hunger for surplus-value without placing its domination at risk. Although this is a question that admits varying responses (it is, after all, a work in progress), in the following section I will examine how neoliberal domination has been structuring its response so far.

State Administration of Criminal Activity

From the foregoing examination of the general features of the contradiction generated by the interrelation of neoliberal economics and neoliberal politics, one basic conclusion can be drawn: neoliberal economics provokes social discontent and neoliberal politics dismantles the institutional channels to address that discontent and seek alternative solutions for society's ills. Neoliberal capitalism does not build avenues to facilitate the resolution of the many economic, social and political problems it generates. If the voracity of capital is not met with any restrictions or initiatives to moderate or civilize it, and it is not prepared to contain the savagery that it unleashes, it will lead, as the logical conclusion to its internal tendencies, to increasing savagery, and its political efforts will be essentially aimed at preventing the problems and social unrest from crystallizing into opposition and resistance by the dominated. It is therefore necessary to examine the basic components of the response that neoliberal domination has been developing, to construct, as a complement to its economic and political dimensions, a mechanism designed to administrate the problems that neoliberal capital creates and fails to resolve: state administration of criminal activity as a pillar of the pattern of domination, replacing state administration of concessions.

Production of Criminals

It is easy enough to demonstrate that, if there is anything in which neoliberalism is extraordinarily efficient, it is in the production of criminals[11] and the organization of what is officially referred to as the war on crime. But the purpose here is to demonstrate that crime is essentially produced by the neoliberal economic, political and ideological dynamic and that the war against it serves to support the development of that same dynamic; the neoliberal state organizes both the production of and the war on crime, and this dual function acquires strategic importance in neoliberal capital domination and the preservation of the order that it imposes on society.

---

[11] Examining the rate of construction of new prisons in Great Britain, Bauman observes that "it is higher than any other sector of the British economy," and nevertheless "as impressive as the prison construction boom may be in Great Britain, it is nothing compared to that of the United States" (Bauman, 1999: 22).

This process is based on a transmutation that is characteristic of neoliberal domination: social problems become criminal problems, and social efforts to find solutions to these problems are substituted and blocked by the war on crime. Neoliberal domination thus sets up a dynamic that enables it to operate with the savagery that it produces, using it as a means of support for the continued production of savagery. Thus it is necessary to examine the methods whereby criminals are produced and to show how the different methods of criminal production, together with their corresponding forms of crime fighting, ultimately converge, becoming politically functional as complements to neoliberal governance so that, in the absence of a working class front to oppose it, the logic of capital can dominate the stage of social organization and close off all avenues of escape.

It is possible to identify four major methods for the production of criminals in neoliberal society: illegal migration, individual crime, organized crime and international terrorism. The core of the state administration of criminal activity is the promotion and war on organized crime, which has been extended to the war on international terrorism, particularly since September 11, 2001 and the imposition of the U.S. anti-terrorist agenda on the rest of the world. All are part of the state administration of criminal activity and constituent elements of the neoliberal pattern of domination. All find their social basis, the objective condition for their establishment, in the processes analyzed above: economic and political transformations[12] that sterilize democratic institutions as viable forums for defending rights, while also producing unemployment and debasing the living and work conditions of a significant proportion of workers, atomizing them and reducing them to the desperate search for individual options of subsistence.[13] But they also have developmental goals with differentiated political, social and even economic dimensions.

---

[12] "Half of the workers of the world – close to 1.4 billion impoverished workers – currently live on less than 2 U.S. dollars per day per person. They work in the vast informal sector – from agricultural operations to fishing, from farms to city streets – without benefits, social security or social assistance... Unemployment, in terms of people currently without jobs, is at its highest levels and continues to rise. In the last ten years, official unemployment grew by more than 25 per cent and now affects close to 192 million people in the world, or 6% of the total work force" (Rudnik and Goransky, 2007).

[13] In its own way, *even* the World Bank recognizes the profound economic inequality that currently prevails as a source of violence: "in its World Development Report for 2005, the World Bank suggests that the growing economic inequality between the different regions of the world and within countries themselves is a decisive factor in violence and the risk of [civil] war, and doubts that it would be possible even to come close to, much less to reach, the goal for the millennium set by the 1995 World Summit in Copenhagen to cut world poverty in half" (Krätke, 2007).

Illegal Migration

The more developed free trade and free capital mobility become, particularly between developed and underdeveloped countries, the more unemployment, casualization and marginality grow, especially in the underdeveloped world[14], and, as a necessary correlate, the greater the numbers are of people migrating to the developed world in search of employment and a means of existence.[15] Faced with this wave of poverty and migration, capital has positioned itself on both sides of the process to close the pincer on the workers.

On the side of the underdeveloped countries, transnational capital and its administrators (the United States, the IMF, the World Bank, etc.), together with their local delegates (the local political class), promote openness and competitiveness in the country in question to make it attractive to transnational capital investment – the only possible way, they claim, of generating the employment that the country so desperately needs. In the discourse and in neoliberal practice, to oppose this process, which subordinates everything to the supreme purpose of being attractive to foreign capital, would be madness and, probably, a criminal act.

On the side of the developed countries, the same capital represented by the same global administrators accuses migrants of being the main cause of the deterioration of the living conditions of local workers, and its political class, particularly the segment on the right of the political spectrum, coordinates the defense of their privileges while promoting hatred of

---

[14] "A significant portion of the periphery is affected by a process of deindustrialization and deconstruction of production that translates into an unprecedented expansion of unemployment and marginalization" (Arceo, 2002).

[15] "The increased exploitation of dependent countries and the concentration of wealth and employment opportunities in industrialized countries and regions provoke huge waves of migration of the most energetic, well-trained and youthful sectors of the labor force from the regions punished by neoliberal policies" (Almeyra, 2005). According to the UN, international migration reached 191 million worldwide in 2005: Europe was home to 34 per cent of total migrants, North America to 23 percent and Asia to 28 percent. Only 9 percent lived in Africa, 3 percent in Latin America and the Caribbean and another 3 percent in Oceania" (UN, 2006). As for Mexico, 400,000 Mexicans immigrate each year to the United States, which is home to 20 million legal or undocumented Mexican migrants. (Román, 2005). Mexico, following its promised entry into the "First World" thanks to NAFTA, has now become the world champion in this field: "The World Bank, in its 'World Development Report 2006: Equity and Development', ranks Mexico in first place out of 134 nations for the number of international migrants, with a total of 2 million for the period 1995–2000. In second place was China with 1.95 million, and in third was the Democratic Republic of Congo, followed by India" (Castro, 2006).

migrants.[16] Thus workers are trapped in a spiral of racism and xenophobia which takes shape in neo-Nazi political projects; one of the preferred platforms for winning votes among right-wing extremists consists in attacking immigrants.

In reality – at least up to now – the solution has not been a radical closure of borders to the flow of undocumented migrants, but the promotion of the incorporation of migrant workers into the economy under conditions of "illegality."[17] This tends to lead to the creation, within the developed countries, of a segment of workers without political or labor rights, who are denied the opportunity of permanent residency or citizenship, who live in permanent fear and who, in their defenselessness, are easily made to work under extremely casual labor conditions. This group of workers, whose most persecuted members will accept the lowest wages, thus becomes an inexhaustible supply of defenseless labor that can be regulated at will, allowing capital greater control over the labor market in developed countries.[18]

Globalization began with the capital of the developed nations crossing borders in search of the surplus population of the underdeveloped nations; now the circle has closed as this growing surplus population is laying siege to the developed countries and infiltrating them.[19] So far incapable of presenting a common political front against capital, workers are compelled to compete with each other and to hate one another, fighting for the crumbs that capital leaves them.[20] In the developed world,

---

[16] "Metropolitan democracies are transformed into *apartheid* regimes, which exhaust all their energy in the militant repulsion of any who might threaten the privileges that still remain" (Hirsch, 2000).

[17] According to Sergio Zermeño, in spite of all the controls on the border between Mexico and the United States, every day "4,600 *illegals* jump the wall, of which around half succeed in making a home north of the border" (Zermeño, 2005b).

[18] "Involuntary facilitators of the expansion of the informal economy, of deregulation of the work force, and of the elimination of rights, undocumented workers help to maintain the competitiveness of the developed economies" (Hernández Navarro, 2005b).

[19] "In the industrialized nations, the working class not only has two sexes, but many nationalities. Willing to work more hours for lower wages and without social security, undocumented workers make it possible for the wealthy nations to prosper." (Hernández Navarro, 2005a).

[20] Playing the cards that capital deals them, workers find it increasingly hard to improve the circumstances of the most underprivileged without this entailing a regression in the conditions of the most "privileged." For example, to reduce unemployment, capital has proposed, under certain conditions, to reduce the working-day... with a proportionate reduction in wages; its best offer thus consists in a strategy whereby workers must *share the poverty* which, of course, is unacceptable. Something similar occurred in France with the initiative to promote youth employment by legally establishing their *casualization* with the so-called First Employment Contract (see Iturriaga, 2006).

while their own poverty increases, workers watch as whatever remains of what were once their rights turn into privileges which they must defend against the starving hordes of immigrants. Reduced to destitution in the underdeveloped world and forced to migrate, lacking citizen and worker rights in the developed world, migrant workers are labeled illegal and, with the reinforcement of the barrier that the poverty of the underdeveloped world establishes around the privileged, they are transformed into criminals, threats to national security for the developed nations.

In the United States, laws are proposed which "locate immigration squarely within the purview of the war against terrorism" (Carlsen, 2006), turning what was previously a civil offense into a crime, limiting access to federal courts for those who wish to appeal deportation orders, speeding up the expulsion of undocumented migrants and criminalizing people who help them; meanwhile, the government orders the construction of reinforced barriers with cameras, lights and sensors on the Mexican border in zones with the highest levels of migrant crossings (Brooks, 2005): "the politicians of this country built by immigrants have chosen to divide families, persecute workers as if they were criminals and deny those who have no papers the right to work, forcing them to live in the shadows" (Brooks, 2007).

In Europe, as Mireille Mendès France and Hugo Ruiz Diaz explain, multilateral treaties are promoted to reinforce cross-border cooperation with a view to fight against terrorism, cross-border crime and illegal immigration, all in a single package, pointing to a policy that has the objective of fostering confusion between immigration, social movements, terrorism and crime, while legitimizing and legalizing liberticidal practices contrary to all European and international regulations on human rights protection, institutionalizing xenophobia and seeking to anchor in the collective unconscious the idea that immigrants are "natural" carriers of the virus of terrorism and crime. "Fortress Europe... fully adopts the logic of the U.S. government on the clash of civilizations, legitimizing *the state of international exception established by the powers against the people*" (Mendés and Ruiz Diaz, 2007, emphasis added).

Individual Crime

As the basic challenge for a growing sector of the population in contemporary capitalism is the challenge to survive, migration and integration into the so-called "informal economy," as well as organized or individual crime, constitute possible survival options[21], although these last two are reinforced because neoliberalism produces not only unemployment but deterioration of the whole social fabric. In a downward spiral aggravated by migration, families and communities disintegrate, the fabric of mediation and social and political cohesion is devastated[22] and the social construction of ethical reference points is likewise destroyed. The need to survive and the destruction of ethical reference points, promoted by the mass media of big transnational capital, transform criminal activity into something that could be called a normal employment option for many unemployed workers.

For the purposes of this analysis, further exploration of individual crime is unnecessary, beyond the recognition that it is clearly a survival strategy for homeless delinquents. What is of interest to this study is how this individual crime establishes a social basis, a source of labor it might be said, for organized crime.

Organized Crime

Between individual and organized crime there is a qualitative difference. The first is a means of individual and family survival; the second is a capital accumulation strategy; organized crime constitutes a capitalist enterprise, necessarily tied in with the framework of the capitalist economy.[23] Organized crime constitutes a successful cluster, the most profitable and dynamic production and commercial chain in the world economy today, the jewel in the crown of neoliberal capitalism, covering a wide range of

---

[21] "Hand in hand with unemployment and an unpromising future, crime, gangs and drug addiction have grown among youth" (Hernández Navarro, 2006).

[22] "Conflicts between the various communities tend to be resolved by violence, due to the decreased possibility of mediation by official institutions, such as political parties, the different churches, the unions... Conflicts within families are also intensified due to the obligation upon women, children and the elderly to look outside the family unit for the supplementary income they need to survive... Violence against women and children has become endemic, the bonds between neighbors and in small communities are broken, crime grows, and so does fear, which in turn provokes violent reactions" (Almeyra, n.d.).

[23] For example, between the women who sell drugs in the street as a means of income to maintain their family because they do not have access to paid employment, or rural workers who grow coca because they are unable to find any other reasonably profitable crop, and the gangster, there is a difference similar to that which exists between the *employer* (the entrepreneur) and his employees: the latter appropriates the *profit* while the former receive a relatively high *wage* (possible thanks to the *high profitability of the enterprise*) for work subject to high *professional* risks. Of course, prisons are filled with the former, while the latter are much harder to catch, and even if imprisoned they maintain a privileged *status*.

entrepreneurial options, officially labeled criminal activities: illicit drug handling (production, trafficking and consumption); arms trading and human trafficking (women, children, illegal immigrants[24], slaves); diverse forms of kidnapping, extortion and blackmail; theft and marketing of stolen goods (especially automobiles); human organ trafficking, and all kinds of illegal products (contraband, robbery, piracy); prostitution; imposition of protection fees on small and medium businesses; etc.

This is the illegal branch of the neoliberal economy, closely associated with the most dynamic elements of its legal branch, directly linked to arms trafficking and money laundering, which constitutes the fundamental condition for its existence (where would organized crime be without guns and money?), and expanding its influence over the global economy as a whole. The key factor behind these criminal operations, on the scale that they have reached, is their extremely high profitability, and money laundering and "tax havens" constitute their institutional framework (globalization brothels as Sader calls them[25]). Tax havens are another clear illustration (if one is needed) of the fact that "global capital" and the entire institutional framework placed at its service have the basic objective of

---

[24] In the south of Mexico, as in many parts of the world, organized crime has discovered how *profitable* the poorest of the poor can be. Migrant women ("more than 20,000 Central American women are currently working as prostitutes in brothels, hideaways and bars in Mexico's south-southeast"), especially the young and attractive ones, are kidnapped and subjected to *different production processes* involving a wide range of *commodities* characteristic of the neoliberal *free market*: they are filmed while being raped to produce porno films which have *high market demand*; sold by kidnappers to bars and clandestine brothels often owned by "local politicians, bankers and people with economic power, operating in the shadows and earning a significant income," where "they are held against their will in a situation of slavery, forced to take drugs, to cover their food and accommodation expenses" and to work as prostitutes, thereby becoming part of the *tourist package* offered to the *customer*. In some cases, their captors will negotiate with their family members for their release or to pay the cost of a *pollero* (smuggler) who will ultimately take them to the United States. Others less fortunate are sold as slave labor to clandestine factories, thereby closing their *productive cycle* (Hernández, 2009). According to the UN Office on Drugs and Crime (UNODC) human trafficking has become "a highly lucrative activity of transnational organized crime, associated and/or competing with drug and arms trafficking" (UNODC, 2009b).

[25] "[Tax havens] are micro-territories or States with loose or non-existent tax legislation, which engage in the anonymous receipt of capital through a kind of marketing of their sovereignty. Numerous banks located in these places – Switzerland, Monaco, the Cayman Islands, the Bahamas or Luxembourg, to name a few of the 60 to 90 that exist in the world – receive money from anywhere on the planet, from any person or company, without having to justify the origin of the funds. They are located on the peripheries of the major economic centers of the world – the United States, Europe and Asia… They are effectively factories for laundering the money of mafias, corrupt political leaders and corporations" (Sader, 2004.)

facilitating immediate profitability, with no concern whatsoever for any other type of consideration.

On the one hand, tax havens are associated with the strategy designed by big multinational corporations to evade taxes[26] and, on the other, with money laundering, "the indisputable reality of tax havens as a safe refuge for illicit funds... crimes of corruption, fraud, laundering, swindles, high technology crime, etc." (Jiménez, 2004). However, according to strict neoliberal logic, these tax havens are respectable places of residence of financial and banking institutions which, as a customer service, offer forms of investment which simply avoid the identification of the actual investors, taking advantage of both the laxity of local legislation (wherein lies the strategy of establishing tax havens to achieve international competitiveness) and the tolerance of the international institutions[27] interested in preserving the free flow of international capital, a basic condition of the whole neoliberal economic framework.

In this way, the criminal branch of the neoliberal economy is interwoven with its legal branch and the huge resources derived from the former[28] contribute to dynamize the latter, particularly at the hegemonic level.[29] The world leader in the laundering of money originating from this criminal branch is the United States. For example, in the case of narco-dollars,

---

[26] The pernicious and degrading effects of tax evasion on society as a whole are numerous: "tax havens and harmful preferential tax regimes affect the location of tax activities and other services, erode the tax bases of other countries, distort trade and investment patterns and undermine justice, neutrality and broad social acceptance of tax systems in general.... they reduce global welfare and weaken the confidence of tax payers in the integrity of taxation systems... thereby contributing to the 'normalization' of a profoundly unjust and regressive tax regime, which causes so much damage to the wellbeing and community of all the world's citizens" (Jiménez, 2004).

[27] "The OECD and the FATF, a body associated with the OECD, not only fail to launch any concerted action against tax havens, but in fact tolerate and accept them... European and international conventions continue to omit express reference to tax havens as spaces outside the law where all kinds of undeclared income are hidden. All of this facilitates the preservation of these territories outside the international legal framework with absolute impunity... There is a global tendency toward formal and real tolerance, if not toward the integration of tax havens into the international community" (Jiménez, 2004).

[28] "The profits derived from criminal activities such as drug or arms trafficking, terrorism, kidnapping, crimes against the financial system, diversion of pubic funds or the result of the activities of any illegal organization, before being used by the holders, must pass through an operation that disassociates the funds from their illicit origin. This process is commonly referred to as money laundering and involves 2% to 5% of the annual gross domestic product of the world, which represents 600 billion to 1.5 trillion U.S. dollars per year, according to data from the IMF" (ATTAC, 2004).

[29] The literature that can be reviewed to document the interconnection between the *criminal and legal* branches of the neoliberal economy is now quite extensive. For an operative, empirical and concrete view of the question, see Saviano, 2007.

Catherine Austin Fitts asserts that "the U.S. launders about $500 billion to $1 trillion annually... this explains the importance that this money has on the New York stock exchange, its interest in keeping it circulating in the market and the threat to its interests represented by any attempt to decriminalize narcotics trafficking" (Austin Fitts, 2001).

From this perspective, it is evident that the "war on drugs" launched by the United States around the world has purposes distinct from those ascribed to it in the official discourse. For example, Plan Colombia has, among other objectives, the purpose of ensuring that narco-dollars continue circulating within the U.S. economy: "Plan Colombia is proceeding apace to try to move narco-deposits out of FARC's control and back to the control of our traditional allies and, even if that does not work, to move Citibank's market share and that of the other large U.S. banks and financial institutions steadily up in Latin America" (Austin Fitts, 2001). The criminal branch of the neoliberal economy, like any other industry, particularly those that are globalized, produces and/or acquires its basic supplies, transforms them into finished products, transports them and markets them, forming a chain running backwards to its suppliers (construction, chemical and pharmaceutical, automotive industries, etc.) and forwards to its transport, marketing and consumption networks; it generates employment and invests in the banking system and the stock market, and engages with government authorities at national and international levels. The interests associated with organized crime are many, and very powerful, and it seems unlikely that within the top levels of neoliberal political and economic power there exists any serious intention of putting an end to it – in the United States much less than anywhere else – at least, as made evident above, not in terms of control of money laundering. What follows below is a brief overview of the arms trafficking sector of this industry, at least in the case of the United States.

In the U.S., the opposition of the powerful National Rifle Association (which unites the main arms producers in the country) against any attempt to regulate arms sales is well known. Cason and Brooks explain that at "arms fairs" the purchase of arms requires no customer record check and that "critics of the weak gun control laws warn that the alleged terrorists are also buying them in the United States to use them against citizens of this country... For the terrorists of the world, the United States is the great arms bazaar."[30] Nevertheless, Cason and Brooks add,

---

[30] "When U.S. troops searched the Al Qaeda camps in Afghanistan, they found a training manual that informed its operatives that it is 'perfectly legal' to buy high-powered

"Attorney General John Ashcroft has been a fierce opponent against the application of greater controls on sales and possession of firearms in this country," which is understandable, given that the election campaign of his boss, President George W. Bush, had been financed – at least in part – by funds provided by none other than the National Rifle Association.[31]

Arms manufacturers, like bankers who launder money and any other legal industry linked to the criminal branch, are interested in selling their products and making profits; their customers are anyone with money. They don't ask them who they are, or what they want them for; whether they are thugs or terrorists is no business of theirs. The impact of the criminal branch of the neoliberal economy is not only economic. Its politico-electoral influence is also clear; its capacity to make "donations" and finance political campaigns, particularly now that electoral processes are increasingly a matter of political marketing and costly media publicity, enables it to influence the critical moment of neoliberal democracy – the electoral moment. As a result, it may influence the composition of the staff who administrate the government apparatus.

According to Catherine Austin Fitts, the four U.S. states with the largest market share in drug trafficking and money laundering of narco-profits and other profits of organized crime, well known as banking power strongholds, are New York, California, Texas and Florida. Austin Fitts then raises the question: "Who were the governors of these four states in 1996? Well, let's see. Jeb Bush was the governor of Florida. Governor Jeb was the son of George H.W. Bush, the former head of an oil company in Texas and Mexico, the former head of the CIA and the former head of the various drug enforcement efforts as vice president and president. Then George W. Bush, also the son of George H. W. Bush, was the governor of Texas. So the governors of the two largest narco dollar market share states just happen to be the sons of the former chief of the secret police" (Austin Fitts, 2001).

With so many economic and political interests articulated around the criminal branch of the neoliberal economy, it is not surprising that this

---

firearms in the United States, and advised Osama bin Laden's followers to 'take advantage of the weak U.S. firearms laws to acquire training as snipers and participate in military exercises'" (Cason and Brooks, 2001). For the case of Mexico, the *Washington Post* published a series of articles documenting the traffic of arms from the U.S. to the Mexican cartels (see for example, Grimaldi and Horwitz, 2010).

[31] During the 2004 election campaign, "Kerry accused Bush of giving into the National Rifle Association, which supports the president's election campaign," while Bush "proposed the granting of immunity in civil trials to arms manufacturers and... supported moves by Congress to allow the expiration of the prohibition on assault weapons imposed by Bill Clinton 10 years ago" (Clarín, 2004).

branch would become an affair of state. Austin Fitts tells of a notorious criminal in New York who, when interrogated regarding whether he was involved in narcotics trafficking, replied "no, who can compete with the government?" and adds that "according to the CIA's own Inspector General, the government has been facilitating drug trafficking... the CIA and the DOJ [Department of Justice] created a memorandum of understanding that permitted the CIA to help its allies and assets to traffic in drugs and not have to report it" (Austin Fitts, 2001). Chossudovsky explains that the Bush administration projects an increase in its military expenditure to "an astounding 451 billion dollars," and adds that "This colossal amount of money allocated to America's war machine does not include the enormous budget of the Central Intelligence Agency allocated from both "official" and undisclosed sources to finance its covert operations... this amount excludes the *multi-billion dollar earnings from narcotics accruing to CIA shell companies and front organizations*" (Chossudovsky, 2002c, emphasis added).

Nor is it surprising that, with these priorities, the truly important ones for today's world rulers, no concern is given to the side effects (collateral damages, they might be called) of the operations of the criminal branch; for example, that hundreds of millions of youth around the world destroy their lives through drug addiction, that corruption invades the government infrastructure, or that society is ethically and culturally debased. As Austin Fitts explains, "you've got to have an underworld. If it does not exist, you need to outlaw some things to get one going... Imagine what would happen to the economy in Philadelphia if this stock market value suddenly disappeared because all the teenagers in Philadelphia stopped dealing or buying drugs... what would happen to the stock market if we decriminalized or legalized drugs? The stock market would crash... What would happen to financing the government deficit if we enforced all money-laundering laws?" (Austin Fitts, 2001).

LEGALITY AND CRIMINALITY

Examining the process in this way from the perspective of social relations and relations, it is evident that criminal activity, which in a diverse and complex array of modalities has been spreading throughout the social framework of neoliberal capitalism, is a product wholly produced by financial capital, the dominant faction of contemporary capitalism. When I examined neoliberal democracy (Chapter 7) from the perspective of social class analysis, I proposed a distinction between real citizens, the global financial oligarchy who make the decisions that define the social order, and imaginary citizens, who merely vote to choose the political personnel who will administrate the social order defined by the real citizens. In the examination of neoliberal crime, it is also necessary to distinguish between employer and employee; in capitalism the former always produces the latter. Earlier, I explained in some detail how the class of those dispossessed of the means of production and subsistence, compelled to sell their labor-power to capital for a wage in order to survive, are on a constant search to make themselves useful, a search for a function to fulfill within the complex social structure of capitalism, and that it is the capitalist class that assigns a place to the different segments of the dominated class, according to its needs of domination and exploitation, and distributes them throughout the economic, political and cultural structure of bourgeois society – which, it should be added, has both legal and illegal elements.

Capital produces the employees it needs; the greater the vulnerability of the employees, the greater ease capital will have in producing them. In the same section, I indicated that without a political organization that would give them some degree of identity and class consciousness and enable them to build some kind of defense mechanism, the dispossessed will be compelled to offer themselves up to the unconditional satisfaction of any capital need. In the sphere of democracy, the distinction between real citizens and imaginary citizens is significant. In the sphere of neoliberal crime, there is an important distinction between criminal capital and criminal employees produced by that capital; the crime that afflicts contemporary society is the product of the domination of neoliberal capital. It should be added here in passing that this is not the first time in its history that capital has undertaken large-scale criminal activities, even as state policy. A mere few examples (as an exhaustive list would require whole volumes) are the piracy of the 17th and 18th centuries and the black slave and drug trades of the 19th century; these examples illustrate the complex nature of the large-scale criminal activities of capital and their significance not only in economic terms of the search for immediate profit, but also in terms of the development of wide-ranging strategies with economic, political, ideological, geopolitical and geoeconomic dimensions.

However, while recognizing its long and extensive experience in the field, it must be admitted that never before in the history of capital had the development of criminal activity reached the global scale that it has today, nor has its consequences been as oppressive upon world society as a whole as they are now. It is with good reason that the authors of the Rome Statute of the International Criminal Court remark that "during this century" (referring to the 20th century, not yet having witnessed the promising start of the 21st, which looks certain to outdo its predecessor in the production of barbarism), "millions of children, women and men have been victims of atrocities that deeply shock the conscience of humanity" (ICRC, 1998). Even within the legal branch of the neoliberal economy, it is not unusual to find illegal activities. Although they may be disguised with an appearance of legality, many of the activities in this branch in fact represent serious crimes; one need only compare many of the habitual practices of the big multinational corporations and their states against the definitions of genocide, crimes against humanity and war crimes provided by the Rome Statute to appreciate the extraordinary dimensions of the problem. The criminal activity of neoliberal capital and the impunity with which it operates are reaching truly outrageous levels.[32] Although tracing its development is a task far beyond the intentions and possibilities of this work, two cases are worth noting here.

During 2008, successive waves of speculation on food products, energy and mortgage loans led to a profound global economic crisis and a process of conversion of public resources into private hands at a rate without precedent in history. In spite of the recurrence of these speculative surges – which gravely affect the living conditions of our society – no serious effort has been made to contain them. Even former senior officials including Jacques Delors acknowledge that "financial markets have become increasingly opaque... The size of the lightly or not-at-all regulated 'shadow banking sector' has constantly increased in the past twenty years... Inadequate incentive schemes, short-termism and blatant conflicts of interest have enhanced speculative trading... epitomizing *the loss of business ethics!*" (Delors et al, 2008, emphasis added). Meanwhile, as a result of these speculative dealings in the context of a systematic effort to destroy rural production in favor of the agri-food multinationals, famine (a product of food shortages and increased food prices) is devastating the most impoverished regions of the world.[33]

---

[32] According to the *preamble* of the Statute, it is necessary "to put an end to impunity for the perpetrators of these crimes and thus to contribute to the prevention of such crimes"; without doubt it is necessary, but the current correlation of forces between social classes, far from reducing crime and impunity, actually increases them.

[33] For a particularly enlightening view on this topic, see Bello, 2008.

More or less simultaneously, the world has begun suffering from a new emerging threat, the so-called swine flu, a new product of the criminal activity of neoliberal capital with the complicity of the state: "Authorities knew of the pandemic threat, but gave no importance to the warnings of scientific institutions and social organizations *as they did not wish to interfere with the economic interests of the huge farm and livestock industry and the pharmaceutical and biotechnology multinationals that profit from diseases.* To this end, fragmentary focuses that do not question the causes of the problem are useful, such as taking emergency measures when the dead and sick can no longer be overlooked, while asserting that the crisis can be resolved with more technology controlled by the multinationals. For any new viruses, new vaccines will be found – patented and sold by corporations. Even if a vaccine is found against the latest virus, the industrial breeding of animals continues to be a time bomb for the creation of *more* new viruses... Instead of attacking the causes of the epidemic, those who produced it are rewarded" (Ribeiro, 2009b, emphasis added). A threat to the lives of an undetermined number of human beings is rendered secondary to the interests of big capital; there can be no clearer definition – and this is but one among a thousand examples – of what matters to neoliberal capital.

The Multifunctional Nature of Organized Crime and Crime Fighting

The preceding sections have provided a general overview of how big global capital and its institutions shape the basic conditions for the existence of all the criminal activities characteristic of the neoliberal world, and particularly how the top levels of neoliberal political and economic power are closely associated with organized crime. The legal branch, which is becoming increasingly criminal, engages with the criminal branch and vice versa; their respective production chains and business networks are interlinked at diverse points, and it is becoming increasingly difficult to distinguish one from the other.[34]

Neoliberal capital and its institutions work to promote (it is not merely a question of tolerance, and certainly not of powerlessness, as its ideologues claim) and to appropriate the profits produced by organized crime. However, in an apparent paradox, they also work to fight organized crime, which raises an obvious dilemma: if, as I have argued, the criminal branch is so interconnected with the legal branch that to eradicate the former

---

[34] For a detailed examination of these cross-links, see Chossudovsky, 2007b.

would have catastrophic consequences for the neoliberal economic network, and if, therefore, capital has no intention of eliminating organized crime, we must ask what the purpose of the so-called war on organized crime really is.

Two points require clarification before attempting an answer to this question. The first is to recall that this analysis of the neoliberal pattern of domination is not so concerned with the economic impact of the criminal branch of the neoliberal economy, or even with its influence on political elections, but with how it is shaped, through the war on crime and in the context of the state administration of criminal activity, into a political design that closes the pincer on the structure of class domination, complementing the elements examined in the previous two chapters. The second is to stress that, although the official discourse presents criminal activity as "the great problem of our time," and although it can be reasonably argued that it has dysfunctional dimensions for the reproduction of capital viewed as a whole, my priority here is to analyze its basic functional dimensions in terms of the pattern of domination.

The state administration of criminal activity is associated with a historical form of domination which, like all forms, is provisional, following a specific course and then coming to an end. The fact that it is a mechanism plagued with contradictions and that it ultimately aggravates the internal contradictions of capital does not mean that it is not, under certain conditions and for a certain time, functional for capital domination and, more specifically, for the domination of the hegemonic faction of capital. It constitutes the form that neoliberal capital has established to operate in the context of its basic contradictions: "The change to functions of the state is the form in which the contradiction between increasing socialization of productive forces and private appropriation can operate provisionally; *it does not make the contradiction disappear, but creates the form in which it can operate*; this is the only means of resolving real contradictions"[35] (Hirsch, 1979: 64, emphasis added).

---

[35] For example, keeping criminal activity restricted to the margins of what is *functional* for capital accumulation and domination is problematic: organized crime, the product of *private initiative*, like any *normal* business, seeks to expand the *scale* of its operations and its *markets* and diversify its *products*, and it will not hesitate to levy charges, to kidnap for ransom and even to kill other *business leaders*, especially those of small and medium businesses, terrorizing and virtually paralyzing whole cities and segments of economic activity. But these are *collateral damages* – like the uncontrolled surge in the speculative activities of big financial capital which drain billions of dollars of public funds – which do not threaten the basic principle of neoliberalism: *freedom for private enterprise.*

Having offered these clarifications, I will now attempt to provide a schematic view of the meaning of the so-called fight against organized crime, and of its multifunctional nature in the structure of neoliberal domination. I have already made reference to the extremely high profitability of the criminal branch of the neoliberal economy and, at least as a general idea, that this extraordinary profitability is guaranteed by the state itself; one of the functions of the state administration of criminal activity is the production of extraordinary profits, particularly for the international financial sector and for the armaments industry.

The issue is so important in the current neoliberal economy that the phenomenon needs to be placed in relation to the basic tendencies of capitalist development and considered as a particular historical form, promoted and used by big neoliberal capital, in a counter-tendency to the tendency of the rate of profit to fall, the importance of which becomes more acute in moments of economic crisis. According to the World Report on Drugs for 2009 issued by the UN Office on Drugs and Crime, "money laundering is rampant and practically unopposed, at a time when interbank lending has dried up. *The recommendations devised to prevent the use of financial institutions to launder money today are honored mostly in the breach. At a time of major bank failures, 'money doesn't smell,' the bankers seem to believe*" (UNODC, 2009a, emphasis added).

According to ATTAC, money held in "tax havens" amounts to a total of 7 trillion U.S. dollars, which is 13 percent of world GDP, while "according to the IMF, 1.5 trillion U.S. dollars derived from activities with organized criminal groups, tax fraud and corruption, are laundered each year in these havens." ATTAC also notes that "the European Union estimates that if drug trafficking activity were halted the U.S. economy would shrink by 19% to 22%. *The lack of willingness on the part of economic and political authorities to take action against tax havens is therefore understandable*" (Serrano, 2009, emphasis added).

Moreover, this extraordinary profit, under conditions of labor casualization and growing unemployment, enables the "economic" (labor and wage) management of part of the surplus population; these activities offer relatively high wages[36] and create expectations (of obtaining

---

[36] This capacity of the *criminal branch of the neoliberal economy* to produce *employment and high wages* is modified as the branch itself is transformed according to the general logic of capitalist production; for example, the *employment and remuneration* opportunities for rural workers who participate in it shrink as drug production becomes more industrialized and natural drugs are replaced with synthetic varieties.

wealth, women, etc.)[37] among certain segments of the excluded population. As the commercial and production chain associated with criminal activities expands, veritable social frameworks are constructed in
urban districts and neighborhoods and in rural towns – what might be
referred to as Crime Promotion Brigades. For example, the so-called *tien-
ditas* (stores where drugs are sold to consumers) often work in tandem
with local police and, in some cases, with bodies that are supposed
to liaise between local residents and the municipal authority, such as
the Citizen Action Committees. This process is sometimes associated
with the promotion of the so-called urban tribes and gangs and the
conflicts between them.[38] The result is that the possibility of organizing
spaces for cohesion and solidarity among those excluded by capital is
undermined from within, and ordinary citizens – those who are neither
criminals nor police officers – are reduced to a state of isolation and
defenselessness.

Whereas in the previous period, under the Keynesian pattern of
domination, the legitimacy of the state was built on the administration of
concessions, under the neoliberal pattern the state administration
of criminal activity constitutes the new strategy for the construction of
legitimacy for the bourgeois states. The first step is the development of
public demand: "in the face of so much terrible, shocking insecurity,"
runs the official discourse, "our society demands security." And in effect,
society is restricted to demanding the minimum: security. Simply not
to be killed while crossing a street, not to be mugged, not to be kidnapped
are the new demands of society, while any demands (employment, progress, justice, welfare, equity) which during the Keynesian period were

---

[37] It is common to hear among young males in excluded communities, or at least those
who still seek opportunities within the law, complain of "girls who prefer *drug dealers*."

[38] Consider, for example, the following news article on a conflict between youth gangs:
"The *emos*, whether we like it or not, are a new generation, but I don't think that it will be
the *anarcho-punks* or the *goths* who attack them... the conscious objective is to divide
them [youth], because they can't be offered expectations for the future... The violence
between different youth gangs is nothing new; it has always existed, but now it has
increased considerably. This campaign is dangerous and could grow... The government
prefers to have youth divided rather than critical and demanding... the levels of frustration
and rage keep growing in the country and suddenly they look around not to find 'who did
this to me', but 'who will pay for it'. In Latin America there are nearly 30 million youth who
don't have the chance to study or work, and their logic, viewing it more as survival than
crime, is inclined toward drug dealing, piracy or contraband. Unless the State addresses the
employment and education problem, there will be more conflict" (Vargas and Olivares,
2008). According to this logic, the *Mara Salvatrucha (MS13)* and skinheads are extreme
cases.

considered reasonable and desirable, even by capital itself, are now forgotten.

The state closes the pincer by offering security, the war on crime, zero tolerance, and similar initiatives.[39] However, of course, insecurity is not generally reduced by this approach; on the contrary, it increases. With an audacity that works by virtue of the extreme ideological defenselessness that prevails today at the societal pole of the dominated, neoliberal capital uses its own brutality to build a particular space of legitimation that allows it to commit more brutality, not only free of the widespread condemnation of society but even with the approval of one sector. This "legitimacy" constructed through the state administration of criminal activity finds various ways of complementing and reinforcing itself. As capitalism today lurches from one crisis to another (environmental, economic, public health and other crises), capital itself attempts to exploit each of these crises to its economic, political and ideological advantage. Regardless of how they arise, whether they were planned in the centers of power or the simple result of spontaneous capital activity, nobody knows better than neoliberal capital that every crisis is an opportunity: "Today's preferred method of reshaping the world in the interest of multinational corporations is to systematically exploit the state of fear and disorientation that accompanies moments of great shock and crisis" (Klein, 2008a).

Even public health crises, like the swine flu epidemic, offer significant lessons and possibilities: "With the support of the main radio and television networks under monopolistic control, acting in the current environment as a power mechanism for the contemporary structure of class domination, the government succeeded in removing millions of Mexicans from public spaces and quarantining them in their houses, passive prisoners of the television duopoly and its talking heads... In another clear action of media terrorism, the opinion makers once again sowed alarmism, fear and desolation, and helped to construct in the collective imagination the idea of a new, devastating hidden enemy. In this manufactured environment, Calderón's health care dictatorship successfully enforced a *de facto* curfew without any formal declaration or tanks in the streets – *an*

---

[39] That this strategy of constructing *legitimacy* can prove highly effective is clearly proven by the political strategy adopted by U.S. President George Bush following September 11, 2001. In Mexico, President Felipe Calderón's strategy to *legitimize* his government has been none other than *the war on organized crime*. However, it is also a strategy with a limited life, as indicated by the growing difficulties experienced by the U.S. government to convince its citizens of the *need to continue the war on terrorism*.

extraordinary experiment in population control and social discipline" (Fazio, 2009, emphasis added).[40]

Dragged from one crisis to another and from one scare to another; all indications are that this is the future that awaits humanity for as long as it remains subjugated to the domination of neoliberal capital. These crises are the result of the profound contradictions faced by capitalism today; but such crises are also viewed as opportunities by capital, which not only fails to solve the problems it creates, but also bases its economic expansion and domination on the promotion of a brutality that is compounded exponentially. And, although it may be obvious, it is worth reiterating (because there are many people who, out of naivety or malice, declare the end of neoliberalism every time the state intervenes in the economy) that what defines neoliberalism is not the alleged opposition/mutual exclusion of the state and the market (in reality the neoliberal state is radically interventionist), but a power structure involving a specific faction of the capitalist class. It is a whole historical period, which may only be brought to an end through a profound change in the relation between social classes, between capital and labor. Neoliberalism will not be brought to an end because a frankly sinister U.S. president is replaced by a pleasant one; this change may be significant if it is truly indicative of a moment of change in the correlation of forces between social classes, but it may simply be a case of capital shedding some dead weight, just as trees periodically shed their dead leaves. Nor will neoliberalism be defeated because, in the face of the magnitude of the bankruptcies provoked by financial speculation, the neoliberal states abandon the free market and, according to Le Monde, "turn socialist" (London, 2008).[41]

International Terrorism

International terrorism, its promotion and the war against it (although it has specific dimensions, particularly in terms of the global geopolitical

---

[40] "Beyond the comparative theories, all the elements of the shock doctrine are present in Mexico. This includes economic shock therapy, the words used last week in the United States by Mexico's treasurer, Agustín Carstens; the minister said that shock therapy worked during the *Mexican flu* emergency, and that the government is preparing additional structural reforms for the second part of the year. After the elections in July – another fear campaign – the worst will be unleashed, including, perhaps, another timely outbreak of the H1N1 virus, our new Al Qaeda" (Fazio, 2009).

[41] In reality, this article by Frédéric London makes fun of the idea, but the lack of conceptual rigor in its discussion of "neoliberalism", "socialism", etc. does little to help clarify

and geoeconomic strategy of the United States[42], the analysis of which goes beyond the purposes of this work), constitutes an extension of the war on organized crime, an element of the state administration of criminal activity. With the war on organized crime, particularly when extended to the so-called war on international terrorism, society is reduced to choosing between freedom or security ("if you want security, you must renounce your freedom" is the basic argument of the U.S. Patriot Act) and is subjected to a new institutional framework which, while subordinating the human rights and civil rights enshrined in every bourgeois constitution since the great revolutions of the 18th century to the supreme objective of fighting organized crime and terrorism, grants a whole new framework of repressive powers to the neoliberal state.[43]

The state administration of criminal activity is a strategy to wage and legitimize in the eyes of society a war against society itself: big capital and its states, while maintaining a complex, multi-dimensional domination strategy, are preparing a violent challenge to the increasing resistance of a growing number of people who reject the domination of capital and its effects.[44] In its specific historical sense, the so-called war on organized crime and its extension to the war on international terrorism means that big capital is not prepared to negotiate with labor, to moderate its voracity, or to make concessions to the rest of society, but is determined, considering only its insatiable hunger for surplus-value, to pursue its purpose while violently imposing its interests.[45]

This explains why the repressive strategy of big capital has been escalating and acquiring added dimensions and increasing complexity. It would thus be possible to establish a line of continuity – not only logical but

---

the issue. In the same edition and with the same flippancy, Ibrahim Warde speaks of "a change of epoch."

[42] How useful the *war on international terrorism* has been in helping big U.S. capital to appropriate strategic natural resources, such as Iraqi oil, should not be underestimated. But more generally, while free trade has furnished the conditions for the spread of the new technological revolution, *the war on terrorism* has furnished the conditions for the spread of the U.S. *military revolution*, the most convincing of its arguments for establishing its hegemony in "the new American century."

[43] It is clear that the consequences of the *anti-terrorism* strategies expressed, for example, in the Patriot Act, Plan Mexico or the SPPNA (Security and Prosperity Partnership of North America) represent a very *real* military and repressive framework.

[44] Recommended reading on this topic includes Zibechi, 2008 and Davis, 2007.

[45] This is the meaning behind the open debate at the core of military intelligence, particularly in the United States, regarding "the three dominant theories on the war of the future that are currently being discussed in military magazines – the Fourth Generation War, the Third Wave War and the Fourth Epoch War" (Bunker, 2006).

by means of a specific process which, although involving innumerable threats[46] at its basic level – running from the war on drug-trafficking (the preferred branch for publicizing the war on organized crime) to the war on terrorism. And within this process, there is in turn a clear path that can be traced from the "selective deterrence" of the Reagan era to September 11, 2001, encompassing the Carter Doctrine of 1980 and the "Project for a New American Century" drafted in 1992: a "tendency, explicit since September 11 and implicit before it, which seeks to establish the issue of terrorism and security as one of the core issues on the agendas of the multilateral bodies, government meetings and defense and security programs of the industrialized nations" (Contreras Natera, 2007).

What began decades ago as the war on organized crime, and in particular, the war on drug trafficking, has now been interwoven with the war on terrorism and, ultimately, with a whole design based around what is labeled the war of the future; at the core of this war, according to its theorists, "lies a universal crisis *of legitimacy of the state*, and that crisis means many countries will evolve Fourth Generation war on their soil" (Lind, 2004, emphasis added).

Free trade is complemented by a preventive military positioning according to a strategy outlined in 1996 by William Perry, then U.S. Defense Secretary: "our defense strategy can be summed up in three words: prevent, deter and defeat... today there is a greater role for preventive defense measures, as more opportunities exist to prevent the conditions for conflict, and therefore to create the conditions for peace" (Perry, 1996). According to Perry, this preventive military positioning requires the construction of what he calls security alliances: "One of the most effective ways of creating the conditions for peace is to develop working relationships between military and national defense institutions around the world, including all levels from defense secretaries to sergeants in the field... We want to build security alliances in all regions, both in the Asia-Pacific region and here in our own hemisphere. And we want to promote openness, trust and cooperation between all countries with mutual security interests, cooperation which may lead to joint activities such as peace

---

[46] "Many big businesses promote crime and live off crime. There has never before been so much economic concentration and scientific and technological knowledge dedicated to the production of death. The countries that sell the most arms are the same countries responsible for world peace. *Fortunately for them, the threat of peace is weakening,* and its dark clouds are rolling away, while the war market recovers and offers promising prospects of profitable slaughter. *The armaments factories are working as hard as the factories that manufacture enemies tailored to their needs.*" (Galeano, 2006, emphasis added).

operations training, exercises and even military operations in coalitions... This is crucial for the stability of the region and for continued economic growth" (Perry, 1996).

The state administration of criminal activity operates as a constituent part of the political space which, while enabling the development of preventive military positioning, consolidates the networking of nation-states, and particularly the submission of the nations of the underdeveloped world. In Chapter 7 we saw how, as a result of the characteristics of the free market, nations are networked to compete to attract foreign investment; but the state administration of criminal activity represents another step in this process, as nation-states are networked to fight organized crime, terrorism and the countless new emerging threats that arise each day[47]: "Until the events of September 11, the U.S. military conception for Latin America was based on the definition of drug trafficking as the main threat to democratization and security in the hemisphere, although battle maneuvers had been applied to unleash low-intensity wars in the most conflictive zones of the region... In general terms, the 'war on drugs' was supposed to lead to the formation of a multinational army under supranational control; in other words, with the Pentagon in the role of commander-in-chief, and the local armed forces acting as internal police, concentrating on 'support tasks'... on October 1, 2002, a new military structure came into operation, with serious geopolitical consequences for Mexico, in the form of a joint military force to 'defend' North America: the so-called Northern Command, responsible for homeland defense in the United States against 'new threats' arising from unconventional enemies... which is complemented by the Southern Command, responsible for the Plan Colombia / Andean Regional Initiative" (Fazio, 2003).

This networking of nation-states through the construction of security alliances to fight terrorism and other emerging threats is evident in the influence of the organization and business management models developed by the big multinationals. Klein speaks of "companies that used to produce products announcing with great fanfare that they don't produce products anymore, they produce brands, they produce images, and they

---

[47] "Possible threats to the West are broadened to include phenomena such as terrorism, drug trafficking, immigration and cultural conflicts... The potential sources of threats to the global security system of the emerging New World Order were located in third world countries as a consequence of the multiple causes of conflict existing in such countries (economic disparity, nationalist interests, religious intolerance, racial hatred, demographic pressure and extreme weather conditions), which might, if their problems spill beyond their borders, threaten the security of the global community" (Contreras Natera, 2007).

can let other people, sort of lesser contractors, do the dirty work of actually making stuff. And that was the sort of revolution in outsourcing, and that was the paradigm of the hollow corporation." And, she adds, "Rumsfeld very much comes out of that tradition. And when he came on board as Defense Secretary, he rode in like a new economy CEO that was going to do one of these radical restructures. But what he was doing is he was taking this philosophy of this revolution in the corporate world and applying it to the military. And what he oversaw was the hollowing out of the American military, where essentially the role of the army is branding, is marketing, is projecting the image of strength and dominance on the globe... but outsourcing every function" (Klein, 2007b).

Corresponding to the global financial oligarchy, its governing group (particularly the top-level political bureaucracy of the United States) views itself as the administration of a global government, which it designs in the image and semblance of the global company, as a network with strategic alliances, senior partners and junior partners, designs for relocation and outsourcing, etc., in competition for world supremacy. These are the global players of the world government.

THE "UNIVERSAL CRISIS OF LEGITIMACY OF THE STATE"

The state administration of criminal activity finds its deepest meaning in the efforts of neoliberal capital to blur the class struggle, trapping society in an alleged war on criminal activity, dissolving the class conflict in a huge multiplicity of conflicts, supposedly formless, lacking any structuring focus, so that, in the absence of a united working class front to oppose it, the logic of capital can dominate the stage of social organization and close off all avenues of escape.

"In the Fourth Generation War," argues Lind, "the state loses its monopoly on war... it is a return to the style of war prior to the creation of the state. Now, as then, many different entities, not just governments of states, will wage war. They will wage war for many different reasons... And they will use many different tools to fight war... What will characterize it are not vast changes in how the enemy fights, but rather in who fights and what they fight for. The change in who fights makes it difficult for us to tell friend from foe... The change in what our enemies fight for makes impossible the political compromises that are necessary to ending any war. We find that when it comes to making peace, *we have no one to talk to and nothing to talk about*" (Lind, 2004, emphasis added).

Significant among the points made in the quote above is the notion that "the war of the future" is basically a war not between states, but between states and what Lind calls a "wide variety of non-state actors." If we consider that wars between states have been the expression of conflicts between national bourgeoisies, Lind's suggestion means that the global bourgeoisie sees itself as lacking significant national rivals, and what it is really concerned about is the opposition of the working class under its domination, although this concern is obscured behind all manner of criminals and terrorists. Thus, for big capital "there is nobody to talk to and nothing to talk about"; in other words, it does not recognize the legitimacy of any social interest in opposition to it. By this logic, the state administration of criminal activity will inevitably develop into the administration of chaos and brutality.

Joxe, examining "the political consequences of the absolute militarism of the United States" with reference to the cases of Iraq and Afghanistan, raises the question: "Might it not in fact be a total chaos strategy? ... The quick victory will no doubt turn into a lasting source of hostility against the 'liberators', condemned to the status of occupiers... The huge imperial power appears to be committed to separating the military objective from the political objective... This beginning of the 'war without end' declared by the Bush administration is a war without victory and without peace, and probably without reconstruction" (Joxe, 2003b). Although the "total chaos strategy" is particularly visible in cases like Iraq and Afghanistan, in reality it is the logical result of the development of the state administration of criminal activity, just as this itself is the result of the destruction of the institutional spaces that defined the contained form of capitalist domination (as explained at the beginning of this chapter). With the neoliberal pattern of domination, which constitutes a return to the natural form of capitalist domination, an increasing number of spaces for social organization around the world are being filled by the logic of the state administration of criminal activity and the "total chaos strategy."

The reason behind this "total chaos strategy," in terms of immediate interests, is identified by Joxe himself: "Whatever is necessary will be done to ensure that both destruction and reconstruction are sources of corporate profits, thereby saving corporate morale at the expense of political morale and intelligence" (Joxe, 2003b). But Lind goes beyond immediate interests and, as we saw above, makes it clear that at the core of what he calls the Fourth Generation War "lies a crisis of legitimacy of the state." However, he expresses no interest in exploring the factors behind this "universal crisis," or what the solutions might be to remedy it. Instead, he asserts without the slightest qualm that *"invasion by immigration can be at least as dangerous as invasion by a state army"* (emphasis added) and poses questions that clearly illustrate his intellectual concerns: "What can the U.S. military team learn from cops? How would the mafia do an occupation?" (Lind, 2004). This is his class perspective for understanding the problem, and this is the solution he offers: Fourth Generation War and the mafia as examples to follow in the construction of a social and political order.

CHAPTER NINE

IDEOLOGICAL DOMINATION – A REFLECTION ON THE INTELLECTUAL AND MORAL LEADERSHIP OF NEOLIBERAL CAPITAL

Contemporary hardships and sufferings are fragmented, dispersed and scattered; and so is the dissent which they spawn. The dispersion of dissent, the difficulty of condensing and anchoring it in a common cause and directing it against a common culprit, only makes the pain more bitter. The contemporary world is a container full to the brim with free-floating fear and frustration, desperately seeking outlets.

Zygmunt Bauman
In Search of Politics

Earlier, I noted that, for Gramsci, the state is "political society plus civil society," connecting the conditions of political and economic domination with those of ideological domination, and those of consensual domination with coercive domination. The state relates the conditions of domination to the conditions of exploitation and establishes an organic link between structure and superstructure. Moreover, I remarked that the dominant class produces its own ideology according to Gramsci's analysis. Its general conception of the world is a necessary condition for its homogeneity and consciousness of its own function in the economic and political spheres and, therefore, for its cohesion as a class. This ideology is not external either to the economics or the politics of the capitalist class, as class practices (economic and political) are interconnected, and mutually determined, with an awareness of class.

Ideology is constructed and performed, made visible and present, within the economic and political practices of the dominant class and, although it preserves its basic principles and its class-based nature throughout the history of capitalism, it evolves and is transformed along with the development of capitalism, with the emergence of new dominant factions and new challenges that arise. But this ideological production not only gives cohesion to the dominant class; it also constitutes a level (along with the economic and political levels) of class-based domination. The dominant class spreads its ideology to society as a whole, adapting it to the conditions of different social groups, organizing the culture[1] to ensure that the dominated class, as a whole and in its diversity, is subject to its "intellectual and moral direction."

The ideology of the dominant class, developed for internal consumption, examines the current circumstances from the perspective of its class interests, and develops initiatives for the future, aimed at directing decision-making in the class's centers of power. Much of this work is strictly private, undertaken by the most exclusive sectors of the production workshop of domination strategies, and may even take the form of state secrets. However, adapted for consumption by the dominated class, whose interests are always placed in opposition to those of the dominant class, the function of ideology is to conceal the actual contradictions and prevent any possibility of "developing alternative responses to overcome the conditions of subjection in which [the dominated] find themselves... The situation of alienation in which they live is fed constantly to prevent a rediscovery of themselves, a new awareness of their situation and a profound reflection that would enable them to break out of the structure that oppresses and dominates them" (Aruj, 2000).

By its very nature, the social reality of capitalism appears fetishized[2], superficial and fragmented, and, on this basis, the ideological structure of capital establishes its intellectual and moral leadership. Its goal is to achieve consensus (active or at least passive) among the dominated by presenting its projects as being in the general interests of society, as the best for society or, at least, as a necessary evil, aimed at preventing worse evils, with the assurance that there is no other option: "individuals face reality... from a perspective developed by the dominant classes to conceal from them the real circumstances of their existence" (Tagarelli, 2009). In contrast, according to Tagarelli, "the task of science consists in uncovering the dominant material relations underlying the dominant ideas in order to recover the real connections of the theory throughout the social and

---

[1] "Domination is a political relation which, on the one hand, is organized and reproduced as the State; but it is also something that is established through the organization of the culture of a society or nation. Political power is produced in the process of organization of the culture... 'Common sense' is a political production and part of the struggle for hegemony... Politics is a collection of practices instituting the shape of the social; that is, as a process that occurs as organization of the culture, involving the organization and development of the state as well as of a historical block" (Tapia, 2008).

[2] The third section of this chapter explores the issue of the fethishization of social relations in capitalism and its connection to ideological domination.

material process."[3] Meanwhile, popular culture, the purpose of which is "to comprehend and transform the social structure," is necessarily constructed in constant tension with the dominant ideology, and its function is to "reveal those elements that [the dominant ideology] uses to conceal a contradictory social reality and expose an oppressive and unequal reality, plagued with contradictions," as a condition for processes of unity among the dominated, in order to "aid in the establishment of classes and individuals as a popular force, converting the divided classes and separated groups – divided and separated as much by culture as by other factors – into a popular cultural force" (Tagarelli, 2009).

Clearly, Gramsci's theoretical proposition covers an extremely vast object of study, the general aspects of which include the examination of ideology as a construction aimed firstly at fostering internal cohesion within the dominant class, and secondly at fostering ideological domination, as well as the examination of counter-hegemonic oppositions and/or constructions developed by the dominated class. It is not possible to review this complex topic here, as the purpose of this chapter is rather more modest.

The first two sections of this chapter will therefore be limited to a general outline of the intellectual and moral leadership that capital exercises over contemporary society, in order to complete my overview of the neoliberal pattern of domination, with a basic sketch that brings together economics, politics and ideology in the current historical context; i.e. the link between the economics and politics of neoliberal capital and its intellectual and moral leadership. The last two sections constitute a reflection on neoliberal capital's project for the future, the project of civilization that it offers humanity, based on which it exercises its intellectual and moral leadership and its economic, political and ideological practices, in order to contextualize the project of an increasingly necrophiliac and genocidal capitalist class that believes itself to be at the end of history and preparing the advent of the last man.

From Collective Bargaining to Individual Competition: Neoliberal Life Options

I earlier explained how a pattern of domination results from a combination of ideological, political and economic circumstances and class

---

[3] This necessarily entails, under the conditions of capitalism, the representation of the "real" social order as conflictive, "that is, combative by nature" (Tagarelli, 2009).

practices that express wills and intentions in conflict, operating in a context of structural relations with a tendential development independent of the will and consciousness. The chapters examining the neoliberal pattern of domination include reflections which define this as a class project with an intentional, voluntary and conscious component, i.e. as the result (at least in part) of the creation by the hegemonic faction of the dominant class of an ideology that promotes political initiatives to control decision-making in its centers of power and foster the cohesion (although with internal conflicts) of capitalists as a class. I further discussed how the projects of neoliberal capital are presented ideologically to promote consensus among (or at least to defuse the resistance of) the dominated class; for example, by promoting globalization and the free market as a "response to the world economic crisis" and promising "a new era of wellbeing and economic growth," or by presenting the transformations undergone by the Keynesian state in its conversion into a neoliberal state as a "transition to democracy," or by defining state administration of criminal activity as a "fight against organized crime and terrorism to guarantee the security of all citizens."

The aim of this chapter is to examine the structural characteristics of the intellectual and moral leadership of neoliberal capital in some detail, beginning with a brief reflection on its role at the time of transition from the Keynesian to the neoliberal pattern of domination, followed by an analysis of the basic features of this leadership once it had been fully established.

The Transition to the Neoliberal Pattern

Ideological domination requires the articulation of a conception of the world and of the era and a project arising from that conception; it requires the establishment of intellectual and moral direction. In Chapter 5, I explained how, in the context defined by the world economic crisis, both "real socialism" and Latin American developmentalism, which had become obstacles to the neoliberal restructuring of world capitalism,[4] were subjected to an intense process of ideological vilification, accused of being the sources of infinite evils. With this attack, neoliberal capital was

---

[4] "The strengthening and democratization of these nation-states became obstacles to the processes and strategies of exploitation and domination of the centers of world capitalist accumulation... neoliberalism is a strategy to dismantle the complex political constructions of the 20th century which had turned into restrictions on transnational capitalist accumulation" (Tapia, 2008).

able to present its strategic initiatives as the solution to the evils of the previous period, thereby winning public support for its new projects.

The transition of the Soviet bloc from state capitalism (self-acclaimed "real socialism") to neoliberal capitalism was presented as a response to a "popular demand for democracy and universal prosperity." In the developed capitalist states of the West, this process was argued to be a "victory for democracy and the free world," and "the end of history."[5] In Latin America, the economic crisis aggravated the loss of prestige of the developmentalist state, thereby facilitating the presentation of the transition from developmentalism to neoliberalism as the solution to its deficiencies and as a "transition to democracy and modernity."

On the level of ideological domination, the key to the Latin American transition lies in the vilification of the developmentalist state; on this basis, neoliberalism launched an offensive to "replace the predominantly nationalist beliefs, through which the majority of the population organized its understanding of the country, the region and the political and economic world," with the goal of "making the privatizing content of the new economic policies compatible with the cultural and political composition of the civil societies that would have to support the new configurations of capitalism in Latin America," and promoting a new common sense, "which revolved around the idea of a global market, efficiency, competitiveness and denationalization" (Tapia, 2008).[6]

The Neoliberal Pattern

Ideological domination contributes to the viability of the economic and political projects of the dominant class; that is, it contributes to the production of real transformations. However, as these transformations develop, the conditions of ideological domination itself are reconfigured.

---

[5] "At the level of the conception of the world and of knowledge, neoliberalism articulated a discourse as a strategy to explain the contemporary context... a normative economic discourse – which, under the pretext of rationality, eliminates the possibility of considering alternatives from among which the best way of satisfying social needs might be chosen – and a political discourse that also argued for the superiority of the political culture and competitive party system of liberalism as the synthesis of all political history" (Tapia, 2008).

[6] "To legitimize the privatization processes, it was necessary to create a new common sense; that is, people needed to view the world as a dynamic of production, circulation and consumption of commodities in highly depoliticized processes, and, therefore, to assess the facts and the meaning of those facts according to this mercantile culture" (Tapia, 2008).

Thus, for example in Latin America, "the first years were ones of public and discursive resistance and confrontation. But as privatization processes advanced, and the processes of deconstruction of the nation-states dismantled the material conditions that enabled the maintenance of nationalist beliefs, the people gradually began replacing their beliefs with others that were liberal and neoliberal in nature, particularly in the urban centers where the greatest economic modernization occurred."[7]

The neoliberal ideology, with the conception of the era that it proposed (its explanations of the past and of the problems of the present, as well as its proposed solutions and promises for the future), played its role throughout the period of transition. But once the structures of the previous forms of domination were dismantled, a new reality was imposed on the relation between capital and labor, and new ideological content emerged. The point of departure in the examination of the neoliberal pattern of ideological domination is thus the new historical, economic and political situation, which is configured in the relation between capital and labor. In particular, it is worth recalling here the point made earlier that while in the previous stage (the various modes of the contained form of domination) capital organized corporately, in this stage capital disorganizes, atomizes and pulverizes in order to dominate the workers, particularly in underdeveloped countries. The neoliberal state abandoned the state administration of concessions (which characterized the contained form) as the core element of domination, thereby bringing about the collapse of the old institutional framework constructed to organize and regulate bargaining between capital and labor – parties and unions.

This context of disorganization and reduction to individual isolation engenders the ideological (and political) defenselessness of the working class, allowing neoliberal capital, in spite of its unprecedented capacity to generate inequality, injustice and savagery,[8] to deregulate its relation with labor, to impose submission to its needs and its logic, to promote

---

[7] Neoliberalism "provoked the disorganization of the material conditions for national regulation and government of the economies and countries of Latin America... The dismantling of the economic and political structures that upheld the limits and processes of national coordination and the production and exercise of social and political power from within led people to gradually replace their beliefs, maintaining national and nationalist notions for a time as a memory but no longer as a goal or project" (Tapia, 2008).

[8] "The alchemy between market, hyper-individualist values, media sensationalism, social fragmentation, widespread privatization and disintegration of the public sphere made it possible, among other things, for a model unprecedented in its capacity to generate inequality and injustice to become an essential, genuine reference point for a society seized by the most diverse forms of prejudice and suspicion" (Forster, 2009).

competitiveness and criminal activity as basic features in the construction of its new intellectual and moral leadership, and to produce alienation and fear. Competitiveness, with alienation as its correlate, shapes the life project accessible to the integrated sector of the working class and expresses the level of ideological submission that capital has imposed on contemporary society. Criminal activity – and the fear that it entails – develops on two fronts: as the ideological framework associated with the only life option that capital makes available to a growing segment of the human population, and because, as argued in the following section (taking up the argument of the previous chapter), state administration of criminal activity ultimately replaces state administration of concessions to establish itself as the core of the whole system of the intellectual and moral leadership of neoliberal capital.

Ideological Defenselessness and the Mass Media

The first phenomenon that can be identified in any examination of ideological domination under the conditions of the neoliberal pattern is an increase (in comparison with previous periods of capitalist domination) in the ideological defenselessness of the working class[9] and, in turn, increased control exercised by neoliberal capital. Contributing to this is the development of new and powerful scientific and technological resources at the disposition of capital, expressed in various ways, such as the huge influence that the communications media have acquired in the neoliberal world.

Neoliberalism, which generally fosters the concentration of wealth, also fosters the concentration of ownership and control of media outlets[10], turning them into monopolies for the production and dissemination of ideology, organizing the production of public opinion and the construction of what is important to society.[11] These monopolies control all of

---

[9] After reading various analyses on the topic, one might be tempted to classify it as *absolute defenselessness*, but there are many initiatives in process, the *germination* of considerable social resistance, which compel us to consider the ideological power of capital in the contemporary world *in relative terms*.

[10] The monopolization process underway affects not only "traditional" media (the press, television, etc.) but also new media: "Google is quickly turning into a megacorporation of the future, buying up the competition (Blogger, YouTube), making users dependent on its advertising system, monopolizing the search for information, and becoming the largest database in history, storing virtually everything... Users, without realizing, are being gradually trapped in Google's web..." (Colectivo Troyano, 2009a).

[11] "Most people are guided by the information provided by the big mass media outlets, but these outlets depend too much on the big economic powers, which in turn depend on

society's avenues of information transmission and communication, and, as a result, acquire the capacity to manipulate information and distort reality in keeping with the interests of the dominant class. In the context of a globalized world and an atomized society, they are able to replace the real world with the media world with considerable success.[12]

Capital now has access to knowledge accumulated over many years[13], rooted in extensive experience in the manipulation of information and of the spectacle, and in the evolution of social psychology and marketing. Added to this arsenal of technical and scientific resources are "the lessons learned from the appropriation made by fascism of audiovisual technologies as the core of its propaganda activity," with which it has been able to "influence the production of a new way of conceiving the world and life, penetrating to the very depths of the consciousnesses of the era" (Forster, 2009). But this increased power of the media as a factor in ideological domination[14] is explained not only by the new scientific and technological instruments at its disposition to monopolize and manipulate communication and information in society, but also, and above all, by the new historical situation in the capital-labor relation: the new correlation of force

---

the politicians. Information passes through filters, corporate parameters and self-censorship (direct threats or fear of losing their jobs), or comes so directly from government sources that the final product could be called 'disinformation'... it is the *mass media* communications system itself, so tied up with the interests of big corporations, that prevents the transmission of genuine information, establishing a system of propaganda rather than information – inculcating the world view of those who hold economic and political power... the propaganda model dominates the media" (Colectivo Yachay Red Científica Peruana, 2002).

[12] "The violence of information has made the real world disappear... the sense of reality is disintegrated, creating a different reality... the massive trade in images demonstrates a huge indifference toward the real world... it smothers *Homo-Televisus*, whose inhuman passiveness supports the cruel aesthetic of the spectacle of the destruction of the most sacred moral values... the formidable machine of propaganda, simulation, concealment and rhetoric makes it impossible for people to feel anything" (Jean Baudrillard, as quoted in Marelli, 2007).

[13] The Keynesian period produced a wealth of experience in the field of ideological domination; in Section 4.3.4, I pointed out that during this period the "production workshop of domination strategies," in conjunction with the *education system* and *the mass media*, organized the ideological and cultural messages that circulated in society, monopolizing the spaces for public communication and adapting scientific applications to *discern and influence* culture, ideology and the *behavior* of society: surveys, interviews, advertising, propaganda, marketing, etc. From that time, capital and its ideological universe began working out how to invade the daily world of the working class, although not to the degree that it has today.

[14] The literature on the topic is extraordinarily extensive, but, of the texts I'm familiar with, I would recommend Chiesa, 2008; Valqui Cachi and Pastor Bastán, 2009; and Revuelta, 2008.

between the classes and the new general conditions of domination of capital over labor.

At its deepest level, the defenselessness of the working class today – i.e. its submission to the intellectual and moral leadership of the ruling class and its inability to develop a popular culture and a counter-hegemonic project – is the result of the defeat suffered during the revolutionary crisis provoked by the collapse of the natural form of domination in its first emergence and the subsequent transition to the contained form. But in immediate terms, it is associated with a two-pronged process entailing, on one hand, the dismantling of the organizational structure that made possible and gave meaning to the political and ideological activity of the workers under the conditions of the contained form of domination and, on the other, the atomization of the workers as a result of this dismantling, which has left them with no forum for organization (either revolutionary, or even trade unionist)[15] where they could construct a conception of the era, identities of class, opinions about the problems afflicting them or a project to solve them, at least until they can reconstruct themselves as a class and establish new fields of class organization.

Even traditional institutions such as the family, the school and the church, which once constituted spaces for social bonding, are increasingly being positioned so as to contribute to the promotion of individualism and social atomization. The social network centered on the extended family, so important for the reproduction of the working class throughout the 19th and early 20th century, has practically disappeared, and even the nuclear family has been severely undermined. The status of churches as producers of social collectives has also been severely reduced, and in the place of institutionalized forms, individualized forms of spirituality are promoted, positing the individual construction of the relationship with God. Meanwhile, schools are dedicated to fostering individualism and competition, and urban tribes and cliques emerge as the new forms of socializing according to post-modernist psychologists.[16] Under these conditions, the media move in to fill the void: "the articulating axis of meaning, the mortar that seals the blocs of domination, has shifted from the old politico-ideological structures, what were traditionally called political parties, to the communication-information machine which, through this

---

[15] *Disorganized*, existing simply as a "class in itself", as a reality in the system of production relations, as a basis for the capitalist relations of exploitation, as explained in Section 2.2.

[16] See, for example, Maffesoli, 1996.

economic-cultural turn, became the guarantor of the reproduction of the system and of its logic" (Forster, 2009).[17]

Competitiveness

In Chapter 7, I explained the increased importance given to the promotion of competitiveness, i.e. skills, knowledge and feelings directed fully and energetically at serving capital, in a world where capital reigns virtually unchallenged and where so many human beings are superfluous, all are forced to compete, and all are subordinated to the supreme goal of being useful and attractive to capital. In the same chapter, I explained how the Competitiveness Promotion Brigades constitute a social framework that forms part of the civil society of neoliberalism, part of the downward network that disseminates the neoliberal conception of the world and connects society to the intellectual and moral leadership of neoliberal capital. With the transition from the Keynesian pattern of domination to the neoliberal pattern, the core of the capital-labor relation has shifted from collective bargaining to individual competitiveness.

Even as unemployment rises, as long as the state maintains minimal regulations (in terms of wages, the work day and working conditions) and the unions preserve some capacity for negotiation, some restrictions on the voracity of capital remain. But if, as is the case under the conditions that neoliberalism tends to establish, the state allows the regulations restricting the behavior of capital to become increasingly lax and the bargaining capacity of the unions continues to shrink, the workers will be thrust, as isolated individuals, into the world of free competition, forced to compete on two levels: first, in an individual effort to be useful to capital, although the reward offered – employment and a wage – is scarce and generally poor in quality; second, to compete against all other workers, both the employed and the unemployed (competing to keep their jobs if they have them and to get one if they don't), the integrated and the excluded. The lack of socially constructed alternatives drives workers toward a suicidal persistence to strive to serve capital, clinging to the increasingly implausible illusion (for a growing number of superfluous workers) promising that, ultimately, wellbeing and employment will be

---

[17] "It was the media corporations, the big entertainment and communications companies, that assumed the huge task of generating a new 'public opinion' that could be identified with the values arising from the neoliberal form assumed by contemporary capitalism" (Forster, 2009).

won, or to the illusions propagated by the media that "present a world of prosperity, luxury and abundance which we all can and must attain. A world of big winners in which the losers also win, as they never give in but keep on competing" (Aruj, 2000).

In the Keynesian pattern, the ideological perception constructed around the state administration of concessions linked the fate of the individual to that of the collective, at least in the realm organized by the corporate structures and the various individual positions admitted by those structures; it included social restraints on the voracity of capital and encouraged efforts to increase the capacity for negotiation and, therefore, the organization, if only under trade unions, of the workers. However, in the neoliberal pattern, according to the ideological perception and the immediate or apparent reality on which it is founded, the fate of the individual appears not merely disassociated from that of the collective, but even in opposition to it; the rationale is "for me to succeed, I must ride on the failure of others." But what this ideology and appearance conceal is that it is essentially the whole that defines the fate of the part. The situation of one class is defined by its relation to the other, and the economic, political and ideological conditions that organize the relations between classes are what determine that the fate of an individual belonging to the working class can appear linked to the collective in one case, and disassociated from it in the other.

The relation between classes in neoliberalism ensures that the striving of the individual to please capital contributes to the erosion of the position of the class, and actually results in the deterioration of individual possibilities of winning concessions from capital. Thanks to this dynamic, capital has discovered new conditions under which to impose harsher demands on workers (who are forced to double their efforts to please it) and to foster the emergence of abundant new reasons for new chasms and oppositions, conflicts and hatred among them, both among individuals and among groups (ethnic, national, professional, etc.). Thus, the more workers strive to please capital, the more they facilitate the development of its insatiable need for surplus labor. But this is a dynamic which workers as individuals are unable to stop or challenge; it can only be overcome when workers stop looking to capital in their aim to please it, and look instead to one another, to work together to establish conditions that will make a project of opposition to capital a viable proposition. Until this happens, the workers (subjected to a series of mechanisms that foster their separation and disassociation) will suffocate in their alienation and in a state of unrest that grows, but that fails to crystallize into the construction of a collective will and a collective project.[18]

ALIENATION

Alienation[19] is the necessary correlate to the submission to the demands of competitiveness at the service of capital. Earlier, I outlined two processes that contribute to the alienation of workers from the rest of their class, confining them in their solitude. Firstly, unlike the Taylorist factory (which allowed for a separation and counterpoint between capital and labor), the neoliberal "integrated factory" requires workers to identify the subjectivity of labor with the subjectivity of capital, to make belonging to the company the only subjectivity possible; to think of belonging to a class, differentiated from the class of capital, is dangerous and unacceptable. Secondly, as it destroys the social regulation of the class relation, neoliberalism fractures the construction of a collective order and promotes a wide range of particularities in the class relation, with one basic purpose: to prevent any chance of structuring a class-based political front by pushing class conflict out of view and presenting it as harmless in order to dominate it.

In this way, the class relation is depoliticized, reduced to individual particularities, and any sense of universality is fractured, as the construction of any interests that could transcend individual particularities and bring them together in the recognition of a social relation or relation between social classes is rendered tenuous, if not impossible. According to Alain Touraine, neoliberalism produces processes of "de-normativization" and de-institutionalization (weakening or disappearance of codified norms upheld by legal mechanisms) which, according to the logic of the deregulated free market, tend to invade every aspect of society, shaping "de-institutionalized" societies in which norms are diluted, promoting "behavioral diversity," and arguing in favor of "individual rights and interests." As a result, economic and cultural behavior becomes anti-institutional and anomic (as quoted in Messina, 2009).

---

[18] "Although many express their discontent, when it comes to participating, to mobilizing, to proposing or supporting some kind of transformation, the absence of a collective will leads them to paralysis, producing a progressive annihilation of their subjectivity and turning them into 'actors' who let themselves be led by events" (Aruj, 2000).

[19] It could be argued that alienation tends to invade all spheres of life under neoliberalism, but the purpose here is to identify a process of isolation and estrangement among workers that renders impossible the construction of a working class front in opposition to capital.

In this society made up of individual particularities and anomic behavior, as it eliminates any vestige of class identity and solidarity, destroys ethical referents and promotes meanness and pettiness,[20] workers relate to each other with fear and suspicion:[21] the other tends to be either an unscrupulous competitor submissive to capital or an anomic criminal. Among the working class, neoliberal domination produces individuals with no defense against economic, political and ideological domination, split off from their own kind, alienated from the rest of their class, and uninterested in any possibility of collective construction.[22]

In addition to these factors, which constitute the obstacles created by neoliberalism to prevent the construction of projects of political unity among workers and which help explain the individual alienation of those who have been dispossessed of their means of production in contemporary society, we must also consider those explored in Chapter 7, related to the transformations to the state brought about by neoliberalism. Nation-states are positioned to ensure the conditions for reproduction of global capital within their national borders, and to keep the globalization of the workers from accompanying the globalization of the capitalists. Workers remain trapped in institutions restricted to the realm of the nation-state, deprived of an institutional framework that would enable them to negotiate with internationalized capital, resulting in a regression to the absence of political, economic and social rights and to growing difficulties in the construction of viable projects to oppose capital.

Neoliberalism thus establishes new conditions to reinforce the alienation of workers and their restriction to individual negotiation in one

---

[20] Neoliberalism, as a proliferation of the offshore manufacturing economy, produces a situation of "adversity and disorganization, rife with unhappiness... unemployment, violence and crime... anomie, decadence, destructiveness, disintegration, savagery, chaos, negativity, anti-social behavior... depression, hopelessness, the absence of a future... poverty as dehumanization, as deterioration of the human person, as a return to barbarism" (Zermeño, 2005: 15, 16, 20, 21).

[21] Although they attribute widely different meanings to it, the issue may be viewed from various theoretical approaches, even those sympathetic to neoliberalism: "How can we construct basic notions of 'trust' (Giddens, 1994) when 'the modern ideal of subordination of the individual to rational collective rules has been pulverized,' when hedonistic and personalized individualism has become legitimate?' (Lipovetsky, 1995: 7–9) How can we reconstruct social capital, in the words of Putnam, the organic solidarity of Durkheim?" (Messina, 2009).

[22] "Neoliberalism produced a kind of common sense that contained a strong inclination toward pessimism regarding almost any sort of collective initiative... The ideological development of the 1980s and 1990s led to a belief that nothing collective was possible, desirable or feasible" (Tapia, 2008).

region of the world.[23] According to Aruj, neoliberalism imposes globalization through fragmentation and is dedicated to preventing those subjected to it from reconstructing their bonds of solidarity and working toward a transformation: "uncertainty about the future provokes a rejection of association with any project that places full confidence in a solution based on own initiative and a distrust of collective projects" (Aruj, 2000). Alienation feeds back into fear, uncertainty, resignation[24] and the refusal to develop their own conception of the world, their own counter-hegemonic class project. According to Luis Tapia, ideological domination is a process of "disorganization of social awareness" with "a core that consists of two types of relations... the relation between disorganization and unawareness and the relation between disorganization and awareness;" in the "processes of disorganization as strategies of domination and unawareness and of self-organization as a process of social or inter-subjective awareness, bringing about a moral and intellectual reform... [d]omination asserts itself through a process of disorganization of the social, political and cultural conditions whereby the different social subjects could achieve self-awareness by relating with other subjects in the context of national and international processes" (Tapia, 2008, emphasis added).[25]

CRIMINAL ACTIVITY

The shift from collective bargaining to individual competitiveness resulting from the transition from the Keynesian pattern of domination to the

---

[23] "The fact that many Latin American countries have now lived through two decades of neoliberalism means that the new generations have been educated in an atmosphere of liberal beliefs and liberal common sense; they have learned these beliefs in every sphere – in their schools, their parents' workplace, the media and the news" (Tapia, 2008). For a part of today's society – perhaps more among the young – life appears reduced to the individual and the individual to the sexual, to "those few surviving enclaves... where a pleasure and playfulness not wholly under the heel of power might still be relished," so that "one would accordingly anticipate an enormous inflation of interest in these matters," although "some thinkers would caution how discourse and sexuality were themselves policed, regulated, heavy with power..." (Eagleton, 1996: 4).

[24] In Chapter 6, I examined how the *liberalization* of the international movement of financial capital and the processes that it provokes have given rise to the construction of a form of political discourse that promotes resignation among the dominated; no human power could possibly oppose the omnipotence of *market forces*. I will return to this point later.

[25] "Domination is based on ignorance and on the socialization of intellectual patterns that incorporate subordination, hierarchy and subalternity into the constitution of the subjects... Domination involves disorganizing the conditions for recognition among social subjects, especially in the world of workers. Disorganization produces unawareness – of

neoliberal pattern means that workers are forced into increasingly deregulated submission to the ever greater demands of capital, and that the search for options of employment and subsistence become increasingly disordered and chaotic, as do the searches undertaken by capital for profitable activities and the employment options that it offers, including unlawful and criminal activities.

Before, I pointed out that the extraordinary profits yielded by organized crime employers enables them, given the conditions of labor casualization and rising unemployment, to provide privileged labor and wage conditions to their employees, offering them relatively high wages and creating expectations of status for a segment of the excluded population so that, as the commercial and production chain associated with criminal activities expands, a genuine social framework is constructed in urban districts and neighborhoods and in rural centers, constituting what I referred to as Crime Promotion Brigades. In the world of neoliberal capital, crime is a normal work option that attracts a growing number of applicants and creates jobs[26] with much more dynamism than any other branch of the contemporary economy. Obviously, the problem is also one of ethics and social cohesion; if large masses of the unemployed are turning to crime, society is suffering from a serious breakdown in the mechanisms of social cohesion and the construction of ethical referents. Neoliberalism does not construct any consistent form of social cohesion, but rather fosters the destruction of all ethical referents as it promotes individualism, competition and unscrupulousness, as much among workers as among capitalists.[27]

---

themselves as individual and collective subjects, of other subjects, of the nation and of the world" (Tapia, 2008).

[26] For example, the National Drug Threat Assessment 2009, a report issued by the U.S. Department of Justice's National Drug Intelligence Center, asserts that drug trafficking organizations (but one sector of the *crime economy*) generate 450,000 *jobs* in Mexico alone. This information in fact aroused terrible indignation among Mexican political party leaders, to such an extent that the national leader of the Democratic Revolutionary Party (PRD), Jesús Ortega, accused the U.S. government of *meddling* (!), asserting that the U.S. intelligence report was "a frankly rude declaration that meddles in the country's affairs" and, in a *forceful rejoinder* (!), claimed that there are 50 times as many U.S. citizens living off drug trafficking (Bravo and Padilla, 2009).

[27] "In the current neoliberal era, there is a clear breakdown in compliance with existing legal frameworks, at both national and international levels... The violation of the rule of law has a domino effect... As federal, state and municipal authorities, the political and the business class in general are the first to violate the rule of law, citizens, professional groups and unions also often assume unlawful practices, taking control of public spaces for their own purposes, infringing basic administrative regulations for urban and rural coexistence, stealing union fees, corrupting and being corrupted. Cynicism, arrogance and the

Neoliberal capital has set up criminal activity and the degradation it produces as a normal lifestyle option, as a part of daily life in contemporary society[28], devastating the ethical referents which, even in the previous periods of capital domination, would have fostered a mass response of indignation from society. If status and social recognition are acquired with money, it doesn't matter where the money comes from. It is a simple question of success or failure: if you have money and they haven't killed or imprisoned you, you are a winner.The neoliberal world issues a constant call to break the law, flout ethical and moral standards, and engage in total depravity. It is hard to find a reasonably informed citizen who does not recognize that organized crime is closely tied to government and corporate corruption and impunity and to the criminal defense of privileges, but the social rejection of crime – especially the version promoted in the media – is based on fear provoked by its violence and its most brutal expressions, not on its success or merit as a business. The hypocrisy and cynicism of neoliberal capital, which simultaneously promotes and combats organized crime, ultimately permeates society.

Neoliberal capital creates the cultural framework and the common sense it needs to develop unhindered; it thus receives understanding and tolerance, and even approval and support, at least from the segment of society most permeated by the degradation it fosters.

Fear

Neoliberal capital is also an enormous factory of fears. In addition to those produced by health, ecological and environmental crises, its economics generates fear because, as a threat or as a reality, it deprives many of access to their means of subsistence, and its politics provokes fear by generating defenselessness and a lack of forums in which solutions could be sought.[29]

---

supremacy of private over collective interests take the place of civil responsibility and collective empowerment; a popular culture of corruption is constructed, in which honesty is synonymous with stupidity" (López y Rivas, 2005).

[28] "Crime spreads like a cancer... Impunity has created a vicious circle revolving around the perception that in our society turning to crime is a low-risk business which, as such, is increasingly attractive in a social stew seasoned with unemployment and poverty" (Iruegas, 2005.)

[29] "The fears may be or appear irrational, but they are not unwarranted. There are fears arising from the uncertainties generated by global processes, such as employment casualization and unemployment, the depreciation of skills and specializations, the loss of limits and referents in the territories inhabited, the absence or weakness of institutions or organizations of social integration, and the general crisis affecting many services of the welfare state" (Borja, 2007).

In the drive to be competitive there is a strong dose of fear, and the criminal activity fostered under neoliberalism produces fear among those outside the growing underworld of crime and feel threatened by it, but also among the criminals themselves. All of these fears are produced by the domination of neoliberal capital. But at the same time, with the state administration of criminal activity, neoliberal capital creates fields in which these fears are condensed, which serve to perpetuate its domination; it creates culprits and solutions as well as new fears. Fears produced by neoliberal economics and politics go much further than those directly associated with criminal activity, but neoliberal domination condenses them and disperses them, firstly because it constructs illusory culprits, and secondly because it encapsulates society in an illusory solution: security. The ideological defenselessness of the workers and the media ensure that the true culprits and the real solutions remain outside the focus of perception and social inquiry.

This construction of illusory culprits and solutions operates both in developed and underdeveloped countries. Around the world, fear (of terrorism, of violence, of crime, etc.) and the offer of security has become the discursive core of neoliberal politics. In developed countries, the focus is on the threat of terrorism, while in underdeveloped countries it is the threat of crime, although in both cases the pattern is flexible, allowing variants, a multiplicity of threats, some of which emerge while others disappear; what matters is that there must always be one on hand when needed. Fortunately, to ensure the solid development of the ideological domination of neoliberal capital, there are many threats, ranging from criminal gangs like Mara Salvatrucha[30] to the prospect of China and India as emerging superpowers, the battle against terrorism and counterinsurgency, climate change and its potential geopolitical consequences, failed or fractured states, cyberspace as a new terrain of conflict, the rise of new powers, the growing influence of non-state actors, the spread of weapons of mass-destruction and other destructive technologies.[31] With such an overabundance of threats we can comfort ourselves with the certainty

---

[30] "The U.S. Attorney General, Alberto Gonzales, declared that the war against Central American youth gangs in general, and against the Mara Salvatrucha (MS-13) in particular, *is second only in importance to the war against al-Qaeda...* the evidence indicates that the 'maras'... have become larger, meaner and better organized, *raising the threat that they represent to Central America and the United States to an alarming level*" (Díaz, 2007, emphasis added).

[31] The U.S. Defense Department, in its "Quadrennial Defense Review" presented in February 2010, reports new supranational threats (see Brooks, 2010).

that the state administration of criminal activity is here to stay, at least from the point of view of the representatives of neoliberal capital; our security is in good hands and is guaranteed... our well-being is not, but at this point nobody remembers such minor details.

The state administration of criminal activity, erected on the fear that permeates contemporary society, constructs a mechanism of externalization of the contradictions of neoliberal capitalism: the ideological view that promotes the slogan that contemporary society is essentially healthy. The problem is a group external to it: criminals and terrorists. This enables the construction of the culprit, which becomes a catalyst and focal point of fear[32] with a solution developed by capital itself, amalgamating fears and intolerance and turning the fears of the public (at least in the discourse) a political priority.[33] This externalization of its internal contradictions is particularly visible in developed capitalist countries where the construction of culprits focuses on criminalizing immigrants, accusing them of being criminals, terrorists and threats to social welfare.

The result is of course the opposite of the supposed aim, but capital creates new conditions to impose its intellectual and moral leadership on society, based on "the most reactionary thought, which denies the possibility of a social transformation that could overcome the exclusions of the present, and also denies the legitimacy of sectors that express the contradictions of contemporary society. Consequently, it seeks to eliminate them from the public stage" (Borja, 2007).[34] Violence and insecurity tend to grow but, far from seeking to rectify the situation, neoliberal capital uses this failure as grounds for escalating the war on crime with the support of

---

[32] "The fears and consequent demands for public security have provoked official responses, populist in character, which arouse the irrational dimension of fear, generically designating social collectives as potentially dangerous, upon which first falls public stigma, and then preemptive repression. It goes without saying that these policies are aimed at producing perverse effects, helping to arouse the most irrational fears and provoking growing demands for more security" (Borja, 2007).

[33] Borja explains this dynamic with what he calls *reactionary populism*, "equivalent at the local level to that used by the Bush government at the global level"; the first step is *to make a political priority out of the fears of the people*, integrated but worried about the uncertainties and worked up by the campaigns of conservative politicians and some media outlets; then, to construct a discourse that threatens anything that is bothersome, and finally, to pass laws that impose penalties on anyone capable of offending normal citizens by their presence in the public space" (Borja, 2007).

[34] The result of this is that "any behavior contrary to the established order" is deemed "illegitimate and dangerous to coexistence", thereby justifying "repressive action against any unpleasant or disagreeable social groups, which are confused with criminal or violent minorities" (Borja, 2007).

a segment of the public that is increasingly terrified and anxious for security; "it is a long war," they claim, "but we cannot abandon it and one day we will win."

In reality, the very nature of this war means it will never be won;[35] but, indeed, it cannot be abandoned. In the previous chapter, I examined the state administration of criminal activity and its role in linking the economics and politics of neoliberal capital, noting that on the level of ideological domination it allows the promotion of a world view that externalizes its internal contradictions, criminalizing and dissolving the class opposition against its domination, reducing society to powerlessness and legitimizing[36] its preventive positioning of police and military forces against society. The ideological defenselessness of contemporary society is such that the repression imposed on it is presented as a response to its own demands.

In the state administration of criminal activity, neoliberal capital encodes its most precious hopes – economic, political and ideological. It had been waiting too long to waste the opportunity to bring them to fruition when it finally came: "what the U.S. needed to be able to dominate much of humanity and the world's resources was 'some catastrophic and catalyzing event – like a new Pearl Harbor'. The attacks of 11 September 2001 provided the 'new Pearl Harbor' described as 'the opportunity of ages.' The extremists who have since exploited 11 September come from the era of Ronald Reagan, when far-right groups and 'think tanks' were established to avenge the American 'defeat' in Vietnam. In the 1990s, there was an added agenda: to justify the denial of a 'peace dividend' following the Cold War. The Project for the New American Century was formed, along with the American Enterprise Institute, the Hudson Institute and others that have since merged the ambitions of the Reagan administration

---

[35] These policies, explains Borja, are aimed at producing perverse effects; the repressive logic leads to preemptive repression of entire social collectives, turning a once innocent populace into criminals, fostering greater injustice and aggravating the very problems of coexistence that it is supposed to resolve, generating more violence than existed previously, contributing to the arousal of the most irrational fears and provoking increased demands for more security (Borja, 2007).

[36] Fear "is a way of postulating the future, perhaps the contemporary way of forging consensus on the dictates of time... it has become a kind of metagram that organizes the subjectivity of every aspect of life... Strictly speaking, the big modern States no longer require political repression to 'maintain order', as we were accustomed to seeing up until the 1980s. The society of fear established in the proliferation of trafficking seeks to introject into each citizen the security guard of his own civil impotence... the exception turned into the rule. How can we explain the origins of this new form that legitimizes order based on the routine collapse of order itself?" (Semo, 2005).

with those of the current Bush regime" (Pilger, 2002).[37] Thus, it is simply too useful to be abandoned, at least not willingly. Only intense social pressure could force it to do so.

THE ORGANIZATION OF THE INTELLECTUAL AND MORAL LEADERSHIP OF NEOLIBERAL CAPITAL

Over the course of the historical development of the liberal pattern, the workers were processing their ideological, political and organic separation from the capitalist state, until they were forced to make the transition to the contained form of domination. During the Keynesian period they were closely connected to the state, organized under its hegemony through their integration into civil society; capitalist domination organized a social framework in which ideological creation and dissemination, that is, the organization of civil society, were closely associated with bargaining for and granting improved material conditions in the lives of the workers. In the Keynesian pattern of domination the framework of the state administration of concessions was established as the setting in which ideological domination is organized. In the neoliberal pattern, this setting is occupied by state administration of both competitiveness and criminal activity.

The Crime Promotion Brigades constitute, in the sub-world of criminal activity, the equivalent of the Competitiveness Promotion Brigades in the sub-world of legal activity. Both are internal to the ideology of neoliberal capital, an expression of a dominated society incapable of making an ideological break with capital. They complete the downward network which, by promoting the life options offered by neoliberal capital, disseminates its conception of the world and binds society to its intellectual and moral leadership. However, as the historical trajectory of the neoliberal pattern advances, this framework organizing the structure of its civil society becomes increasingly tied up with the state administration of criminal activity, firstly because, although competition and alienation (and the discontent they provoke) are mutually connected and reinforced, they are ultimately subsumed in crime and the fear it produces, and secondly, because the future trajectory of neoliberal capital inevitably fosters increasing criminal activity, as will be shown later in this chapter.

It hardly needs stating that the intellectual and moral leadership of neoliberal capital is not of the same progressive nature that characterized

---

[37] Others have compared September 11 with the Reichstag fire (Kagarlitsky, 2001).

the Keynesian pattern, but regressive, fostering degradation and break-down, insecurity and fear, in a context of fragmentation and social atomization, but functional for fostering its sole priority – the insatiable search for profit – and clearly effective for maintaining its ideological hold over a significant segment of society. At least up to now, although there is a trend toward increasing exclusion, capital has maintained the capacity to integrate a segment of the workers, even recruiting them into the Competitiveness or Crime Promotion Brigades, and has maintained its intellectual and moral leadership even while becoming increasingly structured around the state administration of criminal activity and sustained by alienation and fear.

Capital has found a way of producing a particular kind of intellectual and moral leadership (which is actually anti-intellectual and immoral) that recalls the nightmarish worlds created by George Orwell and Aldous Huxley, and has erected a complex apparatus, effective up to now, for maintaining its ideological domination. Meanwhile, as a class, in spite of an abundance of opposition groups, the working class has not been able to distance itself ideologically and politically, or to produce new forms of organization that would create the conditions necessary to launch new projects in opposition to capital. Whether, how and when the working class is able to do so will determine the direction that the process will take over the course of the 21st century.

The ideological domination of capital is not a simple matter of "ideas." Competitiveness and alienation, as the implementation of its ideology, are based on economic and political realities. In Chapter 6, I explained how, in redefining its relationship with the nation-state, capital redefined its structure of economic, political and ideological domination. And the organization of the state administration of criminal activity is not only grounded in propaganda but also in real threats to the lives of ordinary everyday citizens.[38] The neoliberal state, perfected and globalized, adopts the same structure assumed by its older brother, the Nazi State, in its day. The success of Nazi propaganda lay in the combination of "the clever application of propaganda techniques" with the help of "a complex propaganda machine affecting all spheres of German life, appropriately

---

[38] Bearing witness to the *reality* of criminal activity fostered by neoliberal capital are the nearly 20,000 deaths in 5 years in Mexico (Sánchez, 2010), although these are related only to the *war on drugs*, the *soft version* of criminal activity. In Iraq and Afghanistan, where the *war on terrorism* is being waged (the *hard version* of criminal activity), the deaths have surpassed 850,000, as well as more than 1.5 million injured (Dufour, 2008).

planned and with an exhaustive application," which "completely immersed the German people, numbing the senses of the population, restricting each of the activities of individual daily life, submerging them in an unreal world... based on fear and repression... In this way, the German people were subject not only to continuous psychological but also physical violence" (Rodero, 2000).

The rule of capital is imposed as a reality that must be overcome ideologically through a counter-hegemonic construction, but that must also be overcome really as a construction with the effective capacity to transform the relationship between classes, possible both through the resistance posed by workers and through capital's entrapment in its own restrictions and internal contradictions, as will be discussed in the next and final chapter.

The Hegemony of Neoliberal Capital

Neoliberal capital, like its predecessors, liberal and Keynesian capital, in their day, is hegemonic because it successfully imposes its philosophy, its moral perspective and its habits, and because it is able to orchestrate a social framework within which to develop and disseminate its conception of the world, to promulgate the life options it offers, to bind society to its intellectual and moral leadership and to define the "common sense" of its subalterns. It must be stressed, however, that there is a qualitative difference: the hegemony of its predecessors was progressive, while that of neoliberal capital is increasingly regressive. In the liberal period, the bourgeoisie, which rose up revolutionary and victorious from among the ashes of feudalism, basked in the glory of the promise of modernity, taking command of reason and marching purposefully toward progress[39], while in the Keynesian period capital set itself up as benefactor and guarantor of the welfare of its subalterns. In both these periods the capitalist class had reasonably solid arguments (as solid as its nature would allow) to present itself as the class best suited to ensure the development of society.

---

[39] "The revolutionary element that constituted Modernity was the break from the theological world view of the social order and the constitution of a new world view in which Reason, as an attribute of man, was an instrument of transformation of the world, through which he could reflect on himself in his subjectivity... The individual became conscious and objective, and things lost any quality of mystery. Man creates himself and becomes self-referential... the notion of perfection lies ahead... For modernity, there are no limits. It is Man who constructs the meaning of his own actions. There is no prior external orchestration. Individuals are lords of their own actions" (Aruj, 2000).

Neoliberal capital has come into being – as its own intellectuals explain – in the era of postmodernity (i.e. the era of the failure of modernity), the period which gave it life and defined the promises that lent legitimacy to its rule and gave meaning to its infancy. Having now grown old, capital renounces those promises[40], declaring the collapse of modernity's institutions and the failure of its ideology, and building its particular intellectual and moral leadership on the administration of competitiveness and criminal activity, on alienation and fear. The arguments supporting its claim as the class best suited to continue leading society are not at all convincing. Nevertheless, it maintains its hegemony over much of contemporary society. In spite of the factors examined so far, the fact of this hegemony is still extraordinary, and requires at least two additional considerations. The first involves what might be called (paraphrasing Marx) flowers on the chain and their complex relationship with the thanatophilia promoted by the cultural design of neoliberalism, while the second involves fetishism as a natural condition of the capitalist social relation and a constant support upholding its ideological domination which, under the conditions of neoliberal domination, makes humanity look like passengers on a spaceship running on autopilot.

FLOWERS ON THE CHAIN

Even under the most oppressive conditions, human beings need to find reasons for living that make life tolerable and livable. In the world of neoliberal capital, some of these reasons are provided by capital itself. It sells these reasons (because it never gives anything away) and, therefore, they are only accessible to people who are integrated (either through competitiveness or criminal activity), who are able to function as consumers. They are plastic flowers, which nevertheless give some color to the oppressive bleakness of real life and help explain the continued success of capital domination. There are also real flowers, grown by life itself, which (although capital attempts to appropriate them and present them as

---

[40] "Vattimo considers that the philosophies of Nietzsche and Heidegger are the foundations for all future ideology. Using these authors, he constructs what he calls the philosophies of difference, which are based on fragmentation and multiplicity, in opposition to the dialectic vision as a globalizing vision based on Hegel and Marx. This perspective is also referred to as 'weak thought' or the post-modern condition, and is defined as a distancing from the basic ideals of modernity: progress, avant-gardism, critical thinking and surmounting of obstacles. The crisis of modernity thus affects all aesthetic, cultural and social values" (Palenga, n.d.).

products of its garden, mixing the plastic flowers with the live ones, so that the former might sap some of the life of the latter) grow not because of, but in spite of capital.

Heading the list of flowers sold by capital is consumption itself[41] and, in particular, an increasingly spectacular array of electronic products, such as the computer and Internet with their many possibilities, as well as a diverse range of software and virtual games, capable of immersing their many users in a matrix, an illusory, simulated world. The social world is perceived through the virtual communities and replaced with video addictions and second-life websites, to such an extent that normal life and virtual existence become confused, and it almost seems possible to construct one's entire existence around the computer and its range of associated products, provided that one has the real money to buy them and to satisfy all the old necessities which are neither virtual nor admit virtual solutions, such as food, housing and clothing.

Unlike the conventional media that previously monopolized public entertainment and recreation (film, radio and television), which are one-way, admitting spectators only, these new media forms are interactive, offering a reasonably wide margin for users to participate in the creation of their own virtual products within which they may weave something of their own vitality: from on-line chat and making virtual friends and even lovers (which, according to the experts, may potentially convert into real ones) to creating their own spaces for information, reflection and amusement. This universe of electronics and its potential to produce a huge quantity of virtual products is a complex, multifaceted phenomenon with a vast range of open possibilities for the future. The Internet in particular has even turned into a site of conflict between opposing perspectives, from its conversion into a simple commodity at the service of the consolidation and enrichment of the new giant monopolies (IBM, Microsoft, Intel, Apple, Yahoo, Amazon and Google) or free access for the free exchange of use value, music, books, images, etc., to its use as a resource for the global connection of social movements[42] or for the purposes of

---

[41] "When night falls, when the lights of the shopping malls go out and the neon world disappears, the individual takes refuge in his house, opens the shopping bags (the only daily moment of pleasure) and feels a sense of fulfillment of the consumer status awarded by the market. As this pleasure is momentary – lasting only as long as the act itself – a few minutes later, in solitude, he returns to his natural state of inaction: the passivity typical of the democratic societies of the 21st century" (Toledano, 2008).

[42] "The Internet allows the organization of local alternative projects through global protests, which ultimately take place in a particular place, for example, in Seattle, Washington,

police control, as will be discussed below. However, in the context and from the perspective examined here – a world dominated by capital, with a disintegrated and ideologically defenseless working class – the Internet plays a role similar to that attributed by Marx to religion: an illusory happiness, an expression of a social reality in need of illusions.[43] The presentation of mass spectacles (music and sports events, with soccer as the most outstanding example), the communications and entertainment media and this conglomeration of interactive electronic products go hand in hand with religion as producers of illusions, in some cases replacing it, in others complementing it.

Other flowers on the chain, currently in danger of extinction, are survivors from the Keynesian past (employment stability and the recognition of basic rights to education, health, leisure[44], etc.) duly regulated by capital and only accessible to a segment of fortunate ones who have yet to suffer the fate of either labor casualization or unemployment. However, as general propositions, the old useful promises such as progress, development and welfare have fallen completely out of use.

Last of all are those flowers that bloom without external intervention, as life itself produces reasons for finding a sense of purpose. Grandparents are touched by the first steps of their grandchildren, parents proudly witness the growth of their offspring, lovers explore one another (virtually and physically), couples share their dreams and fears, friends offer care and sympathy, and even street children find reasons to play and laugh as they beg for change, simply because they are children. Even under the most oppressive conditions, as the Spanish singer-songwriter Joaquín Sabina suggests, life finds "more than a hundred words, more than a hundred reasons, to hold back the blade from our wrists, more than a hundred pupils in which we can see ourselves alive, more than a hundred lies that make life worthwhile."[45]

Prague, etc., but which are established, organized and developed via the online connection, i.e. the global connection, of local movements and local experiences. The Internet is the global-local connection, which is the new form of control and social mobilization in our society" (Castells, 2003).

[43] "To abolish religion as the illusory happiness of the people is to demand their real happiness. The demand to give up illusions about the existing state of affairs is the demand to give up a state of affairs which needs illusions" (Marx, 1844: Abstract).

[44] "Reality has been masked under the blue veil of anti-depressants, and social cohesion depends on the work calendar: holidays, long weekends and public entertainment events" (Toledano, 2008).

[45] "Más de cien palabras, más de cien motivos, para no cortarse de un tajo las venas, más de cien pupilas donde vernos vivos, más de cien mentiras que valen la pena" (Joaquín Sabina, "Mas de cien mentiras", 1994).

Social Anchoring, "Creative Destruction" and Thanatophilia

This voracity of life for self-preservation has been extremely useful to capital because, while "the maintenance and reproduction of the working class is, and must ever be, a necessary condition to the reproduction of capital," explains Marx, "the capitalist may safely leave its fulfillment to the laborer's instincts of self-preservation and of propagation" (Marx, 1867: Ch. 23).[46] Capital needs to leave some margin, some degree of chaos, for life to develop its own motivations. Thus, in its first period, the domination of capital was intertwined with the extended working class family, the rural community and the urban working class neighborhood. With the arrival of the second period, this space for socialization (which made the initial domination of capital bearable, but which was also the framework for the resistance against it) was destroyed, and was interwoven with the nuclear family, with capital even presenting itself as its protector until, with the advent of neoliberalism, it determined that to continue playing this role was costly and unnecessary.

As it ultimately destroys what it had once supported, capital resorts to the strategy of presenting the damage it causes to society in the same light in which it presents damage done in the realm of production: as creative destruction. Thus, now that the nuclear family has been largely destroyed by the social disaster fostered by neoliberalism, capital declares it obsolete and in decline[47] and, in search of a new focal point for society, offers the recognition of rights to diverse groups and minorities and presents itself as promoter of individual freedom, diversity and multiculturalism (ecologists, feminists, homosexuals, ethnic minorities, etc.). However, in the hands of capital these issues are useful only insofar as they promote association with multiple identities, with the aim of denying the only identity that troubles it – class identity;[48] anyone who discovers their connections

---

[46] "The fact that the laborer consumes his means of subsistence for his own purposes, and not to please the capitalist, has no bearing on the matter. The consumption of food by a beast of burden is none the less a necessary factor in the process of production because the beast enjoys what it eats" (Marx, 1867: Ch. 23).

[47] Consider, for example, this *exemplary* reasoning: "Marriage is an outdated institution, created by the nobility at a time when human life expectancy was 35 years; as such, today in the 21st century, if we want a more just and equitable society, we need to transform the conjugal bond and create a system that truly gives us greater freedom and dignity" (Norandi, 2010). According to this line of reasoning, marriage is to blame for the problems produced by neoliberalism and, of course, if that is where the cause is, the solution is to be found there also.

[48] "The battle, the open field, is the place where the multiple identities invented by capitalism, the mermaid songs of plural subjectivity, disappear, and identity of class, of

to class relations will be suppressed, and even more so if they go in search of those responsible (in terms of social relations) for their afflictions.

No serious analysis can examine, for example, ecological disasters and the rights of children, women and indigenous peoples in Latin America, or of immigrants and ethnic minorities in the United States, without linking them to class relations. Thus, if individual freedom, diversity and multiculturalism manage to prosper, it will not be thanks to capital but, like many other signs of life, in spite of it, as was once the case with the extended family and its community, and subsequently the nuclear family. It is also worth noting that, although capital and the class it represents need the reproduction of the working class, they have never been particularly concerned about the death or the hardships of specific individuals, as great as their number may be. Indeed, for neoliberals, more than for their predecessors, the liberals and the Keynesians, a large proportion of the human race is superfluous. As a result, respect for human life, which has in any case been a fragile notion in every historical period of capitalism, is drastically reduced, and the nature of that respect becomes increasingly complex; on the one hand, neoliberalism leaves glimmers of life, while on the other it repudiates the human drive to live and promotes a cultural design which, in multiple forms, fosters thanatophilia.

Drug addiction, which affects millions of young people around the world, is one of these forms; but the whole framework of the state administration of criminal activity is profoundly thanatophilic. For example, in Mexico there is a long history of femicides, to which has been added a new craze of neoliberal culture: juvenicides.[49] This is not only the product of external aggression killing young people; youth are learning how to be victims of and victimize one another; for example with practices such as cyber-bullying[50] as a way of relating between friends and peers, undermining any vestige of emotional support or solidarity. They thus become accustomed to living in a world that attacks them from without and from within. Even the presentation of the spectacles offered by

---

belonging to a specific historic subject, acquires the dimension of political discourse" (Toledano, 2008).

[49] "It isn't bullets; it's a perverse state policy at political economic, social and cultural levels which is killing our youth. In Juárez, but not only in Juárez, throughout the nation, whether they are the murderers or the murdered, all of our youth are victims" (Quintana, 2010).

[50] "Among the new mechanisms of harassment and victimization is so-called *cyber-bullying,* whereby cell phones and the Internet are used to 'record humiliating acts and broadcast them, with the purpose of causing the social death of the victim via the social networks." (Velasco, 2010).

capital – innocent spaces for amusement – is impregnated with this culture of death; in soccer, for example, the fans of a team turn into veritable religious fanatics, willing to beat and even kill the infidels, that is, fans of the opposing team.

The thanatophilia of neoliberal capital promotes and trivializes death. It vulgarizes death to the point of offering death pornography as a new cultural product:

> "A war unleashed by a Global Empire against a globalized world necessitates the desacralization of death. This war is global because (among other reasons) it is preemptive. The United States decides where the enemy is, who it is and how to fight it. Nobody knows when they will be transformed into an 'enemy' of the Global Empire and be included in its 'preemptive war'. *If the war covers the planet, death must be depicted (through the mass media) as an 'everyday landscape'.* War is the legalization of death. The 'war' is that space within which killing is permitted and required. To kill 'in' the war is to be a hero. 'Out' of it, it is to be a murderer. Therefore, the war must be seen. That is, it must be made obscene. The obscene is fully visible, as is the pornographic. Pornography is boring because its brutal naturalism is overwhelming and quickly tiring. Eroticism, which appeals to creativity, to the imagination, is infinite. What is needed then is to show death pornographically. The cause: *this whole planet at war should assume that death is a spectacle.* One more. One among many. Something that is out there; on the front page of the daily papers. And which we will forget about as soon as we turn the page" (Feinmann, 2005, emphasis added).

Finally, because profit is all that matters, neoliberal culture is a design of global trivialization, of sex, love, life and death, as well as of politics or philosophy: "Just as the reality show fosters the pornographic exploitation of life, the information phenomenon, by and large, appears to play the same role for death... Ultimately, 'sex pornography will be succeeded by death pornography'... What the infinite production of audiovisual events focused on death does (just as pornography does with sex) is feed a consumerist logic... Death is one of the indispensable stars in the spectacle of the image" (Pacheco Benites, 2008). This turn taken by history might prompt us to recall an observation of Marx, that "[c]riticism has torn up the imaginary flowers from the chain not so that man shall wear the unadorned, bleak chain, but so that he will shake off the chain and pluck the living flower" (Marx, 1844).[51] The chain is real and heavy, and life requires an increasing effort to adorn it with flowers that make it livable.

---

[51] "To call on them to give up their illusions about their condition is to call on them to give up a condition that requires illusions. The criticism of religion is, therefore, in embryo, the criticism of that vale of tears of which religion is the halo" (Marx, 1844).

The Spaceship

Associated with this dearth of colors to adorn its domination is a peculiar, paradoxical fact: neoliberal capital denies its role as the producer of its own product. A brief example will serve to illustrate a few general features of the technique it has developed.

At the meeting of the Intergovernmental Panel on Climate Change to assess the results of the Kyoto Protocol to reduce fossil fuel consumption, the U.S. president, George W. Bush deemed the question closed: "Let's quit the debate about whether greenhouse gases are caused by mankind or by natural causes; let's just focus on technologies that *deal with* the issue" (ETC Group, 2007, emphasis added). In other words, when a problem becomes undeniable, the first step is to open a debate about its causes; in step two, it proves impossible to reach agreement about the causes and, therefore, about those responsible; in step three, the search for causes and culprits is abandoned and the focus turns to solutions, for which the appropriate package has already been prepared. Of course, this technique can be combined with the shock doctrine explored by Naomi Klein as mentioned earlier. But what is significant here is that the producer vanishes: the product (the problem) is orphaned. While liberals and Keynesians could show their products with a certain pride to all mankind and affirm emphatically "this is my work," under the conditions of neoliberalism, viewing the situation as whole, there is not much to boast about.

The result is that when globalization becomes overwhelmed with problems – including excessive concentration of wealth, unemployment, poverty, hunger, migration and social uprooting, crime, economic, and environmental and public health crises – the producer vanishes, and the promised global village – a global community, a world without borders, with progressive harmonization and homogenization (Ianni, 1996: 5–6) – quickly turns into a spaceship traveling without a pilot, destination unknown, transporting individuals who are lost, in decline, and threatened with extinction (Ianni, 1996: 8–9).

The Fetishism of Capital

The renunciation of the pleasures and responsibilities of paternity should not be mistaken for mere cynical trickery or misplaced modesty. In this apparent lack of a producer, there is an acknowledgment of a profound reality: it is not the capitalists, but capital, that is guiding the process.

The examination of capital, rather than capitalists, as the controlling force behind the process, is closely tied to the issue of fetishism. I will examine here three of the properties attributed to it by Marx: in capitalism, as things (commodities, money, means of production and subsistence), are turned into agents and functional forms of a social relation, firstly, they are invested with social properties; secondly, they acquire autonomous action, independent of the will and consciousness of human beings, and, thirdly, in acquiring their own action, they assume command over producers, and over society as a whole.

In Chapter I of *Capital, Volume I,* Marx explains how, when the product of labor assumes the form of a commodity, it appears to acquire a life of its own and to assume, as a thing, an inanimate object, social properties and autonomous action[52]: "this I call the fetishism which attaches itself to the products of labor, so soon as they are produced as commodities, and which is therefore inseparable from the production of commodities" (Marx, 1867: Ch. 1, Sect. 4). Fetishism, as Marx indicates when he revisits the topic in Chapter 48 of *Capital Volume 3,* "transforms the social relations for which the material elements of wealth serve as bearers in production, into properties of these things themselves (commodities) and still more pronouncedly *transforms the production relation itself into a thing* (money)" (Marx, 1894: Ch. 48, emphasis added). This fetishism, explains Marx, arises from the fact that commodities are products of private labors exercised independently from one another. These private labors taken collectively are what constitute the global social labor and as producers do not enter into social contact until they exchange the products of their labor, the specifically social attributes of these private labors are expressed only within the framework of that exchange.[53]

To producers, therefore, "the relations connecting the labor of one individual with that of the rest appear not as direct social relations between individuals at work, but as what they really are, *material relations between persons and social relations between things*" (Marx, 1894: Ch. 48, emphasis

---

[52] In the commodity form, the "social character of men's labor appears to them as an objective character stamped upon the product of that labor; properties pertaining to them by nature, as objective determinations of the products of labor themselves... reflecting the social relation which mediates between producers and global labor, as a social relation between objects, existing outside the producers" (Marx, 1867: Ch. 1, Sect. 4).

[53] "The category of 'abstract labor' is closely associated with the critical theory of fetishism because it is the indirect sociability, performed *a posteriori*, of global social labor that is reified in the products that take on lives of their own and ultimately take over in the capitalism of our times" (Kohan, 2007).

added). And in the chapter "The Trinity Formula," Marx notes that "all forms of society, in so far as they reach the stage of commodity-production and money circulation, take part in this perversion. But under the capitalist mode of production and in the case of capital, which forms its dominant category, its determining production relation, this enchanted and perverted world develops still more" (Marx, 1894: Ch. 48). It is not only that things (products) acquire social properties, but that they acquire autonomous action, independent of the will and the consciousness of their producers. Thus, for example, quantities in commodity exchange relations "vary continually, independently of the will, foresight and action of the producers" (Marx, 1894: Ch. 48). And in this action, producers fall under the command of their products; the social action of the producers "takes the form of *the action of objects, which rule the producers instead of being ruled by them*" (Marx, 1894: Ch. 48, emphasis added).

As the processes unfold, the more mediations intervene, the more the internal connection – "the nexus, the link and the passage between two moments of development and the action" (Kohan, 2009) – that joins them is concealed, the more the action of things shifts beyond the control of the producers and the more accentuated the command of these things over their producers becomes. Marx traces a line that follows the general development of this process. In "The Fetishism of Commodities and the Secret Thereof" (Marx, 1867: Ch. 1), he examines the difficulties associated with identifying the internal connection between value and the value form, while in "The Trinity Formula" (Marx, 1894: Ch. 48) he takes the same approach to identify the internal connection between the product of value and its distribution in profit, income and wages.

In the direct production process, he notes, the relation is still very simple, and "the actual connection impresses itself upon the bearers of this process, the capitalists themselves, and remains in their consciousness. The violent struggle over the limits of the working-day demonstrates this strikingly. But even within this non-mediated sphere, the sphere of direct action between labor and capital, matters do not rest in this simplicity. With the development of relative surplus-value... whereby the productive powers of social labor are developed, these productive powers and the social interrelations of labor in the direct labor process seem transferred from labor to capital. Capital thus becomes a very mystic being since all of labor's social productive forces appear to be due to capital, rather than labor as such..." (Marx, 1894: Ch. 48). And he adds: "Then the process of circulation intervenes, with its changes of substance and form, on which all parts of capital, even agricultural capital, devolve... This is a sphere where the relations under which value is originally produced are pushed completely into the background... the surplus-value contained in the commodities seem not merely to be realized in the circulation, but actually to arise from it... This sphere is the sphere of competition which, considered in each individual case, is dominated by chance; where, then, the inner law, which prevails in these accidents and regulates them, is only visible when these accidents are grouped together in large numbers, where it remains therefore invisible and unintelligible to the individual agents in production" (Marx, 1894: Ch. 48).

To sum up, "the actual process of production, as a unity of the direct production process and the circulation process, gives rise to new formations, in which the vein of internal connections is increasingly lost, the production relations are rendered independent of one another, and the component values become ossified into forms independent of one another... the inner connection [is] completely disrupted... precisely because the relations of production, which are bound to the various material elements of the production process, have been rendered mutually independent... we have the complete mystification of the capitalist mode of production, the conversion of social relations into things... it is an enchanted, perverted, topsy-turvy world" (Marx, 1894: Ch. 48).

FETISHISM AND IDEOLOGY

The concept of fetishism, which explains how things acquire social properties, autonomous action and command over human beings, reflects a reality generated by the capitalist relations of production; it is an appearance that necessarily corresponds to an essence, which is modified only when that essence changes.[54] This fetishized form of social relations, according to Kosik's analysis, shapes the world of the pseudo-concrete, made up of the different phenomena that crowd the everyday environment, which with their regularity, immediacy and self-evidence penetrate

---

[54] "Whence, then," asks Marx, "arises the enigmatical character of the product of labor, so soon as it assumes the form of commodities? Clearly from this form itself... fetishism... attaches itself to the products of labor so soon as they are produced as commodities, and... is therefore inseparable from the production of commodities." And he adds: "The recent scientific discovery, that the products of labor, [in] so far as they are values, are but material expressions of the human labor spent in their production, marks, indeed, an epoch in the history of the development of the human race, but by no means dissipates the mist through which the social character of labor appears to us to be an objective character of the products themselves" (Marx, 1867: Ch. 1).

the consciousness of individuals, assuming an independent and natural quality; it is the world of the external phenomena, of procuring and manipulation (fetishized praxis) of ordinary representations, of the fixed objects that appear to be natural conditions and are not immediately recognizable as the result of social activity (Kosik, 1976: 2).

Individuals create their representations of things and a system of "concepts" (a set of representations or categories of "routine thinking") with which they capture and fix the phenomenal aspect of reality. However, as Kosik explains, "these phenomenal forms of reality are diverse and often contradict the law of the phenomenon, the structure of the thing, i.e. its essential inner kernel, and the corresponding concept... Immediate utilitarian praxis and corresponding routine thinking allow people to find their way about in the world, to feel familiar with things and to manipulate them, but it does not provide them with a comprehension of things and of reality" (Kosik, 1976: 1–2). The phenomenon simultaneously reveals and conceals the essence. The essence is manifested in the phenomenon only partially; mediated by the phenomenon, it is shown as something other than what it is. The real contradictions and connections between the part and the whole, the appearance and the essence, remain concealed, and only scientific investigation can uncover the link the joins them: as Marx notes, "all science would be superfluous if the outward appearance and the essence of things directly coincided" (Marx, 1894: Ch. 48).[55]

Fetishism is not a simple ideological construction, but the necessary form assumed by social relations in capitalism. However, insofar as this appearance expresses the command of things, i.e. of the logic of capital, it is an appearance assumed by the capitalist – who "is merely capital personified and functions in the process of production solely as the agent of capital" (Marx, 1894: Ch. 48) – who at once becomes the spokesperson for the command of capital, while fetishism becomes a permanent condition of the ideology of capitalism (and opposition to the command of things is established as criticism of fetishism). As high priests of the capital-god, all the intellectual efforts of capitalists are dedicated to responding to control by capital, to diligently monitor and study the market indicators so as to follow to the letter the instructions of the invisible hand; in short, to codify

---

[55] On this basis, Marx contrasts classical political economics with vulgar economics: "..by Classical Political Economy, I understand that economy which, since the time of William Petty, has investigated the real relations of production in bourgeois society, in contradistinction to vulgar economy, which deals with appearances only..." (Marx, 1894: Ch. 48, fn 33).

the command of 'things' over human beings. Their ideology, designed to explain their mission to themselves and affirm their credibility to the dominated, is based on a fetishized reality created, as Marx explains, by vulgar economics, which "does no more than interpret, systematize and defend in doctrinaire fashion the conceptions of the agents of bourgeois production," who are themselves prisoners of bourgeois production relations: "vulgar economy feels particularly at home in the estranged outward appearances of economic relations... these relations seem the more self-evident the more their internal relationships are concealed from it, although they are understandable to the popular mind... As soon as the vulgar economist arrives at this incommensurable relation, everything becomes clear to him, and he no longer feels the need for further thought. For he has arrived precisely at the 'rational' in bourgeois conception" (Marx, 1894: Ch. 48).[56]

THE SPACESHIP AND ITS PILOT

Although fetishism is a general condition of social relations under capitalism, the capacity for rule developed by the logic of capital is affected by various conditions. First of all, fetishism is more greatly accentuated when the activity developed in social relations becomes more complex and mediated: "In our description of how production relations are converted into entities and rendered independent in relation to the agents of production, we leave aside the manner in which the interrelations, due to the world-market, its conjunctures, movements of market prices, periods of credit, industrial and commercial cycles, alternations of prosperity and crisis, *appear to them as overwhelming natural laws that irresistibly enforce their will over them, and confront them as blind necessity*" (Marx, 1894: Ch. 48, emphasis added).

Secondly, it is also more greatly accentuated as the development of the logic of capital becomes more uncontrolled, as the natural form of domination is more firmly established, and as subjects lose "their autonomy, their rationality, their capacity for democratic planning of social relations and their control over their conditions of existence and coexistence with their environment" (Kohan, 2007). These two conditions appear to be fully

---

[56] According to Kosik, "*agents of social conditions feel at ease*, as fish do in water, in the world of phenomenal forms that are alienated from their internal connections and are in such isolation absolutely senseless" (Kosik, 1976: 2, emphasis added).

developed under the conditions of neoliberal capital domination, which brings together the circumstances of globalized capital which, as it spreads around the world, has effectively taken apart all of the controls constructed under Keynesianism and has returned to the conditions of the natural form of domination. The spaceship does not lack a pilot; it is governed by the logic of fetishized things, by the logic of capital.[57]

In the final section of this chapter, I will examine the direction being taken by this ship, at least according to the spokespeople for the pilot who, as its personifications, are convinced that their master is immortal[58] and, as such, humankind and its historical development have no alternative but to submit to the command of the fetish.[59] But first, I will offer a reflection on the power of the fetish in the neoliberal world.

THE COMMAND OF THE FETISH

In the previous section, I examined three of the properties of the fetishism of capital, related to how things acquire social properties, autonomous action and command over producers. To these properties, a fourth must be added: capitalist production relations are presented as eternal.

"Capital," says Marx, "*is not a thing*, but rather a definite social production relation, belonging to a definite historical formation of society, which is manifested in a thing and lends this thing a specific social character. Capital is not the sum of the material and produced means of production. Capital is rather the means of production transformed into capital, which in themselves are no more capital than gold or silver in itself is money" (Marx, 1894: Ch. 48, emphasis added). The means of production and labor are eternal conditions for human production, unlike the social relation,

---

[57] According to Ianni, the metaphor of the *spaceship* carries with it the idea of the decline of the status of individuals, either singular or collective, as a subject of reason and of history, now reduced to "producing the material and spiritual conditions of their subordination and probable dissolution." And he adds, quoting Robert Kurz: "*Universal reason, supposedly absolute, has been debased to mere functional rationality at the service of the process of appreciation of money (which has no subject), even to the point of the contemporary unconditional capitulation of the so-called sciences of the spirit*" (Ianni, 1996: 8).

[58] "These formulae, which bear it stamped upon them in unmistakable letters that they belong to a state of society in which the process of production has the mastery over man instead of being controlled by him... appear to the bourgeois intellect to be as much a self-evident necessity imposed by Nature as productive labor itself" (Marx, 1867: Ch. 1).

[59] In contrast with this *submission to the fetish*, Marx asserts that "the life-process of society, which is based on the material process or production, does not strip off its mystical veil until it is treated as production by freely associated men, and is consciously regulated by them in accordance with a settled plan" (Marx, 1867: Ch. 1, Sect. 4).

which converts them into capital, and converts capital into wage-labor. But fetishism identifies the social relation with the thing itself, and the latter thus appears just as eternal as the former.

Fetishism, as a support to the eternal nature of capitalism, is the ultimate basis of bourgeois ideology: the social properties, autonomous action and command over producers associated with things are not, to the fetishizing mind, individual conditions of a moment in the history of humanity, but their general, immutable and eternal conditions[60] and, as such, are insuperable: "The formal independence of these conditions of labor in relation to labor, the unique form of this independence with respect to wage-labor, is then *a property inseparable* from them as things, as material conditions of production, an inherent, immanent, intrinsic character of them as elements of production. Their definite social character in the process of capitalist production bearing the stamp of a definite historical epoch is a natural and intrinsic substantive character belonging to them, as it were, from time immemorial, as elements of the production process" (Marx, 1894: Ch. 48, emphasis added).

Thus, at least for those who are ideological prisoners of capitalist production relations, against the power of the fetish there is nothing that can be done. Consequently, the starting point for emancipation from the ideological domination of capital consists in social questioning of capitalist ownership, the abandonment of the fetishist perception of its eternal nature and of the need to submit to its command. Once we break free of this fetishism, we find that both the competitiveness and criminal activity that dominate the world today are at the service of the fetish, that their needs are derived from the needs of the fetish. Thus, at least on the ideological level, we experience a radical liberation which is necessary, although by no means sufficient, to give the working class the capacity to oppose the power of capital (economic, political and ideological).[61]

---

[60] "The changed form of the conditions of labor, i.e. alienated from labor and confronting it independently, whereby the produced means of production are thus transformed into capital, and the land into monopolized land, or landed property – this *form belonging to a definite historical period* thereby coincides with the existence and function of the produced means of production and of the land in the process of production in general... [I]f labor as wage-labor is taken as the point of departure, so that the identity of labor in general with wage-labor appears to be self-evident, then capital and monopolized land *must also appear as the natural form* of the conditions of labor in relation to labor in general" (Marx, 1894: Ch. 48).

[61] "The recent scientific discovery, that the products of labor, [in] so far as they are values, are but material expressions of the human labor spent in their production, marks, indeed, an epoch in the history of the development of the human race, but, *by no means*

In the following chapter, I will examine the general conditions for this process, but it is worth noting here that liberation from the ideological domination of capital is associated with a general process of decline of capitalism that makes it necessary to overcome it by transforming it into a society of freely associated human beings who submit the material production process to their planned and conscious control, "instead of being ruled by it as by a blind power." However, in the world today we are faced with a paradox: the same conditions that are making it increasingly urgent to break free of the domination of capital are also rendering that liberation more difficult. The fetish is weakened but at the same time increasingly fierce and threatening, like an old man refusing to die, forcing humanity to pay the heavy price of suffering a long and destructive terminal phase.

The defeat of capitalism as the fulfillment of a historic need is an open process, involving the conditions under which the transformation may take place, that is, the degree to which the logic of the fetish will develop before humanity frees itself from its command, and the possibility that such liberation may be thwarted if the fetish and its personifications end up destroying humanity, as warn some of the more pessimistic assessors of both the magnitude of the destructive capacity that capital has attained in the contemporary world and the growing and increasingly radical contempt it shows for life.

Globalization: The Enhanced Power of the Fetish

In previous chapters, I examined the economics of neoliberal capital as an apparatus employed to achieve its most basic and intimate goal, to concentrate all of the world's wealth, and its politics as a systematic design to position nation-states in line with this purpose by establishing them as spaces of global political power that guarantee the free movement of capital and the global administration of competitiveness and criminal activity, both to strengthen its economics and its politics and to resolve the problems of what it calls social governance, meaning the obstacles raised by social resistance.

---

dissipates the mist through which the social character of labor appears to us to be an objective character of the products themselves... The fact that in the particular form of production with which we are dealing, viz., the production of commodities, the specific social character of private labor carried on independently, consists in the equality of every kind of that labor, by virtue of its being human labor, which character, therefore, assumes in the product the form of value – *this fact appears to the producers, notwithstanding the discovery above referred to, to be... real and final"* (Marx, 1867: Ch. 1, Sect. 4, emphasis added).

In dismantling the nation-state as the historic space for the regulation of its behavior,[62] neoliberal capital established conditions unparalleled in the history of capitalism for the full deployment of the power of the fetish and gave rise to "economic forces that impose on society the quest for profit as an *absolute priority*... a financial and economic *system that has been placed out of the reach of any social and political intervention*" (Touraine, 2010, emphasis added).

Subjugated more than ever before in the history of capitalism to the command of the fetish, "human beings and concepts of life are disappearing from economic concepts... the theory and the praxis of economics no longer has the real needs of humanity as its point of departure; society loses its primacy over economics and any reflection on society has vanished" (Kurnitsky, 2000).[63] In the words of Samir Amín, "capitalism... has done away with any system of human values, replacing it with the exclusive exigencies of submission to the supposed laws of the market;" (Amin, 2003a) and, according to Kohan, "it is the capitalist mercantile society – which today has reached truly global dimensions, although potentially it has had such dimensions since its infancy – which erases human beings, eliminates any possibility of their deciding rationally on the social order, annihilates their political sovereignty and exercises a despotic control over their daily lives and their mental health" (Kohan, 2007).[64]

PROBLEMS... WITHOUT SOLUTIONS

Under these conditions problems are plentiful, and perusing any newspaper can reveal what daily life has turned into in this world dominated by neoliberal capital: on almost any day in the last two years, in any of the countries of the world, the menu of news includes competitiveness, poverty, unemployment, terrorism, crime, and crises of various kinds (economic, environmental, health crises, etc.). Opinions of the spokespeople for neoliberal capital abound, invariably focused on arguing for

---

[62] "Freeing up trade and industry from any state protection or control is today the aim openly stated by politicians and big industrialists" (Kurnitzky, 2000).

[63] "Free competition of private economic interests is ultimately replacing all forms of social coexistence" (Kurnitsky, 2000).

[64] "The apparent 'absolute objectivity' of the social order ends up predominating over the subjectivities subjugated to the fetishist order... The rules governing the life of this objectivity, which are beyond all human control, assume absolute autonomy and take the helm of the ship of society. They become independent of the collective conscience and will" (Kohan, 2007).

the unavoidable need to pursue and develop their policies, explaining that the problems are due to their constantly inadequate application.[65] In some periodicals at least, reflective opinions also appear. For example, Touraine examines the economic and environmental crises and asserts that

> "we have to acknowledge that we have reached the limits of the possible trying to maintain our way of life and our methods of financial management. The combination of these two orders of problems places us indisputably under *a risk of a greater catastrophe*. To this must be added a third crisis – a crisis of political action... We find ourselves facing three crises that mutually reinforce one another, and there is currently no assurance that we will be capable of finding a solution to any of them. In other words, instead of dreaming irresponsibly of a way out of the crisis which tends to be defined, all too cheerfully, according to the recovery of profits by the banks, we need to acknowledge *the need to renew and transform political life* so that it may be capable of mobilizing all the forces possible against *several fatal threats*" (Touraine, 2010, emphasis added).[66]

FETISHISM AND POSTMODERNITY

But what is alarming is not only the magnitude of the problems but the inability to resolve them: "in the near future, in the next ten years, we run the risk of becoming victims of new economic crises, of an exacerbation of the ecological hazard and of increasing political confusion... If we had to say today what the most likely future is, the exacerbation of the crises or the conception and construction of a new type of society based on respect for human rights by the vast majority, we would have to respond honestly that the pessimistic hypothesis is more probable than the optimistic option, which places its confidence in the capacity of human beings to save their own future" (Touraine, 2010).

---

[65] Consider, for example, the following from two articles published in the January 6, 2010 edition of the Spanish newspaper *El País*: "They didn't need three hours to work out that they were in agreement on the basic point: to strengthen the economic government of Europe, because this is *the only possibility* that the Old Continent has to compete with the United States and emerging powers like Brazil, China and India" (Aizpeolea, 2010); "the unsuccessful attempt of the suicide bomber has prompted the introduction of a controversial system of body scanning... In 30 seconds, the traveler is stripped naked... The White House has been quick to remind us that *the loss of privacy may be a minor necessary evil in the great struggle against terrorism*" (Oppenheimer and Alandete, 2010, emphasis added).

[66] This quote is taken from an article published on the same day as the two quoted above.

I have already examined how this inability to resolve the problems it generates is structurally grounded in the domination of neoliberal capital, deriving from the fact that strategies are not designed to resolve them but to administrate them, and the fact that neoliberal capital defines the problems it creates as opportunities to pursue the development of its logic. It should also be noted that postmodernity, which has become the official ideology of neoliberal capital, is used to construct a discourse hostile to the search for solutions; a profoundly fetishized discourse, carefully elaborated to confirm the power of the fetish. Although postmodernity pervades the work of many authors and (either as an explicit theme or as implicit content) virtually all branches of knowledge today, in some of its versions, such as that of Lyotard (1984), one of its main theorists (and the one I will refer to here because, apart from his consistent and systematic approach, his work has the advantage of dealing specifically with the question of knowledge, and thus has a direct affinity with the subject of my analysis), we find the examination of capitalism as a "self-regulated system" that is "self-programmed like an intelligent machine," which dismisses what opposes it and which, although its logic exacerbates society's afflictions, offers no alternative or possibility of solution to the problems it creates: the post-modern narrative, to put it in his own language, is the narrative of the ultimate victory of the fetish.

Eliminating Dead Weight

According to Lyotard, "in the 1950s with Parsons's conception of society as a self-regulating system... the theoretical and even material model is no longer the living organism; it is provided by cybernetics." But in Parsons's work, "the principle behind the system is still, if I may say so, optimistic; it corresponds to the stabilization of growth economies and societies of abundance under the aegis of a moderate Welfare State" (Lyotard, 1984: 11). In contrast, says Lyotard, "in the work of contemporary German theorists, *Systemtheorie* is technocratic, even cynical, not to mention despairing; the harmony between the needs and hopes of individuals or groups and the functions guaranteed by the system is now only a secondary component of its functioning; the true goal of the system, *the reason it programs itself like a computer*, is the optimization of the global relationship between *input* and *output*, in other words, *performativity*" (Lyotard, 1984: 11, emphasis added).

Liberal capitalism, says Lyotard, after having been subdued by Keynesianism, has reasserted itself and, at its height, has eliminated both Keynesianism and the "communist alternative"[67] (Lyotard, 1984: 5). Under these new conditions, "knowledge has become the principal force of production... In the postindustrial and postmodern age, science will maintain and no doubt strengthen its preeminence... [it] is already, and will continue to be, a major – perhaps the major – stake in the worldwide competition for power," and the process "goes hand in hand with a change in the function of the state... functions of regulation, and therefore of reproduction, are being and will be further withdrawn from administrators and *entrusted to machines*" (Lyotard, 1984: 14, emphasis added).

Subjugated to the new exigencies of power and competition, knowledge can no longer be legitimated by the narrative of speculation favored by truth[68], or by the narrative of emancipation favored by justice[69], and even less by a narrative that attempts a synthesis of truth and justice, whereby "the scientific search for true causes always coincides with the pursuit of just ends in moral and political life... the only role positive knowledge [denotative utterances referring to what is true] can play is to inform the practical subject about the reality within which the execution of the prescription is to be inscribed [referring to what is just]" (Lyotard, 1984: 32, 36). Thus, in the context of the fall of Keynesianism and of the "communist alternative" and as an "effect of the blossoming of techniques and technologies... which has shifted emphasis from the ends of action to its means... the grand narrative has lost its credibility... the project of the system-subject is a failure, the goal of emancipation has nothing to do with science" (Lyotard, 1984: 37, 41).

The modern alternative (legitimation by truth and by justice) is dismissed, and rising up in its place, defining "the nature of the social bond",[70]

---

[67] This obviously refers to the form of state capitalism that claimed the title of "real socialism", to which I referred in Chapters 4 and 5.

[68] Science seeks "knowledge for its own sake... science obeys its own rules... Speculation is here the name given the discourse on the legitimation of scientific discourse... that is to say, philosophical. Philosophy must restore unity to learning, which has been scattered into separate sciences... to realize this project of totalization" (Lyotard, 1984, 32, 33, 34).

[69] "The subject... is humanity as the hero of liberty. All peoples have a right to science... The State receives its legitimacy not from itself but from the people... the State... assumes direct control over the training of the 'people' under the name of the 'nation' in order to point them down the path to progress... knowledge finds its validity not within itself... but in a practical subject – humanity... its epic is the story of its emancipation from everything that prevents it from governing itself" (Lyotard, 1984: 31, 32, 35).

[70] This is the title of Chapters 4 and 5 of Lyotard's book.

is the postmodern form of legitimation, legitimation by performativity: "it was more *the desire for wealth* than the desire for knowledge that initially enforced upon technology the imperative of performance improvement... the goal is no longer truth, but performativity[71] – that is, the best possible *input/output* equation. The state and/or company must abandon the idealist or humanist narratives of legitimation in order to justify the new goal: in the discourse of today's financial backers of research, *the only credible goal* is power. Instruments are purchased not to find the truth, but to augment power.... The question posed by the state or institutions of higher education is no longer 'Is it true?' but 'What use is it?' In the context of the mercantilization of knowledge, more often than not this question is equivalent to 'Is it saleable?' And in the context of power-growth: 'Is it efficient?'" (Lyotard, 1984: 45, 46, 51, emphasis added).

Even the variant explored by Lyotard, which he calls "legitimation by paralogy" (postmodern science as research into instabilities, which "per se has little affinity with the quest for performativity," as the expansion of science is not achieved "by means of the positivism of efficiency," but through searching and inventing), is ultimately subjugated to legitimation by performativity: "*permissiveness toward the various games is made conditional on performativity. The redefinition of the norms of life consists in enhancing the system's competence for power*," unless the scientist refuses to "cooperate with the authorities," and makes "a move in the direction of counterculture, *with the attendant risk that all possibility for research will be foreclosed due to lack of funding*" (Lyotard, 1984: 54, 64, emphasis added).

The personifications of capital, the decision makers[72] to use Lyotard's term, attempt to adapt all social life "to input/output matrices, following a logic which implies that their elements are commensurable and that the whole is determinable. They allocate our lives for the growth of power. In matters of social justice and of scientific truth alike, the legitimation of

---

[71] According to Lyotard, the terms *performance* and *performativity* (of a system) refer to "optimal performance and measurable efficiency in *input/output* relations" and he adds that, unlike a denotative utterance (in which "the addressee is put in a position of having to give or refuse his assent"), the distinctive feature of a performative utterance "is that its effect upon the referent coincides with its enunciation... [*it*] *is not subject to discussion or verification on the part of the addressee*, who is immediately placed in the new context created by the utterance" (Lyotard, 1984: 26, emphasis added).

[72] "The ruling class is and will continue to be the class of the 'decision makers'. It is no longer composed of the traditional political class, but of a composite layer by corporate leaders, high-level administrators, and the heads of the major professional, labor, political and religious organizations" (Lyotard, 1984: 35).

that power is based on its optimizing the system's performance – efficiency. The application of this criterion to all of our games necessarily entails a certain terror, whether soft or hard" (Lyotard, 1984: 10).[73]

In the postmodern form of legitimation, legitimation by performativity, it is easy enough to identify a radical submission to the logic of the fetish. Capital does away with the dead wood represented by the old, obsolete narratives and banalities such as truth and justice. However, more generally, what Lyotard's examination reveals is the need, wholeheartedly assumed by both its ideologues and its personifications, to unburden capital of any consideration that is opposed to its self-regulation.

Rejecting Humanism

If the legitimation of postmodern knowledge is constituted by the performativity of the fetish, it is a given that the old discourses – such as humanism or the political principle of the general public interest, which were appealed to when seeking solutions to the problems afflicting humankind (and now more than ever our problems truly affect all of humankind) – would be dismissed as obsolete and irrelevant. Although throughout this study I have been advocating not only the relevance of, but the urgent need for, an examination of the reality of the contemporary world from the perspective of the analysis of class and from the position of those dispossessed of the means of production, the gravity of the problems affecting contemporary society, the risk that they represent to all human beings, prompts consideration of the need to examine them from a humanist,[74] universalist perspective.

Edward Said defended humanism as "the only, and I would go so far as saying the final resistance we have against the inhuman practices and injustices that disfigure human history" and the recovery of "the rational interpretative skills that are the legacy of humanistic education… as the active practice of a worldly secular, rational discourse" (Said, 2003).

---

[73] Lyotard defines terror as "the efficiency gained by the elimination or by the threat of elimination of a 'player' from the language game one shares with him. He is silenced or consents, not because he has been refuted, but because his ability to participate has been threatened…" There are many ways in which he might be deprived of this ability. The threat is essentially: "Adapt your aspirations to our ends, or else…" (Lyotard, 1984: 64).

[74] The basic principle of humanism, according to Sader, is that "men make their own history, even when they are not aware of the fact" (Sader, 2007). This allows criticism of views that displace people as the center of the world, with its *problems*, but also with its *solutions*, in favor of diverse fetishes (including capital, which is what concerns us here).

According to Touraine, the search for solutions "must have a universalist character, as it represents the defense of the whole of humanity... We appeal to human rights against economic globalization... We speak less and less of interests and more and more of rights. Such is the chief transformation of our society. It is so deep that it is hard for us to perceive it, and, above all, we lack the institutional means necessary to resolve our problems" (Touraine, 2010). And indeed, if we step back and remove the blinders with which the fetishism of neoliberal ideology obscures our vision, we will be struck by the profound irrationality that pervades the contemporary world in relation to human needs: "everything is organized, planned, prevented or induced with profit in mind," a profit enjoyed only by "the small number holding power, and for whom human lives outside their private circle... have no existence... except as utilitarian assets" (Forrester, 1999: 13, 126).[75] The logic that capital imposes on society is in profound contradiction with any humanist construction that we have, even the most impoverished.

Of course, the perspective of the capitalist class is always biased and hostile toward universalist integration but, given the nature of the problems – at least those that threaten the very survival of humanity – it should be more receptive and tolerant, yet it is not; Said himself complained of the scornful dismissal of the humanism he defended "by sophisticated postmodern critics" (Said, 2003). This should not greatly surprise us; capital is far too concerned with its own affairs – the gestation of the last man absorbs all its energy – and lacks the time, interest and conditions to concern itself with the affairs of humanity. What is new, however, lies in the fact that there is not only a virtual contempt, but a detailed theoretical elaboration to dismiss any concern for anything as irrelevant as humanity: "This swaggering boastfulness of a deregulated capitalism, as the best of all possible worlds, is a novelty of the current hegemonic system" (Anderson, 2004: 36).

In fact, far from viewing it as a contribution to possible solutions to problems, they see in humanism a threat: Gustavo Ogarrio remarks on the "attack of a kind of postmodernity against humanism, identified without nuances or contextual framing, which views any formulation departing from any of the dimensions of the concepts of historicity and subject as a

---

[75] "While social ferocity always existed, it had imperative limits, because labor resulting from human lives was indispensable to those who held power... Never has humanity as a whole been so threatened in its survival... human beings until now were always given a guarantee: they were essential to the function of the planet" (Forrester, 1999: 126).

metanarrative or transcendentalist temptation" (Ogarrio, 2003). And indeed, a humanism like the one proposed by Said is extremely dangerous, as he describes it as "the ability to use one's mind historically and rationally for the purposes of reflective understanding," in opposition to "the tightening of the grip of demeaning generalization and triumphalist cliché, the dominance of crude power allied with simplistic contempt for dissenters and "others," on the part of "our leaders and their intellectual lackeys" (Said, 2003).[76]

Rejecting Politics

In Chapters 7 and 8 I examined how nation-states – particularly underdeveloped ones – have been systematically disabled as spaces for regulating the behavior of capital in deference to a supreme principle: the all-powerful market forces, which no human power can oppose. Capital rules all and is ruled by nothing. The logic and rationale of transnationalized capital is imposed upon the nation-state in the privileged position of reason and the public interest constructed by bourgeois political science and, in the absence of any institutional framework to replace it, the door is left open for the wildest irrationality and particularization to be unleashed: "to free the economy from the protection of the state means to free the economy from the primacy of politics.

In so doing, democracy, the social contract, the rule of law and human rights are cancelled, and the conquests of the French Revolution are all rolled back. Because the French Revolution not only brought down absolute monarchy; its historic conquest also consisted in making society master of its own house, making representatives elected by universal suffrage those who made the decisions on the forms of social coexistence based on a social contract, and creating a rule of law whereby society could decide on the structure of its economy" (Kurnitsky, 2000). Neoliberal

---

[76] In Latin America, although the development of antagonisms has been less intense than in the Arab world, there is no shortage of authors who offer a more extreme description of the *danger* that humanism represents for neoliberalism: "the countries of ALBA [Bolivarian Alliance for the Americas] are building an economic system *without precedent*, with the human being at the heart, based on solidarity, cooperation, redistribution and complementariness. In contrast, the government and legislature of the United States retain only a few remnants of a humanist and humanitarian vision of political economics. It is worth examining this contrast further, because it clarifies the basic motive behind the imperialist military aggression of the United States and its allies, which will probably lead the region into war" (Solo, 2009, emphasis added).

capital, while provoking the disorganization of the material conditions for national regulation and economic governance, has introduced a new common sense: "people needed to view the world as a dynamic of production, circulation and consumption of commodities in *highly depoliticized processes* and, therefore, *to assess the facts and the meaning of those facts according to this mercantile culture*" (Tapia, 2008, emphasis added).

Politics and reflection on the public sphere is replaced, according to Tapia, "by a culture of 'entertainment', where every politician, rather than offering a project for life and society, tries to appeal most to the audience," and by the mass media as forums for expression and production of public opinion. The public sphere is just a show because it does not matter, because its purpose is precisely to reinforce the conviction that it is irrelevant, that the important decisions have already been taken and the course of history is already determined. Politics is thus rejected by neoliberal capital as a producer of solutions to the problems it generates, thereby producing a crisis in the political sphere as a sphere of reflection, of proposals of projects for existence with the capacity to make a real impact on the regulation of relations between social classes. The irrationality of the whole coexists with the rationality of the part as society as a whole is fragmented into unconnected segments.

If politics is, as Moulian argues, "the art of choosing goals" and "always involves critical discussion, both historically and contextually, of the goals that society adopts," neoliberalism has eliminated it and, in doing so, has eliminated the discussion of alternatives: "politics has been reduced to administration... nobody seriously considers the replacement of any of the core aspects of the system" (Moulian, 2000). This sterilization even affects philosophy. Most philosophers, according to Mario Bunge, "do not address new problems, or explore what is happening in science and technology, or concern themselves with the main problems confronting humanity. Ontologists imagine possible worlds but ignore the only real one; moral philosophers debate the problem of abortion in depth, but overlook the much more serious problems of hunger, oppression and fanaticism. Exaggerated attention to mini-problems and academic games; insubstantial formalism and formless substantiality; fragmentarism and aphorism... postmodernism, and, in particular, so-called 'weak thought', have wreaked havoc in humanities departments" (Bunge, 2003).

In this way, the depoliticization fostered by the domination of neoliberal capital is permeating all branches of knowledge and expanding throughout the citizenry of its democracy. The model citizen, solidly integrated into the Competitiveness Promotion Brigades, does not reflect on the hierarchy of society's goals; but then neither does the pariah, the criminal, the informal worker, the illegal immigrant, or the racist, xenophobic neo-Nazi.[77]

TURNING DEAD WOOD INTO INPUT

Let us return now to Lyotard to observe how dead wood like truth and justice (although the same procedure can be extended to any uncomfortable narrative, such as humanism, democracy or the political theories of the social contract or the common good) can be turned into input that enhances the performativity of capital. But first, to avoid any confusion, it is worth reiterating where the absolute priority lies: "Having competence in a performative-oriented skill does indeed seem saleable... *and it is efficient by definition. What no longer makes the grade is competence as defined by other criteria, such as true/false, just/unjust, etc.*" (Lyotard, 1984: 51, emphasis added). Nevertheless, in relation to truth, it is important to recall a few salient points.

Firstly (as is obvious), that the aim is not to reject the production of knowledge in general, but to encourage the production of relevant knowledge. Those who have resources to fund research, even for the dissemination of the knowledge, are the state and the companies, but the funds are allocated "in accordance with this logic of power growth. Research sectors that are unable to argue that they contribute... to the optimization of the system's performance are abandoned... The criterion of performance is explicitly invoked by the authorities to justify their refusal to subsidize certain research centers... *The desired goal becomes... the best performativity of the social system...* The general effect [of the performativity principle] is to subordinate the institutions of higher learning to the authorities" (Lyotard, 1984: 47–48, emphasis added).

Secondly, this truth, which is partial, biased and relevant only to the logic of the development of the fetish, can be promoted to the category of the socially prevailing truth: "No money, no proof – and that means... no truth. The games of scientific language become the games of the rich, in which whoever is wealthiest has the best chance of being right" (Lyotard, 1984: 45).

---

[77] "Life is lived in immediate terms, never thinking in perspective; the world has no future, [because] 'the future is already here'. History has no meaning in relation to what lies ahead" (Aruj, 2000).

Thirdly, a circle is closed around wealth, performativity and truth: "An equation between wealth, efficiency and truth is thus established... no technology without wealth, but no wealth without technology... science becomes a force of production, in other words, a moment in the circulation of capital... since performativity increases the ability to produce proof, it also increases the ability to be right: the technical criterion, introduced on a massive scale into scientific knowledge, cannot fail to influence the truth criterion" (Lyotard, 1984: 84, 86).[78] It is thus clear that the aim is to establish a relevant relation between truth and performance.

In Chapter 7, I examined how democracy is turned into neoliberal democracy, i.e. stripped of all of its critical potential, of all that might hinder the development of the logic of the fetish; reduced in theory to a procedural issue disconnected from any construction of socioeconomic totality and in practice to the act of filling in and submitting a ballot paper, it becomes a "performative" democracy, an input that enhances the performativity of capital. And once the technique has been acquired, the procedure[79] can be applied, in general terms, to various objects. For example, with regard to "the relationship between justice and performance: the probability that an order would be pronounced just was said to increase with its chances of being implemented, which would in turn increase with the performance capability of the prescriber," with the result that *the normativity of laws is replaced by the performativity of procedures*" (Lyotard, 1984: 46, emphasis added).

Rejecting Criticism

Thus, the postmodern program does not reject truth, justice, humanism, the common good, democracy, or the social contract in general. What it explicitly posits is the concept of the relevant relationship between these narratives and the performativity of capital. It is thus concerned with

---

[78] "Whence its credibility: it has the means to become a reality, and that is all the proof it needs. This is what Horkheimer called the 'paranoia' of reason" (Lyotard, 1984: 12).

[79] "This procedure operates within the following framework: since 'reality' is what provides the evidence used as proof in scientific argumentation, and also provides prescriptions and promises of a juridical, ethical and political nature with results, one can master all of these games by mastering 'reality'. That is precisely what technology can do. By reinforcing technology, one reinforces 'reality' and one's chances of being just and right increase accordingly" (Lyotard, 1984: 47).

turning them from dead wood into input that will enhance this performa-tivity. In other words, it is concerned with eliminating criticism made from these perspectives of the logic of the fetish, eliminating any construction based on them that might be turned into a project of emancipation, in order to make them relevant to the development of the logic of the fetish. "[T]his realism of systematic self-regulation, and this perfectly sealed cir-cle of facts and interpretations" Lyotard argues "can be judged paranoid only if one has, or claims to have, at one's disposal a viewpoint that is in principle immune from their allure. This is the function of the principle of class struggle in theories of society based on the work of Marx" (Lyotard, 1984: 12).

Thus, if this viewpoint is eliminated (i.e. if Marxism is eliminated[80]), we will be happily settled in this paranoid realism of the systematic self-regulation of the fetish: "This is how legitimation by power takes shape. Power is not only good performativity, but also effective verification and good verdicts... It is self-legitimating, in the same way a system organized around performance maximization seems to be" (Lyotard, 1984: 47). The elimination of this viewpoint thus becomes the core purpose of the post-modernist narrative.

This viewpoint, as I indicated in the first chapters of this work, was constructed by Marx from two intersecting perspectives: the first refers to necessary relations, independent of the will and consciousness of human beings, relations which have a tendential development and which neces-sarily lead to the end of the capitalist mode of production, while the sec-ond relates to the struggle of the classes. Lyotard, as will be shown below, does not commit the vulgarity of declaring the internal contradictions of capitalism resolved, as do some other postmodernists, but positions his argument that the critical model has been invalidated at the level of the class struggle. The delegitimation of the emancipation narrative is based on the retreat of Keynesianism and the defeat of "the communist alternative." According to his assessment of Marxism, "in the countries with liberal or advanced liberal management," the struggles inspired by Marxism have been transformed into "regulators of the system," while "in communist countries, the totalizing model and its totalitarian effect

---

[80] Although the discourse of "the decline of the unifying and legitimating power of the *grand narratives*" is targeted at any criticism of the logic of the fetish, its privileged target is Marxism. According to Lyotard, "it would be easy to show that Marxism has wavered between the two models of narrative legitimation [of speculation and emancipation]" (Lyotard, 1984: 36).

have made a comeback in the name of Marxism itself, and the struggles in question have simply been deprived of the right to exist" (Lyotard, 1984: 13).[81]

In this way – and this is his final argument – "the social foundation of the principle of division, or class struggle, was blurred to the point of losing all of its radicality; we cannot conceal the fact that the critical model in the end lost its theoretical standing and was reduced to the status of a 'utopia' or 'hope', a token protest raised in the name of man or reason or creativity, or again of some social category – such as the Third World or the students – on which is conferred in extremis the henceforth improbable function of critical subject" (Lyotard, 1984: 13). In contrast with the postmodernist position, over the course of these chapters I have explained the historical trajectory taken by the different eras of capitalist domination, and the conclusion that can be drawn from this examination (particularly in the case of the neoliberal pattern) – the need to further develop this criticism – is exactly the opposite of that put forward by the postmodernists.

The domination pattern concept is useful for analysis, but also for political purposes. It is useful for analysis because it links the history of domination to the tendencies that have directed the historical development of capitalism and to the circumstances of the class struggle. It is useful for political purposes because it reveals the subject of the process (class or a faction thereof), helping to dismantle the most intrinsic tactic of bourgeois ideology aimed at defusing any inquiry by the dominated classes who seek the cause of and the solution to their woes: to present the order of capitalist society as an expression of human nature, the needs of capital as natural needs and the process of capital as natural, as a process without a subject. If, as its ideologues take for granted, the laws governing the operation of capital are as natural and eternal as the law of gravity, the afflictions of the workers are natural, eternal and irremediable and the only rational response is resignation. But as capital is in fact a product of society and history, resignation is not only irrational but impossible and, although for Lyotard it is merely a "token protest raised in the name of man," the project of emancipation of humanity from the power of the fetish – the incorrigible utopia referred to in a song by Spanish songwriter

---

[81] "Everywhere the Critique of political economy (the subtitle of Marx's *Capital*) and its correlate, the critique of alienated society, are used in one way or another as aids in programming the system" (Lyotard, 1984: 13).

Joan Manuel Serrat,[82] which "is not satisfied with the possible," and "raises hurricanes of rebellion" – is as inalienable a feature of the working class as the will to live itself. "Without utopia, life would be a rehearsal for death" sings Serrat, and he is right for two reasons.

First, because the class struggle in capitalism remains unaltered: the weakness and defeat of those dispossessed of the means of production, which under the current circumstances has resulted in their resistance being "blurred to the point of losing all of its radicality," has as a necessary correlate the reinforcement and the fierce radicalization of the struggle on the side of capital. Second, because with its development, capital tends to aggravate the social ills that it provokes, as Lyotard himself acknowledges: "The logic of maximum performance is no doubt inconsistent in many ways, particularly with respect to contradiction in the socioeconomic field: it demands both less work (to lower production costs) and more (to lessen the social burden of the idle population). But," he adds, in keeping with a discourse convinced of the eternal nature of the fetish, "our incredulity is now such that we no longer expect salvation to rise from these inconsistencies, as did Marx" (Lyotard, 1984: xxiv). He subsequently confirms this point of view: "Even when its rules are in the process of changing and innovations are occurring, even when its dysfunctions (such as strikes, crises, unemployment, or political revolutions) inspire hope and lead to belief in an alternative, what is actually taking place is an internal readjustment, and its result can be no more than an increase in the system's 'viability'. The only alternative to this kind of performance improvement is entropy, or decline" (Lyotard, 1984: 11–12).

ETERNALIZING THE IMPOTENCE

The invalidation of criticism is precisely the eternalization of the subjugation of humanity to the logic of the fetish, and its resigned submission to decline, at the mercy of the entropy of the system, with all the enthusiasm for necrophilia and genocide that this entails. And postmodernism pursues its work in relation to this declared supreme purpose and goes a step further: if the working class has been expelled from the position it had reached under Keynesianism, and "real socialism" and its collapse in the current historical context constitute arguments to abandon all criticism

---

[82] "¡Ay! Utopía incorregible que no tiene bastante con lo posible... que levanta huracanes de rebeldía... Sin utopía, la vida sería un ensayo para la muerte." (Joan Manuel Serrat, "Utopía", 1992).

of the logic of capital forever, what follows is the eternalization of the workers' fallen status, maintaining them in a condition of isolation and atomization.

I have already examined how the globalization of capital is constructed on the basis of the fragmentation of the working class; after destroying the corporate structures that upheld the forms of socialization under Keynesianism and confining the working class in conditions of competitivity and alienation, oppressed by crime and fear, capital discovers the wonders of fragmentation (the local, the micronarrative, the isolated and the separate) and tribalization as companions to steer the spaceship and as counterparts to the supposed death of the metanarratives of modernity, i.e. Marxism, which is the only metanarrative that really worries the personifications of capital.

Kohan argues that "the critical view of domination and capitalist exploitation underwent a shift... from the grand theory – centered, for example, on the explanatory concept of the 'mode of production' understood as an articulated whole of social relations in history – to the micronarrative, from the questioning of the classist nature of the state apparatus to the description of the individual confrontation and the 'autonomy' of politics, from the attempt to politically transcend the immediate consciousness of social subjects to the populist apology for specific discourses belonging to each segment of society" (Kohan, 2007).

Postmodernism, as an "ideology legitimizing political impotence," explains Kohan, has promoted a "fetishist dismemberment",[83] isolating the different instances of social relations, separating them rather than locating them as integral parts of a social whole, which, through their calculated dispersal, prevents the comprehension of capitalism as an organized entity and eliminates the very notion of social class. The subject[84] is replaced "by a proliferation of multiplicities, or 'agents', with no unitary

---

[83] "The instances and segments that comprise the social framework become absolutely 'autonomous'... The local fragment takes on a life of its own. The micro-unit began to claim autonomy and turn its back on any logic of struggle at a global level. The specific code of each rebellion (the code of the colonized, of ethnicity, of an oppressed community or people, of gender, of a sexual or generational minority, etc.) no longer recognized any level of connection with the others... Each instance of domination... could only be challenged from its own particular context, turned into an isolated ghetto and into a 'language game' disconnected from any global perspective or universal translation" (Kohan, 2007).

[84] "The subject of Marxism is a collective subject that is constituted as such (incorporating the multiple individualities and group identities) in the struggle against its historic enemy. It is the working class as a whole, and thus constitutes a subject that is not only individual, but collective" (Kohan, 2007).

meaning connecting them or structuring them as a collective identity based on class consciousness and experiences of struggle... With history forgotten and the class struggle negated, the subject also vanishes, his identity is annulled and his memory filed away; in other words, any possibility of criticism of or radical opposition to capitalism is eliminated" (Kohan, 2007).[85]

Situated in this recognized and acceptable field of conflict are the so-called "new social movements" (ecologists, feminists, homosexuals and lesbians, ethnic minorities, etc.). But if capitalist society is eternal, conflicts are merely "skirmishes and protests at a local level, in a micro-world of social movements,"[86] or "external and alien to the core of capitalist social relations" and as such can be solved or overcome without affecting the capitalist regime. The constant in postmodernist discourse is, as Kohan astutely notes, the transformation of political logic "into an infinite collection of diverse, fragmented and brutally scattered logics," (Kohan, 2007) whether this social fragmentation is considered to express multiple conflicts and a plurality of struggles[87] or as sites for the construction of festive and emotional expression.

For example, in relation to the so-called urban tribes, analyses are constructed that interpret them as sites of conflict. According to Carlos Reina, heavy metal is an expression of an urban society that offers few alternatives to its youth: "it channels the violence that the world offers young people. As a result, they assume a violent appearance, expressing themselves in this way... Metal lovers do not present themselves as the perpetrators of violence, but as its victims. They are trying to show what adults have done to them and to the world... This is exactly what metal is all about: the wars, the pollution, the corruption, the political violence, and the death that plague the individual daily because of the irrationality of people, of religions and of systems of domination. Metal and the 'metaller' are a reflection of the world that surrounds us... It is thus not a widespread

---

[85] "If there is no longer a central power to fight, if there no longer exists a privileged space of confrontation where the diverse collective of exploiters and oppressors find a common fortification to guarantee the reproduction of the social order, then there is no way of forming a radical opposition to fight for complete changes to the system" (Kohan, 2007).

[86] "But with the condition that each one must remain confined to its own issues and that all maintain a mutual distance from one another" (Kohan, 2007).

[87] "Instead of the universalist aspirations of socialism and the integrating politics of the struggle against class exploitation, we have a plurality of essentially disconnected individual struggles, leading to submission to capitalism... an excuse for disintegrating the resistance to capitalism" (Ellen Meiksins Wood, as quoted in Kohan, 2007).

form of anarchy, but a critique of society, although in reality it rarely proposes solutions to the problems it exposes" (Reina, 2006).

Other authors interpret these tribes as places for recreational or emotional expression: instead of faith in the future, they argue, we find an emphasis on the present, and instead of the predominance of reason, we witness the return of the emotions, of feelings and festivity.[88] Society is crumbling, the institutions have collapsed, ideologies have lost their force, and, in the place of a society of the masses, new figures take shape, presenting a richly complex, multifarious society: the old social contract, they argue, has been replaced by the idea of belonging to a group, to a tribe; feelings and emotions replace the ideals of reason and the logic of identity gives way to the logic of belonging. We thus witness the rise of the time of the tribes (sexual, musical, artistic, sporting, cultural, religious), of the networks, of the factions, of the fleeting, evanescent groupings and of nomadic beings who wander from one tribe to another, who have no single ideological, sexual, professional or class identity, who do not allow themselves to be pigeon-holed in roles that were once definitive, and who can belong to various tribes simultaneously.[89]

However, the enthusiasm produced by tribalism and its charms[90] should not allow us to forget (in the world of ideas, because in practice they are imposed as an unavoidable reality) certain minor details such as the following: (1) the basic condition of the existence of social classes under capitalism is not altered by this "richly complex, multifarious society"; (2) the members of the tribes still need a means of subsistence and can only obtain them, as in the old pre-postmodern times of capitalism,

---

[88] "In opposition to reason, which proposes that individuals unite for a common project that is reasonable and logical for all... in postmodernity we find a 'being together' that is informed by a sensitive, erotic reason, that is, a 'being together' out of sentimental interest, not common interest in a political or religious project... In opposition to a faith in the future of modernity, there appears in postmodernity a special attention to the present, to the experience of here and now... Tribes are junctions that form part of a network – a network that connects them to each other. This network is the masses... an entity unto itself, i.e. without a purpose... by which it may be differentiated from the notion of society, in which it was understood that specific common purposes existed... the masses breaks up constantly into tribes" (Cassián et al, 2006).

[89] This line of interpretation can be found in works of authors such as Michel Maffesoli (see Maffesoli, 1996) or the interviews he has given to the newspapers *La Nación* (Corradini, 2005) and *El Clarín* (Martiniuk, 2009).

[90] "The term 'identification' implies a process of participation, somewhat magic or mystical. You lose yourself; when I lose myself in a particular tribe, I experience ecstasy. I am no longer myself – I am the group. Through the multiplicity of facets I will participate in a multiplicity of tribes and the interlinking chain of these tribes makes up the masses" (Maffesoli, as quoted in Martiniuk, 2009).

through profits, income or wages; and, (3) in a world with billions of human beings wallowing in poverty, unemployment and labor casualization, competitivity and/or criminal activity constitute the only real life options that neoliberal capital offers to those who, although they may be tribalized, continue to be its modern slaves and, while they may move freely from one tribe to another, nomadic wandering from class to class is impossible, except in the highly unlikely event that the tribe of the worldwide financial oligarchy, perhaps out of boredom[91], should dissolve of its own volition, convert into something with a more relaxed, personal character, and place the means of production and subsistence that it has concentrated at the service of the satisfaction of the needs of humanity.

Without a doubt, this imaginary generous disposition of capital would be gratefully welcomed, but, as it has not happened nor is it at all likely to happen in the future, what capital actually offers in cultural terms is clear. While it continues to globalize, the rest of humanity, in order to escape individual alienation, must tribalize; the tribes may be festive and amorous or sinister and necrophiliac, or even conflictive and rebellious. The argument of weak thought is aimed at fostering an unhealthy weakness in critical thinking, and the death of the metanarrative of emancipation is joyously celebrated in order to strengthen the metanarrative of capital. The only thing that is forbidden, from the perspective of the personifications and ideologues of capital, is the recovery and development of a criticism of the logic of the fetish that would create the conditions for reestablishing the political viability of the project of human emancipation.

In terms of ideological domination, the discourse of postmodernity asserts the hegemony of neoliberal capital in opposition to a counter-hegemonic cultural proposal by the working class: "the homogeneity of the consciousness of a social collective and the disintegration of its enemy takes place precisely in the territory of the cultural battle... Hegemony is a process of articulation and organic unification of diverse heterogeneous, scattered, fragmentary struggles, within which specific groups are able to shape a perspective of unitary confrontation on the basis of a political strategy and a cultural direction... Through hegemony, a social collective (national or international) can broaden the confrontation against

---

[91] Maffesoli contrasts the myth of Dionysus, god of festivity, with the myth of Prometheus, god of progress: "The citizens of the booming modern, progressive, hardworking metropolis, dying of boredom, end up opening their doors to let in Dionysus" (as quoted by Corradini, 2005).

its enemy by threading together many different individual rebellions"
(Kohan, 2007).

Up to this point I have examined the neoliberal pattern of domination on
a level of abstraction corresponding to the concept, with a greater focus
on its general features and its internal logic than its actual manifestation
in history. I now hope to offer some reflections on the project for the future
that this logic entails: the mission and vision of neoliberal capital, to use
the terminology currently in fashion.

THE END OF HISTORY

A basic and undisputed component of this vision is the eternal nature of
capital and, consequently, the end of history. According to Francis
Fukuyama, liberal democracy – which has conquered "rival ideologies like
hereditary monarchy, fascism and most recently communism," represents
"the end point in mankind's ideological evolution," the "final form of government and, as such, constitutes the end of history." As it is "free from
fundamental internal contradictions" (as its problems are due more to
"incomplete implementation of the twin principles of liberty and equality" on which it is based than to any fault in the principles themselves),
"the ideal of liberal democracy could not be improved upon." And, as the
evolution of human societies was not infinite, but ended when mankind
achieved "a form of society that satisfied its deepest and most fundamental longings... there would be no further progress in the development of
underlying principles and institutions, because all of the really big questions had been settled" (Fukuyama, 1992: xi-xii).

This dimension of its vision is not at all surprising given that we know
that it is an eternal[92] characteristic of the fetishist ideology to view the

---

[92] More than 160 years ago, Marx wrote: "Economists have a singular method of procedure. There are only two kinds of institutions for them: artificial and natural. The institutions of feudalism are artificial institutions; those of the bourgeoisie are natural institutions.
In this they resemble the theologians, who likewise establish two kinds of religion. Every
religion which is not theirs is a religion of men, while their own is an emanation from
God... Thus *there has been history, but there is no longer any*" (Marx, 1847: Ch. 2, emphasis
added).

social relations of capitalism as eternal, and as we have seen how the shift from the contained form to the natural form of its domination is celebrated as a great triumph – an eternal triumph over the working class.

"The Last Man"

It is nevertheless worth pausing briefly to examine the notion of the last man. Following Maffesoli, we might think of this as referring to those Dionysian, nomadic peoples who happily wander from one tribe to another. But as Maffesoli does not discuss the concept explicitly, I will turn back to Fukuyama, who argues that, as we have reached the end of history, of the ideological evolution of humanity and the final form of government, and that "liberal principles in economics – the 'free market' – have spread, and have succeeded in producing unprecedented levels of material prosperity," (Fukuyama, 1992: xiii) modern man – "those who live in the old age of mankind" – is the last man: "preoccupied with material gain... devoted to the satisfaction of the myriad small needs of the body ... disabused of the possibility of a direct experience of values... [with] a certain tendency toward relativism, that is, the doctrine that all horizons and value systems are relative to their time and place, and that none are true but reflect the prejudices or interests of those who advance them" (Fukuyama, 1992: 305–307). Yet neither Maffesoli's Dionysian nomadic men nor this modern man explicitly posited by Fukuyama constitute the last man that is being gestated by neoliberal capitalism.

We ought to recall that Lyotard himself repeatedly reminds us who is in charge, and makes it clear that, from the perspective of the one in charge, these little men, Dionysian and/or disillusioned, are of no importance, making it difficult to identify them as the last man. The system is the one in charge and, as Lyotard points out, it is concerned only with its own performativity: "it must induce the adaptation of individual aspirations to its own ends... to guide individual aspirations... in order to make them compatible with the system's decisions." To put it more clearly, the system's decisions "do not have to respect individuals' aspirations: *the aspirations have to aspire to the decisions*... Administrative procedures should make individuals 'want' what the system needs in order to perform well" (Lyotard, 1984: 62, emphasis added).[93] As far as the system is concerned,

---

[93] Elsewhere, Lyotard quotes Claus Mueller: "In advanced industrial society, legal-rational legitimation is replaced by a technocratic legitimation *that does not accord any importance to the beliefs of the citizen or to morality per se*" (Lyotard, 1984: 97, emphasis added).

the aspirations, demands and suffering of individuals – the modern nomadic little men – have no legitimacy: "Within the framework of the power criterion, a request (that is, a form of prescription) gains nothing in legitimacy by virtue of being based on the hardship of an unmet need." Or, expressed more clearly: "The technocrats declare that they cannot trust what society designates as its needs... society cannot know its own needs since they are not variables independent of the new technologies... society can only be aware of the needs it feels in the present state of its technological milieu. It is the nature of the basic sciences to discover unknown properties which remodel the technical milieu and create unpredictable needs" (Lyotard, 1984: 63, 101).

In this way, Lyotard, clearly and with brutal sincerity, invites us to take note of what is important from the perspective of the logic of the fetish: "Rights do not flow from hardship, but from the fact that the alleviation of hardship improves the system's performance. The needs of the most underprivileged should not be used as a system regulator as a matter of principle... [as] their actual satisfaction will not improve the system's performance, but only increase its expenditures... It is against the nature of force to be ruled by weakness" (Lyotard, 1984: 63). Thus, there is only one situation in which the system will take an interest in aspirations, requests or hardship: "The only counterindication is that not satisfying them can destabilize the whole" (Lyotard, 1984: 63); in other words, when social pressure forces the system to divert its valuable resources to attend to a demand in order to avoid the risk of a greater conflict that could reduce its performativity.

Maffesoli's happy nomad and Fukuyama's last man share the common feature of lacking class characteristics, as well as a lack of interest in the narrative of emancipation, in those grand narratives that Lyotard, Vattimo (1991) and others have dismissed. It is quite clear that what would least please the master is that slaves should become interested in their own emancipation, but it is equally clear that the capitalist system's last man cannot reside among the disdainfully treated little men whose half-smiling, half-terrified faces resemble more that of a slave who adapts his aspirations to what his master wants of him, hoping for a pat on the back and an encouraging word in return: "You couldn't be happier, kid!"[94]

---

[94] According to Vega, the paradox of the political pessimism of postmodernism "lies in the fact that, at the same time, it is based on a very optimistic interpretation of the operation of the capitalist system, or more exactly, on the possibilities offered by its prosperity and the widespread nature of mass consumption... they appear still to be living in 'Les

Thus, in essence, the subject is the fetish and the capitalist is merely its personification; its incarnation must be sought for elsewhere.

According to Marx, "it is only because his money constantly functions as capital that the economic guise of a capitalist attaches to a man... Except as personified capital, the capitalist has no historical value, and no right to that historical existence... And so far only is the necessity for his own transitory existence implied in the transitory necessity for the capitalist mode of production" (Marx, 1867: Ch. 23, 24). The right to existence must be defended in competition with other capitalists to earn the right to reach the finishing line; if the subject of the process of capitalist development is the flourishing of the fetish, the last man is its final incarnation, the incarnation of Absolute Monopoly of the means of production and subsistence, i.e. the result of the full development of its internal tendencies.

Following the thought of Heidegger, Roberto Aruj suggests that postmodernism "eliminates the historic subject as the reconstructor of reality, as reconstructor of history... Subjects do not exist; rather, *there are beings that become Being*, in the sense of an entity involved in a transformation in which *the subject is the recipient of the dynamic*" (emphasis added). And these individuals turning into Being, that is, capitalists chosen by the Being to be incarnated, "attempt to maintain their status through competition with no restrictions on its development... Their ultimate goal is to stay in the game because only those who can integrate and adapt to the dynamic established by the system will make it through the elimination rounds. The rest will vanish... the lives of millions of people is worth nothing." (Aruj, 2000)[95] According to Kurnitzky, neoliberalism proclaims that "might is right," and total competition under the precepts of laissez faire turns society into a battleground of individual economic interests, with no limit on the actions of "the ablest and the fittest" (Kurnitzky, 2000).

Treinte Glorieuses' (1945–1975), when European and global capitalism experienced a golden age of booming prosperity, expressed in the politics of the Welfare State, full employment and the material improvement of significant sectors of the population in Western countries... the fundamental ahistoricism of postmodern authors is such that, for them, the golden age of capitalism has continued up to the present day, and they boldly continue to consider its benefits, but not its huge contradictions... they believe that the 'market economy' can only be judged from the comfortable point of view of the few who benefit from capitalism and not from the vast majority that suffers its costs" (Vega, 1997).

[95] It is worth recalling here that according to Marx, the actions of the capitalist "are a mere function of capital – endowed, as capitalism is, in his person, with consciousness and a will," and that "competition makes the immanent laws of capitalist production to be felt by each individual capitalist as external coercive laws. It compels him to keep constantly extending his capital, in order to preserve it..." (Marx, 1867: Ch. 24).

Earlier on, I offered an analysis of the global financial oligarchy, the personification of global financial capital, which aims to concentrate all the world's wealth, while in Chapter 7 I explained how its ruling group (particularly the high-level political bureaucracy of the United States) views itself as the administration of a global government, responsible for bringing all the nation-states into the network in its global administration of competitivity and criminal activity, to compete in the provision of the most profitable conditions and to fight everything that threatens the unhindered development of the free market and the domination of financial capital and the global financial oligarchy. The implementation of this project of economic and political expansion of global financial capital is the project for the future that neoliberal capital offers humanity and is what explains why it bases its ideological domination on the promotion of competitivity, alienation, criminal activity and fear, and why it is so radically hostile to any opposition to the logic of the fetish.

In this global oligarchy, still in fierce competition with itself and in a voracious pursuit of the means of production and subsistence that remain outside its control, lies neoliberal capital's last man, still seeking the full implementation of his mission and vision, i.e. Absolute Monopoly. No doubt, he will continue this pursuit to the extent that society and the project's own internal contradictions allow. Unless the power of the fetish is contained, its logic, and the development of its internal tendencies, will continue to grow.

THE GESTATION OF THE LAST MAN

The gestation of Absolute Monopoly, the last man of neoliberal capital, the implementation of his mission and vision, has various goals, including concentration of wealth and competition, preservation of its intellectual and moral leadership, degradation, surveillance and murder. All of these goals are contained in the development of the productive force of labor and scientific and technological research, and are a basic condition for the development of capitalist relations of production. The first of the above-mentioned goals, concentration of wealth, refers to the substance of capitalist relations. From the first chapters of this work, I have examined how the essence of the power of capital over labor lies in the appropriation of the means of production, offering an analysis of neoliberal economics as an instrument that pursues, as its ultimate goal, the concentration of all the means of production in the world. The notion of the last man as Absolute Monopoly relates to this internal impulse toward concentration and centralization that constitutes one of the essential dimensions of the development of capitalism.

The second goal, competition, is the necessary correlate of the first. Monopoly is constructed in conflict with the dispersal of the means of production. Like the first, it is a permanent condition in the history of capitalism which although it appears to be aimed at transforming the internal relations of capital, is in fact the cause and effect of the transformation of the capital/wage-labor relation, initiated because the form of competition is overdetermined by the relation between capital and labor; to be able to compete unhindered, capital needs to be freed from restrictions in its relations with labor.

In neoliberalism, in contrast with Keynesianism, capitalist competition has two peculiarities: first, it is generally established without state regulation (as deregulated, privatized free market and free competition economics)[96] and second, it is ideologically constructed as a mechanism of self-legitimation. The first aspect has already been examined in this work, and so I will add just a brief note here regarding the second: it is not just that capitalists compete, but that their competitivity is constructed as synonymous with legitimacy.

This issue is explicitly addressed by Lyotard. Since performativity is what matters, the question is whether this discourse of power "can constitute a legitimation." According to Lyotard, "[a]t first glance, it is prevented from doing so by the traditional distinction between force and right, between force and wisdom – in other words, between what is strong, what is just and what is true." But (postmodernist) "force" does not appear to be derived from anything more than the "technical game (in which the criterion is the efficient/inefficient distinction)... 'Context control', in other

---

[96] Competition, according to De Brie, "has little to do with the tournaments between brave knights who move to the beat of the drum of the liberal movement, in which the winner, touched by the grace of the Market-God, is the best product and the best service at the best price. As in the battles of feudal times, anything goes in the economic war, and hitting below the waist is the preferred tactic. The wide array of weapons is in good supply: agreements and cartels, abuse of high positions, social dumping and forced sales, crimes of insider trading and speculation, mergers and dismantling of competitors, false balance sheets, fiddling with accounts and transfer values, tax fraud and evasion through offshore affiliates and shell corporations, embezzlement of public funds and distorted markets, corruption and covert commissions, undeclared earnings and abuse of company assets, surveillance and espionage, blackmail and betrayal, violation of regulations related to the right to work, the freedom of the unions, safety and hygiene, partner contributions and the environment... added to which are the practices in place in the free trade zones that have multiplied around the world... zones that are totally or partially outside the law, especially in terms of corporate, tax or financial regulations" (De Brie, 2000).

words, performance improvement won at the expense of the partner or partners constituting that context (be they 'nature' or men) can pass for a kind of legitimation. De facto legitimation" (Lyotard, 1984: 86–87). Thus, having eliminated irrelevant distinctions (right, wisdom, etc.), competitive efficiency provides the specific legitimacy of neoliberal capital: a de facto legitimacy based on force.

Preservation of Its Intellectual and Moral Leadership

In relation to this third goal, there is also little to add, except to note that as the gestation of the last man progresses and the irreconcilable contradiction that exists between him and the rest of humanity becomes more brutally evident, the use of the mass media to manipulate, control and direct social behavior for political purposes, based on the argument of a situation of a permanent global war on terrorism and organized crime, becomes increasingly perverse and cynical.

We can find an example of this in the war on terrorism, although it could also easily be found in the war on organized crime or, more generally, in any situation in which neoliberal capital seeks to promote its anti-popular or pernicious projects. Rouleau suggests that, "with the pretext of 'communicating', all governments – to varying degrees – practice disinformation," but in times of war, "manipulation of information becomes common currency, whether through the dissemination of half-truths or lies, commission through omission or the spreading of unverifiable rumors." Thus, in preparation for the war against Iraq and to generate a climate of confidence and support for the government's anti-terrorist policy among Americans, there flourished "in the White House and in the Pentagon, in the CIA and in the Department of State" a multitude of "communication departments" and "public relations" advisers and, "in the greatest of secrecy," the Pentagon created "an Office of Strategic Influence, whose mission was to misguide public opinion – a supreme skill – through non-U.S. press agencies (chiefly, the Agence France Presse and Reuters)" (Rouleau, 2003).

It is certainly not surprising that the Pentagon has "decided that even lying is valid," given that "these types of techniques have always been used by the CIA in disinformation campaigns and operations to destabilize foreign governments, for example, in Cuba or Iraq" (Baron, 2002). But there is one substantial difference between past and present models: these campaigns were once directed against foreign enemy governments; now they are directed against the whole world. "According to an article published on the front page of the New York Times, the newly created Office of Strategic Influence is planning to disseminate information to international agencies and media outlets as part of *an effort aimed at influencing public opinion in the heart not only of enemy countries but also of those considered to be friends*, with the aim that all the information broadcast by agencies such as Reuters or Agence France Press *ends up published in the American dailies*"[97] (Baron, 2002, emphasis added).

In February 2002, a scandal broke out when the existence of the Office of Strategic Influence was made public: "in the face of the outrage generated in the Congress and in the press, Donald Rumsfeld, Secretary of Defense, was compelled to offer his apologies and announce the closure of the department, *which was quickly replaced by another* bearing the more discrete name of Office of Special Plans" (Rouleau, 2003, emphasis added). However (and this point is of particular significance), "one of Washington's most notorious 'hawks' and a personal friend of Rumsfeld, Frank Gaffney, published a virulent attack against a 'left' that sought to deprive the United States of *an indispensable instrument of war*" (Rouleau, 2003, emphasis added). In fact, as the gestation of the last man progresses, what is clear above all else is the war that this last man has launched against the rest of humanity; the outstanding feature of the state administration of criminal activity is combat and its establishment as a situation of permanent war (on organized crime and/or international terrorism and/or any useful enemy), which means, as a logical correlate, that everything – from human and civil rights to information and communication[98] – is submitted to the rules of war, thereby legitimating (at least for the personifications of capital) the planned use of propaganda aimed at social and political control.[99]

---

[97] "The main target would be the moderate Islamic Arabic nations, where the discontent and unease provoked by the anti-terrorist war is on the rise and, according to the Pentagon, threatens to destabilize the whole region. But the information, or rather, disinformation, would also be aimed at allied nations in Europe, Asia and Latin America" (Baron, 2002), and at U.S. society itself.

[98] Information and communication *via all forms of media*, including the Internet, which has increasing priority: "For decades, the battle of ideas has been waged on radio and television. Today, that battle has entered a new dimension. It is now being waged on the World Wide Web, as demonstrated by two websites sponsored by the United States European Command" (Coon, 2007).

[99] When questioned about illegal spying on U.S. citizens, President Bush refused to comment: "We don't talk about ongoing intelligence operations to protect the country... Any sources and methods of intelligence will remain guarded in secret," and he explained that the "reason" was that "there is an enemy stalking us who would like to know exactly what we're doing in order to stop it" (AFP, 2005).

The necessity for lies is itself grounded in lies[100] and the circle is thus closed; who, other than the enemy, would be opposed to misleading the enemy? In a state of war, normal democratic conditions cannot be established, as lying, misleading and concealing are necessities of war and true information is only available to Chiefs of Staff; troops and civilians must simply place their trust in the commands, as inquiring into the truth is equated with serving the enemy. And as the enemy also misleads, i.e. there is no nor can there be any reliable, verifiable information on the enemy, about whom we only know what the authorities tell us,[101] society is trapped in a truly Orwellian "Ministry of Truth" (which, to reduce the obviousness of its filial association with Big Brother, might well be named the Office of Strategic Influence or Special Plans).

With a design that echoes the media manipulation presented in the film Wag the Dog or the story lines of comic strips like Batman and his arch-criminal enemies, or the films depicting James Bond's struggle against the diabolical organization SPECTRE led by the supervillain Blofeld, mythical enemies of the free world can be created, like Goldstein en 1984 or Bin Laden and Al Qaeda[102] after 9/11, or any other enemy that may appear in the future once the media effectiveness of the existing supervillains has been exhausted.

Having established the war on terrorism, the next natural, logical step is to feed the fear, multiplying infinitely the effects of terrorism "through the manipulation and spin of mass media presentation around the globe" (Freytas, 2007).[103] The use of "media terrorism" (media operations directed

---

[100] *"Covert propaganda...* produces *devastating results,* given that the mass audiences of television, radio and newspapers consume it unaware of the interests and political objectives that drive it, believing that it has no other purpose than to *inform*" (Guevara, 2005).

[101] "In the real world, there are no precise data on the existence or the death of Bin Laden, and nobody has yet revealed how he was able to escape from the military siege and missiles in Afghanistan. Nobody questions why the CIA, with its countless networks of infiltration into Islamic terrorism, has not been able to detect or assassinate him, nor even why Osama has disappeared without a trace in spite of the fact that officially every intelligence service in the world is searching for him night and day" (Freytas, 2006a).

[102] Chossudovsky reminds us that "the alleged mastermind behind 9/11, Saudi-born Osama Bin Laden, was recruited during the Soviet-Afghan war, ironically under the auspices of the CIA, to fight Soviet invaders" (Chossudovsky, 2008a). See also Chossudovsky, 2001 and Tarpley, 2004.

[103] "The 'fear of terrorism' process is in turn fed by the major international agencies and networks responsible for the worldwide broadcasting (as if taken from the pages of a spy novel) of stories, leaks, press releases, letters, videos with new threats, 'secret information' on terrorist groups, leads, etc... and keeping the 'terrorism of Al Qaeda' up their sleeve like a trump card to be pulled out whenever the international (or local) situation so requires" (Freytas, 2007).

by experts in mass communications and mass psychology for the social, political and military purposes of "terrorism") has become widespread as an "advanced system and strategy of manipulation and social control" (Freytas, 2006c).

According to Naomi Klein, "remaking people, shocking them into obedience" is a powerful idea that as early as the 1950s caught the attention of the CIA, which funded a series of experiments and produced a secret handbook on how to break down prisoners using shock treatment to reduce them to a childlike state: "but these techniques don't only work on individuals; they can work on whole societies: a collective trauma, a war, a coup, a natural disaster, a terrorist attack puts us all into a state of shock. And in the aftermath, like the prisoner in the interrogation chamber, we, too, become childlike, more inclined to follow leaders who claim to protect us" (Klein, 2007b). The situation of permanent war (on terrorism or on organized crime) established by neoliberal capital is a strategy to keep society in a permanent state of shock and malleable at will.[104]

There is, incidentally, a friendly exchange of technology between the world powers on this point. For example, Russia learns from the United States, and vice versa. According to Pineda, "the doctrine of the 'Revolution in Military Affairs', the emphasis of which is on information warfare and the presentation of force, arose in the former Soviet Union in the late 1970s... this approach was officially adopted and developed by the U.S. army and... in reciprocal fashion, the Russian military has adopted the information warfare designs developed by the United States" (Pineda, 2003). After the failure of the war against Chechnya in 1994, Pineda explains, Russian army commanders concluded (like Nixon after Vietnam) that they had lost the information war, as they had not been able to present the Chechen armed resistance as a band of criminals and terrorists and that, for this reason, they had not been able to win over public opinion. Consequently, they sought to "reprogram" the propaganda, with so much success that while 82 percent of Russians accepted Chechnya's independence in 1998, by November 1999, 63 percent supported the idea of

---

[104] For this reason, for example, Bin Laden makes periodical reappearances: "he threatens Europe and the United States with a holy war, promises attacks and mass murders with chemical and biological weapons, and then disappears as mysteriously as he came... Al Jazeera shows the videos with his communiqués and threats, the U.S. and European networks broadcast them around the world, and the CIA – along with the rest of the intelligence services of the central powers – announces all kinds of terrorist catastrophes looming, mainly in the United States or Europe" (Freytas, 2006a).

conducting armed operations until the Chechen combatants were completely annihilated.[105]

It is worth reflecting briefly on this idea of total annihilation. If the identity and rationality of people struggling for independence is denied and the enemy is presented as an irrational, satanic, dangerous threat looming over the innocent ("they attacked us" is the key idea), the logical solution is their extermination, and it is easy to shift "from the defensive to the offensive, that is, from the acceptable idea of ensuring security to the will to annihilate" (Pineda, 2003).[106] The aim of extermination develops more clearly in the case of terrorism, but is also present in the case of the war on drugs, especially when this war is associated with guerrilla movements, as in Colombia, or with violence spilling over borders as in Mexico. More generally, it is necessary to examine the link with the thanatophilia promoted by neoliberal capital discussed earlier. The reality is, viewing the situation as a whole and even including conflicts between bourgeois nation-states, that the enemy of neoliberal capital is the working class, some segments of which need to be exterminated, while others need to be misled into supporting the extermination of the first.

In these circumstances, it is no surprise that the suffering and extermination of whole peoples is perceived by the segments of the working class that support it as an image that produces a mild sensation of satisfaction and security, at the same time mixed with increased fear and insecurity: a threat was annihilated, but others will follow it until, possibly, their turn comes to be treated as threats to the free world, i.e. as hindrances to the gestation of the last man.[107]

---

[105] It is not hard to see the similarity between the pattern followed by Russia in Chechnya and that followed by the United States in Afghanistan: "The tactic that radically tipped the balance in favor of the new war was the propaganda on the explosions in Moscow. The presentation of these events had a dramatic effect on public opinion. The reports underlined the idea that Chechnya was a nation of bandits, with no law or order, and that kidnappings were commonplace; therefore, the country was a direct threat to the Russian population... and society would never be safe until the Chechen threat was eliminated completely... The propaganda put the Chechen independence leader, Shamil Basayev, in first place among the men most hated by Russia's urban population" (Pineda, 2003).

[106] This shift occurs even more easily if blame is added to the mix: 'The intolerable rise of crime in Russian cities was associated with the image of 'bandits' attributed not only to the guerrillas but to the whole Chechen population" (Pineda, 2003).

[107] "What is wrong with the human race, that it can be moved to crying over 22 hired men running behind a ball, and yet doesn't shed a single tear over the mass murder of its own species? How did we come to this aberration, this atrocious individualism, this dehumanization, this indifference to life and death, where the only forces of collective mobilization are sports idols and entertainment figures?" (Freytas, 2006b).

Degradation

The global spread of social degradation is the necessary correlate to a world in which free competition, war and crime are set up as dominant daily forms of social coexistence moving toward the gestation of the last man. What follows are some examples related to specific issues, countries and regions, with no intention other than to illustrate the process.

In Mexico, according to Gilberto López y Rivas's analysis, laws are amended or violated to favor transnational corporate interests and ensure the prevalence of private profit. Justice enters the market as merely another commodity and the violation of the rule of law has a domino effect: "As federal, state and municipal authorities, the political and the business class in general are the first to violate the rule of law, citizens, professional groups and unions also often assume unlawful practices, taking control of public spaces for their own purposes, infringing basic administrative regulations for urban and rural coexistence, stealing union fees, corrupting and being corrupted. Cynicism, arrogance and the supremacy of private over collective interests take the place of civil responsibility and collective empowerment; a popular culture of corruption is constructed, in which honesty is synonymous with stupidity" (López y Rivas, 2005).

Yet in the face of all kinds of growing problems, Mexico's so-called political class responds with scandals. According to Castaingts, calm, rational communication, which seeks to comprehend in order to guide actions, is nonexistent. There is only what is expressed in terms of political scandal; and the television and radio media, which foster outrage over the scandal, merely exacerbate the situation. "The result is clear: civil society harbors a growing distrust of political society and government... We live under the rule of mediocrity, lacking analysis, in the absence of serious proposals. The language of scandal not only destroys political society, but also affects civil society, which, subjected to economic stagnation, the poor distribution of wealth, exclusion, growing crime, the deterioration of the idea of nation and of state, and bombarded by scandals, suffers the deterioration of its ties and bonds, and faces growing problems in its reproduction and cohesion as it is pushed toward disorder or anomie" (Castaingts, 2004).

I will not dwell further on Mexico or on the so-called war on drug trafficking launched by President Calderón, with its wide range of perverse consequences, but will turn to Colombia, which illustrates certain dimensions of this war that are of great relevance to the topic that concerns us. According to Hernando Calvo Ospina, the strategy adopted by the Colombian government in its attempt to defeat the country's guerrilla organizations has been to destroy, or neutralize, the social fabric that really, supposedly or potentially supports it. To achieve this objective, Colombia has become one of the biggest violators of human rights in the world: "This 'dirty war'... has rested on two fundamental pillars: covert or secret operations by the Military Forces and paramilitary actions... the clandestine, illegal arm of the government" (Calvo Ospina, 2003).

The military high command, involved liberal and conservative party bosses, landowners and mafia gangsters in the development of paramilitary structures that perpetrated the crimes, thus initiating one of the bloodiest, most macabre marriages of convenience in Colombia's recent political history: "The organization Human Rights Watch, in its 1996 report, reveals that the CIA and the Pentagon aided in the reorganization of 'the intelligence systems that resulted in the creation of networks of hitmen who identify and murder civilians suspected of aiding the guerrillas', networks of hired killers at the service of the drug traffickers and landowners... a new form of exercising unlimited legal repression, which some analysts have dubbed 'violence by delegation'" (Calvo Ospina, 2003).

According to Calvo Ospina, these networks are what make up the so-called United Self-Defense Forces of Colombia (AUC, for its initials in Spanish), with more than 11,000 members spread across the country, chiefly in strategic zones where multinational corporations are present and major projects are being planned. Their leader, Carlos Castaño, "in addition to acknowledging that he received training from the Israeli and Colombian armies... accepts without reservation that not only is the AUC financed by drug trafficking, but that it manages a significant proportion of the drug trade. This has not prevented the AUC from enjoying 'friendly' relations with the DEA and the CIA in the persecution of other drug traffickers such as, for example, Pablo Escobar... With the disappearance or imprisonment of the leaders of the drug cartels in Medellín and Cali... the AUC took over control of drug processing and exportation... it is now a new militarized mafia cartel, the world's biggest cocaine exporter with an anti-guerrilla discourse" (Calvo Ospina, 2003).

In August 2002, a landowner whose father had a background in the drug trade, Alvaro Uribe Vélez ("the man closest to our philosophy," according to the head of the AUC), became president of Colombia. His central goal, explains Calvo Ospina, is the total paramilitarization of the state and of society: the recruitment of up to one million Colombians as informers; the creation of a contingent of 25,000 rural workers and indigenous people who, after receiving military training, are reintegrated into their communities in a manner reminiscent of the Civil Patrols in Guatemala; the establishment of local security fronts in neighborhoods and businesses, etc. And, to serve as an example to other countries (like Mexico), in case anyone had failed to work out the right way to wage the war on drugs, U.S. Secretary of State Colin Powell enthusiastically congratulated President Uribe during a visit to Colombia, declaring that Colombia had "created a great strategy and assembled all the pieces needed to fight the phenomenon of insecurity and terrorism" (Calvo Ospina, 2003).

This is not surprising as, "by the mid-nineties, state terrorism, making use of paramilitarism (referred to as 'hit teams', 'death squads' or any of the many other names given to them to conceal their true identity) had killed or 'disappeared' 25,000 leftists and prominent progressives... for which Colombia has been charged by the United Nations with 'political genocide'. *Not even the dictators of the Southern Cone went so far*" (Calvo Ospina, 2003, emphasis added). It is also no surprise that whenever a Colombian president (first Betancur and then Andrés Pastrana) agrees to engage in dialogue with guerrilla groups, paramilitary violence multiplies to sabotage the attempt: "In keeping with the terms of the National Security Doctrine, the efforts to find a non-violent or political solution to Colombia's internal conflict have been perceived by the military high command as advances by the 'communist guerrilla forces' in their attack on power" (Calvo Ospina, 2003). And this is but one of many examples of the world created by neoliberal capital.[108]

While in Latin America the kidnapping industry and other related industries continue to grow to the point that they represent the most successful of all of the region's industrial districts,[109] in Afghanistan and Iran the mafia economy is being globalized. The West, the biggest consumer of drugs, forces them to embark on a useless war ("we'll do everything possible, but we cannot control the whole border") that costs them

---

[108] It is not my purpose to explore the topic further here, but for more information see the Washington Office on Latin America, 2008, and Rojas Aravena, 2008, among many others.

[109] "Mass poverty is incompatible with social harmony and public stability. Latin America has become a flagrant example of this. Added to organized crime, the illegal levies of paramilitary groups and the practices or deviations of some guerrilla forces, the outrageous gap between rich and poor, the cynicism of the elite, the widespread corruption of the police, or the disrepute of the justice system (due, among other factors, to the impunity that has accompanied so many state crimes), have weakened civic values, undermined social solidarity and fostered a wave of crime which, in some countries, is characterized by the multiplication of sexually motivated kidnappings... symptomatic of societies in crisis, and of an accelerated societal breakdown" (Prolongeau and Rampal, 1997).

lives ("our martyrs bear witness to it"), erodes their government structures ("the temptation that the manna of trafficking must represent to a poorly paid government employee") and their productive and social structures: "in Afghanistan, there is nothing but opium. What is needed is to pull this country out of poverty and develop alternatives for rural workers... the U.S. offensive has only encouraged the option of poppy growing, which is the means of subsistence for 3.3 million Afghans" (Gouverneur, 2002).

In Iraq, local corruption is entwined with corruption in the West[110] and they have been working together, even since before the war in 2003, to ruin the country. The sanctions against Baghdad, in force since August 1990, had a devastating effect on Iraqi society: in addition to "problems in obtaining food and medicine, the infrastructure began to deteriorate,[111] essential services for the population, ministries, electrical power plants, drinking water, all dropped to extremely precarious levels... Corruption, which until then had been nonexistent, began to develop at every level. Crime grew at a dizzying rate... Much of the middle class emigrated and the country lost its professionals. The education system, which previously covered all children, recorded a spike in student dropouts, as many had to work to help their families survive, thereby producing a semi-illiterate generation... The country took a fifteen-year leap backwards, which will take a lot of work to redress... they destabilized one of the most important states in the region and increased its chances of fragmentation. Who will be judged for these errors? What commission will assess these mistakes for which the whole Middle East pays so dearly?" (Gresh, 2005).

Up to this point, the examples offered have been taken from the defenseless underdeveloped world (although always with the enthusiastic collaboration of developed nations). Not included in this analysis are the many other notable cases of social degradation in the contemporary world, such as the recurring humanitarian crises that especially affect the

---

[110] "Between 1996 and 2003, the 'Oil for Food' program allowed Iraqi president Saddam Hussein to divert hundreds of millions of dollars. At the same time, several high officials in the United Nations (UN) pocketed large commissions... Moreover, foreign political leaders, chiefly French, have also taken advantage of the system" (Gresh, 2005).

[111] "And, in the midst of this collapse, the desire of the United States to monopolize all of the reconstruction contracts should not be underestimated. To be able to reestablish electricity, it would have been necessary to turn to the corporations from Germany (Siemens) and Switzerland (ABB) that had installed the modern electrical grid in place in Iraq. To repair the phone lines, the best option was to call Alcatel (a French firm), which had installed the existing system and was familiar with the terrain. But Washington wanted to punish the governments of Old Europe, and at the same time guarantee the juicy contracts to companies that funded the Republican Party" (Gresh, 2005).

countries of Southern Africa and the Horn of Africa, or the shocking working conditions suffered by large numbers of workers in India and China.
However, examples can also be found in the developed world. In France,
while they expand the "law-free zones handed over to the parallel economy and the law of the gangs" and their suburbs appear to have become
their biggest threat,[112] they are exploring the best responses to their problems: "We are witnessing a massive expansion of penalization of behaviors
which until now were not prosecuted under the law, as well as a toughen-
ing up of the penalties imposed for minor crimes... we have shifted from a
global approach to problems (social development of neighborhoods, construction improvement and crime prevention), that is, from the idea that
these problems have social causes, to the idea of the individual responsibility of offenders and their capacity to choose rationally" (Bonelli, 2003).

Indeed, in France, as around the world, "they are working hard on the
task of social demolition," eliminating 10,000 jobs in education while
simultaneously hiring 10,000 prison guards, and amending a range of laws
(related to dismissal, reduction of work hours and control of public funds
allocated to businesses), "all of which are considered detestable obstacles
to the 'liberation of the forces that be', i.e. employer arbitrariness" (de Brie,
2003).[113] The French Right "is committed to the policy of the right to plun-
der, developed under the aegis of the World Trade Organization (WTO),
which negotiates – under the framework of the General Agreement of
Trade in Services (GATS) – for the progressive submission of all public services, including health and education, to the law of the market." De Brie
explains in detail the method used in these cases, whereby the "extremists" call for exaggerated reforms and the government, after sizing up
the terrain, offers reasonable, moderate measures: "they use the proven
method of cutting the problem into slices; social demolition in stages"
(de Brie, 2003).

But this is not only happening in France. Throughout the European
Union social dumping is being legitimated in the common market, establishing "a clear hierarchy between the rights of companies and social

---

[112] 'Against a background of spikes in crime, self-proclaimed security experts prophesy
about the advent of a kingdom of criminals who are increasingly young, recidivist and
violent... youths can no longer be integrated into a world in marked decline, nor can they
accept the new under-qualified jobs that their lack of qualifications makes them objec-
tively fit for" (Bonelli, 2003).

[113] The only justification for this demolition, de Brie suggests, "is to meet the demands
of the employer lobby, align France together with countries with less social support, and
integrate it into the policy of forced globalization that capitalism seeks to impose on the
whole world."

norms, in which the former prevail over the latter," and although the Court of Justice of the European Communities "admits that union action constitutes a 'fundamental right' (which is indeed an advance in the social wasteland of Europe) it immediately empties it of content by subjecting it to the obligation of not 'hindering' the freedom of establishment or the free provision of service of the companies in the common market... the defense of the minimum wage thus proves incompatible with European law if it is likely to make the conditions offered to companies of another member state 'less attractive, or more difficult'" (Robert, 2010). And since the EU is filled with "millions of voters who are victims of the brutalities engendered by globalization in the postindustrial world... with multitudes of disposable workers, suburban new poor, *mileuristas*, the excluded, retirees in the prime of their lives, casualized youth, middle-class families on the brink of poverty... the many common people who have fallen victim to neoliberal shock treatment," the social democratic parties, which in 2002 governed in 15 countries while in 2010, "in spite of the fact that the financial crisis has demonstrated the moral, social and ecological impasse of ultra-liberalism, govern in only five nations (Spain, Greece, Hungary, Portugal and the United Kingdom) because they have not known how to take advantage of the failure of neoliberalism. And the governments of three of these countries – Spain, Greece and Portugal, attacked by the financial markets and affected by the 'debt crisis' – will fall into discredit and lose their popular support when they begin, with an iron hand, to implement the austerity programs and unpopular policies demanded by the logic of the EU and its main gatekeepers" (Ramonet, 2010).

"Some time ago," adds Ramonet, "Europe's social democrats decided to encourage privatization, promote the reduction of government budgets at the expense of the public, push up the retirement age and dismantle the public sector, while spurring on the concentrations and mergers of megacorporations and allowing the banks to do as they pleased. For years they have been accepting, without much regret, a shift toward social liberalism. They no longer view as priorities any of the objectives that once formed part of their ideological DNA, for example, full employment, the defense of the social benefits won in the past, the development of public services or the eradication of poverty" (Ramonet, 2010). It is thus no surprise that, in light of this vacuum of options, right, extreme right and even neo-Nazi projects thrive.

The United States offers a great deal of material for analysis in this area, but I will limit myself to a brief overview drawn from a report issued by the Truth Commission for Economic, Social and Cultural Rights in the U.S.[114] With regard to what could be called "foreign policy," the Commission echoes the "growing concern of the international public opinion about the United States government['s] obvious contempt for national sovereignty and the peaceful international coexistence rules which have allowed for balances, although rather formal, in the post-war world; amidst the public and notorious will of the United States government to refuse to limit its actions, as decided by most of the nations, by instruments intended to avoid the impunity of War Crimes and Crimes Against Humanity."

With regard to "domestic policy," the report points to the "existence of more than 31 million American citizens living under the poverty level, and about 45 million people with no access to healthcare" and has "reached the general conclusion that human, economic, social and cultural rights are indeed violated in the United States of America; the Federal Government, the legislative and judicial authorities, and the private mega-companies can be identified as those responsible for these violations; [and] that such human rights violations were in most cases totally pre-ventable." In the face of "this alarming panorama of deterioration, it was necessary to suggest proposals to the audience," and this was made all the more urgent by the fact that "amidst the enactment of domestic laws, such as the Patriotic Act, that limit individual and political rights and legitimize endangering democracy in their own territory, the situation of the eco-nomic, social and cultural rights of the poor in the United States of America still remains invisible" (Truth Commission, 2006).

Indeed, in the neoliberal context, all myths – even the most devoutly cultivated – vanish into thin air: "The 'American dream' is very simply defined: that the next generation should enjoy a better standard of living than the last one. But this fundamental myth in the United States is quickly vanishing" (Brooks, 2008). And as the myths vanish, even in the country of myths, and that country's political class lurches from one scandal to the

---

[114] In preparing this report, the members of the commission reviewed "documentation and listened to dozens of emblematic testimonies by poor, white and black, Latin and Asian, young and old women and men, veterans of Iraq and mothers who had lost their children in that war of occupation, homeless people, victims of the Katrina hurricane, unemployed, migrants against whom walls are built and restrictions are implemented, while their work and human exploitation is legitimized under neo-slavery conditions, physically handicapped people, mothers whose children have been unjustly removed by the State because of their poverty, and citizens with no healthcare, among various sectors in American society" (Truth Commission, 2006).

next,[115] its government has no qualms about arguing that it has the right to deny the rights of others,[116] including, of course, its own people: "The U.S. government has responded to the evidence being arrayed against its outlandish 9/11 conspiracy theory by redefining the war on terror from external to internal enemies. Homeland Security Secretary Janet Napolitano said on February 21 that *American extremists are now as big a concern as international terrorists*. Extremists, of course, are people who get in the way of the government's agenda" (Roberts, 2010, emphasis added).

It isn't for nothing that the oligarchy of the United States is the one that most openly promotes its own candidacy for the honor of last man as, according to Samir Amín, "deprived of the tradition in which social democratic workers' and communist parties marked the formation of modern European political culture, U.S. society lacks the ideological instruments that would enable it to resist the unchallenged dictatorship of capital... and it is capital that shapes the society's mode of thinking in all its dimensions" (Amin, 2003a). But even under these conditions of the society's ideological and political weakness, the project of the U.S. oligarchy "cannot for long be sustained without active repressions, or even tyranny, at home" and without doing substantial damage to its internal democratic institutions: "The popular tradition within the United States is anticolonial and anti-imperial and it has taken a very substantial conjuring trick, if not outright deception, to mask the imperial role of the US in world affairs or at least to clothe it in grand humanitarian intentions over the past few decades. It is not clear that the US population will generally support an overt turn to any long-term militarized Empire (any more than it ended up supporting the Vietnam War). Nor will it accept for long the price, already substantial given the repressive clauses inserted into the Patriot and Homeland Security Acts, that has to be paid at home in terms of civil liberties, rights and general freedoms" (Harvey, 2004: 82).

In short, social degradation, which dislocates communities, afflicting them with multiple conflicts and isolating them in contained fury and impotence, acting like a cancer that gradually spreads throughout the whole body of society, is not accidental or circumstantial, but rooted in profound tendencies of neoliberal capital related to the gestation of the last man and, more generally (as will be shown in the last chapter) to the

---

[115] For a few examples of the scandals, see Brooks, 2005a and Brooks, 2006. U.S. Senator John McCain, with an undeniable hint of humor, remarks of Washington that "this town has become very corrupt, there's no doubt about it" (as quoted in Brooks, 2006).

[116] For an exploration of this question, see Chomsky, 2005.

period of decline of capitalism. According to the UN Office on Drugs and Crime, "transnational organized crime, illegal drug trafficking and terrorism have become social, political and economic forces capable of altering the fates of nations and whole regions... and... have given rise to the appearance of phenomena such as widespread bribery of public officials, the growth of 'crime multinationals', human trading and the use of terrorism to intimidate communities large and small" (UNODC, 2008).

The gestation of the last man is not an act of creation of life but the trajectory of the last survivor: an aging capitalism no longer has the strength to support life, and its last offspring staggers onward, killing its surviving siblings and anything that opposes it, hinders it, or is simply superfluous to it. The last oligarchies of globalization fight over living space in an effort to consummate their status as the last man and, as they energetically and fiercely pursue the goals yet to be examined – surveillance and murder – they learn how to thrive in the midst of the chaos and butchery. According to Klein, the economic prosperity of Israel is based on the fact it "has learned to turn endless war into a brand asset, pitching its uprooting, occupation and containment of the Palestinian people as a half-century head start in the 'global war on terror'... Israel has struck oil. The oil is the war on terror, the state of constant fear that creates a bottomless global demand for devices that watch, listen, contain and target 'suspects'. And fear, it turns out, is the ultimate renewable resource" (Klein, 2007a).[117]

Surveillance

The contenders for the title of last man monitor one another on a global scale as a necessity of competition, but they also monitor their slaves in order to prevent (or, when required, to repress) any outbreak of resistance or rebellion. To address this point and take note of the trend (a growing systematic effort to enhance surveillance capacities, and the use of scientific and technological research and development for espionage and societal control), highlighting its significance and relevance and outlining

---

[117] "Many of the country's most successful entrepreneurs are using Israel's status as a fortressed state, surrounded by furious enemies, as a kind of twenty-four-hour-a-day showroom – a living example of how to enjoy relative safety amid constant war" (Klein, 2007a). Among other successful products and services, these salespeople offer high-tech fences for an apartheid planet, unmanned drones, biometric IDs, video and audio surveillance gear, air passenger profiling and prisoner interrogation systems. "Palestinians," says Klein, "are no longer just targets. They are guinea pigs...." in laboratories "where the terrifying tools of our security states are being tested" (Klein, 2007a).

some of its dimensions without going into an exhaustive exploration, I draw chiefly from the report "An Appraisal of Technologies of Political Control," a study commissioned by Science and Technology Options Assessment (STOA), a European Parliament committee established to assess public policy options in science and technology.

According to this report, "surveillance technology can be defined as devices or systems which can monitor, track and assess the movements of individuals, their property and other assets" (STOA, 1998). The report discusses the growing prominence of a form of pre-emptive policing known as "data-veillance," based on military models for gathering huge amounts of low-grade intelligence, and the wide range of surveillance technologies that have been developed, including night-vision goggles, parabolic microphones to detect conversations over a kilometer away and laser versions that can pick up any conversation from a closed window in line of sight, the Danish Jai stroboscopic camera, which can take hundreds of pictures in a matter of seconds and individually photograph all the participants in a demonstration or march, and automatic vehicle recognition systems, which can track a car around a city using a computerized geographic information system.

The document indicates that most surveillance up until the 1960s was extremely low-tech, but by the 1980s new forms of electronic surveillance began to emerge, many of which aimed at the automation of communications interception. The report goes on to cover the following general topics in the development of technologies of political control:

> Algorithmic surveillance systems: systems that can scan crowds and match faces against a database of images held in a remote computer. It has now become possible to analyze data using complex algorithms which enable automatic recognition and tracking. There are also vehicle recognition systems that can see both night and day, to identify a vehicle number plate and then track it around a city.
>
> Bugging and tapping devices: a wide range of devices for recording conversations and intercepting telecommunications traffic. Lap top computers are adapted to tune into mobile phones active in the area simply by moving the cursor over their number.
>
> National and international communications interception networks: global surveillance systems that facilitate the mass supervision of all telecommunications including telephone, email and fax transmissions.

Under this last heading, the report examines two global surveillance systems in particular: the UK/USA system and EU-FBI system. The UK/USA System: is employed by U.S. military intelligence agencies such as NSA-CIA and operates on a system known as ECHELON, "a global surveillance system that stretches around the world to form a targeting system on all of the key Intelsat satellites used to convey most of the world's satellite phone calls, Internet, email, faxes and telexes" (STOA, 1998). According to the report, this system works by indiscriminately intercepting huge quantities of communications, and then picks out those of value using artificial intelligence aids.

ECHELON routinely intercepts all telecommunications in the European Union, is designed for primarily non-military purposes (governments, organizations and businesses) and has been used to obtain privileged information which – and this is what truly outraged European business and political leaders[118] – has benefited U.S. companies involved in arms deals and strengthened Washington's position in crucial World Trade Organization talks with Europe. But while ECHELON exhibits features that tie in with the competitive strategies of the U.S. oligarchies[119] in relation to their European counterparts, in the case of the EU-FBI the two sides are in cooperation:

The EU-FBI Global Telecommunications Surveillance System: links the different police authorities of the European Union with the FBI. According to a Statewatch report, the EU accepted the "requirements" established by the FBI focusing on the systematic recording and storage of all information traffic in telecommunications: "every phone call, every mobile phone call, every fax, every e-mail, every website's contents, all internet usage, from anywhere, by everyone, to be recorded, archived and be accessible for least seven years," in addition to making it compulsory for network and service providers to provide law enforcement agencies with data from intercepted communications and real-time access to transmissions (Statewatch, 2001).[120] Included as part of this deployment of technological resources to monitor and control society is direct intervention into personal computers: "it is now totally possible to gain remote access to any

---

[118] According to Ornelas Bernal, "ECHELON is at the center of conflict between the United States and Europe... The disputes have been reignited as a result of various cases in which 'privileged information' enabled U.S. companies to take contracts away from their European competitors... The existence of international espionage has shifted from being an element of the 'Western alliance in defense of the free world', to a factor of confrontation between the dominant powers" (Ornelas Bernal, 2000).

[119] "The U.S. government – in collaboration with its Anglo-Saxon allies – designed and implemented an intelligence instrument known as ECHELON... a vast system capable of intercepting all kinds of communications and appropriating key information (mainly economic and political) used to support the interests of the family of Anglo-Saxon states, with the U.S. at the head" (Memoria, 2002).

[120] For more information on this topic, see Moeche, 1999 and Mathiesen, 2000.

computer with an Internet connection (and other devices such as mobile phones, electronic diaries...) and not only to see their content; with the right program, it is also possible to manipulate it, modify it and/or activate controls without its user realizing" (Ateneu, 2010).[121]

The so-called cloud computing technologies constitute a huge step in this direction; user information is stored permanently in online servers (controlled by major corporations in the industry like Microsoft and Google) instead of being stored in their personal computers. Thus, as the use of these technologies continues to spread, it will not even be necessary to tap into personal computers to access all kinds of information about the user; the incalculable "power that this represents for corporations and governments of the First World to access the details, interests, preferences, friendships, habits, culture, ideas and photographs of millions of people around the world" is patently obvious (Colectivo Troyano, 2009b).

Included among these interceptable devices and services is Facebook and the other so-called social networks, which constitute "a mine of information on their users that will wind up on the hard drives of the U.S. intelligence community, used with equal enthusiasm on both the internal and external 'enemy' since the Bush era" (Carmona, 2009).[122] Lisandro Pardo notes that "the information available on social networks is constantly growing. This source of data is a goldmine for any on-line business project, but it also constitutes a real-time information source that no intelligence agency can afford to ignore," and he adds: *it would be a very interesting exercise to try to ascertain the point at which a simple case of data monitoring can turn into full-scale surveillance"* (Pardo, 2009, emphasis added). Also included in this category are video surveillance systems:[123] cameras installed on streets and highways, and inside and outside public buildings. Using closed-circuit cameras, companies spy on their employees and governments on their citizens, but with the webcams installed on personal

---

[121] "At the end of 2001, the American television network MSNBC leaked that the FBI was using the Magic Lantern virus to spy on computers. This Trojan virus and others like Back Orifice, Netbus and Sub7 can be introduced into the computer via any online operation: downloading a song, receiving an email, opening a picture... once installed, the computer is accessible to the virus owner, who not only can see what is happening on it, but even intervene and usurp the identity of its users, passwords included" (Ateneu, 2010).

[122] For more information on this topic, see also Rodríguez, 2009 and Alandete, 2009.

[123] "We understand video surveillance systems to refer to any systems equipped at least with a camera connected to a screen where the image is viewed... All such cameras and those who operate them come under social control, forming part of the para-policing infrastructure" (Ateneu, 2010).

computers it is possible to monitor any user connected to the Internet, if his or her computer has been previously tapped (Ateneu, 2010).

Of course, this vast array of surveillance devices is not deployed without resistance and contradictions: the same Statewatch report notes "the enormity of the threat to data protection, individual privacy and funda-mental freedoms" and "the battle between the Data Protection officials and the law enforcement agencies over the retention of data." Law enforce-ment agencies structure their agenda "in quasi-secret international fora," and the governments of the EU "tell the European Commission (and European Parliament) that the demands of the law enforcement agencies take precedence over the privacy and freedoms of people" (Statewatch, 2001).[124] Ultimately, these agencies are relying on their capacity to mold the minds of the public: "what one generation perceives as repression, the next accepts as a necessary part of an increasingly complex everyday life" (Ateneu, 2010).

The threat that these surveillance systems represent should not be underestimated. According to Statewatch, "it is the interface of the ECHELON system and its potential development on phone calls com-bined with the standardization of 'tappable' telecommunications centers and equipment being sponsored by the EU and the USA which presents *a truly global threat over which there are no legal or democratic controls*" (Statewatch, 2001, emphasis added). What is troubling is the "trend toward convergence and integration of the different recording and surveillance systems... On the horizon we can glimpse the features of an extensive, increasingly integrated multinational recording and surveillance system... Furthermore, there is international cooperation on telecommunications surveillance... Both the EU-FBI system and Echelon can be partially or wholly integrated very easily; the advanced technology of Echelon is expanding and soon it will be able to be used by the EU-FBI system. The technological similarities overlap and exchanges of personnel encourage integration" (Mathieson, 2000).

---

[124] According to the UK's Data Protection Commissioner, "the routine long-term preser-vation of data by ISPs [Internet Service Providers] for law enforcement purposes would be disproportionate general surveillance of communications." Nevertheless, "the EU has agreed in secret on the creation of an international phone tapping network through a secret network of committees and the EU's network and service providers will be required to install 'interceptable' systems, and to put any person or group under surveillance when-ever they receive an interception order... These plans have never been submitted for review to a European government, nor to the European Parliament's Committee on Civil Liberties, in spite of the evident issues of public freedoms posed by such an uncontrolled system. The decision to go ahead was simply adopted in secret" (Statewatch, 2001).

MURDER

Earlier in this chapter, I indicated that in dismantling the nation-state as the historic space regulation of its behavior, capital established conditions without precedent in its history for the full deployment of the power of the fetish. According to Kurnitzky, "the expansion of unlimited economic power... [and] making free competition the regulator of society means making violence the universal method in social confrontations... *Around the world a vacuum has been created in which violence can be intensified without limits*: everyday violence, civil and gang warfare, religious or ethnic warfare, violence arising from mafias and cartels and the violence with which the economic powers impose their interests worldwide on all societies" (Kurnitzky, 2000, emphasis added).

The gestation of the last man is necessarily conflictive and, although the main purpose is not necessarily to kill but to pursue the logic of capital and the gestation of the absolute monopoly of the means of production and subsistence, murder is a necessary component of the march toward the goal and, as the march goes on, it tends to become capital's most universal approach: to kill those who hinder it, those superfluous to it, those who resist it, its competitors; to kill as a direct condition for the pursuit of its goal of gestation or as a collateral effect, as simple incidental damage; to kill in situations of war or other military operations, but also as the result of "broad economic, social and institutional mechanisms, as well as the environmental consequences of war and economic collapse" (Chossudovksy, 2007a).

Without doubt, the economic and political oligarchy of the United States, which most explicitly manifests its aspiration to establish as absolute monopoly and the last man, is the world champion in this area. What follows is a brief review of its evolution to illustrate the developing trend.

THE UNDERDEVELOPED WORLD AND THE PROMOTION OF CONFLICTS

Throughout the neoliberal period so far, the pursuit of the goal has been very intense in underdeveloped countries: "Countries are destroyed, often transformed into territories, sovereignty is foregone, national institutions collapse, the national economy is destroyed through the imposition of 'free market' reforms, unemployment becomes rampant, social services are dismantled, wages collapse, and people are impoverished... In turn, the nation's assets and natural resources are transferred into the hands of foreign investors through a privatization program imposed by the invading forces" (Chossudovsky, 2007a). These processes of destruction, with varying degrees of intensity and coordination between nation-state and national economy – dismantling the capacities of state regulation to facilitate the concentration of wealth into the hands of neoliberal capital and promote tribalism to help neutralize resistance – have already been examined in the chapters on the neoliberal economy and the neoliberal state, where it was noted that they constitute a promotion of death, linking together with the state administration of criminal activity and/or direct military aggression.

But in relation to the issue that concerns us here, it is worth recalling that in the neoliberal period so far the United States has asserted itself as the military superpower of globalization and, while the global powers have not confronted one another militarily (although this possibility is not excluded for the future, depending on the number of competitor oligarchies that survive and how far they are willing to go toward mutual extermination), they have used the underdeveloped nations to compete against each other, seeking to position them as sites of conflict where they can wear out their rivals. The underdeveloped world has thus revealed its usefulness not only as a source of resources, markets and cheap labor, but also as a source of conflicts which, appropriately handled, may be of considerable competitive value. Up to now, the deaths – an already enormous heap of corpses – have occurred mainly among the populations of underdeveloped countries as a result of the strategies for the gestation of the last man implemented by the developed nations.

For example, as Chossudovsky explains, to wear down the former Soviet Union, Washington deliberately provoked a civil war in Afghanistan that lasted for more than 25 years. In fact, the 'Militant Islamic Network' "was created by the CIA. The 'Islamic Jihad' (or holy war against the Soviets) became an integral part of the CIA's intelligence ploy. It was supported by the United States and Saudi Arabia, with a significant part of the funding generated from the Golden Crescent drug trade... The history of the drug trade in Central Asia is intimately related to the CIA's covert operations" (Chossudovksy, 2008a).[125] Chossudovksy also points out that after the

---

[125] According to Chossudovsky, when Brzezinski, National Security Advisor to President Jimmy Carter, was asked in an interview whether he regretted having supported Islamic fundamentalism, giving arms and advice to future terrorists, he responded: "Regret what? That secret operation was an excellent idea. It had the effect of drawing the Russians into the Afghan trap... The day that the Soviets officially crossed the border, I wrote to President Carter: We now have the opportunity of giving to the USSR its Vietnam War. Indeed, for almost 10 years, Moscow had to carry on a war unsupportable by the government, a conflict that brought about the demoralization and finally the breakup of the Soviet empire" (Chossudovsky, 2008a).

Cold War, the CIA continued to support Islamic brigades that served "as a catalyst for the disintegration of the Soviet Union and the emergence of six new Muslim republics in Central Asia," but that would also operate in Bosnia and Chechnya and promote secessionist Islamic insurgencies in India's Kashmir and on China's western border with Afghanistan and Pakistan, while at the same time separatist forces in Tibet have received support from the United States.[126]

The fostering of conflicts, while aimed at debilitating the competitors, also seeks to organize new economic benefits by appropriating strategic resources like oil,[127] and creating highly profitable business sectors such as the drug trade.[128] Chossudovksy explains that what he calls "Washington's hidden agenda," which "consists in sustaining rather than combating international terrorism, with a view to destabilizing national societies and preventing the articulation of genuine secular social movements directed against the American Empire... Washington continues to support—through CIA covert operations—the development of Islamic fundamentalism, throughout the Middle East, in the former Soviet Union as well in China and India... Throughout the developing world, the growth of sectarian, fundamentalist and other such organizations tends to serve U.S. interests. These various organizations and armed insurgents have been developed, particularly in countries where state institutions have collapsed under the brunt of the IMF-sponsored economic reforms" (Chossudovsky, 2008a).

---

[126] In the case of China, "Washington is attempting to trigger a broader process of political destabilization and fracturing of the People's Republic of China. In addition to these various covert operations, the U.S. has established military bases in Afghanistan and in several of the former Soviet republics, directly on China's Western border" (Chossudovsky, 2008a).

[127] "Russia's main pipeline route transits through Chechnya and Dagestan. Despite Washington's condemnation of 'Islamic terrorism', the indirect beneficiaries of the wars in Chechnya are the Anglo-American oil conglomerates which are vying for complete control over oil resources and pipeline corridors out of the Caspian Sea basin" (Chossudovsky, 2008a).

[128] Afghanistan "is a strategic hub in Central Asia... it is also strategic for its opium production, which today, according to UN sources, supplies more than 90% of the world's heroin market, representing multi-billion dollar revenues for business syndicates, financial institutions, intelligence agencies and organized crime... Protected by the CIA, a new surge in opium production unfolded in the post-Cold War era. Since the October 2001 US invasion of Afghanistan, opium production has increased 33 fold... The Golden Crescent drug trade was also being used to finance and equip the Bosnian Muslim Army (starting in the early 1990s) and the Kosovo Liberation Army (KLA)... Albania and Kosovo lie at the heart of the 'Balkan Route' that links the 'Golden Crescent' of Afghanistan and Pakistan to the drug markets of Europe" (Chossudovsky, 2008a).

Constructing the Future

It is also important to note that the need for murder entailed in the gestation of the last man defines the prospects for the future and the plans of the personifications of neoliberal capital in several senses:

First, as an extension of the "global war on terrorism" declared by the United States; Chossudovksy explains that, according to U.S. military doctrine, "[a] terrorist attack on American soil of the size and nature of September 11, would lead – according to former US Central Command (USCENTCOM) Commander, General Tommy Franks, who led the invasion of Iraq in 2003 – to the demise of Constitutional government." Such an event "would be used to galvanize U.S. public opinion in support of a military government and police state. The resulting crisis, the social turmoil and public indignation would facilitate a major shift in US political, social and institutional structures" (Chossudovsky, 2008a). Thus we find that, while "supporting international terrorism,"[129] U.S. government agencies (according to the logic of the shock doctrine) are preparing their preemptive plan for a terrorist attack: "General Franks was not giving a personal opinion on this issue. His statement is consistent with the dominant viewpoint both in the Pentagon and the Homeland Security Department as to how events might unfold in the case of a national emergency... The 'massive casualty producing event' is an integral part of military doctrine" which is used to "create conditions of collective fear and intimidation, which facilitate the derogation of civil liberties and the introduction of police state measures" and allow the government to "to galvanize public opinion in support of a global military agenda" (Chossudovsky, 2008a).[130]

Second, as an extension of the notion of the "enemy" being anyone who gets in the way: Chossudovksy explains that in March 2005, the Pentagon released the summary of a document that outlines the U.S. government's agenda for global military domination, which "calls for a more 'proactive' approach to warfare, beyond the weaker notion of 'preemptive' and defensive actions, where military operations are launched against a

---

[129] And this is true, according to Chossudovsky, both before and after September 11: "the 'Islamic terror network' is a creation of the U.S. intelligence apparatus... There is ample evidence that Al Qaeda remains a U.S. sponsored intelligence asset... [which] remains firmly under the control of the U.S. intelligence apparatus" (Chossudovsky, 2008a).

[130] In another article, Chossudovsky quotes David Rockefeller: "We are on the verge of global transformation. All we need is the right major crisis and the nations will accept the New World Order" (Chossudovsky, 2007a).

'declared enemy' with a view to 'preserving the peace' and 'defending America'. The document explicitly acknowledges America's global military mandate... *This mandate also includes military operations directed against countries, which are not hostile to America, but which are considered strategic from the point of view of US interests*" (Chossudovsky, 2005, emphasis added). Third, as an extension of the global arms race: the aforementioned Pentagon document of March 2005 "points to shifts in weapons systems as well as the need for a global deployment of US forces in acts of worldwide military policing and intervention" (Chossudovsky, 2005).

With this panorama before us, it is no surprise that the Stockholm International Peace Research Institute (SIPRI) has reported that worldwide military expenses have been increasing constantly since 1998,[131] or, as Jules Dufour asserts, "the worldwide rearmament process is happily moving forward in 2009 as military expenses continue to rise, taking a significant part of the resources that should be used for human development. At the same time, the financial crisis that is having such a harsh effect around the world is prompting governments to dedicate astronomical amounts of their national budgets to saving the assets of the richest. *These two phenomena combined are causing a process of widespread impoverishment and contributing to the disintegration of whole societies*" (Dufour, 2009, emphasis added).

Dufour adds that both the rescue plans and the military expenditure could be used for other purposes. Without even including military expenditure, "the resources assigned to rescue the global financial system [during the 2008 crisis] would be sufficient to *end world poverty for the next 50 years*" (emphasis added), and he concludes: "with the great rearmament and the financial crisis, the world has entered a spiral of huge deficits and public debt that places the protection of human rights and fundamental freedoms at risk. More than ever, the process of impoverishment of the majority appears to be developing at an accelerated rate because *the solutions adopted by the governments only serve to accentuate the dynamic of this spiral of precariousness, slavery, sickness and death, and*

---

[131] According to the 2009 SIPRI Yearbook, worldwide military expenditure in 2007 reached a total of 1.339 trillion dollars, of which 45% was spent by the U.S., with an investment of 541 billion dollars – 3.4% more than in 2006. Great Britain held second place with an expenditure of 59.7 billion dollars. China was next with around 58.3 billion, followed by France with an expenditure of 53.6 billion. In 2008, the national defense budget in the United States amounted to a total of 604.4 billion dollars (Stockholm International Peace Research Institute, 2009).

all with the exclusive aim of safeguarding the assets and increasing the power of the richest people on the planet" (Dufour, 2009, emphasis added).

There is no doubt that (as Dufour points out) investments in education, health and environmental conservation and recovery would be much more profitable and beneficial for all, but this is not in the script of neoliberal capital, which is becoming increasingly necrophiliac and genocidal as complements to its unbridled globalphilia. The UN millennium development goals are not the goals of neoliberal capital.

SCIENCE AND TECHNOLOGY FOR DEATH

Of course, this vocation for war and death, which goes hand in hand with its voracious desire to concentrate control of the means of production and subsistence, has never been foreign to the spirit of capitalism,[132] but what is significant is the qualitative difference between the development of this general tendency of capital throughout its previous history and its current level. This difference does not consist in the current personifications of capital having a greater inclination toward killing to pursue their interests than their predecessors had, but in the level of development of science and technology and their use in the pursuit of the interests of capital.

To illustrate this point, it will be sufficient to cite a few brief examples related to global warming, worldwide pollution, and the proposition of geoengineering, i.e. technologies for restructuring the stratosphere and/or the oceans, as a solution: "the manipulation of the planet as a whole, or of large slabs of the planet or whole ecosystems in order to, theoretically, slow down climate change" (Ribeiro, 2009a). The reports of the ETC Group assert that geoengineering uses additional technology to counteract collateral damage without eliminating the problem that causes it; its application ensures that the industry will continue to pollute the planet and makes the problem more complex by contributing massively to particle pollution (ETC Group, 2007). According to the research, "all these projects entail a hazard to the natural balance of ecosystems and further upset the climate" (Ribeiro, 2009a) as they involve "experiments that tinker with the

---

[132] Including during its golden era, the post-war boom: "What is referred euphemistically as the 'post war era' is in fact a period of continuous war and militarization. Since the end of the Second World War, this 'long war' seeks to establish US hegemony worldwide... This entire 'post war period' [1945 up to the present] is marked by extensive war crimes resulting in the death of more than ten million people... This figure does not include those who perished as a result of poverty, starvation and disease" (Chossudovsky, 2007a).

planet's complex climate system" (ETC Group, 2010). Put simply, "its benefits are speculative and its risks are planetary... *geoengineering is deadly serious*" (ETC Group, 2009, emphasis added).

Nevertheless, it is the solution preferred by the United States, which didn't care for the "focus on the negative effects" of a report drafted by the International Panel on Climate Change (IPCC), or for its "rejection of voluntary agreements," and pushed for "techno-fix strategies to be given a prominent place in the final report's recommendations" (ETC Group, 2007). The reason for this, according to the ETC Group, is that the large-scale nature of all geoengineering technologies means they are highly centralized, and have commercial applications as well as a strong potential for military application (ETC Group, 2009). In business terms this technology is "incredibly lucrative," so much so that "it's really more of a business experiment than a scientific experiment" (ETC Group, 2007).

It is worth digressing briefly here to consider further the potential military uses of this technology. The ETC Group explains that the potential for using environmental modification technologies as a weapon against other nations makes weather control "fascinating" to many of the world's military powers: "A US Air Force report entitled 'Weather as a Force Multiplier: Owning the Weather in 2025' concluded that the weather 'can provide battlespace dominance to a degree never before imagined,' including the ability to thwart an enemy's operations by enhancing a storm or by inducing drought and making fresh water scarce" (ETC Group, 2007).

According to Chossudovsky, "the US military has developed advanced capabilities that enable it selectively to alter weather patterns. The technology, which is being perfected under the High-frequency Active Auroral Research Program (HAARP), is an appendage of the Strategic Defense Initiative – 'Star Wars'. From a military standpoint, HAARP is a weapon of mass destruction, operating from the outer atmosphere and capable of destabilizing agricultural and ecological systems around the world... Weather-modification, according to the US Air Force document AF 2025 Final Report, 'offers the war fighter a wide range of possible options to defeat or coerce an adversary', capabilities, it says, [which] extend to the triggering of floods, hurricanes, droughts and earthquakes: Weather modification will become a part of domestic and international security and could be done unilaterally... It could have offensive and defensive applications and even be used for deterrence purposes. The ability to generate precipitation, fog and storms on earth or to modify space weather... and the production of artificial weather all are a part of an integrated set of [military] technologies" (Chossudovsky, 2007c).

HAARP "is a weapon of mass destruction... an instrument of conquest capable of selectively destabilizing agricultural and ecological systems of entire regions," and also has several associated uses: "HAARP could contribute to climate change by intensively bombarding the atmosphere with high-frequency rays... Returning low-frequency waves at high intensity could also affect people's brains, and effects on tectonic movements cannot be ruled out. More generally, HAARP has the ability of modifying the world's electro-magnetic field. It is part of an arsenal of 'electronic weapons' which US military researchers consider a 'gentler and kinder warfare'" (Chossudovksy, 2002d).

As an aside, it is worth considering Chossudovsky's argument that "[a]lready in the 1970s, former National Security advisor Zbigniew Brzezinski had foreseen in his book *Between Two Ages* that 'technology will make available, to the leaders of major nations, techniques for conducting secret warfare, of which only *a bare minimum of the security forces* need be apprised" (Chossudovsky, 2002b, emphasis added). This reminds us that, for capital, human beings are a necessary but undesirable evil and that, both in the factory and in the army, as in any other sector of society, it is working tirelessly to dispose of them.[133] Thus, considering the huge economic and political-military potential of geoengineering, it is obvious why geoengineers should wish to continue with their research and experiments – even those that constitute "high risk planet-altering schemes," such as "'solar radiation management' (SRM), a way of 'cooling down the planet's thermostat' by reflecting a portion of the sun's rays back to outer space, through a variety of techniques ranging from sunshades in space, to aerosol sulfates in the stratosphere, to whitening clouds" (ETC Group, 2010).

All of these schemes, which, informed by the logic of the gestation of the last man, place the natural balance of ecosystems at risk and further destabilize climatic conditions, are gambling with the life of the whole planet. Even a slight increase in the Earth's temperatures could unleash a crisis that could "affect the water and food supplies of more than 2 billion people" (ETC Group, 2010). But the neoliberal doctrine is more

---

[133] Clearly, U.S. oligarchs have not forgotten that, at least at one point during the Vietnam War, "their" youth refused to go and kill and die for them, and they have been implementing a range of schemes (which are not explored here) to ensure that it doesn't happen again.

than clear: risks, appropriately taken, are opportunities. "It is not a question of identifying the causes of the problems in order to resolve them, but to make use of the crises and the disasters as new sources of business, even when the proposed 'solutions' pose even greater threats to the environment, ecosystems, health and life" (Ribeiro, 2009a).

For example, by combining geoengineering with genetic engineering, an environmental crisis transformed into a food crisis could result in a need to abandon all precautions and allow the proliferation of genetically enhanced crops. "Claiming concern about contamination, companies will insist on using 'Terminator' (sterile seed) technology. Global food security will depend on a handful of agribusinesses" (ETC Group, 2007: 2).[134] Promoting transgenics means handing food sovereignty over to a handful of transnationals, as all GM products are patented and owned by six companies: "to hand over seed sovereignty is to give these companies the key to the entire food chain" (Ribeiro, 2009a). This would be a way of consolidating the excessive power that transnationals have acquired in this sector in recent decades: "they have increasing power to decide what is planted, what we eat, what quality (or lack thereof) it will have, etc. Transgenic crops are the greatest expression of this corporate control; all are patented and inevitably contaminate other crops – which turns into a crime for the victims, because they are accused of 'unauthorized use' of their patented genes" (Ribeiro 2009a).[135]

In light of the above, we shouldn't be surprised by the fierceness with which Monsanto attacks farmers around the world – including those of the United States – to keep them "and everyone else from having any access at all to buying, collecting, and saving of normal seeds" (Cohen-Cole, 2009), or that "there is a large group of conservative think tanks with strong links to big oil that have abandoned the old tactic of denying climate change and joined the chorus in favor of a techno-fix... At any point the climate engineers feel they've got a geoengineering scheme ready to audition on the world stage, they've got ample data showing that the climate emergency is already underway" (ETC Group, 2009).

---

[134] Of course, "the world's 1.4 billion people who depend on farmer-saved seed – most of whom farm on marginal lands – will be left to fend for themselves," (ETC Group, 2007: 2), but this is insignificant "collateral damage."

[135] "All agribusinesses... have enjoyed extremely high profits since the food crisis was announced in 2007, much higher than in previous years... The same companies that created and benefit from this debacle, which now with the food crisis have immorally increased their profits, promise us more of the same, or worse: further expansion of industrial, transgenic, polluting agriculture, to continue raking in profits... They are veritable vultures of hunger" (Ribeiro, 2009a).

Privatization and Death

Examples of neoliberal capital's contemptuous indifference toward human life are so great in number that a whole library would not be big enough to record them, but it is worth adding a few particularly significant cases here:

It is well-known that disease is a simple matter of business for pharmaceutical companies, and that the more diseases there are the better. For example, flu vaccines "are big business because the viruses are constantly mutating, and companies see in this an endless (what we might cynically call 'renewable') source of profits... mass vaccination will not be very useful to public health, as the virus will keep mutating, but the government purchases and the drain on public resources to the benefit of the transnationals are excellent business... With the officially orchestrated hysteria to vaccinate the whole world, fast-track approvals are being processed for new vaccine production methods that have not been properly evaluated and could have very hazardous consequences, as they are experimental methods which in most cases involve the use of transgenic organisms and manipulated viruses, *adding new risks as yet unknown*" (Ribeiro, 2009a, emphasis added).

It is also worth noting that "synthetic biology" – the production of synthetic living organisms or the alteration of existing organisms with synthetic DNA – "entails an exponential increase in risks and dangers to the environment and to health posed by transgenics,"[136] and that "nanotechnology" – manipulation of living or inert matter at the scale of the nanometer (one millionth of a millimeter) – has a high toxicity potential for living organisms: "it is the size that is the riskiest aspect: the immune systems of living organisms have no way of detecting synthetic nanoparticles, which therefore pass unnoticed, with the potential to harm the DNA" (Ribeiro, 2009a). But perhaps the most hazardous of all, according to Silvia Ribeiro and the ETC Group, is the convergence of new technologies promoted by the U.S. Government's National Science Foundation (NSF): "In the USA, senior science policy makers and industry players" are devising a project whose aim is "to combine biotechnology, information technology and cognitive (neural) science with atom technology at the nano scale... The fundamental building blocks of bio, info and neuro are

---

[136] "Unlike transgenics, which take genes from existing organisms and insert them into other existing organisms, synthetic biology aims at creating artificial genes and living organisms, wholly created in a laboratory" (Ribeiro, 2009a).

'materially unified' at the nano-scale and therefore can be combined, or otherwise manipulated through atom technology... Merging these technologies into one, proponents say, will drive a huge industrial revolution and a societal "renaissance" that *will guarantee American dominance – military and economic – through the 21st century...* [the] theory seeks to wire together tools that could extend human control over all matter, life, knowledge and even the collective mind – fundamentally changing nature and society in the process... [it] could be about the end of society and nature as we know them" (ETC Group, 2003: 7, emphasis added).[137]

The ETC Group warns about the extreme significance of these theories of technological convergence: "there is sufficient scientific reality and political muscle [behind the concept of converging technologies] to take it very seriously. We have entered a point in history where technologies are so powerful and their risks so great that government/industry cohabitation will be seen as essential for security and progress. Converging technologies make almost everything possible or (worse) plausible. In such a world, our focus must not be on techno-toys, but on governance and social self-defense" (ETC Group, 2003: 6–7). While it may sound like science fiction, the risks and threats are real, and even more alarming when we consider: (1) all of capital's scientific and technological advances are developed without any degree of control by society; (2) for capital, anything that can be appropriated is automatically its property; and (3) not only is capital unconcerned with safeguarding life, but what it deems to be excess population is viewed as a threat to its interests.

In relation to the first point (society's lack of supervision or control over the scientific and technological ventures of capital), the various reports issued by the ETC Group point emphatically and repeatedly to "the urgent need for an international framework to evaluate new technologies, so that governments, in consultation with civil society and the scientific community, can make reasoned and equitable decisions regarding their possible development" (ETC Group, 2009: 7). According to the ETC Group,

---

[137] Among the projects included is the "Socio-Tech" or "predictive science of social behavior" project, which would enable users to "identify drivers for a wide range of socially disruptive events and allow us to put mitigating or preventive strategies in place before the fact," or the "memetic engineering" project, which would allow the prediction and administration of cultural issues and "could help us deal with challenges to American cultural supremacy." The report "places enormous importance on the use of converging technologies for military and police purposes. The belief is that the proliferation of unmanned vehicles, remote sensors, and augmented biological and chemical technologies will reduce the likelihood of war by providing an 'overwhelming US technological advantage'" (ETC Group, 2003: 4).

governments need to tell the big transnationals that they do not have the right to redesign the planet, but instead of doing so, they have "opted for an 'inverted' principle of caution: as long as there are enormous scientific uncertainties and a lack of public awareness, nothing should prevent corporations from *continuing to use everyone as their guinea pigs*" (Ribeiro, 2009a, emphasis added). This means that "the scientific debate and the government/commercial experimentation is taking place, once again, in the absence of public discussion" (ETC Group, 2007: 1), while big corporations engage in "dangerous planet-tinkering schemes with minimal transparency and even less public participation" (ETC Group, 2009: 1). As Silvia Ribeiro points out, "there are no regulations applicable to nanotechnology anywhere in the world, and governments continue to allow it to be marketed 'in the meantime'" (Ribeiro, 2009a).[138]

Worse still, capitalist governments, plagued by mutual distrust (as no government believes that international negotiations will be able to halt climate change) and trapped in a competitive dynamic, are part of the problem rather than the solution: "one of the most dangerous aspects of geoengineering is that it could be unilaterally deployed. A single country, corporation or individual, or some coalition of the willing convened by those who possess the technology, could conceivably attempt to geoengineer the planet... It's not hard to imagine different countries wanting to control the climate's thermostat in conflicting ways. Multilateralism is the only option here" (ETC Group, 2009: 6).

As for the second point (capital's increasingly voracious push for privatization), public resources continue to be sold off regardless of how hazardous this may be to the general conditions of human life. Chossudovsky, for example, examines the efforts to privatize food, water and fuel corporations: "These three essential goods or commodities, which in a real sense determine the reproduction of economic and social life on planet Earth, are under the control of a small number of global corporations and financial institutions... The fate of millions of human beings is

---

[138] This is why the recommendations of the ETC Group are so important: "There is an urgent need to engage all sectors of society in a comprehensive debate about the future that is being planned for them. The sweeping economic, social and political issues raised by converging technologies range far beyond the boundaries of any single country and must be debated worldwide through the United Nations. The international community must have the capacity to monitor and regulate the public and private governance [i.e. to control governments and participate in key decisions] as well as control and ownership of technologies... Beyond governance, the international community must create the capacity to track, evaluate and accept or reject new technologies and their products through an International Convention on the Evaluation of New Technologies" (ETC Group, 2003: 6).

managed behind closed doors in the corporate boardrooms as part of a profit driven agenda... We are at the crossroads of the most serious economic and social crisis in modern history. The process of global impoverishment... has reached a major turning point, leading to the simultaneous outbreak of famines in all major regions of the developing world" (Chossudovsky, 2008b).

One of the legal methods of privatizing public resources consists in intellectual property systems – "which have nothing to do with public acknowledgment of those who created something in particular" – and particularly patents: "knowledge is common property; each of us relies on the knowledge of others, and we are all interdependent... The idea of privatizing this reciprocal flow, inherent and basic to the subsistence of human societies, is absurd and perverse. In reality they are systems to privatize and restrict access to resources and knowledge" (Ribeiro, 2009a). It is no coincidence, as Ribeiro notes, that 97% of the world's patents are in OECD countries, that 90% of them are the property of transnational corporations, or that two thirds of what is patented is never ultimately used (Ribeiro, 2009a); patents exist to prevent others from having access to the object of the patent.

But to all this it is necessary to add two circumstances peculiar to the period. Firstly, that the advances of science and technology have made previously unimagined elements of nature prone to control. Secondly, that everything that scientific and technological advances enable us to control is privatized and "patented" by capital, from living organisms to seeds, plants, animals and their genetic codes to the elements of the periodic table (thanks to nanotechnology): "the grab for patents on nano-scale products and processes could mean mega-monopolies on the basic elements that are the building blocks of the entire natural world. If current trends continue, nanoscale technologies will further concentrate economic power in the hands of multinational corporations" (ETC Group, 2005a: 5–6).[139] All of the common property of mankind, the very basis of human life throughout its history, is in the process of being appropriated by capital: "in a world where privatization of science and unprecedented corporate concentration prevail, democracy and human rights are being eroded and national sovereignty is undermined" (ETC Group, 2005a: 5).

---

[139] The report adds that "almost as soon as scientists figured out how to manipulate life through genetic engineering, corporations figured out how to monopolize it" (ETC Group, 2005a: 6).

According to Chossudovsky, "in the more advanced phase of water privatization, the actual ownership of lakes and rivers by private corporations is contemplated" (Chossudovsky, 2008b). By this logic, it is not surprising that there are moves to privatize and sell air,[140] to expand the promising market for oxygen, and, based on the principle that "every crisis is an opportunity," it makes sense to allow pollution to flourish until the air provided by nature is unbreathable so that it will become essential for "private initiative" to resolve the problem.

It would be a simple variant of the modus operandi employed by capital, for example, to privatize the water supply. The World Bank demands austerity measures of countries in debt, which it uses to foster the deterioration of water supply systems; as a result, a "crisis" occurs, which is to be resolved by privatizing the water supply: "The World Bank serves the interests of water companies... through its regular loan programs to governments, which often come with conditions that explicitly require the privatization of water provision... The privatization of water under World Bank auspices feeds on the collapse of the system of public distribution of safe tap drinking water" (Chossudovsky, 2008b). And with regard to the third point, it should be noted that, on the one hand, this voracious push for privatization is not only a matter of business but a basic part of capital's whole power structure, and, on the other, as I indicated above, not only is capital unconcerned with safeguarding life, but, given that what it deems to be excess population is viewed as a threat to its interests, the implementation of the power structure itself encompasses the aims of protecting itself against this threat and disposing of this excess.

According to Chossudovsky, the agenda had already been laid out by Henry Kissinger as early as the 1970s – "*Control oil and you control nations; control food and you control the people*" (Chossudovsky, 2008b, emphasis added) – as part of an explicit design to dispose of those who are

---

140 According to an advertising portal on the Internet, "cans of oxygen are sold in many stores in Japan. Each can costs 600 yen. There are various flavors in case you get bored with the taste of 'regular oxygen', and they come with a comfortable adapter to enable to absorption without a problem. The business of the future!" "They shudder," remarked an anonymous source, "because our great grandparents say they never paid a single penny for water..." (García, 2006). A search confirms that this is now *an emerging market with a lot of potential* in Latin America. "The experts at the service of the transnationals have demonstrated an unlimited capacity for invention to better serve their employers. For them, nothing is impossible, absurd, or immoral. Among their most recent achievements is their success in putting nature itself on sale, disguised as so-called 'environmental services'. Expressions such as 'oxygen sales' and 'carbon sink sales' are now common currency, particularly in the countries of the South" (Movimiento Mundial por los Bosques Tropicales, 2006).

superfluous (and, as such, a hindrance) to capital: "President Richard Nixon at the outset of his term in office in 1969 asserted 'his belief that overpopulation gravely threatens world peace and stability.' Henry Kissinger, who at the time was Nixon's National Security adviser, directed various agencies of government to jointly undertake 'a study of the impact of world population growth on U.S. security and overseas interests'... Although the NSSM 200 [National Security Study Memorandum: Implications of Worldwide Population Growth for U.S. Security and Overseas Interests] report did not assign, for obvious reasons, an explicit policy role to famine formation, it nonetheless intimated that the occurrence of famines could, under certain circumstances, provide a de facto solution to overpopulation" (Chossudovsky, 2008b).

There is no doubt that the implementation of this de facto solution has produced satisfactory results and that its future looks extremely promising, if we also consider, for example, wars for natural resources, among other equally promising concepts that could be applied in the near future. Michael T. Klare reports that "British Defense Secretary John Reid warned that global climate change and dwindling natural resources are combining to increase the likelihood of violent conflict over land, water and energy... With sea levels rising, water and energy becoming increasingly scarce and prime agricultural lands turning into deserts, *internecine warfare over access to vital resources will become a global phenomenon*" (Klare, 2006, emphasis added). According to Klare, "the greatest danger posed by global climate change is not the degradation of ecosystems per se, but rather the disintegration of entire human societies, producing wholesale starvation, mass migrations and recurring conflict over resources," and he quotes a Pentagon report which asserts that "[a]s famine, disease, and weather-related disasters strike due to abrupt climate change... many countries' needs will exceed their carrying capacity," i.e. "their ability to provide the minimum requirements for human survival." This "will create a sense of desperation, which is likely to lead to offensive aggression" against countries with a greater stock of vital resources (Klare, 2006).[141]

Thus, Klare points out, together with the "concern over the inadequate capacity of poor and unstable countries to cope with the effects of climate change, and the resulting risk of state collapse, civil war and mass

---

[141] Klare quotes here from a 2003 Pentagon Report "An Abrupt Climate Change Scenario and Its Implications for United States National Security." The full text of this report is available at: http://www.climate.org/PDF/clim_change_scenario.pdf

migration," there is "a growing trend in strategic circles *to view environmental and resource effects – rather than political orientation and ideology – as the most potent source of armed conflict in the decades to come...* a major shift in strategic thinking may be under way. Environmental perils may soon dominate the world security agenda" (Klare, 2006, emphasis added).[142]

CAPITAL'S RIGHTS

In short, neoliberal capital has decided that it has rights of ownership over life and death all over the planet. The project for the future which neoliberalism (i.e. capitalism in its gestation of the last man of the end of history) offers humanity is expressed in widespread necrophilia and war as its increasingly dominant form (war on what it identifies as organized crime or international terrorism, war for natural resources, etc.) because it seeks not to solve the problems it creates, but to turn them into opportunities for profit and the deployment of force.

Its mission and vision require a radical and increasing abandonment of any commitment to life on the planet: it is dismantling the framework constructed during the Keynesian period to attend to the most basic needs of society, destroying the environment and privatizing nature. Its intellectual and moral leadership consists in submerging humanity in savagery, leading it into all kinds of sterile wars in order to keep it at the service of the perverse and criminal logic of the fetish and its insane personifications.

But this insanity is anchored in a reality. Underlying the situation is a crisis in the capital/wage-labor relation, a single crisis disguised as multiple crises (health, economic and financial, overproduction, realization, underproduction, food, climate, environmental, etc.). The march toward Absolute Monopoly is transforming the relation among capitalists themselves and between capitalists and the working class – it is the march toward the Last Man. But it also confirms that society has reached the end of capitalism itself, its period of decline, as will be argued in the following chapter. And here we find a great paradox: the conditions that indicate that we have reached the end of the capitalist relation are defined by capital as the end of life itself and, in an attempt to prolong its own life at the

---

[142] And, as if that weren't enough, the Pentagon report predicts: "In this world of warring States... nuclear arms proliferation is inevitable" (as quoted in Klare, 2006).

expense of human life, it imposes a dictatorship that is increasingly cynical, grotesque, brutal and predatory.[143]

In the first chapter, I explained the central role played by the development of science and technology in the structure of the capital/wage-labor relation and in the constitution of the social power of capital (economic, political and ideological). This question will be revisited in the following chapter, but by way of conclusion here, I offer the following reflections:

1. The development of the productive force of labor resulting from the advances in science and technology sets the parameters for the development of the capital/wage-labor relation and marks the end of the capitalist relation.
2. This development of the productive force of labor and of science and technology in general is still – and will continue to be until the working class effectively challenges it – the property of capital.
3. It has become a principle of neoliberal capital, personified in a rapidly shrinking number of human beings, to make use of its as yet undisputed ownership of this development to promote its dystopia and to display its willingness to turn the crisis of the end of its history into the end of the history of humanity.
4. Neoliberal capital is set in opposition to the vast majority of humanity, which has not yet managed to develop a sense of separation from capitalist domination, to build a united political front and outline a project of its own for the future that would enable the initiation of a new phase of history, leaving behind the savagery and destructive chaos of the present one.

---

[143] A few decades ago, Spanish filmmaker Luis Buñuel found the bourgeoisie to possess a *discreet charm*: cynical, perverse, drug-addicted, drug-dealing and criminal... Clearly, their *discretion* has diminished and their *charm* has been somewhat refined.

PART THREE

CONCLUSION

CHAPTER TEN

THE PATTERN OF DOMINATION AND HISTORICAL CYCLE OF CAPITAL

This absolute contradiction between the technical necessities of modern industry and the social character inherent in its capitalist form dispels all fixity and security in the situation of the laborer... This antagonism vents its rage... in the most reckless squandering of labor power and in the devastation caused by a social anarchy that turns every economic progress into a social calamity... But the historical development of the antagonisms, immanent in a given form of production, is the only way in which that form of production can be dissolved and a new form established.

Karl Marx
Capital

Although the main purpose of this work has been to elaborate a theoretical framework for the examination of the forms of capitalist domination and an introduction to their historical analysis, with a special focus on the neoliberal form of domination, it is fitting to conclude by presenting a note (as I proposed in the third chapter) on the relation between the historical succession of patterns of domination and the long-term trends they produce in the life cycle of capitalism.

To this end and remaining always at the level of abstraction on which this work has been developed, as an intermediate theoretical field between general theory – the analysis of the forces that generate, develop and produce the disintegration of capitalism – and its specific manifestations in history, I will turn my attention again to the relation between capital and wage-labor, the essential relation under capitalism, which has served as the basis for everything discussed so far; the theoretical space that allows us to link the pattern of domination to the long-term history of capitalism derives from the capital relation.

SOCIAL POWER AND THE CAPITAL RELATION

In the first chapter, I explained that the essential relation under capitalism, the underlying social relation of its social classes, consists in the separation between direct producers and the means of production and subsistence, and the fact that this same essential relation, the capital relation, constructs the basic articulation between economic, political and ideological dimensions of class relations. The class relation constitutes the core from which it is possible to explain domination and to link it to capitalist exploitation. Domination and exploitation are mutually interdependent and both are constructed on this common foundation: the capital relation. Exploitation is not possible unless it is sustained through domination, and domination has no purpose except to support exploitation.

I also argued that, insofar as the capital relation organizes a form of social power, the rule of one class over another, founded in all its dimensions (economic, political and ideological) on the same social relation, the basic distinction between the general forms of capitalist domination must arise from a point of articulation between domination and exploitation based on the capital relation itself. I therefore proposed that this basic distinction must consist in the recognition or denial of the material interests of the workers, the willingness or capacity of the capitalists (always under the pressure of worker resistance) to give concessions to the workers to moderate the exploitation, i.e. the degree to which capital is willing or able to share the product of value, that is, the value created by the working class itself.

While the content of domination consists in supporting exploitation, its form derives from the nature of its relationship with exploitation. Based on this proposition, I distinguished two general forms of capitalist domination: the natural form and the contained form. There is a link between exploitation and domination, between the economic and the political, built around the conditions in which the capitalist class is likely to grant concessions to the working class. And although these conditions arise from two sources – the struggle of the workers and the evolution of the capital relation itself – it is the second of these, its evolution, which defines the objective conditions in which concessions from the capitalist class are likely. Ideological, economic and political domination are not independent variables. As components of the social power of a class, their fate is tied to the basic relation (the capital relation), which, as it evolves, transforms the conditions of domination of the capitalist class, the conditions of its social power; the capital relation develops, and this is the essential point.

The Development of the Capital Relation

The development of the relation between capital and wage-labor, and the development of the capital relation itself, depends on the development of the productive force of labor. In Chapter 2, I noted that in *Capital*, Marx demonstrates that the capital relation articulates tendencies of development, general trends that organize the future of capitalist society: an increase in the productivity of labor and an increase in the organic composition of capital; expulsion of the work force from the labor process, expansion of the industrial reserve army and the creation of an absolute surplus population; and concentration and centralization of capital. Moreover, Marx shows how these tendencies are expressed in downward pressure on the rate of profit and that the same tendencies that provoke the reduction of the rate of profit generate counter-tendencies that slow down the development of the tendency to its fullest, with a constant reduction of capital and an increase in its technical composition that is more intense than the increase in its value composition. Capital's search for counter-tendencies to prevent the drop in the rate of profit includes a wide range of possibilities, the examination of which reveals the particular features of each historical period, but the basic counter-tendency sought, which ultimately supports all others, is to increase the rate of surplus-value. These counter-tendencies, it should be noted, slow down but do not stop the main tendency.

Capitalist development, the development of the capital relation, is thus necessarily the development of the productive force of labor. Marx constructs the concept of the organic composition of capital and its tendency toward growth as a synthetic expression of this process. From this perspective, the tendencies toward reduction of the rate of profit and expulsion of the work force from the labor process become clearly visible. As I had further pointed out in the second chapter, the development of the capital/wage-labor relation can be investigated on different analytical levels, constructed on the basis of the examination of the development of its tendencies over time; that is, the examination of the historical process of capitalism and its articulation in the short, medium and long term. I argued that it is necessary to begin with the most direct and immediate features of the capital relation in the consciousness and the practice of capitalists in order to identify the general forms of capitalist domination; the forms which, in their specific historical manifestations, appear as

patterns of domination, but which, to appreciate the historical significance of each pattern of domination, need to be placed in relation with
the medium- and long-term history of capitalism.

The Medium Term in the Development of Capital

The general features of the medium term in the history of capitalism – and
the corresponding periodization – were also explained in the second
chapter. The historical development of capitalism appears as a series of
phases of economic expansion, the fundamental condition for which is
the existence of a historical set of economic, political and ideological circumstances that ensure a rate of profit satisfactory for capital, and phases
of depression that express the exhaustion of the conditions that ensured
an increased rate of profit during the period of expansion that preceded it
and the search for new counter-tendencies.

If we compare the periodization of the medium term in the history of
capitalism with what I proposed as the period of prevalence of each pattern of domination, we will find that the liberal pattern covers the first
three expansive periods (1770–1830, 1850–1873 and 1896–1914) followed
by two corresponding periods of depression (1830–1850 and 1873–1896)
and the decisive shift to the Keynesian pattern did not occur until the middle of the third period of depression from 1914 to 1945 (with the stimulus
of the crisis of 1929), although in Western Europe this shift had been developing since the second period of depression (1873–1896).

On the other hand, the Keynesian pattern, at least as a relatively general
form of capitalist domination, had a much shorter life, which, in the strictest sense, not including its prolonged and turbulent process of transition,
is limited to the period of expansion after World War II (1945–1967); with
the onset of the subsequent period of depression (from 1967 onward), the
shift began toward the currently prevailing neoliberal pattern.

The Long Term in the Development of Capital

It is worth reiterating here that between one stage and another in the
medium term there is a basic continuity in terms of the tendential laws of
capitalist development; each stage begins with the levels of labor productivity, organic composition and concentration of capital with which the
previous stage ended. The return to a phase of expansion after one of
depression is not circular but might better be described as a spiral: the

long term, the full historical duration of the capitalist mode of production, develops over the course of the stages that make up its medium term. Thus the analysis of the medium term offers explanatory dimensions and precise historical meanings when placed in relation to the long term.

The long term of capitalism covers the period from its birth as a social model for organizing production until its death. From the perspective of this analysis there are only three periods to consider: infancy, maturity and decline. And the delimitation of each of these periods should be drawn from the decisive moments in the productive force of labor, i.e. decisive moments in the development of the capital relation.

In the infancy of capitalism, formal subsumption and absolute surplus value prevailed; the first industrial revolution had just begun to make its effects felt in some countries and certain sectors, and ownership of capital, i.e. of the means of production and subsistence of the workers, was spread out among many capitalists. The move toward its maturity began at the end of the 19th century in Western Europe, culminating in the technological transformations fostered by Fordism. Real subsumption and relative surplus value dominated the scene; science became the decisive productive force with the establishment of what Figueroa calls the workshop of technological progress, and general labor and immediate labor were separated. The dispersed nature of the ownership of capital that typified the previous period was transformed and replaced by a clear tendency toward concentration and centralization, although the separation between producers and the means of production and subsistence assumed a wide variety of forms, from extreme nationalization of capital in real socialism to a combination of state and private monopoly capital in the rest of the world, with priority given to private monopolies in the developed nations and state capital in the underdeveloped world.

The decline of capitalism (which will be examined below) corresponds to the current period, with its technological revolution and its extreme concentration of capital in the hands of a handful of gigantic transnational monopolies. A correspondence can thus be identified between the long-term periods of the history of capitalism and the historical sequence of patterns of domination.

The first pattern of domination was the liberal pattern (the first historical expression of the natural form of domination), which represented the infancy of capitalism, characterized by the powerlessness of workers faced with a capital that had yet to fully stabilize the forms of extraction of relative surplus value and that unleashed its voracious appetite for growth.

The second pattern of domination was the Keynesian pattern (the first and only historical expression of the contained form of domination), which represented capitalism in maturity; a rise in productivity derived from advances in scientific research and their conversion into technology coupled with the developments of Fordism and *Taylorism*, under conditions of a certain degree of development of the organic composition of capital, allowed for the construction of a delicate balance that permitted the granting of concessions to workers together with increases in the rate of profit.[1]

The neoliberal pattern of domination, the second historical expression of the natural form of domination, represents the decline of capitalism.

Decline of Capitalism and the Neoliberal Pattern

I will not go any further here to argue for the correspondence between historical periods and the liberal and Keynesian patterns. However, still without leaving the level of abstraction on which this work is developed, it is necessary to further explain the argument for the relationship between the decline of capitalism and the neoliberal pattern, beginning on the logical plane and concluding on the *historical* plane.

The Logical Plane

First of all, it must be remembered, as Figueroa Sepúlveda notes, the basic theoretical proposition of Marxism lies in the demonstration of the historicity of capitalism: "the notion of the collapse of capital arises directly from dialectical materialism. According to this method, capitalism is historically determined production, one mode among others, with a beginning and an end... If Marx addressed the study of capital in a historical mode, we would expect to find in his work at least the basic elements for a theory of its collapse, and that theory should be constructed chiefly on the basis of the contradiction between the development of productive forces and production relations" (Figueroa Sepúlveda, 1989: 12–13).[2]

---

[1] In the second chapter, I indicated that the crucial condition for the consolidation of the *contained form* of domination was that it was supported by advances in labor productivity, i.e. with the relevant mediation, by advances in the rate of exploitation and the rate of profit. If capital cannot find a form of compensation, it will maintain constant and incessant opposition to any limitation upon "freedom" and "free enterprise" and will defend its *unrestricted right* to exploit labor.

[2] This is of course the explicit proposition that Marx sets forth in what he calls his "guiding principle" (see Marx, 1859: Preface).

Secondly, Figueroa Sepúlveda distinguishes between crises and collapse. The first "occur in conditions in which the development of the productive forces still admit the presence of capitalist production relations" (Figueroa Sepúlveda, 1989: 25), while "a theory of collapse is simply a theory of the transformation of this conflict into an insoluble problem, forcing a change to a new social form of production. In other words, it differs from the theory of other manifestations of the same conflict that may be solved or overcome within the context of capitalist production" (Figueroa Sepúlveda, 1989: 14).

Thirdly, the concept of crisis is associated with the medium-term history of capitalism, while the collapse is associated with the historical end of capitalism. It is also necessary to distinguish between the collapse and decline of capitalism, as the latter of these two is associated with the move toward the end and, as such, constitutes the final period in the history of capitalism.

Fourth, on the logical plane, the conditions of the period of decline are represented in the natural form of domination. For capital, decline means an increasing organic composition and a decreasing rate of profit, and as a result, a renewed need to increase the rate of surplus-value in a final effort to reestablish the level of the rate of profit, and a renewed hostility toward making concessions to the working class, becoming ever more intense as it draws closer to its end.

In this sense, the development of the relation between capital and wage-labor, the relation that separates producers from the means of production and subsistence, entails its necessary negation. The conflict between capital and labor is not eternal, nor is the development of capitalism limited to a scenario of struggles between the political wills of social classes in a perpetual dispute over concessions, as these struggles unfold in the context of objective conditions defined by the capital relation, which lead toward its end and which determine that, in the period of its decline, capital should become particularly hostile toward granting concessions to workers.

The Historical Plane

As mentioned above, the decline of capitalism is the characteristic of the current period, with its technological revolution and its extreme concentration of capital in the hands of a handful of gigantic transnational monopolies. The particular features of this new boost in labor productivity provided by the current technological revolution, with their consequences of the increased organic composition of capital, the expulsion of the work force from the labor process, the concentration and centralization of capital and its effects on the rate of profit, constitute the general context of the neoliberal pattern of domination, as noted throughout this analysis. However, a detailed examination of these features in their current manifestations is beyond the scope of my study. Therefore, returning to the central idea with regard to the capital/wage-labor relation – that the development of this relation is contingent upon the development of the productive force of labor – I will point to just a few features that seem particularly relevant to the analysis proposed here.

First, with regard to the potential of the new technologies to increase the intensity of labor and exploitation, while expelling the work force from the labor process, it is patently clear that "since the beginning of the 1980s the increase in productivity and exploitation – intensification of the pace of work, falling wages, the loss of the social advances made previously – has provoked a huge shift of value from labor to capital" (Astarita, 1997), and, as Luis Gómez notes, the confluence of the development of microelectronics, electromechanics, hydraulics, pneumatics, new materials, energetics, robotics and organizational theories has facilitated the emergence of the concept of flexibility, a concept referring to the technical, real, concrete possibility for the first time in history of the design of completely automated production systems (without direct human labor). Electronic components make it possible to introduce full-scale production process control technology, encompassing control, command and regulation (which were previously handled by qualified workers). Robotics and flexible production systems represent an articulation between the production of means of production that design traditional automation systems (electromechanics, hydraulics and pneumatics) and the industry of computerized means of production for control and command of the production processes. The mechanical machine is transformed into an automated machine, the relation between operating machines and command and control machines is given priority, and the trend toward making the machine independent of direct labor (qualified and unqualified) is consolidated, thereby enhancing the transformational power of automation systems (transformation of material, loading and unloading, and even control of maintenance and cleaning processes) that depend on another type of intellectual, abstract labor, focused on the development of microelectronics, information technology and design and programming: command and regulation, orders and running procedures.

The most complex innovations are produced in the experimentation laboratories of the big corporations. The operator is removed from direct supervision of the machine to supervision via control panels, involving a new form of labor organization, with the use of central computers for the operational coordination of machine-tools and a reformulation of the concept of a workshop, which is transformed from a collection of individual machines organized in systems of production lines into computerized networks of machine-tools organized in modules covering individual complete processes. The aim of the flexible workshop is to achieve consistency in production systems by giving the relation between machines priority over the relation between humans and machines; this is its essential difference from Taylorism and Fordism (Gómez E., 1993).

Second, with regard to the potential of the new technologies to organize production on a global scale and, as a result, to promote the concentration and centralization of capital on that scale, as Dabat, Rivera and Suárez note, "the historic transformation that global capitalism is experiencing has its main driving force in the revolutionary changes to the technological base, which are opening up huge possibilities of interconnection of human activities on different continents, in different countries and cities. The innovations in the fields of information technology and telecommunications have brought about a structural and spatial-temporal change that encourages a new form of organization of social, economic and political activities, characterized by its capacity to have repercussions over large distances in a form of interconnection that is increasingly intense, systematic and rapid" (Dabat et al, 2004: 39).

And according to Fröbel, Heinrichs and Kreye, "it was capital itself which in its centuries-long development created the set of conditions for its own appreciation and accumulation, particularly a worldwide industrial reserve army, widespread fragmentation of the production process and efficient transportation and communications technology... This whole set of new conditions for capital appreciation and accumulation became decisive for the first time in the 1960s. It has created a global work force market and a global market of production centers which, for the first time, integrate both the traditional industrialized countries and the underdeveloped nations. The individual capitalists who are faced with this set of conditions are able to enjoy increased profits with the appropriate reorganization of their production, by making use of the industrial reserve army at a global level through the fragmentation of the production process and advanced technology in transportation and communications. The demands of competition turn this possibility into a necessity... in order to guarantee the appreciation of individual capital" (Fröbel et al, 1981: 49, 50).

The selected features of the new technologies – the potential to intensify labor and, at the same time, to expel the work force from the labor process, as well as to promote the concentration and centralization of capital on a global scale – are directly associated with the basic trend present in the development of the relation between capital and wage-labor, the trend that guides the fate of the social classes, capital and labor under capitalism, which Marx considers to be the general law of capitalist accumulation (Marx, 1867: Ch. 25): extreme concentration of the means of production and subsistence on the side of the capitalist class, and exploitation and extremely intense competition in the workplace among the fortunate workers who have jobs, coupled with exclusion and extreme poverty among the industrial reserve army and a growing absolute surplus population on the side of the working class.[3]

The capital relation articulates developmental tendencies, general trends that shape the future of capitalist society and which, although they have a common foundation, unfold in two directions that are clearly differentiated, both of which are relevant to a reflection on the period of decline and the course taken toward the end of capitalism as a social mode of organizing production. The first guides the fate of the working class, while the second guides the fate of the capitalist class. The increase in labor productivity and in the organic composition of capital means, for the working class, expulsion from the labor process, expansion of the industrial reserve army and the creation of an absolute surplus population, while for the capitalist class it means concentration and centralization of capital and a reduction in the rate of profit.

THE SOCIAL LIMIT

The first of these two directions is associated with what might be called the social limit of capitalism – the limit imposed on capital by the working

---

[3] Figueroa Sepúlveda distinguishes between *relative surplus population* (equivalent to the industrial reserve army, the worker population superfluous to the needs of the capital in operation, but necessary to the expansion of production) and *absolute surplus population*: "the general tendency of capital culminates in the creation of a consolidated surplus population that must arise in an advanced stage of production as a result of the extension of the relative surplus population beyond the point at which it effectively constitutes a need for appreciation" (Figueroa Sepúlveda, 2008). Here we are speaking of an *absolute surplus population*.

class – and this limit in turn has a relative and an absolute dimension. The relative social limit of capitalism is the effect of the working class struggle and operates in direct relation with the effectiveness of workers in opposing and destroying the domination of capital. The absolute social limit lies in the growing inability of the bourgeoisie to ensure the reproduction of life of its slaves: "in order to oppress a class, certain conditions must be assured to it under which it can, at least, continue its slavish existence... the bourgeoisie is unfit any longer to be the ruling class in society... It is unfit to rule because it is incompetent to assure an existence to its slave within his slavery... Society can no longer live under this bourgeoisie, in other words, its existence is no longer compatible with society" (Marx and Engels, 1848: I). The absolute social limit is reached when the relative social limit proves incapable of converting the decline of capitalism into the transition to socialism. In this case, the bourgeoisie "cannot help letting [its slave] sink into such a state, that it has to feed him, instead of being fed by him" (Marx and Engels, 1848: I) and/or leave an increasing percentage of the excess slaves to die or simply kill them off.

It would not be possible to overstate the current dimensions or the worsening trends of the diverse phenomena characteristic of the period: unemployment, the billions of people lacking the most basic elements of life, the famines afflicting growing masses of people, the huge dimensions of the migratory movements of human beings who wander the world in a desperate search for a place to survive, along with the increasing necrophilia of the neoliberal bourgeoisie. As Joachim Hirsh notes:

> "Viewed globally, ever greater numbers of human beings are no longer useful to capital, even as objects of exploitation, and are left to their fate by governments and, in the worst cases, are treated only as objects to be monitored, controlled and attacked with counter-insurgency strategies involving police intervention... The fact that an increasing number of human beings are marginalized and excluded from the formal context of appreciation at the same time means a new context of socio-political crisis: the less assured the relation between capital, labor and sustenance is, the more superfluous capital becomes" (Hirsch, 2000).

And according to Samir Amin:

> "The new organization of labor (the so-called 'network society') entails a dramatic reduction in total labor, made possible thanks to the use of new technologies or, to put it another way, to their increased productivity. But in the actual operation of the system this economy of the labor factor is accompanied, through exclusion, by a brutal reduction in the number of workers used by capital... The theory of the supporters of capitalism is that those excluded today could be working tomorrow, thanks to the expansion

of markets... [but] in its senility, capitalism cannot produce anything other than growing exclusion... Today, a subsequent expansion of capital in the peripheries (even a marginal one) entails destruction of unimaginable scope... The only prospects it offers are a world of shanty towns and of five billion excess, surplus human beings... Capitalism has entered its declining senile phase, as the logic that governs this system is no longer capable of assuring the most basic survival of half of humanity. Capitalism is turning into savagery, directly inviting genocide" (Amin, 2009).

THE INTERNAL LIMIT

The other limit, as mentioned earlier, is associated with the tendency of the rate of profit to fall and is also connected to the development of the capital relation through the development of the productive force of labor; the limit of capital is capital itself. Capitalism is exhausted through the unfolding of the laws of its own development, and contains a tendency, as shown above, toward collapse.[4] In the context of contemporary capitalism, the behavior of the rate of profit has been examined by Anwar Shaikh (1990), Fred Moseley (2005) and Robert Brenner (2009a), among others. Brenner in particular identifies a "long fall" – a period of prolonged stagnation and crisis beginning as early as the late 1960s and continuing up to the present – in the rate of growth of the global GDP, the basic reason for which lies in the prolonged decline of the average rate of profit in the private sector as a whole.

Chris Harman identifies diverse attempts to calculate the long-term behavior of the rate of profit: "the results" he says "are not always fully compatible with each other, since there are different ways of measuring investment in fixed capital, and the information on profits provided by companies and governments are subject to enormous distortions." Nevertheless, he adds, "there is general agreement that profit rates fell from the late 1960s," and that the partial recoveries revealed an inability to produce a lasting reversal of the trend, even when they had been contextually significant. Although "it is wrong to describe the situation as one of permanent crisis – rather it is one of recurrent economic crises," capitalism has not been able "to return to the 'golden age' and it will not be able

---

[4] According to Katz, the declining trend in the rate of profit is a necessary process that is not a contingent occurrence or a passing phase, but an internal result of the process of accumulation, whose evolution responds to a predictable pattern of development (Katz, 2002).

to do so in future. It may not be in permanent crisis, but it is in a phase of repeated crises from which it cannot escape, and these will necessarily be political and social as well as economic" (Harman, 2007).

This behavior of the rate of profit provokes a complex array of consequences associated with diverse problems of overaccumulation, overproduction, underconsumption, financial parasitism, overextended credit, and the new place of the state in the economy, among others. The response should not be "limited to merely recording a statistic [of the level of the fall in the rate of profit], but should consider every conclusion on the historical conditions under which capital accumulation develops. The fall in profitability is, more than anything, a qualitative indicator, in other words, whether we are in the presence of a system that is maturing or developing or in full decline and disintegration... If the law holds, the decline in the rate of profit must result in increasing obstacles, ever more insuperable for capital appreciation. And this is what we are witnessing in the economy today."[5]

"Flexibilizing" the Internal Limit

However, although it will ultimately exacerbate the systemic problems, a general reduction in the rate of profit is relatively compatible with an increased rate of profit for a handful of capitalists if that handful can, on the one hand, demonstrate the ability to concentrate the production and appropriation of worldwide surplus-value into their hands, and on the other, prove capable of unleashing truly global assaults in order to appropriate the world's wealth.

The sixth chapter of this study was dedicated to an examination of the strategies of neoliberal capital to concentrate production and appropriation of surplus-value. According to Wim Dierckxsens, "with a low rate of profit in the production sector, capital seeks accumulation not through economic growth, but through the concentration of existing income." Neoliberalism has thus focused on increasing transnational and financial capital at the expense of the redistribution of income and of national and

---

[5] "All these contradictions, which have acquired explosive characteristics, are a measurement of the capitalist *impasse*. The excess of unsaleable products that flood the markets, whatever the sector or activity considered, and of surplus capital unable to find profitable employment, is an indicator of the current relevance of the law formulated by Marx that makes his work truly exploratory, in spite of what his detractors may say" (Heller, 2003).

local markets. A veritable economic war was unleashed by the existing markets on behalf of transnational corporations, leading to exclusion, increased levels of labor exploitation and the plundering of the economies of the periphery: "accumulating capital without economic growth is only possible by means of the concentration of income... The concentration of markets and of global income into fewer hands has succeeded in saving the rate of profit of the transnationals, but has deteriorated the demand for products and services of immense majorities... Now it threatens growth even in the superpowers themselves... A distribution of global income in decline only serves to aggravate the world recession... This cannot be a sustainable long-term project as its final result will be economic contraction, i.e. recession" (Dierckxsens, 2002: 13).[6] Associated with this logic of concentration of wealth (and this explains the importance they have acquired in the neoliberal world) are diverse forms of accumulation ranging from speculation to flagrant crimes, and including what David Harvey calls "accumulation by dispossession" (Harvey, 2004).

With regard to accumulation by speculation, Dierckxsens explains that "accumulation based on concentration of income essentially consists in making money with money without creating wealth. The most profitable methods are stock market and currency speculation... This form of unproductive accumulation was fostered in the 1970s when the Keynesian policies expressed in the Welfare State took a backwards step. During the post-war period, investment was closely tied to the production process through a whole arsenal of economic regulations... The falling rate of profit in the sphere of production towards the late 1970s gave rise to neoliberalism, which liberated capital flows from these restraints" (Dierckxsens, 2002).

According to Harvey, these recurring speculative raids are orchestrated by "a powerful Wall Street/U.S. Treasury financial regime... with controlling powers over global financial institutions (such as the IMF) and able to make or break many weak economies through credit manipulations and

---

[6] "The policies of structural adjustment fostered the replacement of national markets with transnational ones, the replacement of public companies with transnationals, the acquisition of companies, the mergers of transnationals and currency speculation in the periphery... All these measures contributed to saving the rate of profit of transnational and financial capital... All these investments do not generate new wealth, or expand the total market, or foster growth; they only foster the redistribution of income and the existing market in the world" (Dierckxsens 2002).

debt management practices" (Harvey, 2004: 70).[7] Harvey argues that these raids form part of the strategy of accumulation by dispossession, "a 'vulture capitalism' dedicated to the appropriation and devaluation of assets, rather than to building them up through productive investments" (Harvey, 2004: 72), which is characterized by violence, swindling, oppression, pillaging and fraud. He adds that "wholly new mechanisms of accumulation by dispossession have also opened up," among which he notes biopiracy and the pillaging of the world's stockpile of genetic resources by a few large multinational companies, the depletion of the global environmental commons (land, air, water) and the proliferation of environmental degradation, the privatization of water and other public services (constituting a new wave of "enclosing the commons"), and the reversion to the private domain of common property rights won through past class struggles (the right to a state pension, to welfare, to education or to national health care) (Harvey, 2004: 75).

As far as unlawful forms of accumulation are concerned, the excellent business represented by diverse modes of "organized crime" has already been explored. Jorge Beinstein suggests that the rise of "gangster capitalism" needs to be viewed in connection with widespread deregulation and the complicity of the state in forms of accumulation that encourage social pillaging in its broadest sense: "we could identify a kind of 'logical sequence' based on the diversion of funds originating in the productive sector (with decreasing profitability) towards 'classical' financial operations (purchase of public deeds, shares, etc.) and from there (once these operations were saturated) towards new, increasingly fast and complex forms of speculation ('derivative' products, etc.), ultimately leading to illegal businesses, plundering, etc. (from dismantling public companies in the periphery to drug trafficking)" (Beinstein, 2000).

---

[7] Harvey suggests that the structured destruction of assets by means of inflation, the promotion of indebtedness levels which even in the advanced capitalist countries reduce whole populations to servitude through debt, corporate fraud and dispossession of assets like pension funds constitute "central features of what contemporary capitalism is about" (Harvey, 2004: 75). But above all, he says, "we have to look at the speculative raiding carried out by hedge funds and other major institutions of finance capital as the cutting edge of accumulation by dispossession in recent times." He illustrates this point with the case of Southeast Asia: "by creating a liquidity crisis throughout Southeast Asia, the hedge funds forced profitable businesses into bankruptcy. These businesses could be purchased at fire-sale prices by surplus capitals in the core countries, thus engineering what Wade and Veneroso refer to as 'the biggest peacetime transfer of assets from domestic (i.e. Southeast Asian) to foreign (i.e. U.S. and Japanese) owners in the past few years anywhere in the world'" (Harvey, 2004: 75).

Disdain for the Absolute Social Limit

From the above we may conclude that the absolute priority of neoliberalism has been to ensure that, even in the midst of economic stagnation, transnational capital thrives[8], regardless of the social consequences that such a priority entails. All these barbaric forms of accumulation to which neoliberal capital resorts to compensate for the drop in the rate of profit increase the damage to the lives and wellbeing of virtually every sector of the people dispossessed of the means of production and subsistence. But as long as these forms aid accumulation, capital will continue to use them, will intensify them if it can[9] and will have no qualms about resorting to other even more barbarous measures. In the decline of capitalism, a perverse logic is taking root: the harder it becomes to maintain capital accumulation, the more brutal its compensatory strategies become, and the more destructive these strategies are, the more problematic a reasonably sustainable accumulation becomes. István Mészáros describes it as a "structural crisis of the system," which is spreading everywhere, undermining the basic conditions for the survival of the human species (Mészáros, 2010).[10]

However, the move toward what I have called the absolute social limit of capitalism by leaving a growing number of its slaves to die, fostering homicide among them and/or killing them is not something that will cause much concern for a genocidal capital, in the embryonic phase of Absolute Monopoly, which is preoccupied only with efforts to raise the relative social limit. Although I have systematically excluded an analysis of the inter-imperialist contradictions from this reflection in order to concentrate on the analysis of the capital-labor relation, it is essential to bear in mind that "a distribution of global income in decline only aggravates the global recession... With a low rate of profit in the sphere of production, capital does not seek to accumulate through economic growth but through

---

[8] "We have therefore witnessed for the last dozen years or so the extraordinary spectacle of a world economy in which the continuation of capital accumulation has come literally to depend upon historic waves of speculation, carefully nurtured and rationalized by state policy makers" (Brenner, 2009b).

[9] "In the absence of any strong revival of sustained accumulation through expanded reproduction, this will entail a deepening politics of accumulation by dispossession throughout the world in order to keep the motor of accumulation from stalling entirely" (Harvey, 2004: 81).

[10] "The enormous expansion of financial adventurism... is by its nature inseparable from the deepening of the crisis in the productive branches of industry as well as from the ensuing troubles arising from the utterly sluggish capital accumulation" (Mészáros, 2010).

the concentration of existing income... as the world market is divided up among an ever smaller number of transnationals, the new distribution of the existing market becomes increasingly disputed, even more so when this market is shrinking due to a fall in global demand. As sales contract, so do profits... To postpone this crisis in a nation is possible, but it requires more than just an economic confrontation. The war for the market becomes total... *The continuous division of the global market will not provide a way out for all transnational capital. The war for the global market requires extra-economic measures in order to emerge victorious. This means a threat of war at the global level"* (Dierckxsens, 2002, emphasis added).

Nobody is preparing more keenly than the U.S. oligarchy to resolve the final dispute for Absolute Monopoly with war. According to Chossudovsky, its "killing machine is deployed at a global level, within the framework of the unified combat command structure... It is part of the Pentagon's 'long war', a profit driven war without borders, a project of world domination... upheld by the institutions of government, the corporate media and the mandarins and intellectuals of the New World Order in Washington's think tanks and strategic studies research institutes" (Chossudovsky, 2010).[11]

Thus, the priority given to the rate of profit by the transnationals confirms the genocidal vocation of neoliberal capital and its characterization as capitalism in gestation toward the last man. As long as it maintains this direction, that is, as long as what I've called the relative social limit of capitalism (working class resistance) fails to impose another option, capital will continue on its course toward the absolute social limit, constructing its "criminal project of global destruction, in which the quest for profit is the overriding force" (Chossudovsky, 2010). It is thus no surprise to find that, as Dufour notes, "the Earth's surface is being conceived as a wide battlefield... an integrated network of military bases and installations which covers the entire planet (continents, oceans and outer space)... distributed according to a command structure divided up into five spatial units and four unified combatant commands" (Dufour, 2007).

Quoting Iraklis Tsavdaridis, Secretary of the World Peace Council, Dufour adds that "the establishment of U.S. military bases should not of course be seen simply in terms of direct military ends. They are always

---

[11] "The medium term strategic objective is to target Iran and neutralize Iran's allies, through gunboat diplomacy. The longer term military objective is to directly target China and Russia" (Chossudovsky, 2010).

used to promote the economic and political objectives of U.S. capitalism."
This is the dynamic *imposed by the logic of the fetish*, even though it *is
directed toward total destruction*. According to Dierckxsens, "in a war for
the global market basically for the benefit of the big capital of one nation,
an increasing number of countries are joining the recession. *There is no
country that can escape it – not even the winning nation, as it destroys its
own environment.* To win in the short term means a more profound recession in the future" (Dierckxsens, 2002, emphasis added).[12]

Mészáros comments that "the objective of the feasible war at the present phase of historical development, in accordance with the objective
requirements of imperialism – world domination by capital's most powerful state, in tune with its own political design of ruthless authoritarian 'globalization' (dressed up as 'free exchange' in a U.S.-ruled global market) – is
ultimately unwinnable, foreshadowing, instead, the destruction of humankind... envisaging war as the mechanism of global government in today's
world underlines the fact that we find ourselves at the precipice of absolute irrationality from which there can be no return if we accept the ongoing course of development" (Mészáros, 2003).[13]

Dierckxsens describes this as "the setting for war: *there is not even
enough room for all the transnationals*. The division of the world must
be redefined by force" (Dierckxsens as quoted in Rodríguez Derivet,
2003, emphasis added). However, the cynical command still exercised by
capital over humankind is such that, according to Chossudovsky, the
"main architects [of war] are rewarded for their contributions to world
peace... realities in an inquisitorial environment are turned upside down:
the warmongers are committed to peace, the victims of war are presented
as the protagonists of war... When the lie becomes the truth there is no
turning backwards. When war is upheld as a humanitarian endeavor, justice and the entire international legal system are turned upside down:
pacifism and the antiwar movement are criminalized. Opposing the war
becomes a criminal act" (Chossudovsky, 2010).

---

[12] "The basic contradiction in the existing rationale is that capitalism has reached the
historic moment where it is impossible to return to linking investment with production in
a profitable way. A greater development of productive forces, in other words, is no longer
possible under the existing economic rationale and social relations. This contradiction will
become visible in the thwarted attempts to solve it" (Dierckxsens, 2002).

[13] "The weapons already available for waging the war or wars of the twenty-first century
are capable of exterminating not only the adversary but the whole of humanity, for the first
time ever in history. Nor should we have the illusion that the existing weaponry marks the
very end of the road. Others, even more instantly lethal ones, might appear tomorrow or
the day after tomorrow" (Mészáros, 2003).

At present, according to Enrique Dussel, the prevailing project is one of "perpetual war": "the state of war is a permanent, universal state of existence." It constitutes an ontology of death in which the "cynical reasoning" of the empire defines what a terrorist act is, and declares specifically who the terrorists are: "this tautological judgment 'legitimately' authorizes (for the judge and military command enforcing the sentence) 'the total destruction of the terrorist.' It has become totally irrational. The Totalized Totality issues a judgment on its own grounds. The Other has been annihilated for being other" (Dussel, 2002).

The Working Class and the Relative Social Limit

It is worth reiterating here that the period of decline does not represent the sudden collapse of capitalism, but a course toward its end. The neoliberal form of organizing the capital-labor relation admits variants, and in capitalism today a significant section of humankind still finds a place within the social relations organized by capital. It is what we might call a "flexible" domination; in contrast to previous periods, with a basically homogeneous design in class relations, capital now fosters competitiveness and criminal activity and "flexibilizes" its design according to its economic and political needs and strategies.

Some workers, particularly illegal immigrants, are radically deprived of any kind of rights (labor, social or political), while labor and wage concessions are granted to a constantly shrinking segment of highly qualified workers, and division and conflict within the working class is fostered to the extreme of assigning certain segments the explicit task of exterminating others by cultivating racism, xenophobia and the whole framework of the state administration of criminal activity. Within the general design to disable nation-states as spaces for the regulation of class relations, variants are also admitted; the most radical differences are found between developed and developing nations, although even in the latter case the so-called "transition to democracy" allows for political tinkering and diverse margins of negotiation between different national and class interests.

However, from the perspective of the long-term trends and the current historical period of capital, the world of the worker surplus population, the waves of illegal migration, the underworld of criminal activity and its professional sector (torturers, hired killers, human traffickers, etc.) and the assault on the living conditions of the whole class dispossessed of the means of production and subsistence, must all inevitably grow: "The anxiety shared by the vast masses in virtually every part of the world arises from the discovery made by the working class, the youth and the oppressed masses of the rapid degradation of the conditions of their existence: a return to or continued unemployment, the precarious nature of their basic living conditions, destruction of social welfare, a return to hunger or, even where hunger is absent, a return to both individual and social decay, and the arrogance of the property owner classes and of a society that once again shamelessly exposes the wealth of the few before the eyes of the many who have none" (Chesnais, 1996).[14]

Such is the logical result of the renewed eagerness of capital to increase the rate of surplus-value – in the current combinations of dealings with workers, capital embraces any means of producing surplus-value, whether relative or absolute[15] – and to concentrate its production and appropriation in the hands of a few huge and insatiable monopolies that dominate production and the global market. Under these conditions, the development of the period of decline must be marked by a growing rebellion of those dispossessed of their means of production and subsistence, and by the increasing fragility of the hegemony of capital: "what is new in this phase of globalization directed by financial capital is the appearance, among vast sectors of the world's population, of cracks in the domination, in the absorption by the dominated classes of capitalist ideas and values and in the fatalistic notion that there is no alternative to neoliberal politics since it is the only possible option" (Almeyra, 2007).

Rebellion and Revolution

Nevertheless, we need to bear in mind that rebellion is not revolution, nor does hegemonic weakness mean resources are lacking to prolong capital domination. "According to Gramsci, we can dismiss the idea that economic crises in themselves produce groundbreaking events: they *can only*

---

[14] According to Raúl Zibechi, "a UN study estimates that 1 billion people live in peripheral slum districts of third-world cities, and that the poor in the world's big cities have hit two billion, one third of humankind. These figures will double in the next 15 to 20 years, as the growth of the world's population will occur entirely in the cities and 95% will be seen in the suburbs of the cities of the South" (Zibechi, 2008).

[15] "This consists in the bloodthirstiness with which employers oppose the reduction of working hours and seek to dismantle the legal frameworks of labor: employers want to overturn what for them represent hindrances to the appropriation of absolute surplus-value" (Chesnais, 1997).

create more favorable ground for the dissemination of certain ways of think-
ing, of proposing and resolving the questions that inform all subsequent gov-
ernment activity... By definition, it is a long process that should not be
confused with its episodic manifestations... The crisis consists precisely in
the death of the old and the birth of the new; on these grounds the most
diverse gruesome phenomena are tested" (Portantiero, 1981: 51, 52, emphasis added). The development of science at the service of capital, in its productive, political and military applications, elaborated in what I have
called the production workshop of domination strategies, provides capital
with new mechanisms for domination and new motivations for competition and division of workers, hindering the construction of viable alternatives to capital domination.[16]

It thus turns out that the very thing that makes the destruction of the
capital relation increasingly necessary also makes that destruction difficult: advances in science and technology, being conditions for deepening
the exploitation process and enforcing its tendential laws, pushing capital
toward its end, are also advances in the domination of the capitalist class
over the working class. Capital can thus prolong its domination and, the
more its period of decline is prolonged, the more threatening its capacity
for brutality and genocide becomes.[17]

To turn into a revolution, it is necessary for rebellion to give rise to the
construction of a counterhegemonic project – with economic, political
and cultural dimensions – which can coordinate an effort to distance the
working class from capital domination, challenge the appropriation of scientific and technological developments and allow the creation of a united
political front with its own blueprint for the future that will lead to the
social appropriation of the material means of production and scientific
and technological knowledge to be used to meet the needs of humanity
and care for the environment.

---

[16] "What continues to stabilize and ideologically legitimate it are not the promises,
exposed long ago in practice, of a better, more peaceful 'world society', but the difficulty
associated with developing specific socio-political alternatives under the changed conditions of globalized capitalism, and in the face of the failure of traditional state-socialist and
social democratic concepts" (Hirsch, 2000).

[17] Iraq, since the U.S. army invaded it to "bring democracy" in 2003, is a good example of
the capacity for brutality displayed by contemporary capitalism; more than a million
deaths (IraqSolidaridad, 2008), without the *Christian* rulers of the United States losing any
sleep or registering in their consciousness any recollection of the old Mosaic command-
ment "thou shalt not kill." Dante could scarcely have imagined more faithful and diligent
servers of *Satan*, the symbolic construction of *evil*, than neoliberal capital and its current
personifications.

Dussel asserts that the "cynical reasoning" of those who dominate, exploit and kill needs to be opposed with both a material and critical argumentation that would constitute the basis of a critical consensus of the oppressed (discovering arguments, communicating and sharing experiences that will help to break the "morale" of the powers that be) as a political organization of material and critical power of the oppressed (Dussel, 2002).[18] Under the conditions of neoliberal domination, an obstacle to the construction of this "political organization of the material and critical power of the oppressed" consists in the new role played by nation-states, which are set up as restraints, in macro-ghettos, designed to foster isolation, competition and conflict among the workers, who are also deprived of rights and lack a political organization that extends beyond nation-states and their institutional structures.

The important decisions are made at supranational levels, while the regulation of class relations remains tied to the institutions of the nation-state: "In the face of the growing power of supranational entities in national affairs, there appears to be no other alternative than to link local struggles to global ones. International unity will then no longer be a mere utopia of the past, but a necessity imposed by the present, although to become a reality it is still necessary to give new meaning to national struggles" (Thwaites and Castillo, 1999). While in its birth the bourgeoisie promoted the political centralization of a nation-state[19], in its decline it promotes – in a highly conflictive manner, as we have seen – the transformation of nations into provincial governments at the service of big transnational capital, aimed at keeping the working class isolated and deprived of rights.And to construct the "critical consensus of the oppressed" and restore their capacity to develop a political initiative, it is necessary to break the ideological and political barriers within which capital confines them. Until the working class can break out of the framework

---

[18] "It is not the dominator who has the right to 'judge' the Other, his victim. It is the consensual and critical community, through its presence and exposure of the side of the victims, that has the duty to judge the despotic dominating power." Dussel also reminds us that "there can be no representation or consensus without 'living citizens', and in the postcolonial peripheral world this is not by any means guaranteed" (Dussel, 2002).

[19] "The bourgeoisie keeps more and more doing away with the scattered state of the population, of the means of production, and of property. It has agglomerated population, centralized the means of production, and has concentrated property in a few hands. The necessary consequence of this was political centralization. Independent, or but loosely connected provinces, with separate interests, laws, governments, and systems of taxation, became lumped together into one nation, with one government, one code of laws, one national class-interest, one frontier, and one customs-tariff" (Marx and Engels, 1848: I).

that prevents it from believing that humanity's problems have a solution outside the logic of the fetish and develops its own design, capital will enjoy universal ubiquity, appearing to define both the problems and the solutions and subjugating society to the eternal omnipotence of the fetish.[20]

The ideological helplessness and lack of political initiative of the working class is associated with its confinement to the ghetto of the nation-state. As discussed earlier, the current situation of workers is reminiscent of Lenin's descriptions of Tsarist Russia in the late 19th and early 20th century, when workers demanded freedom of residence and occupation, freedom to move wherever and whenever they wanted, as a basic condition for their organization and political education, to articulate their interests and develop their class-consciousness. This freedom, which was won with great struggles at the level of the nation-state, has been lost again in the globalized world.[21]

Globalization, according to Piqueras, "is a general offensive by capital, coordinated for the first time as an entity on a global scale... It breaks national boundaries of social regulation in a search for *global space*... As an increasingly conscious and contriving entity, in the last 25 years it has successfully destroyed, subjugated or co-opted the major labor organizations and entities across the planet... It confines many of the previously large labor entities or movements within ever smaller contexts, with self-limiting claims and immediate objectives that hardly ever contemplate social universality... *Micro-entities* expressed in groupings of extremely small dimensions, with a highly limited radius of action and

---

[20] For example, we have seen how big transnational capital imposes "free trade" on developing countries, thereby destroying the local economy while at the same time promoting the *solution* to the problem: more concessions to big capital in order to attract investment. This is also the case of the so-called "transition to democracy" that serves to increase subordination of politico-electoral concerns to the interests and needs of big transnational capital: the *precarious nature* of the *transition to democracy* is resolved with new *reforms to further the "transition." Economic problems* are explained as due to a lack of *competitivity*, and *political problems* as due to *insufficient implementation* of the *transition to democracy*. An agenda is thus organized and imposed on society, whereby, viewed in terms of class relations, big capital is situated on both extremes: *it produces* the problem and *offers* the solution. Other cases have also been examined, such as the migration of undocumented workers, climate change, food production, etc.

[21] "The political institutionalization of class commitments and the guarantee of democratic freedoms have historically been achieved in the context of the national state... Political universalism requires a redefinition that can establish a new version of the traditional meaning, which was coined in the nation-state context, of freedom, equality, democracy and human rights... to move beyond the historic relation between nation-state and citizenry" (Hirsch, 1996: 44, 49).

socio-political influence... On the other hand, the deepening of the politico-ideological domination of [the capitalist] class has the paradoxical effect of preventing most of the population from perceiving reality in terms of class, resulting in a *widespread sense of ideological helplessness*" (Piqueras, 2005, emphasis added).

It is clear that the shift from rebellion to revolution and the construction of a counterhegemonic project poses some difficulties (the whole concept of the neoliberal pattern of domination is considered in order to identify the difficulties to be overcome in order to successfully organize, expand and consolidate the struggle against capital), but they are not insuperable difficulties in a historical context of structural economic crisis that is expanding and fostering a growing rebellion. Thus, while the fact that rebellion is not revolution and the difficulties that the transition from one to the other entails must be acknowledged, it is also important to note that the decline of capitalism is constantly fostering rebellion because what is at stake is survival itself; as Piqueras suggests, "the radical offensive of capital against humanity puts humankind in motion almost by necessity" (Piqueras, 2005). In the first chapter, I pointed out that, following Marx, the basis of domination is the division of the dominated, and that this is produced by the need the dominated experience to serve capital; neoliberalism produces division and conflict among them, but it also invites them to struggle against capital and, therefore, to unite. And even as an effect of the defense of life, of the basic and essential level of rebellion, even if it still appears to lack a counterhegemonic expression, the system of domination tends toward instability. Rebellion produces diverse forms of resistance against the vast and multifaceted genocidal deployment of capital and struggles associated with a wide range of social demands to which the system of domination and exploitation does not respond, nor does it show any disposition toward restoring previous forms of negotiation and concession.

Mabel Thwaites Rey suggests that "capitalism constitutes a social order that needs to validate itself. By means of material reproduction it attempts (generally with success) to legitimate itself by integrating all of society into a hierarchical structure... [but] when capitalism as a social-economic system fails to socialize the whole population in a given territory, cracks appear in the nation-state as an articulating force, unleashing political, economic, social, ideological and cultural crises" (Thwaites Rey and Castillo, 1999).

The recourse to violence on the part of the capitalist class is an expression of its weakness, of its inability to preserve its hegemonic control over society. It needs to resort to violence because it can no longer present its state as representative of the societal whole: "coercion and force appear as a consequence of the inability of the bourgeoisie to present itself to society as 'society itself', and in doing so to engage in compromises with other classes. Because for the dominant class to present the state as the representative body of the people as a whole, this representation cannot be entirely false; the state needs to assume some of the interests of the dominated groups" (Thwaites Rey, 1994).

Rebellion and revolution represent two distinct but connected phenomena and, in the context of a structural economic crisis of capitalism, one can – indeed must, because the defense of life demands it – lead to the other: "The possibility itself of exercising 'hegemonic supremacy' and not mere rule ultimately depends on the chances of ensuring the advancement of society as a whole, of ensuring the 'incorporation' of the popular strata into social-economic development. And it is on this point that it cannot be denied that Gramsci's formula necessarily refers to the structural moment in its most profound sense. The truly hegemonic class would therefore be the one that can present itself as developing productive forces 'in the historical sense', thereby making its particular class interests appear to be the general public interest, to the extent that there is not an absolute, obvious gap between the two. *Otherwise, there may open up a yawning chasm through which the organic crisis may enter*" (Thwaites Rey, 1994, emphasis added).

PERIOD OF DECLINE AND THE HISTORICAL CYCLE OF CAPITAL

In the second chapter I examined the basic principle of the theoretical framework set forth by Marx in his *Preface* to *A Contribution to the Critique of Political Economy,* which is the underlying concept throughout *Capital:* the relation between direct producers and their means of production defines historical eras, and this relation develops together with the development of productive forces, ultimately coming into contradiction with the new level reached by those forces. Feudalism was characterized by the unity between direct producers and the means of production. Small-scale production (household and handicrafts industries) disperses the ownership and/or possession of the social means of production among many producers. The historical development of feudalism is the development of this basic relation and unfolds as the development of land rent over three stages or phases of development, until its dissolution and conversion into capitalism: payment in labor, payment in kind and, finally, monetary payment.

Capitalist social relations are also historical relations, just as historical as feudal relations, and their long term is associated with the historical cycle of their classes, the process that creates, develops and dissolves them. Capitalism unites and concentrates the means of production under a single command: it destroys small-scale production, separates direct producers from the means of production and concentrates the means of production and workers under its command, thereby socializing production. Concentration and centralization make capital grow; i.e. they develop the capital-labor relation, the separation between producer and the means of production. But essentially this separation develops together with the development of labor productivity. Marx's examination of the path leading from cooperation to manufacturing, to machinery and modern industry, identifies progressions in the socialization of production, as well as technical and social transformations: the transition from formal to real subsumption and the division of labor into immediate labor and general labor.

The successive developments in labor productivity mark out the historical course of capitalism, from infancy to maturity and decline, with the forms of exploitation and domination corresponding to each one (liberal, Keynesian and neoliberal). At the same time, an essential contradiction develops, contained in capitalist production relations: the greater society's wealth, the more redundant workers tend to become. This is what constitutes the general law of capitalist accumulation and the tendency of capital to create a worker surplus population:

> "The category of consolidated surplus population was developed by Marx to designate a logical result of the development of capitalism at the level of the essential production relation. *Capital* represents historicity viewed from the perspective of a particular mode of production. The object of study is not a particular stage of this mode of production, but the analysis of capital in general, and includes the analysis of the forces that create and develop it and provoke its disintegration. Moreover, Marx presented his theory of surplus population after introducing his thesis on the concentration and centralization of capital. A consolidated surplus population is one of the elements that inform the process of disconnecting the social relation from production and its contradiction with the development of productive forces" (Figueroa Sepúlveda, 2008).

The period of the decline of capitalism is the process leading to the final crisis of the capital relation, the social relation that separates producers from the means of production. There is a need implicit in the development of this relation: to restore the connection between producers and the means of production through the social re-appropriation of those means, and to use production to satisfy the needs of the producers. In this way, by economizing labor time, technological progress, rather than producing a redundant population, may reduce working hours, providing more free time and work for all, and thus establish the conditions for the full development of all individuals.

The fulfillment of this need is also the fulfillment of freedom[22] in two senses: freedom in relation to nature – exercise of rational control over nature achieved through the development of science and technology – and freedom from domination by things, leading to self-determination and the establishment of human beings as the agents and authors of history – overcoming the logic of the fetish and replacing market mechanisms with "production by freely associated men, consciously regulated by them in accordance with a settled plan."

In opposition to the capitalist state, the historical need still awaiting fulfillment is the socialist state, the organization of the working class, whose basic task is to ensure a connection between producers, organized as a worker collective, and the means of production and subsistence. It is a need contained in the development of necessary relations, independent of the will and consciousness of human beings, but the form that this need takes will depend on the class struggle, on the will and consciousness that develop. The specific historical process results from the articulation between objective and subjective; the tendential laws of the development of capitalism do not organize a mechanical trajectory, but spaces of possibilities for action by the subjects.

Among those who personify the ruling faction of capital today, there is a systematic effort to prolong its domination; they are not passively awaiting its collapse. Ultimately, of course, necessity prevails[23] and, just as all the feudal societies and pre-capitalist societies in general, through a long and complex process, made a transition to capitalism, capitalism itself

---

[22] According to Walicki the conception of freedom – understood as *collective* freedom – in Marx has two aspects: first, the capacity to dominate nature, through the development of productive forces, and second, to eliminate power from reified, alienated social relations. "In this way, man is the one who is in control. Man is the only actor and author of history. Freedom determines its own destiny; freedom is self-determination" (Walicki, 1988).

[23] "Necessity makes its way amid a multitude of contingent manifestations and establishes itself as a unit of potential, of contingency, and of contradiction between the two" (De Gortari, 1972: 128).

will make the transition to socialism, although the form and duration of this transition is no minor matter. In the 19th century, Marx believed that, if it could identify the law that governs its development, a society could shorten and lessen the birth pangs thereof.[24] Perhaps the 21st century will justify this optimism, shortening the period of decline and lessening the birth pangs of socialism.

---

[24] "And even when a society has got upon the right track for the discovery of the natural laws of its movement – and it is the ultimate aim of this work, to lay bare the economic law of motion of modern society – it can neither clear by bold leaps, nor remove by legal enactments, the obstacles offered by the successive phases of its normal development. But it can shorten and lessen the birth pangs" (Marx, 1867: Preface to the First German Edition).

BIBLIOGRAPHY

Abu-Tarbush, José. 2005. "Los 'think tanks': información, poder y opinión pública." *Disenso* 47. <http://www.pensamientocritico.org/josabub1105.html>

AFP, 2005. "Bush autorizó en 2002 espiar a miles de estadunidenses, denuncia el NY Times." *La Jornada,* December 17. <http://www.jornada.unam.mx/2005/12/17/022n1mun.php>

Aizpeolea, L.R. 2010. "Los 'sabios' recuerdan a Zapatero que Europe debe mejora su competitividad." El País, January 6. <http://www.elpais.com/articulo/espana/sabios/recuerdan/Zapatero/Europa/debe/mejorar/competitividad/elpepinac/20100106 el pepinac_6/Tes>

Alandete, David. 2009. "La CIA se enreda en la Red." El País, November 5. <http://www.elpais.com/articulo/tecnologia/CIA/enreda/Red/elpeputec/20091105elpeputec_10/Tes>

Almeyra, Guillermo. n.d. "La violencia y la mundialización."Unpublished Manuscript.

Almeyra, Guillermo. 2003. Revolucion, emancipacion, sujeto revolucionario. Paper presented at First International Conference on the Work of Karl Marx and the Challenges of the Twenty-First Century, Havana, May 5–8, 2003. <http://www.nodo50.org/cubasigloXXI/congreso/almeyra_10abro3.pdf>

Almeyra, Guillermo. 2003a. "¿Dónde se refugia ahora la política?" La Jornada, July 13.

Almeyra, Guillermo. 2004. Política, partidos y poder en la mundialización. Paper presented at Second International Conference on the Work of Karl Marx and the Challenges of the Twenty-First Century, Havana, May 4–8, 2004. <http://www.nodo50.org/cubasigloXXI/congreso004/almeyra_180404.pdf>

Almeyra, Guillermo. 2005. "Mundializacion, neoliberalismo y unidad de los explotados." Diálogo Nacional Website. <http://www.dialogonacional.org.mx/pon42.html>

Almeyra, Guillermo. 2007. "America Latina: el comienzo de una nueva fase." *Cuadernos del Sur* 36.

Amin, Samir. 1975. "Una crisis estructural" in S. Amin et al. (comp.) *La crisis del imperialismo*. Barcelona: Fontanella, pp. 11–46.

Amin, Samir. 2003a. "Estados Unidos: el control militar del planeta." *La Jornada*, March 3. <http://www.jornada.unam.mx/2003/mar03/030305/per-control.html>

Amin, Samir. 2003b. "La economía política del siglo XX." *Tareas* 113: 5–22. <http://www.salacela.net/images/tareas/7_a.pdf>

Amin, Samir. 2009. "El capitalisrmo senil." *La Historia del Día*, November 14. <http://lahistoriadeldia.wordpress.com/2009/11/14/samir-amin-el-capitalismo-senil-descargar-documento-2/>

Amnesty International. 2007. *Report 2007*. London: Amnesty International. <http://archive.amnesty.org/report2007/eng/Homepage.html>

Anderson, Perry. 2004. *The Role of Ideas in the Construction of Alternatives*. Los Angeles: UCLA. <http://bibliotecavirtual.clacso.org.ar/ar/libros/hegeing/Anderson.pdf>

Antunes, Ricardo. 2001. *¿Adiós al trabajo?* Sao Paolo: Cortez.

Arceo, Enrique. 2002. *Hegemonía estadounidense, internacionalización financiera y productiva, y nuevo pacto colonial*. Buenos Aires: Ceceña. <http://168.96.200.17/ar/libros/cecena/arceo.pdf>

Aruj, Roberto. 2000. "El posmodernismo como sustento ideológico filosófico del neoliberalismo a fines del siglo XX." *La Onda Revista Digital* 16. <http://www.laondadigital.com/laonda/laonda/Documentos/El%20posmodernismo%20como%20sustento%20ideologico%20filosofico%20del%20neoliberalismo%20a%20fines%20del%20siglo%20XX.htm>

Astarita, Rolando. 1997. "Sobre las tendencias actuales del capitalismo." *Herramienta* 5. <http://www.herramienta.com.ar/varios/5/5-8-3.html>

Ateneu Llibertari del Casc Antic. 2010. "Sonríe te están grabando: Cámaras, cámaras y más cámaras." *Indymedia Madrid,* February 18. <http://madrid.indymedia.org/node/12868>

ATTAC. 2004. "La desregulación del sistema financiero estimula el lavado de dinero." *Rebelión,* January 15. <http://www.rebelion.org/hemeroteca/economia/040115attac.htm>

Austin Fitts, Catherine. 2001. "Narco-dollars for Beginners: How the Money Works in the Illicit Drug Trade." *Drugwar.com,* October 24. <http://www.drugwar.com/fittsnarco1.shtm>

Ayala, Roberto and Víctor Figueroa. 2001. "Imperialismo y globalización: ¿Es posible humanizar el capitalismo?" *Rebelión,* June 6. <http://www.rebelion.org/hemeroteca/izquierda/rayala060601.htm>

Baron, Ana. 2002. "EE.UU. crea una oficina para dar información falsa." *Clarin,* February 20. <http://www.clarin.com/diario/2002/02/20/i-02801.htm>

Bauman, Zygmunt. 1999. *In Search of Politics.* Stanford: Stanford University Press.

BBV. n.d. "La calificación de riesgo, significado y procedimientos." Bolsa Boliviana de Valores, S.A. <http://www.bbv.com.bo/aula.temario3.asp>

Beinstein, Jorge. 2000. "La gran mutación del capitalismo: Narcomafias, centro y periferia." *América Latina en Movimiento,* December 13. <http://alainet.org/active/1099>

Bellinghausen, Hermann. 2003. "Noveno aniversario del alzamiento zapatista." *La Jornada,* January 2. <http://www.jornada.unam.mx/2003/01/03/006n1pol.php?origen=index.html>

Bello, Walden. 2008. "Cómo fabricar una crisis global." *La Jornada,* May 27 and 30. <http://www.jornada.unam.mx/2008/05/27/index.php?section=opinion&article=018a1pol> <http://www.jornada.unam.mx/2008/05/30/index.php?section=opinion&article=014a1pol>

Bendesky, León. 2003. "El buque hace agua." *La Jornada,* July 14. <http://www.jornada.unam.mx/2003/07/14/019a1eco.php?origen=index.html&fly=2>

Bendesky, León. 2006. "Rubor." *La Jornada,* February 20. <http://www.jornada.unam.mx/2006/02/20/index.php?section=opinion&article=031a1eco>

Bihr, Alain and François Chesnais. 2003. "¿Aún es posible criticar la propiedad privada? Un asunto tabú." *Le Monde Diplomatique,* September. <http://www.pensamientocritico.org/alabih1004.htm>

Blanco, José. 2006. "Turbio año electoral." *La Jornada,* January 10. < http://www.jornada.unam.mx/2006/01/10/index.php?section=opinion&article=020a1pol>

Bloch, Ernst. 1986. *The Principle of Hope.* Boston: MIT Press.

Bobbio, Norberto and Nicola Matteucci. 1981. *Diccionario de Ciencia Política,* Madrid: Siglo XXI.

Boff, Leonardo. 2003. "Porto Alegre, Davos y la globalización." *Rebelión,* January 24. <http://www.rebelion.org/sociales/boff240103.htm>

Bonelli, Laurent. 2003. "Una visión policial de la sociedad." *Le Monde Diplomatique.* February. <http://monde-diplomatique.es/2003/02/bonelli.html>

Borja, Jordi. 2007. "Miedos urbanos, demandas de seguridad y represión preventiva." *La Factoria* 32. <http://www.lafactoriaweb.com/articulos/borja32.htm>

Boron, Atilio. 2000. *Tras el búho de Minerva. Mercado contra democracia en el capitalismo de fin de siglo.* Buenos Aires: Fondo de Cultura Económica.

Boron, Atilio. 2001. "El nuevo orden imperial y cómo desmontarlo." *Rebelión,* August 27. <http://www.rebelion.org/hemeroteca/izquierda/boron270801.htm>

Bravo, Elba Mónica and Liliana Padilla. 2009. "EU debe informar cuántos de sus ciudadanos viven de las drogas, exigen PAN y PRD." *Milenio Online,* March 12. <http://impreso.milenio.com/node/8543726>

Brenner, Robert. 2009a. *The Economics of Global Turbulence,* 2nd ed. New York: Verso.

Brenner, Robert. 2009b. "Overproduction not Financial Collapse is the Heart of the Crisis: the US, East Asia, and the World." *Asia Pacific Journal,* February 7. <http://www.japanfocus.org/-Robert_Brenner__S_J_Jeong/3043>

Brooks, David. 2005a. "El mayor escándalo de corrupción en un siglo sacude a la clase política de EU." *La Jornada,* December 28. <http://www.jornada.unam.mx/2005/12/28/023mmun.php>

Brooks, David. 2005b. "Por ley, será delincuente todo migrante indocumentado en EU." *La Jornada,* December 17. <http://www.jornada.unam.mx/2005/12/17/003n1pol.php>

Brooks, David. 2006. "Más que a azufre, en Washington todo huele a corrupción; proliferan los escándalos políticos." *La Jornada,* September 30. <http://www.jornada.unam.mx/2006/09/30/index.php?section=mundo&article=026n1mun>

Brooks, David. 2007. "Anuncia Washington nuevas medidas para "controlar" la inmigración indocumentada." *La Jornada,* August 11. <http://www.jornada.unam.mx/2007/08/11/index.php?section=mundo&article=027n1mun>

Brooks, David. 2008. "Perciben estadounidenses recesión económica." *La Jornada,* January 2. <http://www.jornada.unam.mx/2008/01/02/index.php?section=economia&article=017n1eco>

Brooks, David. 2010. "Presenta Obama el gasto militar para 2011; es el más grande de la historia." *La Jornada,* February 2. <http://www.jornada.unam.mx/2010/02/02/index.php?section=mundo&article=024n1mun>

Brunhoff, Suzanne de. 1980. "La gestión estatal de la fuerza de trabajo," in Moncayo Victor Manuel and Fernando Rojas, eds., *Estado y economía. Crisis permanente del Estado capitalista.* Bogotá: Sociedad de Ediciones Internacionales.

Bunge, Mario. 2003. "La filosofía no ha muerto, pero está gravemente enferma." *Tendencias 21,* April 26. <http://www.tendencias21.net/Mario-Bunge-la-filosofia-no-ha-muerto,-pero-esta-gravemente-enferma_a150.html>

Bunker, Robert J. 2006. "Guerra de Cuarta Época. Generaciones, modos y época. Formas de guerra y el RPMA." *La Nueva Cuba,* May 18. <http://www.lanuevacuba.com/archivo/robert-bunker-1.htm>

Calvo Ospina, Hernando. 2003 "El paramilitarismo como estrategia contrainsurgente en Colombia." *Le Monde Diplomatique,* April. <http://monde-diplomatique.es/2003/04/ospina.html>

Camil, Jorge. 2005. "Golpe de estado." *La Jornada,* December 16. <http://www.jornada.unam.mx/2005/12/16/021a1pol.php>

Campo Urbano, Salustiano del, Juan F. Marsal and José Antonio Garmendia. 1987. *Diccionario UNESCO de Ciencias Sociales.* Barcelona: Planeta-Agostini.

Carlsen, Laura. 2006. "Bad Blood on the Border." *Counterpunch,* February 4. <http://www.counterpunch.org/carlsen02042006.html>

Carmagnani, Marcello. 1984. *Estado y sociedad en América Latina (1859–1930).* Barcelona: Grijalbo.

Carmona, Ernesto. 2009. "Facebook ¿es de la CIA?" *Rebelión,* May 27. <http://www.rebelion.org/noticia.php?id=86035>

Carrillo, Jorge and Raúl Hinojosa. 2003. "Cableando a Norteamérica: la industria de los arneses automotrices," in Contreras, Oscar and Jorge Carrillo eds., *Hecho en Norteamérica.* Mexico City: Cal y Arena.

Cassián Nizaiá, et al. 2006. "Imaginario Social: Una aproximación desde la obra de Michel Maffesoli." *Athenea Digital* 9. <http://ddd.uab.cat/pub/athdig/15788946n9a11.pdf>

Cason, Jim and David Brooks. 2001. "Frenética compra de armas en EE.UU." *La Jornada,* December 27.

Cason, Jim and David Brooks. 2004a. "Descubre el Pentagono una nueva amenaza en AL: el populismo radical." *La Jornada,* March 29. <http://www.jornada.unam.mx/2004/03/29/030n1mun.php?origen=index.html&fly=1>

Cason, Jim and David Brooks, 2004b. "El FMI recomienda a México acelerar reformas con las hechas en el IMSS." *La Jornada,* September 29. <http://www.jornada.unam.mx/2004/09/30/017n1pol.php?origen=index.html&fly=1>

Castaingts Teillery, Juan. 2004. "Política mexicana: lenguaje y cultura del escándalo." *El Financiero,* October 21.

Castells, Manuel. 2001. "La crisis de lo político." *PoliticasNet.* <http://usuarios.multimania.es/politicasnet/articulos/crisisp.htm>

Castells, Manuel. 2003. "Lección inaugural del programa de doctorado sobre la sociedad de la información y el conocimiento." *Educared.* Buenos Aires: Fundación Telefónica. <http://www.educared.org.ar/vicaria/adjuntos/lab-curr/leccion-inaugural-castells.pdf>

Castro, José Adalberto. Speech given at the opening of the seminar "El fenómeno de las migraciones en nuestro tiempo. Perspectiva comparada entre México y la Unión Europea," Madrid, Spain, January 19, 2006. <http://www.senado.gob.mx/index.php?ver=sp&mn=2&sm=2&id=9893&lg=59>

Chesnais, François. 1996. "Notas para una caracterización del capitalismo a fines del siglo XX." *Revista Herramienta* 1. <http://www.herramienta.com.ar/revista-herramienta-n-1/notas-para-una-caracterizacion-del-capitalismo-fines-del-siglo-xx>

Chesnais, François. 1997. "La caracterización del capitalismo a fines del siglo XX." *Revista Herramienta* 3. <http://www.herramienta.com.ar/revista-herramienta-n-3/la-caracterizacion-del-capitalismo-fines-del-siglo-xx>

Chiesa, Giulietto. 2008. "Guerra y Mentira. El control político y militar de nuestras sociedades." *VoltaireNet.* January 15. <http://www.voltairenet.org/article154345.html>

Chossudovsky, Michel. 2001 "Who is Osama Bin Laden?" *Global Research,* September 12. <http://www.globalresearch.ca/articles/CHO109C.html>

Chossudovsky, Michel. 2002a. *War and Globalization: The Truth behind September 11.* Montreal: Centre for Research on Globalization.

Chossudovsky, Michel. 2002b. "Washington's New World Order Weapons Have the Ability to Trigger Climate Change." *Global Research,* January 4. <http://www.globalresearch.ca/articles/CHO201A.html>

Chossudovsky, Michel. 2002c. "United States War Machine: Revving the Engines of World War III." *Third World Traveler.* <http://www.thirdworldtraveler.com/War_Peace/US_War_Machine.html>

Chossudovsky, Michel. 2002d. "Washington's New World Order Weapons Have the Ability to Trigger Climate Change." *Global Research,* January 4. <http://www.globalresearch.ca/articles/CHO201A.html>

Chossudovsky, Michel. 2003. *Globalization of Poverty and the New World Order.* Montreal: Centre for Research on Globalization.

Chossudovsky, Michel. 2005. "New Undeclared Arms Race: America's Agenda for Global Military Domination." *Global Research,* March 17. <http://www.globalresearch.ca/articles/CHO503A.html>

Chossudovsky, Michel. 2007a. "The Criminalization of U.S. Foreign Policy: From the Truman Doctrine to the Neoconservatives." *Global Research,* February 5. <http://www.globalresearch.ca/index.php?context=va&aid=4659>

Chossudovksy, Michel. 2007b. "La corrupción al asalto de los Estados. Como las mafias gangrenan la economía mundial." *Globalización,* October. <http://www.rcci.net/globalizacion/2007/fg707.htm>

Chossudovsky, Michel. 2007c. "Weather Warfare: Beware the U.S. Military's Experiments with Climatic Warfare." *Global Research,* December 7. <http://www.globalresearch.ca/index.php?context=va&aid=7561>

Chossudovsky, Michel. 2008a. "Al Qaeda and the 'War on Terrorism'." *Global Research,* January 20. <http://www.globalresearch.ca/index.php?context=va&aid=7718>

Chossudovsky, Michel. 2008b. "The Global Crisis: Food Water and Fuel. Three Fundamental Necessities of Life in Jeopardy." *Global Research,* June 5. <http://www.globalresearch.ca/index.php?context=va&aid=9191>

Chossudovsky, Michel. 2010. "Preparing for World War III, Targeting Iran." *Global Research,* August 1. <http://www.globalresearch.ca/index.php?aid=20403&context=va>

Chomsky, Noam. 2005. *El terror como política exterior de Estados Unidos.* Buenos Aires: Libros del Zorzal.

Clarin. 2004. "Los diez principales temas de la batalla electoral en EE.UU." *Rebelión,* October 24. <http://www.rebelion.org/noticia.php?id=6601>

Claudín, Fernando. 1976. *Marx, Engels y la revolución de 1848.* Madrid: Siglo XXI.

Colectivo Troyano. 2009a. "Corporaciones e implantes cerebrales, no están muy lejos." *Rebelión,* November 24. <http://www.rebelion.org/noticia.php?id=95811>

Colectivo Troyano. 2009b. "Reinventando la rueda: ¿'redes sociales' o control social?" *Rebelión,* June 4. <http://www.rebelion.org/noticia.php?id=86432&titular=reinventa ndo-la-rueda:-%BF%22redes-sociales%22-o-control-social?->

Cohen-Cole, Linn. 2009. "Genetically Modified Seeds: Monsanto is Putting Normal Seeds Out of Reach." *Global Research,* February 14. http://www.globalresearch.ca/index .php?context=va&aid=12309

Colectivo Yachay Red Científica Peruana. 2002. "El mundo de la desinformación." *Rebelión,* November 14. <http://www.rebelion.org/hemeroteca/medios/yachay141102.htm>

Committee of Santa Fe. 1980. "A New Inter-American Policy for the 1980s." Washington: Council for Inter-American Security.

Committee of Santa Fe. 1989. "Santa Fe II: A Strategy for Latin America in the Nineties." Washington: Council for Inter-American Security.

Consuegra, Renato. 2006. "Respingan inversores." *La Crítica.* <http://www.lacritica.com .mx/index.php?option=content&task=view&id=126&Itemid=25>

Contreras Natera, Miguel Ángel. 2007. "Imperio y fin de sciécle. 11 de septiembre: una per-spectiva crítica." *Sociologando,* September 19. <http://www.sociologando.org.ve/pag/ index.php?id=33&idn=114>

Coon, Charlie. 2007. "El Departamento de Defensa se lanza a la Web para librar la batalla informática." *Rebelión,* June 22. <http://www.rebelion.org/noticia.php?id=52564>

Cordera Campos, Rolando. 2006. "El enredo." *La Jornada,* March 19.

Córdova, Arnaldo. 1979. *La política de masas y el futuro de la izquierda en México.* Mexico City: Serie Popular Era.

Coriat, Benjamín. 1992. *El taller y el cronómetro. Ensayo sobre el taylorismo, el fordismo y la producción en masa.* Mexico City: Siglo XXI.

Corradini, Luisa. 2005. "'Estamos en la era de los nómades y las tribus' dice Maffesoli." *La Nación,* August 31. <http://www.lanacion.com.ar/nota.asp?nota_id=734590>

Cortada, James and Thomas Hargraves. 1999. *Into the Networked Age: How IBM and Other Companies Are Getting There Now.* New York: Oxford University Press.

Crozier, Michael, Samuel Huntington and Joji Watanuki. 1975. *The Crisis of Democracy: Report on Governability of Democracies to the Trilateral Commission.* New York: NYU Press.

Cueva, Agustín. 1993. *El desarrollo del capitalismo en América Latina.* Mexico City: Siglo XXI.

Dabat, Alejandro. 1993. *El mundo y las naciones.* Mexico City: UNAM.

Dabat, Alejandro, Miguel Ángel Rivera and Estela Suárez. 2004. "Globalización, revolución informática y países en desarrollo," in Dabat Rivera and Wilkie, eds. *Globalización y cam-bio tecnológico.* Mexico City: Juan Pablos Editor.

Davis, Mike. 2007. "Los suburbios de las ciudades del tercer mundo son el nuevo escenario geopolítico decisivo." *Tortuga,* Interview, March 10. <http://www.nodo50.org/tortuga/ article.php3?id_article=5228>

De Brie, Christian. 2000. "Gobiernos, mafias y transnacionales, asociados," *Le Monde Diplomatique, Southern Cone Edition,* April.

De Brie, Christian. 2003. "La demolición social." *Le Monde Diplomatique,* February. <http:// monde-diplomatique.es/2003/02/brie.html>

De Gortari, Eli. 1972. *Introducción a la lógica dialéctica.* Mexico City: FCE-UNAM.

De la Garza, Enrique. 1988. *Ascenso y crisis del Estado social autoritario*. Mexico City: Colegio de México.

Delors, Jacques, et al. 2008. "Financial Markets Can Not Govern Us!" Open letter of elder statesmen on international financial crisis endorsed by International Progress Organization, May 19, 2008. <http://i-p-o.org/ipo-nr-10June08-financial_crisis.htm>

Díaz, Miguel. 2007. "The Other War that Washington is not Winning." *Revista Ari* 27. <http://www.realinstitutoelcano.org/wps/portal/rielcano_eng/Content?WCM_GLOBAL_CONTEXT=/elcano/Elcano_in/Zonas_in/ARI%2027-2007>

Díaz–Salazar Rafael. 2004. "De Porto Alegre a Bombay." *Rebelión*, January 16. <http://www.rebelion.org/hemeroteca/sociales/040116salazar.htm>

Dierckxsens, Wim. 2002. "Fin del neoliberalismo, fin del capitalismo. Surge una nueva utopía." *Alternativas*, 23 (June): 13–28. <http://www.servicioskoinonia.org/relat/313.htm>

Dimas, Eduardo. 2002. "Un jugoso botín: el Plan Puebla-Panamá." *Rebelión*, September 30. <http://www.rebelion.org/hemeroteca/economia/edimas300902.htm>

Dudley, Steven. "Lula Needs a Miracle." *The Progressive*, October 1. <http://www.highbeam.com/doc/1G1-93457090.html>

Dufour, Jules. 2007. "The Worldwide Network of US Military Bases: The Global Deployment of US Military Personnel." *Global Research*, July 1. <http://www.globalresearch.ca/index.php?context=va&aid=5564>

Dufour, Jules. 2008. "Las guerras de ocupación de Afganistán e Iraq." *Global Research*, July 31. <http://www.globalresearch.ca/index.php?context=va&aid=9719>

Dufour, Jules. 2009. "El gran rearme planetario." *Global Research*, July 26. <http://www.globalresearch.ca/index.php?context=va&aid=14539>

Dussel, Enrique. 2002. "Estado de guerra permanente y razón cínica." *Revista Herramienta*, 21. <http://www.herramienta.com.ar/revista-herramienta-n-21/estado-de-guerra-permanente-y-razon-cinica>

Eagleton, Terry. 1996. *The Illusions of Postmodernism*. Oxford: Blackwell.

Engels, Frederick. 1847. "Principles of Communism." Marx/Engels Internet Archive. <http://www.marxists.org/archive/marx/works/1847/11/prin-com.htm>

Engels, Frederick. 1877. "Karl Marx." Marx/Engels Internet Archive. <http://www.marxists.org/espanol/m-e/1870s/cmarx.htm>

Engels, Frederick. 1878. *Anti-Dühring: Herr Eugen Dühring's Revolution in Science*. Marx/Engels Internet Archive. <http://www.marxists.org/archive/marx/works/1877/anti-duhring/index.htm>

Engels, Frederick. 1880. *Socialism: Utopian and Scientific*. Marx/Engels Internet Archive. <http://www.marxists.org/archive/marx/works/1880/soc-utop/index.htm>

Engels, Frederick. 1884. "Origin of the Family, Private Property, and the State." Marx/Engels Internet Archive. <http://www.marxists.org/archive/marx/works/download/pdf/origin_family.pdf>

Engels, Frederick. 1895. Introduction to Karl Marx's *The Class Struggles in France*. Marx/Engels Internet Archive. <http://www.marxists.org/archive/marx/works/1850/class-struggles-france/intro.htm>

Estay, Jaime. 2001. "Economía mundial y polarización económica y social," in Caputo, Orlando, Jaime Estay and José María Vidal Villa, *Capital sin fronteras. Polarización crisis y Estado-nación en el capitalismo global*. Barcelona: Icaria.

Estay, Jaime. 2004. "ALCA: paraíso de inversionistas." *Red de Estudios de la Economía Mundial*. <http://www.redem.buap.mx/acrobat/jaime14.pdf>

ETC Group. 2003. "The Strategy for Converging Technologies: The Little BANG Theory." ETC Group Communique Issue #78. <http://www.etcgroup.org/upload/publication/169/01/combang2003.pdf>

ETC Group. 2005a. *A Tiny Primer on Nano-scale Technologies and the "Little Bang Theory."* Ottawa: ETC Group. <http://www.etcgroup.org/upload/publication/55/01/tinyprimer_english.pdf>

ETC Group. 2005b. "Oligopoly, 2005: Concentration of World Power." ETC Group Communique Issue #91. <http://www.etcgroup.org/upload/publication/44/01/oligopoly2005_16dec.05.pdf>

ETC Group. 2007. "Gambling with Gaia." ETC Group Communique Issue #93. <http://www.etcgroup.org/en/node/4913>

ETC Group. 2008. "Who Owns Nature?" ETC Group Communique Issue #100. <http://www.etcgroup.org/upload/publication/707/01/etc_won_report_final_color.pdf>

ETC Group. 2009. "The Emperor's New Clothes: Geoengineering as 21st Century Fairy Tale." ETC Group Special Report, August 28. <http://www.etcgroup.org/upload/publication/pdf_file/etcspecialreport_rsgeoeng28aug09.pdf>

ETC Group. 2010. "Top-down Planet Hackers call for Bottom-up Governance." ETC Group news release, February 11. <http://www.etcgroup.org/en/node/5073>

Fazio, Carlos. 2003. "ALCA y militarización, dos caras de un mismo proyecto hegemónico." *Visiones Alternativas*, May 7. <http://www.visionesalternativas.com.mx/militarizacion/articulos/geoestrat/23.htm>

Fazio, Carlos. 2009. "Influenza, recesión y teoría del shock." *La Jornada,* May 18. <http://www.jornada.unam.mx/2009/05/18/index.php?section=opinion&article=022a1pol>

Feinmann, José Pablo. 2005. "Pornografía de la muerte," in Bugani, Pedro, ed., *La suma del neoliberalismo y la postmodernidad en la globalización capitalista.* Buenos Aires: Pensar Libre. <http://www.psicoanalisis-s-p.com.ar/textos/modernidad015.doc>

Fernández Lagraña, Luis. 2006. "Centro Latinomericano para la competividad." *ABC Digital,* April 16. <http://archivo.abc.com.py/2006-04-16/articulos/246092/centro-latino americano-para-la-competitividad>

Figueroa Sepúlveda, Víctor. 1986. *Reinterpretando el subdesarrollo.* Mexico City: Siglo XXI.

Figueroa Sepúlveda, Víctor. 1989. *La identidad perdida del socialismo.* Mexico City: Ancien Régime (UAZ-UAM).

Figueroa Sepúlveda, Víctor. 1992. "El librecambio y la gestión estatal de la crisis en los Estados Unidos: primera parte." *Vínculo Jurídico* 11–12. <http://www.uaz.edu.mx/vinculo/webrvj/rev11-12-5.htm>

Figueroa Sepúlveda, Víctor. 1993. "El librecambio y la gestión estatal de la crisis en los Estados Unidos: segunda parte." *Vínculo Jurídico* 13. <http://www.uaz.edu.mx/vinculo/webrvj/rev13-3.htm>

Figueroa Sepúlveda, Víctor. 1995. "La gestión estatal del desarrollo en América Latina." *Revista Problemas del Desarrollo,* Vol. 26: 103.

Figueroa Sepúlveda, Víctor. 2001. "América Latina: el nuevo patrón de colonialismo industrial." *Revista Problemas del Desarrollo* Vol. 32: 126.

Figueroa Sepúlveda, Víctor. 2003. "La actualidad del imperialismo, la actualidad de la crítica," in Figueroa, Víctor, ed., *América Latina en la crisis del patrón neoliberal de crecimiento.* Zacatecas: Political Science Unit, Universidad Autónoma de Zacatecas.

Figueroa Sepúlveda, Víctor. 2008. Excedentes de población. Mimeo, materials from Doctorate in Political Science, Universidad Autónoma de Zacatecas.

Forrester, Viviane. 1999. *The Economic Horror.* Cambridge: Blackwell.

Forster, Ricardo. 2009. "Neoliberalismo, medios de comunicación y democracia." *El País,* September 8. <http://www.pagina12.com.ar/diario/elpais/1-131394-2009-09-08.html>

Fox, Vicente. 2004. "Reunión de presentación del Instituto Mexicano para la Competitividad." Mexican President's Office Online Archive. Feb. 17. <http://fox.presidencia.gob.mx/actividades/discursos/?contenido=7501>

Freytas, Manuel. 2006a. "Bin Laden, el mejor amigo de Bush." *IAR Noticias,* June 15. <http://iarnoticias.com/secciones_2006/norteamerica/0049_bin_laden_imperio_15juno6.html>

Freytas, Manuel. 2006b. "Control mental: Como las grandes cadenas televisivas manipulan la masacre de Israel en Líbano y Gaza." *IAR Noticias,* July 14. <http://www.iarnoticias.com/secciones_2006/medio_oriente/0016_manip_medios_gaza_14julo6.html>

Freytas, Manuel. 2006c. "Guerra de Cuarta Generación." *IAR Noticias*, March 21. <http://www.iarnoticias.com/secciones_2006/norteamerica/0019_guerra_cuarta_generacion_21mar06.html>

Freytas, Manuel. 2007. "La trama funcional y mediática de los ataques terroristas." *IAR Noticias*, July 5. <http://www.iarnoticias.com/secciones_2007/norteamerica/0092_cia_terrorismo_tercerizado_05jul07.html>

Fröbel, Folker, Juergen Heinrichs and Otto Kreye. 1981. *La nueva división internacional del trabajo*. Mexico City: Siglo XXI.

Fromm, Erich. 1978. *Marx y su concepto del hombre*. Mexico: Fondo de Cultura Económica.

Fukuyama, Francis. 1992. *The End of History and the Last Man*. New York: Free Press.

Galeano, Eduardo. 2006. "El gran negocio del crimen y el miedo sacrifica la justicia." *La Jornada*, June 4.

Gallin, Dan. 2000. "Globalización y la política del sindicalismo." <http://www.global-labor.org/A%20la%20hora%20de%20la%20mondializacion%20que%20movimento%20sindical.pdf>

García, Hector. 2006. "De aperitivo, ¿oxígeno a la menta o a la naranja?" *Kirainet—Un Geek en Japón* (blog), November 6. <http://www.kirainet.com/de-aperitivo-¿oxigeno-a-la-menta-o-a-la-naranja/>

Garrido, Luis Javier. 2005. "La otra." *La Jornada*, December 30.

Gereffi, Gary. 2006. "Las cadenas productivas como marco analítico para la globalización." <http://www.cema.edu.ar/~eab/UCEMA/Bloques_Economicos_y_Agronegocios_2006/Gereffi_Gary_Cadenas_productivas>

Gilly, Adolfo. 2004. "Populismo radical: un sujeto político no identificado." *La Jornada*, June 1. <http://www.jornada.unam.mx/031a1mun.php?origen=index.html&fly=1>

Gómez E., Luis. 1993. "Una aproximación a la historia social de la tecnología posindustrial," in Micheli, Jordy, compiler, *Tecnología y modernización económica*. Mexico City: Universidad Autónoma Metropolitana—Xochimilco, pp. 471–499.

González Casanova, Pablo. 2000. "¿A dónde va México?" *América Latina en Movimiento*, July 4. <http://alainet.org/active/840&lang=eshttp://alainet.org/active/840 &lang=es>

Gouverneur, Cédric. 2002. "Mundialización de la economía mafiosa. Guerra del opio en las fronteras de Irán." *Le Monde Diplomatique*, March 11. <http://www.eldiplo.org/login.php3?numero=102&semanal=34/S_B_1_38>

Gramsci, Antonio. 1999. *Antología. Selección, traducción y notas de Manuel Sacristán*. Madrid: Siglo XXI.

Gresh, Alain. 2005. "'Petróleo contra alimentos'. Un escándalo puede ocultar otros." *El Monde Diplomatique*, August 19. <http://www.eldiplo.org/login.php3?numero=102&semanal=75/S_B_1_34>

Grimaldi, James and Sari Horwitz. 2010. "As Mexico's drug violence runs rampant, U.S. guns tied to crime south of the border." *Washington Post*, December 15. <http://www.washingtonpost.com/wp-dyn/content/article/2010/12/12/AR2010121202663.html>

Guevara, Rodrigo. 2003. "Irak y el capitalismo militar de Estados Unidos." *IAR Noticias*, December 25. <http://iarnoticias.com/secciones/mediooriente/irak_y_el_capitalismo_militar_de_estados_unidos.html>

Guevera, Rodrigo. 2005. "Los 'contratistas' de operaciones psicológicas con el Pentágono." *IAR Noticias*, December 19. <http://iarnoticias.com/secciones_2005/norteamerica/0117_contratistas_privad_informacion_19dic05.html>

Harman, Chris. 2007. "The Rate of Profit and the World Today." *International Socialism*, July 2. <http://www.isj.org.uk/?id=340>

Harvey, David. 2004. "'The 'New Imperialism': Accumulation by Dispossession," in Panitch, Leo and Colin Leys, eds., *The New Imperial Challenge: Socialist Register 2004*. Winnipeg: Fernwood, pp. 63–87.

Heller, Pablo. 2003. "Tasa de ganancia y descomposición capitalista." *En defensa del Marxismo*, 30 (May).

Hernández, Evangelina. 2009. "Prostitución forzada, otra cara del yugo a migrantes." *El Universal,* December 2. <http://www.eluniversal.com.mx/primera/34025.html>
Hernández López, Julio. 2006. "Astillero, el mal (estado) del país." *La Jornada,* March 13.
Hernández López, Julio. 2007. "APPO, PRD y elecciones en Oaxaca." *La Jornada,* May 22. <http://www.jornada.unam.mx/2007/05/22/index.php?section=opinion&article=019a1 pol>
Hernández Navarro, Luis. 2005a. "El oso y el tigre." *La Jornada,* October 11. <http://www .jornada.unam.mx/2005/10/11/021a1pol.php>
Hernández Navarro, Luis. 2005b. "Migración y guerra contra el terrorismo." *La Jornada,* December 20. <http://www.jornada.unam.mx/2005/12/20/021a1pol.php>
Hernández Navarro, Luis. 2006. "Optimismo y cambio en América Latina." *La Jornada,* January 31. <http://www.jornada.unam.mx/2006/01/31/index.php?section=opinion &article=027a1pol>
Herrera, Claudia and David Brooks. 2006. "En EU, Calderón se desmarca de la política migratoria del actual gobierno." *La Jornada,* November 10. <http://www.jornada.unam .mx/2006/11/10/index.php?section=politica&article=003n1pol>
Hirsch, Joachim. 1979. "Elementos para una teoría materialista del Estado." *Críticas de la economía política* 12–13.
Hirsch, Joachim. 1996. *Globalización, Capital y Estado.* Mexico City: Universidad Autónoma Metropolitana—Xochimilco.
Hirsch, Joachim. 2000. "¡Adiós a la política!" *Revista Viento del Sur* 17.
Huntington, Samuel. 1996. *The Clash of Civilizations and the Remaking of World Order.* New York: Simon & Schuster.
Ianni, Octavio. 1977a. "Clases subalternas y Estado oligárquico." in Benitez Zenteno, Raúl, ed., *Clases sociales y crisis política en América Latina.* Mexico City: Siglo XXI-UNAM.
Ianni, Octavio. 1977b. *El Estado capitalista en la época de Cárdenas.* Mexico City: Serie Popular Era.
Ianni, Octavio. 1984. *La formación del Estado populista en América Latina.* Mexico City: Serie Popular Era.
Ianni, Octavio. 1996. *Teorías de la globalización.* Mexico City: Siglo XXI.
ICRC. 1998. Rome Statute of the International Criminal Court. Geneva: ICRC. <http://www .icrc.org/ihl.nsf/FULL/585?OpenDocument>
ILO. 2007. *Global Employment Trends 2007.* Geneva: ILO. <http://www.ilo.org/global/ About_the_ILO/Media_and_public_information/Press_releases/lang–en/WCMS _081866/index.htm>
Instituto Mexicano para la Competividad. 2003. *Análisis de la competitividad en México, September 2003.* <http://www.queretaro.gob.mx/sedesu/deseco/esteco/perfeco/reveco/ Documentos/IMCO.htm>
IraqSolidaridad. 2008. "Más de un millón de iraquíes han muerto desde el inicio de la ocupación." *Rebelión,* Feb. 6. <http://www.rebelion.org/noticia.php?id=62888>
Iruegas, Gustavo. 2005. "En defensa propia." *La Jornada,* December 16.
Iturriaga, Yuriria. 2006. "Francia: repudian millón y medio de personas la reforma laboral." *La Jornada,* March 19. <http://www.jornada.unam.mx/2006/03/19/index.php?section =mundo&article=031n1mun>
Jaffe, Hosea. 1976. *Del tribalismo al socialismo.* Mexico City: Siglo XXI.
Jiménez Villarejo, Carlos. 2004. "Delincuencia financiera y paraísos fiscales." *Revista La Factoria* 24. <http://www.revistalafactoria.eu/articulo.php?id=267>
Joxe, Alain. 2003a. *El imperio del caos.* Buenos Aires: Fondo de Cultura Económica.
Joxe, Alain. 2003b. "Una estrategia del desorden sin freno ni fin." *El Monde Diplomatique* May. <http://www.monde-diplomatique.es/2003/05/joxe.html>
Kagarlitsky, Boris. 2001. "El incendio del Reichstag en Nueva York." *Herramienta Debate y Crítica Marxista* 17. <http://www.herramienta.com.ar/revista-herramienta-n-17/el -incendio-del-reichstag-en-nueva-york>

Katz, Claudio. 2002. "Una interpretación contemporánea de la ley de la tendencia decreciente de la tasa de ganancia." *Laberinto*, Feb. 1. <http://laberinto.uma.es/index.php?option=com_content&view=article&id=125>

Klare, Michael T. 2002. *Resource Wars: The New Landscape of Global Conflict*. New York: Henry Holt.

Klare, Michael T. 2006. "The Coming Resource Wars." *Third World Traveler*, March 11. <http://www.thirdworldtraveler.com/Oil_watch/ComingResourceWars.html>

Klein, Naomi. 2007a. "Laboratory for a Fortressed World." *The Nation*, June 14. <http://www.naomiklein.org/articles/2007/06/laboratory-fortressed-world>

Klein, Naomi. 2007b. "Shock Doctrine: Naomi Klein on the Rise of Disaster Capitalism." Interview, *Third World Traveler*, September 17. <http://www.thirdworldtraveler.com/Naomi_Klein/Shock_Doctrine_interview.html>

Klein, Naomi. 2008a. "Disaster Capitalism: State of Extortion." *The Nation*, July 8. <http://www.commondreams.org/archive/2008/07/03/10085>

Klein, Naomi. 2008b. "One Year after the Publication of The Shock Doctrine, A Response to the Attacks." Naomi Klein website, September 2. <http://www.naomiklein.org/articles/2008/09/response-attacks>

Kohan, Néstor. 2007. "Desafíos actuales de la teoría crítica frente al posmodernismo." *Rebelión*, August 2. <http://www.rebelion.org/docs/54445.pdf>

Kohan Nestor. 2009. "Diccionario básico de categorías marxistas." *Nodo 50*, February 1. <http://www.nodo50.org/Diccionario-basico-de-categorias.html>

Kosik, Karel. 1976. *Dialectics of the Concrete*. Dordrecht: Reidel.

Kurnitzky, Horst. 2000. "Una llamada a la violencia: La Concepción Socialdarwinista de la Economía Neoliberal," in Kurnitzky, Horst, ed., *Globalización de la violencia*. Mexico City: Colibrí Editores.

Krätke, Michael R. 2007. "Por vez primera, tenemos estadísticas fiables sobre la distribución de la riqueza en el mundo." *Rebelión*, January 16. <http://www.rebelion.org/noticia.php?id=44875>

Kuhnl, Reinhard. 1978. *Liberalismo y fascismo. Dos formas del dominio burgués*. Barcelona: Fontanella.

Lenin, Vladimir, I. 1903. *To the Rural Poor*. Lenin Internet Archive. <http://www.marxists.org/archive/lenin/works/1903/rp/index.htm#2>

Lenin, Vladimir I. 1914. *Karl Marx*. Lenin Internet Archive. <http://www.marxists.org/archive/lenin/works/1914/granat/ch04.htm>

Lenin, Vladimir I. 1916. *Imperialism, the Highest Stage of Capitalism*. Lenin Internet Archive. <http://www.marxists.org/archive/lenin/works/1916/imp-hsc/>

Lenin, Vladimir I. 1918. *The State and Revolution*. Lenin Internet Archive. <http://www.marxists.org/archive/lenin/works/1917/staterev/>

Lind, William S. 2004. "Understanding Fourth Generation War l." *Antiwar*, January 15. <http://www.antiwar.com/lind/index.php?articleid=1702>

Lipietz Alain. 1991. "Posfordismo y democracia." *Economía Informa* 190.

Lipietz, Alain. 1997. "El mundo del postfordismo." *Ensayos de Economía* Vol 7: 12. <http://lipietz.net/IMG/article_PDF/article_379.pdf>

London, Fréderic. 2008. "Cuando Bush y la Reserva Federal se volvieron socialistas." *Le Monde Diplomatique*. Mexican edition. October 2.

López y Rivas, Gilberto. 2005. "Estado de derecho." *La Jornada*, December 16.

Lyotard, Jean-Francois. 1984. *The Post-Modern Condition: A Report on Knowledge*. Minneapolis: University of Minnesota Press, Minneapolis.

Mac Liman, Adrián. 2002. *El caos que viene*. Madrid: Editorial Popular.

Maffesoli, Michel. 1996. *The Time of the Tribes: The Decline of Individualism in Mass Society*. Thousand Oaks, CA: Sage Publications.

Manzano Ruiz, Alberto. 2006. "Irak y las armas de manipulación masiva. Censura, mentiras y muertes para mantener la supremacía del Imperio." *Rebelión*, June 12. <http://www.rebelion.org/docs/32939.pdf>

Marcos, Subcomandante. "Si nos equivocamos acerca del PRD, ofreceremos disculpas." *La Jornada,* August 11, 2005. <http://www.jornada.unam.mx/2005/08/11/014n1pol.php>
Marelli, Sergio. 2007. "La imaginación y el poder." *Etcétera,* November 1. <http://www.etcetera.com.mx/articulo.php?articulo=2297>
Martin, Hans-Peter and Harald Schumann. 1997. *The Global Trap: Globalization and the Assault on Prosperity and Democracy.* London: Zed Books.
Martínez Peinado, Javier. 2000. "Periferia y fábrica mundial." *Aportes* 15. <http://www.redem.buap.mx/t3javier.htm>
Martiniuk, Claudio. 2009. "Nuestra marca de época es la tribu, lo arcaico, más el desarrollo del Internet." *Clarín,* December 27. <http://edant.clarin.com/diario/2009/12/27/um/m-02108637.htm>
Marx, Karl. 1844. *A Contribution to the Critique of Hegel's Philosophy of Right.* Marx-Engels Internet Archive. <http://www.marxists.org/archive/marx/works/1843/critique-hpr/intro.htm>
Marx, Karl. 1847. *The Misery of Philosophy.* Marx-Engels Internet Archive. <http://www.marxists.org/archive/marx/works/1847/poverty-philosophy/index.htm>
Marx, Karl. 1853. "The British Rule in India." Marx-Engels Internet Archive. <http://www.marxists.org/archive/marx/works/1853/06/25.htm>
Marx, Karl. 1859. *A Contribution to the Critique of Political Economy.* Marx-Engels Internet Archive. <http://www.marxists.org/archive/marx/works/1859/critique-pol-economy/index.htm>
Marx, Karl. 1863. Formal and Real Subsumption of Labour under Capital: Transitional Forms. Marx's Economic Manuscripts of 1861–1863. Marx-Engels Internet Archive. <http://www.marxists.org/archive/marx/works/1861/economic/ch37.htm>
Marx, Karl. 1867. *Capital: A Critique of Political Economy. Vol. I.* Marx-Engels Internet Archive. <http://www.marxists.org/archive/marx/works/1867-c1/index.htm>
Marx, Karl. 1885. *Capital, Vol II.* Marx-Engels Internet Archive. <http://www.marxists.org/archive/marx/works/1885-c2/index.htm>
Marx, Karl. 1894. *Capital, Vol III.* Marx-Engels Internet Archive. <http://www.marxists.org/archive/marx/works/1894-c3/index.htm>
Marx, Karl. 1895. *The Class Struggles in France, 1848–1850.* Marx-Engels Internet Archive. <http://www.marxists.org/archive/marx/works/1850/class-struggles-france/index.htm>
Marx, Karl. 1973. *Outlines of the Critique of Political Economy.* Marx-Engels Internet Archive. <http://www.marxists.org/archive/marx/works/1857/grundrisse/index.htm>
Marx, Karl. 1981. *El Capital. Libro I. Capítulo VI (Inédito).* Mexico City: Siglo XXI.
Marx, Karl and Frederick Engels. 1848. *Manifesto of the Communist Party.* Marx-Engels Internet Archive. <http://www.marxists.org/archive/marx/works/1848/communist-manifesto/index.htm>
Marx, Karl and Frederick Engels. 1883. *Communist Manifesto: Preface to the 1883 German Edition.* Marx-Engels Internet Archive. <http://www.marxists.org/archive/marx/works/1848/communist-manifesto/preface.htm>
Mathiesen, Thomas. 2000. "La Globalización de la Vigilancia." One of a series of documents on ENFOPOL published online by the Universidad de Granada. <http://www.ugr.es/~aquiran/cripto/enfopol/enfo08.htm>
Memoria. 2002. "Echelon en la disputa por la hegemonía." *Memoria* 157 (March), editorial. <http://www.revistamemoria.com/vista.php?id=1286&path=718c4f0612e3d85fcbad>
Mendès France, Mireille and Hugo Ruiz Diaz. 2007. "Hacia una sociedad internacional policial y represiva." *Rebelión,* November 20. <http://www.rebelion.org/noticia.php?id=59017>
Messina, German. 2009. "Las sociedades latinoamericanas en las que (sobre)vivi(re)mos." *Observatorio de la Economía Latinoamericana* 116. <http://www.eumed.net/cursecon/ecolat/la/09/mmf.htm>
Mészáros, István. 1970. *Marx's Theory of Alienation.* Mészáros Internet Archive. <http://www.marxists.org/archive/meszaros/works/alien/index.htm>

Mészáros István. 2003. "Militarism and the Coming Wars." *Monthly Review,* January. <http://
www.monthlyreview.org/0603meszaros.htm>
Mészáros, István. 2010. *The Structural Crisis of Capital.* New York: Monthly Review
Press.
Moeche, Erich. 1999. ENFOPOL: The Creation of a Global Surveillance Network. Paper pre-
sented at the Computers, Freedom and Privacy 99 Conference, Washington D.C., April
6–8.
Mokhiber, Russell and Robert Weissman. 2002a. "Cracking Down on Corporate Crime,
Really." *Focus on the Corporation,* July 3. <http://lists.essential.org/pipermail/
corp-focus/2002/000120.html>
Mokhiber, Russell and Robert Weissman. 2002b. "La acción como respuesta." *Znet,* October.
<http://www.zmag.org/Spanish/1002mokweiss.htm>
Mokhiber, Russell and Robert Weissman. 2005a. "Self Interview: On the Rampage."
Z Space, Feb. 24. <www.zcommunications.org/self-interview-on-the-rampage-by-russell
-mokhiber.pdf>
Mokhiber, Russell and Robert Weissman. 2005b. "El crimen y la violencia de las corporacio-
nes infligen mucho más daño a la sociedad, tanto en dólares como en vidas, que la
delincuencia callejera." *Rebelión,* April 6. <http://www.rebelion.org/noticia.php?id
=13510>
Moore, Stanley. 1957. *The Critique of Capitalist Democracy.* New York: Paine-Whiteman.
Morin, Edgar. 1999. *Sociología.* Barcelona: Kairós.
Moseley, Fred. 2005. "Teoría marxista de las crisis y la economía de posguerra de los Estados
Unidos," in *Razón y Revolución,* 14: Spring. <www.razonyrevolucion.org/textos/revryr/
RyR14/ryr14-moseley.pdf>
Moulian, Tomas. 2000. "El Neoliberalismo como Sistema de Dominación." *Alternativa* 15.
Norandi, Mariana. 2010. "Matrimonio, institución vetusta y obsoleta, dice investigadora." *La
Jornada,* February 8. <http://www.jornada.unam.mx/2010/02/08/index.php?section=so
ciedad&article=040n1soc>
Ogarrio, Gustavo. 2003. "Said: la radical actualidad de algún humanismo." *Rebelión,*
November 18. <http://www.rebelion.org/hemeroteca/said/031118said.htm>
Ohmae, Kenichi. 1997. *El fin del Estado-nación.* Santiago: Editorial Andrés Bello.
Oppenheimer, Walter and David Alandete. "Al Qaeda también nos desnuda." *El País,*
January 6, 2010. <http://www.elpais.com/articulo/sociedad/Qaeda/nos/desnuda/
elpepisoc/20100106elpepisoc_1/Tes>
Ornelas Bernal, Raúl. 2000. "Un mundo nos espía. El escándalo ECHELON." *Revista Chiapas*
9 <http://www.revistachiapas.org/No9/ch9ornelas.html>
Pacheco Benites, Alberto Renaun. 2008. "La muerte de la muerte." *Contratexto* 6. <http://
www.ulima.edu.pe/Revistas/contratexto/v6/index.html>
Palenga, Mima. n.d. "Pensamiento débil." Available from *Free PDF E-Books.* <http://www
.free-pdf-ebooks.com/ebook/vattimo-m%C3%A1s-all%C3%A1-de-la-interpretaci%
C3%B3n.html>
Pardo, Lisandro. 2009. "Redes sociales, bajo el interés de la CIA." *Rebelión,* October 20.
<http://www.rebelion.org/noticia.php?id=93625>
Pérez, Carlota. 1986. "Las nuevas tecnologías: una visión de conjunto," in Ominami, Carlos,
ed., *La Tercera Revolución Industrial: Impactos Internacionales del Actual Viraje
Tecnológico.* Buenos Aires: RIAL, Grupo Editor Latinoamericano, pp. 43–90. <http://
www.carlotaperez.org/Articulos/ficha-lasnuevastecnologiasunavision.htm>
Perry, William. 1996. "La política de Estados Unidos hacia América Latina." *FASOC* Vol. 11(1):
49–53. <http://www.fasoc.cl/files/articulo/ART411926d0889da.pdf>
Petras, James. 2002. "La estrategia militar de EE.UU. en América Latina." *Visiones
Alternativas.*
<http://www.visionesalternativas.com.mx/militarizacion/articulos/geoestrat/1.htm>
Petras, James. 2004. "The Politics of Imperialism: Neoliberalism and Class Politics in
Latin America." *Counterpunch,* November 13–14. <http://www.counterpunch.org/
petras11132004.html>

Petras, James. 2007. "Global Ruling Class: Billionaires and How They 'Made It'." The James Petras Website. <http://petras.lahaine.org/articulo.php?p=1696&more=1&c=1>

Pilger, John. 2002. "Document Revealed: What America Needed was a New Pearl Harbor." *Third World Traveler*, December 12. <http://www.thirdworldtraveler.com/Pilger_John/New_Pearl_Harbor.html>

Pineda, Francisco. 2003. "Irak, Afganistán, Chechenia: la guerra de desinformación en la 'era de la información'." *Revista Rebeldía* 7.

Piqueras, Andrés. 2005. "La mutua conformación del capital y el trabajo desde el capitalismo maduro al capitalismo senil y las formas sociales a que da lugar." *Revista Polis* 12. <http://www.revistapolis.cl/polis%20final/12/pique.htm>

Plihon, Dominique. 2003. *El nuevo capitalismo*. Mexico City: Siglo XXI.

Portantiero, Juan Carlos. 1981. "Estado y crisis en el debate de entreguerras," in *Los usos de Gramsci*. Mexico City: Folios.

Portelli, Hugues. 1998. *Gramsci y el bloque histórico*. Mexico City: Siglo XXI.

Poulantzas, Nicos. 1973. *Poder político y clases sociales en el Estado capitalista*. Mexico City: Siglo XXI.

Prolongeau, Hubert and Jean-Christophe Rampal. 1997. "En América latina, el secuestro se convierte en una industria." *Le Monde Diplomatique*, November.

Quijano, Aníbal. 1977. "Imperialismo, clases sociales y Estado en el Perú: 1895–1930," in *Clases sociales y crisis política en América Latina*. Mexico City: Siglo XXI-IIS-UNAM.

Quintana, Victor. 2010. "Modelo juvenicida." *La Jornada*, February 5. <http://www.jornada.unam.mx/2010/02/05/index.php?section=opinion&article=017a2pol>

Ramonet, Ignacio. 2010. "Socialdemocracia, fin de ciclo." *El Monde Diplomatique*, February. <http://www.eldiplo.com.pe/socialdemocracia-fin-de-ciclo>

Rascon, Marco. 2005. "Emilio Azcárraga y don Osito Bimbo, se apropian de la moral pública." *La Jornada*, September 6.

Real Academia Española. 1992. *Diccionario de la lengua española*. 21st edition. Madrid: Real Academia Española.

Regalado Álvarez, Roberto. 1999. "El manifiesto comunista y la transnacionalización de la dominación política," in Caycedo Turriago, Jaime and Jario Estrada Álvarez, eds., *Marx vive: siglo y medio del manifiesto comunista: ¿superación, vigencia o reactualización?* Bogotá: Universidad Nacional de Colombia, pp. 85–93. <http://www.espaciocritico.com/sites/all/files/libros/mrxvv1/mrxvv1a06p85a93.pdf>

Reina Rodríguez, Carlos Arturo. 2006. "Los Espectros Urbanos: En la era de las tribus, más que pesado, es metal con historia." Carlos Reina website, July 14. <http://carlosreina.espacioblog.com/post/2006/07/14/los-espectros-urbanos-la-era-las-tribus-mas-pesado->

Revelli, Marco. 2004. "8 tesis sobre el postfordismo." *Ediciones Simbióticas*, Nov. 27. <http://www.altediciones.com/t11.htm>

Revista Inter-Forum. 2002. "Reporte Latinoamericano de Competitividad." *Revista Inter-Forum*, December 23. <http://www.revistainterforum.com/espanol/articulos/122301artprin.html>

Revuelta, María José. 2008. "El tratamiento mediático de la globalización." *Rebelión* May 8. <http://www.rebelion.org/docs/67138.pdf>

Ribeiro, Silvia. 2005. "Los dueños del planeta: corporaciones 2005." *La Jornada*, December 31. <http://www.jornada.unam.mx/2005/12/31/019a1eco.php>

Ribeiro, Silvia. 2007. "El 2006 y la plutocracia." *América Latina en Movimiento*, January 18. <http://alainet.org/active/15154&lang=es>

Ribeiro, Silvia. 2009a. "Una red de poderosas trasnacionales juegan a romper las reglas de la naturaleza." Interview, *Armas contra las guerras* 262. <http://www.herbogeminis.com/Entrevista_a_Silvia_Ribeiro.html>

Ribeiro, Silvia. 2009b. "Premiando a las transnacionales de la epidemia." *La Jornada,* May 9. <http://www.jornada.unam.mx/2009/05/09/index.php?section=opinion&article=029a1eco>

Robert, Anne-Cécile. 2010. "La polémica sobre una decisión demasiado favorable a las empresas." *El Monde Diplomatique*, July. <http://guasabaraeditor.blogspot.com/2010/07/la-crisis-social-llega-al-parlamento.html>

Roberts, Paul Craig. 2010. "The Road to Armageddon: the Insane Drive for American Hegemony Threatens Life on Earth." *Global Research*, February 26. <http://www.globalresearch.ca/index.php?context=va&aid=17821>

Rodero, Antón Emma. 2000. "Concepto y técnicas de la propaganda y su aplicación al nazismo," in *Actas del III Congreso Internacional Cultura y Medios de Comunicación*. Salamanca: Publicaciones Universidad Pontificia. <http://www.bocc.ubi.pt/pag/rodero-emma-propaganda-nazismo.pdf>

Rodríguez, Juan Carlos. 2009. "Facebook, de la CIA a la privacidad." *Eco Diario*, June 25. <http://ecodiario.eleconomista.es/internet/noticias/1354212/06/09/Facebook-de-la-CIA-a-la-privacidad.html>

Rodríguez Derivet, Arleen. 2003. "La guerra del fin de la historia." *La Jiribilla*. <http://www.lajiribilla.cu/2003/n097_03/paraimprimir/097_04_imp.html>

Rojas Aravena, Francisco. 2008. "Violencia en América Latina. Debilidad estatal, inequidad y crimen organizado inhiben el desarrollo humano." *Pensamiento Iberoamericano* 2. <http://www.pensamientoiberoamericano.org/articulos/2/51/1/globalizacion-y-violencia-en-america-latina-debilidad-estatal-inequidad-y-crimen-organizado-inhiben-el-desarrollo-humano.html>

Román, Jose Antonio. 2005. "Derbez: migración sin freno por la incapacidad de crear empleos." *La Jornada*, October 4.

Romero, Aldo Andrés. 1998. "El Manifiesto Comunista y la Globalización." *Revista Herramienta* 7. <http://www.herramienta.com.ar/varios/7/7-6.html>

Rossanda, Rossana. 2003. "La doctrina Bush borra los principios de la ONU y dicta las reglas para imponer su ley donde sea." *Creatividad feminista http://www.rebelion.org/noticia.php?id=77871*

Rosselet-McCouley, Suzanne. 2010. "Appendix I: Methodology and Principles of Analysis," in *World Competitiveness Yearbook 2010*. Lausanne: IMD. <http://www.imd.ch/research/publications/wcy/upload/methodology.pdf

Rouleau, Eric. 2003. "La propaganda de guerra y sus deficiencias." *El Monde Diplomatique*, February. <http://monde-diplomatique.es/2003/02/rouleau.html>

Rudnik, Isaac and Jacob Goransky. 2007. "Propuestas alternativas y actores sociales en América Latina." *Rebelión*, February 27. <http://www.rebelion.org/noticia.php?id=47402>

Sader, Emir. 2004 "Paraísos fiscales: Prostíbulos de la globalización." *Rebelión*, July 1. <http://www.rebelion.org/noticia.php?id=1329>

Sader, Emir. 2007. "Oda al humanismo." *Rebelión*, May 18. <http://www.rebelion.org/noticia.php?id=51044>

Said, Edward. 2003. "Worldly Humanism vs. the Empire Builders." *Counterpunch*, August 4. <http://www.counterpunch.org/said08052003.html>

Salbuchi, Adrian. 1999. *El Cerebro del Mundo: La cara oculta de la Globalización*. Cordoba: Ediciones del Copista. <http://www.laeditorialvirtual.com.ar/>

Sánchez, Esther. 2010. "Narcoguerra 2009: Todos perdieron." *El Universal*, January 10. <http://www.eluniversal.com.mx/estados/74251.html>

Sánchez Rebolledo, Adolfo. 2003. "Contrastes de 6 de julio." *La Jornada*, July 10. <http://www.jornada.unam.mx/2003/07/10/021a1pol.php?origen=opinion.php&fly=1>

Sánchez Rebolledo, Adolfo. 2006. "Otro régimen de partidos." *La Jornada*, January 12.

Sánchez Vázquez, Adolfo. 1999. *Entre la realidad y la utopía. Ensayos sobre política, moral y socialismo*. Mexico City: Fondo de Cultura Económica.

Saviano, Roberto. 2007. *Gomorra*. Mexico City: Debate.

Saxe-Fernández, John. 2006. *Terror e imperio. La hegemonía política y económica de Estados Unidos*. Mexico City: Debate.

Saxe-Fernández, John. 2007. "Agenda secreta: anexión y ocupación." *La Jornada*. April 26. <http://www.jornada.unam.mx/2007/04/26/index.php?section=opinion&article=032a1eco>

Semana. 2001. "A vender oxígeno." *Semana.com,* September 3. <http://www.semana.com/
    noticias-economia/vender-oxigeno/20168.aspx>
Semo, Ilán. 2005. "Tráficos." *La Jornada,* June 18. <http://www.jornada.unam
    .mx/2005/06/18/021a2pol.php>
Serrano, Pascual. 2009. "Cómo saber quienes son los dueños del mundo." Review of
    the book *Cosa Nostra: Las mafias en el Costa del Sol." ATTAC Madrid.* <http://www
    .attacmadrid.org/d/11/091028122020.php>
Schmitter, Philippe. 1992. "¿Continúa el siglo del corporativismo?" in Schmitter, Philippe
    and Gerhard Lehmbruch. *Neocorporativismo. Tomo 1.* Mexico City: Alianza.
Shaikh, Anwar. 1990. *Valor acumulación y crisis. Ensayos de Economía Política.* Bogotá:
    Tercer Mundo.
Silva de Sousa, Rosinaldo. 2004. "Narcotráfico y economía ilícita: las redes del crimen orga-
    nizado en Río de Janeiro." *Revista Mexicana de Sociología* 66.1, January-March. <http://
    www.ejournal.unam.mx/rms/2004-1/RMS04105.pdf>
Solo, Toni. 2009. "Dólar militarismo versus ALBA humanismo." *Rebelión,* November 15.
    <http://www.rebelion.org/noticia.php?id=95254>
Sotelo Valencia, Adrián. 1999. *Globalización y precariedad del trabajo en México.* Mexico
    City: El Caballito.
Statewatch. 2001. Statewatch Investigation, Full Report: EU—FBI Telecommunications
    Surveillance System. <http://www.statewatch.org/news/2001/may/03Benfopol.htm>
STOA PUBLICATIONS. 1998. *An Appraisal of the Technologies of Political Control.* STOA
    Interim Study—Executive Summary—September 1998. <http://www.ratical.org/
    co-globalize/GblzOfRepES.html>
Stockholm International Peace Research Institute. 2009. *Yearbook 2009: Armaments,
    Disarmament and International Security—Summary.* Stockholm: SIPRI. <http://www
    .sipri.org/yearbook/2009/files/SIPRIYB09summary.pdf>
Tagarelli, Diego. 2009. "Crisis, cultura popular e ideología." *Globalización,* March. <http://
    rcci.net/globalizacion/2009/fg828.htm>
Tapia, Luis. 2008. "La reforma del sentido común en la dominación neoliberal y en la con-
    stitución de nuevos bloques históricos nacional-populares," in Ceceña, Ana Esther, ed.,
    De los saberes de la emancipación y de la dominación. Buenos Aires: CLACSO. <http://
    bibliotecavirtual.clacso.org.ar/ar/libros/grupos/cecen/07tapia.pdf>
Tarpley, Webster Griffin. 2004. *9/11 Synthetic Terror Made in the USA.* Joshua Tree, CA:
    Progressive Press.
Thurow, Lester. 1992. *La guerra del siglo XXI.* Buenos Aires: Vergara.
Thwaites Rey, Mabel. 1994. "La noción gramsciana de hegemonía en el convulsionado fin
    de siglo. Acerca de las bases materiales del consenso," in Ferreyra, L., E. Logiudice and
    M. Thwaites Rey, *Gramsci mirando al sur. Sobre la hegemonía en los 90.* Buenos Aires:
    K&ai Editor, Colección Teoría Crítica. <http://www.geocities.com/catedragramsci/
    textos/S_la_nocion_gramsciana_de_hegemonia_htm>
Thwaites Rey, Mabel and José Castillo. 1999. "Poder estatal y capital global: los límites de la
    lucha política," in Boron, Atilio A., Julio Gambina and Naum Minsburg, eds., *Tiempos
    violentos; Neoliberalismo, globalizacion y desigualdad en America Latina.* Buenos Aires:
    CLACSO—EUDEBA. <http://168.96.200.17/ar/libros/tiempos/castillo.rtf>
Toledano, María. 2008. "La destrucción de la política." *Rebelión,* December 24. <http://www
    .rebelion.org/noticia.php?id=77939>
Touraine, Alain. 2010. "Las tres crisis." *El País,* January 6. <http://www.elpais.com/articulo/
    opinion/crisis/elpepiopi/20100106elpepiopi_4/Tes/>
Truth Commission for Economic, Social and Cultural Rights in the U.S. 2006. Report
    issued in Cleveland, Ohio July 15–16. <http://www.cubanow.net/pages/print.php?item
    =1269>
UN. 2006. International Migration and Development: Report of the Secretary-General. New
    York: United Nations. <http://www.un.org/esa/population/migration/hld/Text/Report
    %20of%20the%20SG(June%2006)_English.pdf>
UNESCO, 1987. *Diccionario UNESCO de ciencias sociales.* Barcelona: Planeta DeAgostini.

UNICEF. 2005. *Annual Report 2005*. New York: UNICEF. <http://www.unicef.org/about/annualreport/2005/pdf/Unicef2005ar.pdf>

UNODC. 2008. Sociedad "incivil": delincuencia, drogas ilícitas y terrorismo. Vienna: UNODC. <http://www.un.org/spanish/Depts/dpi/boletin/drogas/sociedad.shtml>

UNODC. 2009a. *World Drug Report 2009*. Vienna: UNODC. <http://www.unodc.org/documents/wdr/WDR_2009/WDR2009_eng_web.pdf>

UNODC. 2009b. *Global Report on Trafficking in Persons*. Vienna: UNODC. <http://www.unodc.org/unodc/en/human-trafficking/global-report-on-trafficking-in-persons.html>

Urrutia, Alonso. 1998. "Zedillo: que vengan observadores, pero 'sin agenda previa de qué deben decir.'" *La Jornada*, May 9.

Valqui Cachi, Camilo and Cutberto Pastor Bastán, eds. 2009. *Capital, poder y medios de comunicación: una crítica epistémica*. Cajamarca, Peru: Universidad Privada Antonio Guillermo Urrelo. <http://www.rebelion.org/docs/90146.pdf>

Vargas, Rosa Elvira. 1998. "Zedillo: es injusto que 'progresistas' acusen a México de opresor de indios." *La Jornada*, May 7.

Vargas, Rosa Elvira and Emir Olivares. 2008. "Los emos, blanco del conservadurismo." *La Jornada*, March 21. <http://www.jornada.unam.mx/2008/03/21/index.php?section=soci edad&article=032n1soc>

Vattimo, G. 1991. *The End of Modernity*, Baltimore: Johns Hopkins University Press.

Vega, Renán. 1997. "Postmodernismo y neoliberalismo: la clonación ideológica del capitalismo contemporáneo." *Folios* 7.

Velasco, Elizabeth. 2010. "Víctimas de *cyberbullying*, niños y adolescentes 'podrían suicidarse'." *La Jornada*, February 10. <http://www.jornada.unam.mx/2010/02/10/index.php?section=sociedad&article=038n1soc>

Villamil, Jenaro. 2010. "Zedillo opaca a Salinas." *Proceso*, December 20. <http://www.proceso.com.mx/rv/modHome/detalleExclusiva/86556>

Villegas Dávalos, Raúl. 2004. "La devastación del mundo laboral," in *La devastación imperial del mundo*. Mexico City: Universidad de la Ciudad de México.

Vidal-Beneyto, José. 2002. "Gobernabilidad y gobernanza." *El País*, April 12. <http://www.elpais.com/articulo/opinion/Gobernabilidad/gobernanza/elpepiopi/20020412elpepiopi_7/Tes>

Walicki, Andrzej. 1988. "Karl Marx as philosopher of freedom." *Critical Review: A Journal of Politics and Society, 1933-8007*, 2:4, pp. 10–58.

Washington Office on Latin America. 2008. *The Captive State: Organized Crime and Human Rights in Latin America*, Report issued February 28. <http://www.wola.org/index.php?option=com_content&task=viewp&id=588&Itemid=2>

World Bank. 2003. ¿La globalización incrementa la pobreza al mundo? Washington: World Bank. <http://www.bancomundial.org/temas/globalizacion/cuestiones2.htm>

World Commission on the Social Dimension of Globalization. 2004. *A Fair Globalization: Creating Opportunities for All*. Geneva: ILO. <http://www.ilo.org/public/english/wcsdg/docs/report.pdf>

Zermeño, Sergio. 2003. "¿Qué sigue en el Distrito Federal?." *La Jornada*, July 10. <http://www.jornada.unam.mx/2003/07/10/021a2pol.php?origen=opinion.php&fly=1>

Zermeño, Sergio. 2005a. *La desmodernidad mexicana*. Mexico City: Editorial Océano.

Zermeño, Sergio. 2005b. "Desesperante autismo." *La Jornada*, February 3. <http://www.jornada.unam.mx/2005/02/03/021a1pol.php>

Zibechi, Raúl. 2008. "La militarización de las periferias urbanas." *Pensamiento Crítico*, February 20. <http://www.pensamientocritico.org/rauzib0208.html>

SUBJECT INDEX

INDEX OF AUTHORITIES